DRESSMAKING Made Simple

The Made Simple series
has been created
primarily for self-education
but can equally well
be used as
an aid to group study.
However complex the subject,
the reader is taken
step by step,
clearly and methodically,
through the course. Each volume
has been prepared by experts,
using throughout the
Made Simple technique of teaching.
Consequently the gaining
of knowledge now becomes
an experience to be enjoyed.

In the same series

Accounting
Acting and Stagecraft
Additional Mathematics
Administration in Business
Advertising
Anthropology
Applied Economics
Applied Mathematics
Applied Mechanics
Art Appreciation
Art of Speaking
Art of Writing
Biology
Book-keeping
British Constitution
Business and Administrative Organisation
Business Economics
Business Statistics and Accounting
Calculus
Chemistry
Childcare
Commerce
Company Law
Computer Programming
Computers and Microprocessors
Cookery
Cost and Management Accounting
Data Processing
Dressmaking
Economic History
Economic and Social Geography
Economics
Effective Communication
Electricity
Electronic Computers
Electronics
English
English Literature
Export
Financial Management
French
Geology
German
Housing, Tenancy and Planning Law
Human Anatomy
Human Biology
Italian
Journalism
Latin
Law
Management
Marketing
Mathematics
Modern Biology
Modern Electronics
Modern European History
Modern Mathematics
Money and Banking
Music
New Mathematics
Office Practice
Organic Chemistry
Personnel Management
Philosophy
Photography
Physical Geography
Physics
Practical Typewriting
Psychiatry
Psychology
Public Relations
Rapid Reading
Retailing
Russian
Salesmanship
Secretarial Practice
Social Services
Sociology
Spanish
Statistics
Teeline Shorthand
Transport and Distribution
Twentieth-Century British History
Typing
Woodwork

DRESSMAKING Made Simple

Gidon Lippman and
Dorothy Erskine

Fashion Drawings
Alan Couldridge, Des. R.C.A.

Technical Diagrams
Linda Jones

Made Simple Books
HEINEMANN : London

Made and printed in Great Britain
by Butler & Tanner Ltd, Frome and London
for the publishers William Heinemann Ltd,
10 Upper Grosvenor Street, London W1X 9PA

First Edition, October 1974
Reprinted, March 1982

SBN 434 98546 5 Casebound

SBN 434 98547 3 Paperbound

Preface

In a world of mass production, individual dressmaking undertaken with knowledge and skill is immensely enjoyable and rewarding.

The beginner all too often becomes frustrated, because of the temptation to be over-ambitious as, for instance, choosing a fabric which is difficult to handle, or a too intricate or complicated pattern. This book shows how to do it the *simple* way.

Part One. This is a planned, progressive sequence in the choice of design, pattern and material.

Part Two. Explains how to put together six basic garments, using simple techniques.

Part Three. Contains the additional and the more advanced techniques for anyone wishing to extend their expertise and knowledge of the subject.

Included in the Appendices is a comprehensive Glossary of dressmaking and fashion terms, fabric descriptions and textile terms, which could provide a ready source of reference and interest. Measurements in this book are first given in metric units, followed by the imperial equivalents in brackets. Also, further information about the metrication of fabrics is included in the text where appropriate.

It is a book suitable for all beginners. The general reader either attending recreational classes or working alone, will find that it is a helpful introduction and that it adds to the pleasure and satisfaction of producing her own work. Students working for GCE examinations, The City and Guilds of London Institute Examinations and those on other dress and fashion courses will find it particularly valuable, since it maintains a balance between theory and practice. Lecturers in schools and colleges will also find it a useful book for teaching and demonstration purposes.

The numerous diagrams, charts, illustrations and stage-by-stage instructions will achieve results in a relatively short time. This is important, since if garments are to be crisp, new and professional, the work must be carried out without excessive handling and worrying over. We believe that dressmaking is part of fashion and that with experience the craft of making up can ultimately be combined with the art and design of human decoration. One is complementary to the other.

We offer a word of advice to anyone setting out on this venture. Making it simple is the essence of success. Confine yourself to using fabrics which handle easily (as suggested in chapter three) and begin with our basic garments. Moreover, in order to accumulate experience, try 'variations on a theme', that is use the same basic shape and construction of a garment a few times and ring the changes with different design details or decorations, selecting similar fabrics which have a common handle. This experience will be invaluable in providing a sound background to the subject and so make progress to more difficult garments less discouraging.

However varied the reasons for dressmaking may be, we hope this book will fulfil its aim by making a contribution to the enjoyment of life for many people.

GL and DE

Foreword

There is today an enormous interest in making things; using one's hands, reverting to artisanship. Proof of this is apparent in the variety of magazines now available.

However, for the serious student of professional clothes construction it is rare to find authoritative and up-to-date books which will guide one through every aspect of producing well-cut, well-made professional garments. Whether you are a young student studying to make fashion your career, or whether you simply wish to make your own clothes for economic reasons, I am certain that this book will guide and prepare you in a very sound and logical way.

The authors have had enormous experience, both in the Fashion Industry and in the teaching of students destined to become names in that Industry. For these reasons it will be clear that this book is one in which you can have complete confidence. But it is your diligence to practise what the book preaches which will make your efforts successful; *your* sustained interest and perseverance. As with all skills, constant practice will make perfect, whether learning to play a musical instrument or making a piece of furniture—so it is with producing clothes.

The information and knowledge which abound in this book cover an enormous range, even to the choice of fabrics and indeed the relative behaviour of fibres, both man-made and natural.

Recent decades have brought forth rapid and constant change within the Fashion Industry, in design and technique. Despite the use of highly sophisticated machinery, basic principles remain and are usually elegantly simple. Once learned, they enable one to proceed with inventiveness and freedom. Indeed, these words are synonymous with good fashion, as are innovation and individuality. This book will provide those basic principles and will admirably serve students commencing a training as designers or technicians, as well as those simply wishing to perfect their methods of producing well-made clothes for themselves.

JOANNE BROGDEN
Professor of Fashion
Royal College of Art

Acknowledgments

We offer our sincere appreciation and grateful thanks to our editor Margaret Anderson, for the invaluable help in the presentation of this book, and in particular for compiling the index. We are also indebted to our reader, Mr F. Stillman, CMG(Hons.), ACI, CTI, ASIA, Chief Examiner, City and Guilds of London Institute, for useful comments and advice. Our thanks are due to Bernina Sewing Machines for their co-operation and assistance. We thank the Clothing and Footwear Institute for permission to use excerpts from their publication *Making the Point*. Special thanks go to Pat O'Gorman for giving so much of her time in typing the manuscript.

Table of Contents

PART ONE : INTRODUCTION

CHAPTER ONE

CHOOSING THE DESIGN

Introduction to Design

There are progressive sequences in making clothes. Before you start work the choice of design, pattern, material and their suitability to your figure, colouring and purpose, must be considered. The first step is to choose the design.

The Importance of Design

People wear clothes for a variety of reasons: naturally for protection and warmth, but personal satisfaction always enters into it, as does the need for group identification and admiration. The season and time of day makes a difference; and work, social activities and leisure are all vital factors in the way people want to dress.

Women to-day have far more freedom in the way they dress, since the old dogmas about which design suited a certain shape were abolished and rules on where, when and how to wear stripes, checks, horizontal, diagonal or vertical lines, have gone by the board. The result is that more time and effort must be spent on actually choosing a design. Great care is necessary before taking the final decision and adequate attention must be paid to all details. This is especially true when people are making their own garments, since they do not, of course, have the finished product in front of them. Though the rigid rules have disappeared, the sheer number of possible choices can be overwhelming. With a few guiding principles to help you make the right personal choice, you will avoid the more obvious pitfalls.

Colour and Fabric

When choosing clothes everyone is attracted to certain elements of a **dress design**, the term used to describe the numerous ingredients of a **total look**. The use of colour; the type and quality of fabric, its texture and pattern; and the shape, cut and fit of a garment, are all part of the creative art of dressmaking and contribute to the final result. However, in the process of clothes selection, the first decisive factors are usually the choice of colour and fabric. We find both exciting and often cannot resist purchasing materials for the enjoyment of handling and feeling these fabrics. We love colours and think about the potentially beautiful effect they will create in the finished garment, and, so, fabrics are frequently hoarded! A drawer full of dress lengths, which have never been used for the purpose they were intended, is all too familiar.

The authors hope that the following pages will go some way toward solving that problem. In the course of this book we offer suggestions on what type of fabric to choose, and guidance on how to cut and make up these fabrics.

Colour Defined

Colour is defined as the sensation produced by rays of light on the eye. A particular colour is determined by the frequency of the light. Artists divide colours into (1) primary (blue, red, yellow) and (2) secondary, a mixture of two primary colours—for example, blue and yellow mixed make green. Colours with tones close to each other are harmonious, or contrasting if the tones are apart. There are warm and cold colours. Used separately, or with other colours, they have a vital influence on the effect of a garment design—colour impact can be powerful and is often striking when differences combine. There are, of course, fashions in colours; and colours, or a combination of them, at times thought of as peculiar (such as black in summer), or even vulgar (orange with red), are at other times considered visually pleasing and desirable.

Changes in attitudes towards our surroundings are the result of many events and influences in our society, which is much the better for them. Our lives are enriched by variety, which stimulates and excites our critical faculties.

The Feel for Fabrics

Modern textile technology supplies a multitude of man-made fibres, for fabrics with great versatility, side by side with those made from natural fibres. 'Easy-care' clothes are undoubtedly an asset. But as the range of man-made fibres is now so vast that only the experts know with a degree of accuracy the exact composition of fibre-contents in any given simulated fabric, no attempt is made here to describe or discuss the intricacies of textile technology (but see pages 49 and 295 for more information).

We need to know certain things about fabrics which affect the making of garments. Will a particular material lend itself to soft folds? Will it hang well? Can it be cut on the cross grain? Will it pleat? Will it stretch, or can it be washed? In short, the behaviour of the fabric determines the choice of a design, for each fabric has certain characteristics, constructed by the technologist to provide a determined performance. It is most important that the nature of the material is fully understood, so as to exploit it to the fullest advantage.

In order to understand the nature of fabrics, their characteristics and to learn what they are best suited for, Chapter Fifteen describes a wide range of fabrics and their performances. We confine ourselves to suggesting only a few fabrics, for the first attempts at dressmaking, in Chapter Three.

Selection from both the wide spectrum of colours and the extensive range of present-day textiles available depends in the first instance, on individual preferences and taste. Every woman has her favourite colour and likes to wear it, taking into account and complementing her own hair and skin colouring—she will also have her favourite fabrics. Since the choice is wide, why not put it to good advantage by using imagination and enjoy a little experimentation.

Window Shopping

Inspiration for these new ideas can come from various sources and window shopping, when opportunity allows, is one of them. A well-known journalist and an authority on fashion once described window displays as the *dreams of fashion*. See these displays as often as possible, since fashion colours and fabrics on their own, in the garments displayed in windows, or inside shops and stores, will tell a 'story'. Colours, textures and types of fabric will stand out as being seasonable and will be identical on most fabric counters and in many ready-to-wear clothes. Newspapers and their supplements, magazines and advertisements are other sources for ideas. All these sources complement each other and form part of a co-ordinated fashion picture.

Planning Ahead

Facing the challenge of dressmaking will seem less of an ordeal if the importance of planning ahead is not under estimated—indeed it cannot be stressed often enough. But, then, the act of planning is itself an inherent part of the pleasure of making clothes.

Let us try to understand what initial planning involves and how to solve some of the problems which will be encountered.

Admittedly with the change of fashion development during the past years—from a situation where a mere handful of designers dictated which fashion was 'in' from season to season, to the time where the guidelines and directions come from so many more origins—choice and selection of fabrics and designs may well appear to be more confusing. International influences, changing at an ever growing rate, can easily present perplexing advice.

Before making any firm decisions on design selections, the following hints will be of value.

The Bit Bag

Collect fabric cuttings/samples, the larger the better, from any and every available source, and keep them in a 'bit bag' and have easy access to it. These samples will initially assist you in gaining knowledge and understanding of the various types of fabrics. The 'feel' of any fabric suggests its probable behaviour in wear, its comfort and performance.

Note the construction of fabrics by carrying out the following tests. Try to detect if material is woven, knitted or of bonded type. Feel the weight and compare one with another and get to know the differences between them—ignoring specific fibre contents, does it feel like cotton,linen, silk or wool, irrespective of it being natural or man-made. Hold a cutting in your hand, crush it, open your hand, see if it creases and, if so, does it recover? Does it feel soft or hard, try to stretch it. Pull it and see if there is much, little, or no give at all. These tests will help to develop your knowledge of fabric behaviour. Study cuttings for texture and pattern, if the sample is large enough you will be able to see the repeat of a printed, woven or knitted design (large repeat patterns in any shape or form, affect cutting at a later stage).

Observe colours. Take cuttings and 'play' with them for colour combinations. Move your cuttings around and 'mix' colours, see which blend and which contrast. This will sharpen your colour sense invaluably.

The Scrapbook

Cut out photographs and drawings of interesting designs from newspapers and magazines and build up a small library, perhaps in the form of a scrapbook or notebook. See how parts of garments can be interchanged—for example put the top of one with the skirt of another. The results of these simple tests will point to the right selection to the problem of using the most suitable fabric for any chosen design. This will increase your excitement, the urge to pick up scissors and needle will become stronger and you will approach it with greater confidence. Remember to build up to it gradually and, above all, that the essence of good design is simplicity. Resist the temptation to use decorations excessively, if in doubt leaving off rather than piling on will produce good fashion.

You will soon understand current fashion and learn to discriminate and to combine it with your individual preferences. The ultimate choice need not be either way-out fashion, difficult to carry off for all but a few, or a style devoid of any fashion influences which turns enjoyable clothes into dull clothing. How much better that the choice of garments should be based on an attitude of mind and not purely due to fixed ideas on age or status.

Working Facilities

Finally, give some thought to working facilities. For those people fortunate enough to have a separate work-room at their disposal, dressmaking may seem more pleasant and progress faster. However, with forethought and planning the absence of a separate room does not mean that you cannot manage. A hard top table is most important for cutting out and, if at all possible, arrange to have this and all other tools and equipment in one area. Place the sewing machine close to the ironing board and iron (under-pressing—pressing seams as you proceed from one stage to the next—should take place frequently). Moving from one to the other is tiring and time consuming.

Keep all tools in a work-box for easy access. Prevent the mislaying of vital sewing aids by keeping a tape measure around your neck and a pin cushion on your wrist.

Most important of all—ensure that the lighting is good. Bad or insufficient light can be disastrous and you will tire very quickly from eye strain. This will lead to a host of mistakes and constant unpicking is not only a bore, but makes for over-handling of garments which then look tatty and far less successful.

Last but not least, the working area must be clean, as some stains are stubborn and may withstand all removal efforts.

Changing Fashions

The basic fact about clothes is that arms go in sleeves, coats fasten, skirts start at the waist (wherever they may end) and practically all dresses cover the body from shoulder to hem. Designers can indulge in the wildest flights of fancy, or dip into past decades for inspiration, but one thing remains constant, clothes are still cut out and made up more or less as they have been for centuries. After the toga, worn alike by Roman men and women, the development of shape in clothes led to cutting, fitting and sewing together the different parts.

So to-day, coats, jackets and most dresses sit on the shoulders, with balance and fit from shoulder and bust. All are shaped and joined with darts and seams. Similar rules apply to skirts—whether flared, pleated, straight, long or short—they must fit around the waist area. Trouser legs vary greatly with the prevailing fashion mood, but they still have to fit well over the seat and sit well at the waist.

Even the most far-out shapes in fashion have a basic method of making-up, which is totally unaffected by apparent seasonable changes. Look closely and you will observe that fashion does not change quite so rapidly as reports

A B C

Fig. 1. (A) Blazer; (B) Tailored jacket; (C) Cardigan style jacket.

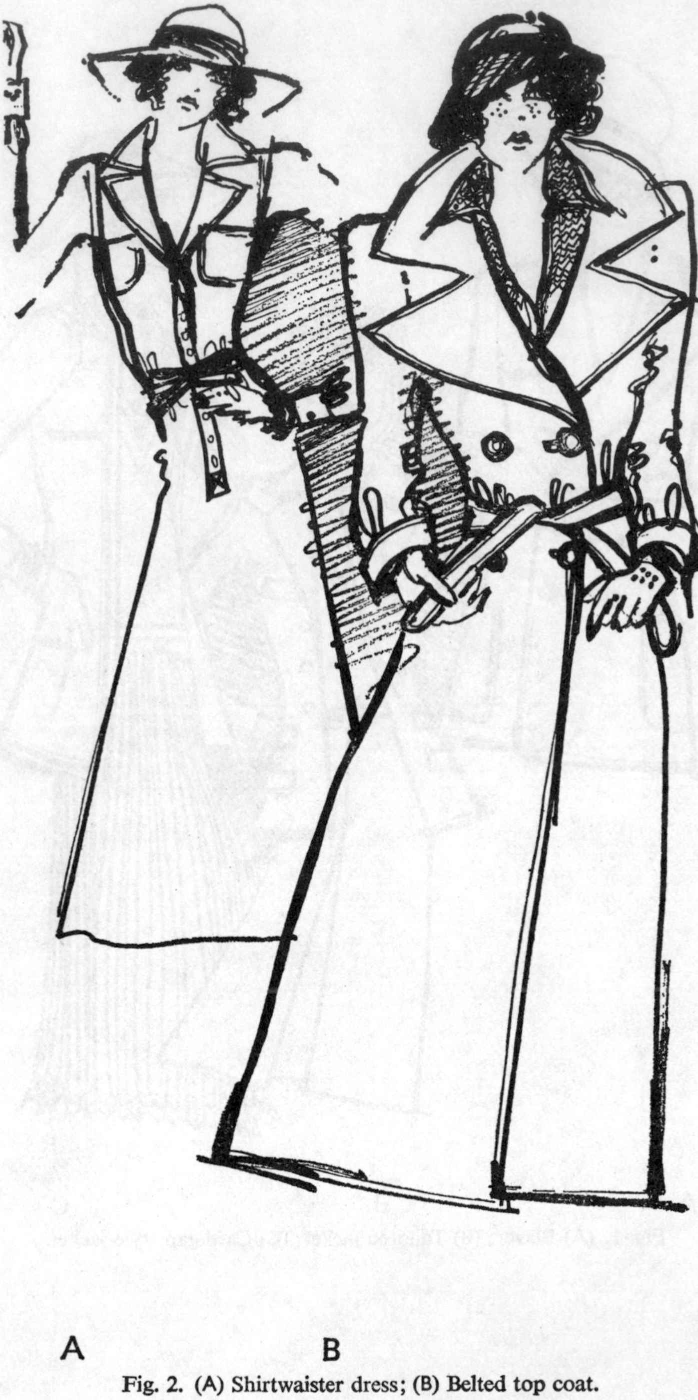

A B

Fig. 2. (A) Shirtwaister dress; (B) Belted top coat.

Fig. 3. (A) Polo-neck sweater; (B) V-neck sweater; (C) Cardigan.

Fig. 4. (A) and (B) Burberry style trench coats.

Fig. 5. (A) Circular skirt; (B) Pleated skirt; (C) Culottes.

Fig. 6. (A) Pyjama style evening trousers; (B) Tailored trousers; (C) Jeans.

seem to show. Careful analysis reveals that trends can appear many years before they are taken up on a wholesale basis. Often the timing is wrong and the public eye misses the message. An avant-garde French designer produced a range of thirties- and forties-styled coats a good ten years before they hit the wider fashion scene. The change is always more gradual than it appears. The function of clothes, as well as the method of putting them together, however, does not change. It is the shape and outline that alter according to the fashion mood of the time.

Classics

Keeping function and method in mind, one is led naturally to the classics. The very name indicates a clean, smooth, undating line and comprises a set of basic designs which can vary their shape enough to fit in with the current fashion look.

The twentieth century has produced some remarkable classics, from ideas that date from way back, were later refined, and have been worn continuously, in some form or other, for more than sixty years.

The shirtwaister dress, the Burberry style trench coat, trousers, tailored suits, skirts and sweaters had been seen earlier, but were accepted generally during the 1914–18 War. Necessity and practicability were two excellent reasons for this acceptance.

Next, leading French designers promoted them as resort-wear for the rich in the post-war years. Finally, when the skirts narrowed and shortened, and the lines simplified to a new elegance, they filtered through to the general public. (It is interesting to note that two or three great film stars of the thirties who are still very much with us, classics themselves, were famous for their raincoats, trousers and the generally sporty image that evolved with them.)

The classics were given a 'Utility' look for the Second World War, when the fashion was for shorter, squarer and more militant-looking clothes. Fuller and longer, once again, they survived through the wilder excesses of the 'New Look' in the late forties and early fifties.

The shirtwaister, in fact, made up in the most luxurious fabrics, gave a new dimension to these classic ideas. It is still here to-day as living proof that good design fits in with any period and is totally adaptable to any situation.

Suitability to Figure

Are you short, tall, fat, thin, average, square-shouldered, round-shouldered, bulging or drooping? Do you know what shape you are? Eating and standing the right way help greatly to improve your figure, but figures do vary individually. An accurate record of measurements and an honest appraisal in the mirror can help you assess your figure type. So can a candid photograph!

Choosing a design suitable for you or for someone else, can be a stimulating exercise. As suggested earlier in this chapter, give a little thought to the current shapes of clothes, fashion lines, colour and fabrics, and learn to know which are most flattering to your particular figure. Keep in mind the following simple points. Generally speaking, vertical shapes, but not necessarily design lines, make you look taller, whereas horizontal lines make you look broader. Straight lines are harder but they can be strong design lines, although a curved line is more graceful. A waist-length jacket looks younger than a hip-length one, but can you afford to be horizontally sliced across the middle? You can keep the short look by simply dropping the jacket length a matter of 5–8 cm (2–3 in). It can be fitted or straight, depending on the current fashion, but remember that the longer the jacket the heavier it looks, especially at the lower hip length. Necklines, sleeve lines, waistlines and hemlines all act as

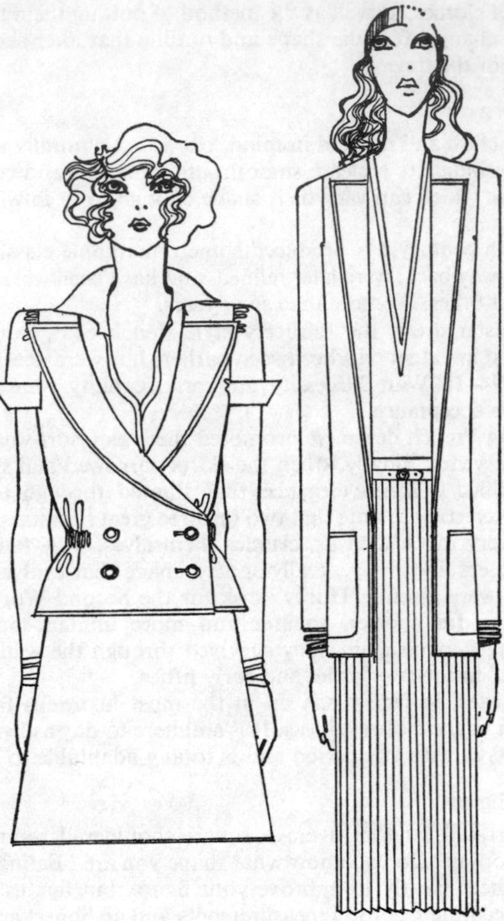

Fig. 7. Bad design lines for (A) a short figure and (B) a tall figure.

dividers. Remember that the length of these can usually be varied enough to suit you, without altering the basic fashion line of the design.

Skirts slightly flared toward the hem are good for all shapes, but especially for heavier hip sizes. Pleated skirts are always attractive, but for larger sizes pleats should be stitched at hip level, or sewn in groups of two or three. Straight skirts are more difficult to flatter, unless the wearer is slim and the skirt length a good balance for her height. Gathered skirts are a downright danger on anyone with an average-plus waistline and plus hips! Circular skirts also tend to increase the appearance of the hip size, but are flattering when the fullness starts at or just below hip level.

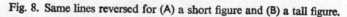

Fig. 8. Same lines reversed for (A) a short figure and (B) a tall figure.

Keep dramatic collars for dramatic occasions. If you like the idea of a cape effect, try it out first to see if you look like a mushroom as opposed to a model.

The burning question of length will always be with us. Let commonsense rule here. Only the Ancient Egyptians solved this one—they hardly changed

the length or style of their garments for 3000 years, which could indicate a stable and happy people. Find the length which suits you best and, in spite of all-seeming fashion changes, vary it no more than 2·5 cm (1 in) up or down. You may end up with your own classic.

CHAPTER TWO

TAKING MEASUREMENTS

Metric and Imperial Measurements

The following is a conversion and comparison chart, with metric measurements rounded up to the nearest 0·5 cm, as approved by the Pattern Fashion Industry (a metric conversion chart for fabric buying is given on page 262). The units of imperial and metric measurements are shown below, but note that this is not part of the comparison chart, i.e. 100 cm is not 1 yd.

Metric unit	*Abbreviation*	*Imperial unit*
Metre (100 centimetres)	m	Yard
Centimetre (10 millimetres)	cm	Inch
Millimetre	mm	

NEAREST MILLIMETRES AND CENTIMETRES TO INCHES

Cm	*Mm*	*In*	*Cm*	*In*
0·3	3	$\frac{1}{8}$	33·0	13
0·6	6	$\frac{1}{4}$	35·5	14
1·0	10	$\frac{3}{8}$	38·0	15
1·3		$\frac{1}{2}$	40·5	16
1·5		$\frac{5}{8}$	43·0	17
2·0		$\frac{3}{4}$	46·0	18
2·2		$\frac{7}{8}$	48,5	19
2·5		1	51·0	20
3·2		$1\frac{1}{4}$	53·5	21
3·8		$1\frac{1}{2}$	56·0	22
4·5		$1\frac{3}{4}$	58·5	23
5·0		2	61·0	24
6·5		$2\frac{1}{2}$	63·5	25
7·5		3	66·0	26
9·0		$3\frac{1}{2}$	68·5	27
10·0		4	71·0	28
11·5		$4\frac{1}{2}$	73·5	29
12·5		5	76·0	30
14·0		$5\frac{1}{2}$	79·0	31
15·0		6	81·5	32
18·0		7	84·0	33
20·5		8	86·5	34
23·0		9	89·0	35
25·5		10	91·5	36
28·0		11	94·0	37
30·5		12	96·5	38

NEAREST MILLIMETERS AND CENTIMETERS TO INCHES

Cm	*In*	*Cm*	*In*
99·0	39	114·5	45
101.5	40	117·0	46
104·0	41	119·5	47
106·5	42	122·0	48
109·0	43	124·5	49
112·0	44	127·0	50

How to take Body Measurements

The cause of many ill-fitting garments can frequently be attributed to the taking of incorrect body measurements. Well-fitting garments require, initially, the correct use of the tape measure. When applied accurately to the main parts of the body, measurements can easily be compared with the flat pattern, checked and adjusted if necessary. Commercial patterns are available in a large variety of sizes, to suit most figure types. Therefore, alterations to patterns from your own body measurements should be minimal, which will make fittings later on easier and more successful. In order to avoid discrepancies, be sure to take your measurements with precision and here is how to do it.

Start by wearing the foundation garments you feel happiest in and which will most likely be worn with the planned garment. Wear it throughout all the fitting stages, because when measuring the body, or fitting your clothes, changing from one type of foundation garment to another leads to enormous differences in measurements. Tie a narrow belt, cord or string around your waist. This places the waist in its natural position, where it is smallest. Stand in front of a full-length mirror. For full-length dresses or trousers wear the type of shoes you normally like best, to give an accurate reading for length.

A plea at this stage: do not use excessive zeal and measure too tightly. It may well be psychologically tempting to do so, but breathing in and holding breath is cheating and ultimately only accentuates any feature meant to be played down. There are better ways of hiding figure faults.

It is also worthwhile to be fully aware of the contours and bone structure of the body and how its limbs work, although a wealth of anatomical knowledge is not essential. By seeing and feeling your body you become aware perhaps as never before, for we take it for granted, that limbs articulate in a certain manner. The lower arm bends forward from the elbow, but cannot do the reverse. Legs bend backwards from below the knee cap, but not forwards. Sitting down is obviously vastly different from standing up.

Clothes must accommodate our requirements for movement and comply with the demands of our physical actions. Garments too-tightly fitting may not only look aesthetically wrong, but also restrict essential normal movements of the body and feel most uncomfortable. Tight fit, desired by some women, can still be realized if applied in the correct form, but the type of fabric to be used must also be taken into account. Where one material gives to pressure of body and limbs, as for example a knitted jersey, others do not. Yet the opposite, of not measuring tautly enough, produces equally undesirable results.

Readers may ask if it is necessary to measure all the parts of the body listed on pages 20–7. Indeed, if no help is available from someone else, measuring some of them would prove a very difficult task, but to obtain maximum accuracy it is obvious that assistance is highly desirable. Should this not be possible, measure only those listed in **bold type**. Commercial patterns are often confined to a minimum number of measurements: these are adequate for purchasing your current size, but garments may require more attention at fittings. The additional measurements mentioned, if available (taking some from old garments made of firm, non-stretch material may help), can be checked against patterns. Adjustments can be made, if necessary, before proceeding to cut out the fabric and you are then prepared for fittings with less problems to face.

The following four figures illustrate the positioning of the tape measure on and around the front of the body.

Measure the girth on the main parts of the body by holding the tape horizontally, keeping it straight and taut and measure the following. (Once your statistics have been taken keep them in a safe place, preferably in the form of a chart as suggested on page 27).

(1) Bust. Place the tape over the fullest part of the bust and around the body. Do not let it slip down at the back.

(2) Waist. A belt, cord or string, tied around the waist, places it in its normal position, where it is smallest. Measure around the waist.

(3) Hips. Measure:

(a) High hips at 7·5–10 cm (3–4 in) below the waist.
(b) Low hips at 18–20·5 cm (7–8 in) below the waist.
(c) From the hips, and with both feet together, slide the tape over the thighs. When these are prominent, take the measurement at the widest part.

(4) Back waist length (centre back neck to waist). Measure from nape of neck to centre back of natural waist.

(5) Front waist length. Measure:

(a) From nape of neck at centre back, pass around the side of neck at shoulder to the most prominent point of the bust.
(b) Over bust to waist. (Note both (a) and (b) measurements).
(c) Base of front neck (hollow between the collar bones) to centre front waist.

(6). Chest. Measure with the tape directly, under the arms, all around the body.

(7) Across front. At 9 cm ($3\frac{1}{2}$ in) below the base of the front neck, from left to right armhole.

(8) Across back. At 12·5 cm (5 in) below the prominent bone at the base of the back neck, measure from left to right armhole.

(9) Neck. Measure the circumference of the neck just above the base.

(10) Shoulder. From the base at the side of neck to the shoulder bone.

(11) Bodice side seam (depth of armhole). Measure from about 2·5 cm (1 in) under the arm pit to the waist at your side. (The measurement between the top of the side seam at the arm pit and the end of the shoulder seam, at the

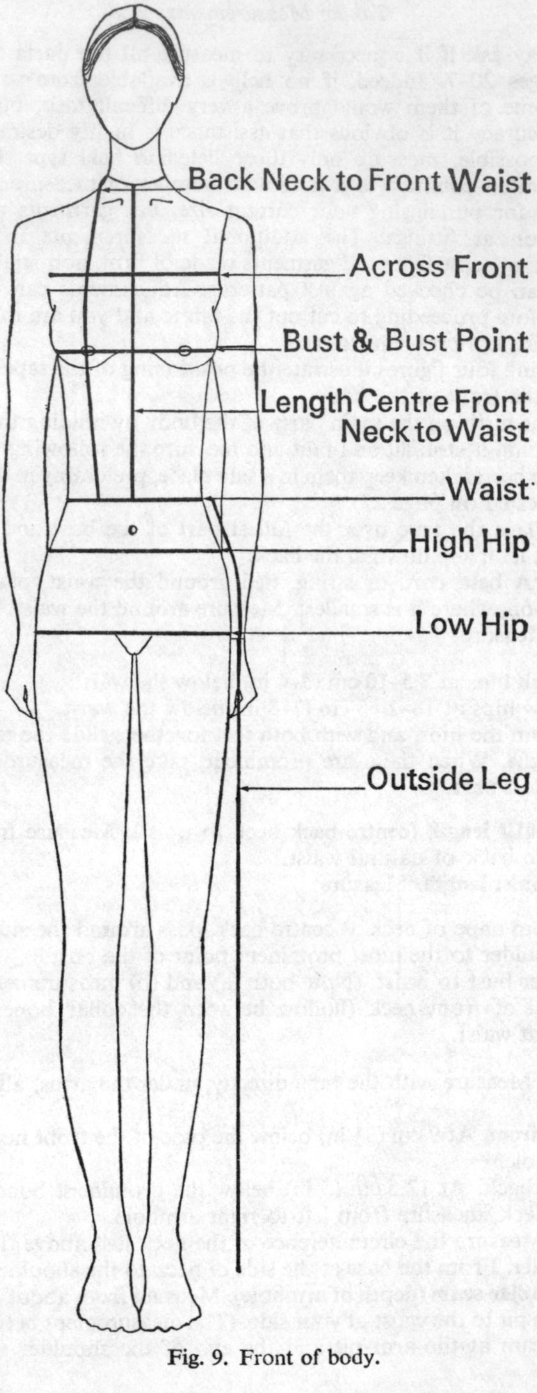

Fig. 9. Front of body.

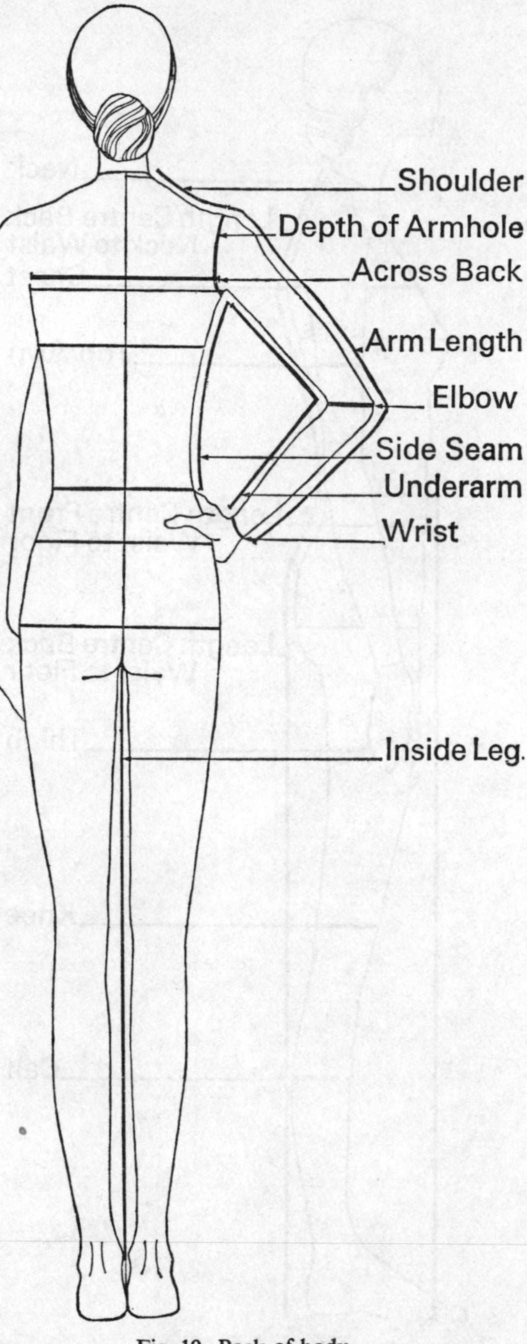

Fig. 10. Back of body.

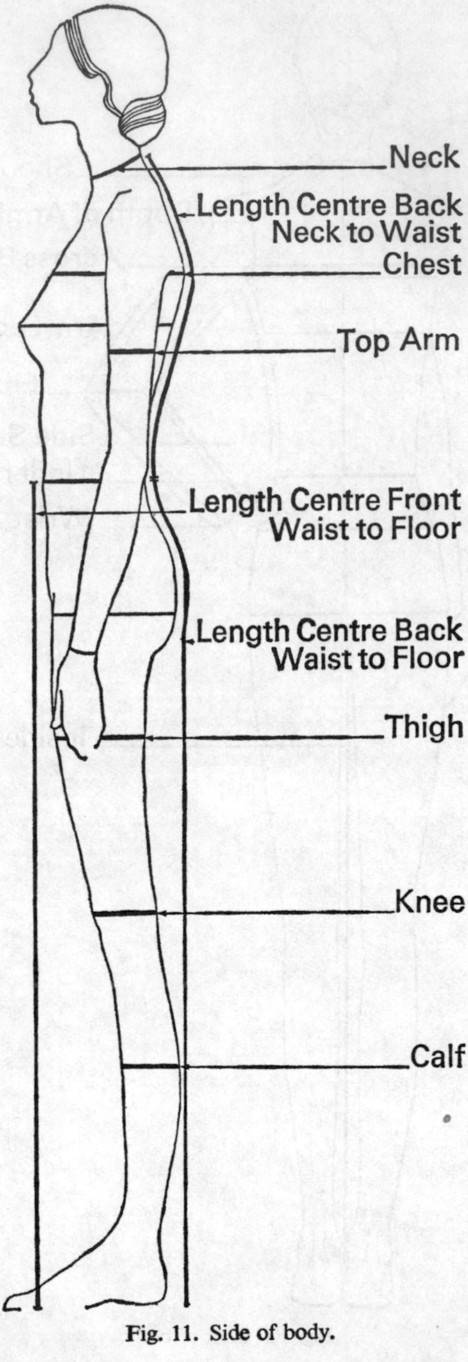

Fig. 11. Side of body.

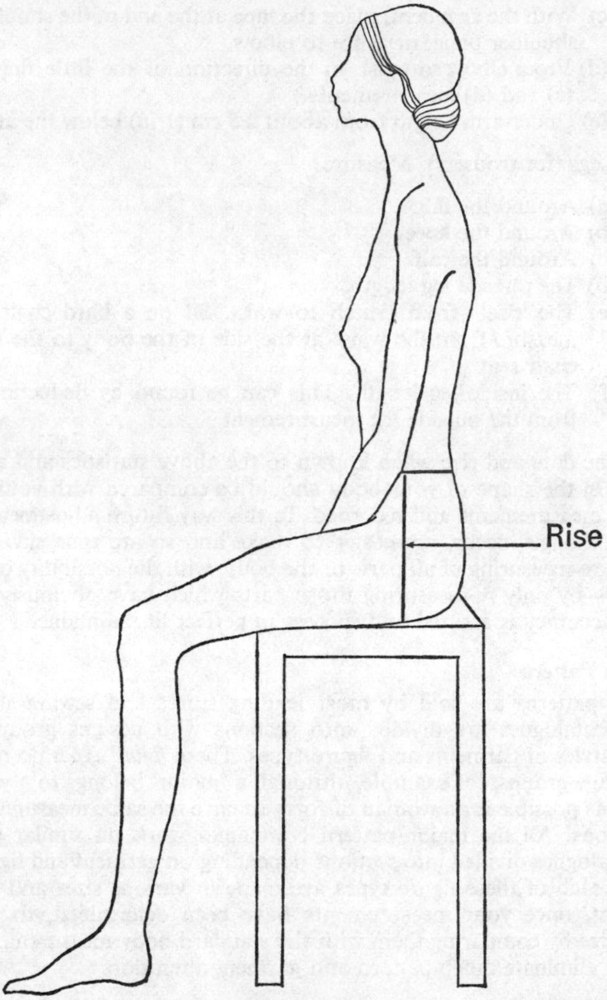

Fig. 12. Waist to crutch (rise).

shoulder bone, equals the depth of the armhole and the height of the sleeve crown.)

(12) Full length (waist to floor). Measure:

(a) Front waist to floor.
(b) Side waist to floor.
(c) Centre back waist to floor.

(13) Arms. Measure:

(a) Fullest part of the upper arm in a bent position.
(b) Around wrist.

(c) With the arm bent, place the tape at the end of the shoulder at the shoulder bone, measure to elbow.
(d) From elbow to wrist, in the direction of the little finger. (Note (c) and (d) measurements.)
(e) Under-arm length from about 2·5 cm (1 in) below the arm pit.

(14) Legs (for trousers). Measure:

(a) Around the **thigh.**
(b) Around the **knee.**
(c) Around the **calf.**
(d) The outside leg length.
(e) The **'rise'**—from crutch to waist. Sit on a hard chair or stool, measure from the waist at the side of the body to the top of the chair seat.
(f) The inside leg length. This can be found by deducting the rise from the outside leg measurement.

Add the date and size when known to the above statistics and any future changes in the shape of your body should be compared with your previous chart of measurements and recorded. In this way future adjustments to patterns, if changes occur, are easier to make and so are time saving. Avoid frequent re-measuring of all parts of the body, with the possibility of different readings—by only re-measuring those parts which have obviously changed, greater accuracy is assured and success in perfect fit maintained.

Buying a Pattern

Paper patterns are sold by most leading stores and sewing shops. The pattern catalogues are divided into sections with designs grouped under various styles of garments and figure types. These *figure types* do not always refer to age groups, for example, although a 'junior' belongs to a young girl, it is just as possible for a woman of forty to have the same measurements and proportions. All the major pattern companies work on similar lines with their catalogues divided into sections depending on garment and figure types. In turn, each of these figure types are made in various sizes and it is most important, once your measurements have been determined, to find your correct size by comparing them with the standard body measurements given. This will eliminate much pattern and garment alteration.

Pattern Measurements

Some confusion may arise as soon as a comparison between your body measurements and the pattern measurements is made. Having bought the 'correct' size, it may come as a surprise to find that the pattern exceeds your body measurements, but remember that when you measured your body you made no allowance for body movement, as previously discussed. A given amount of ease is incorporated into every pattern and these allowances in measurements, over and above those of the body, vary considerably. As already mentioned, the amount will depend on the type of fabric used and taking its give and stretch into account. For example, about 7·5 cm (3 in) on the bust, 2·5 cm (1 in) at the waist, and 5 cm (2 in) on the hips is allowed on 'misses' patterns, with much less allowed for knit fabrics.

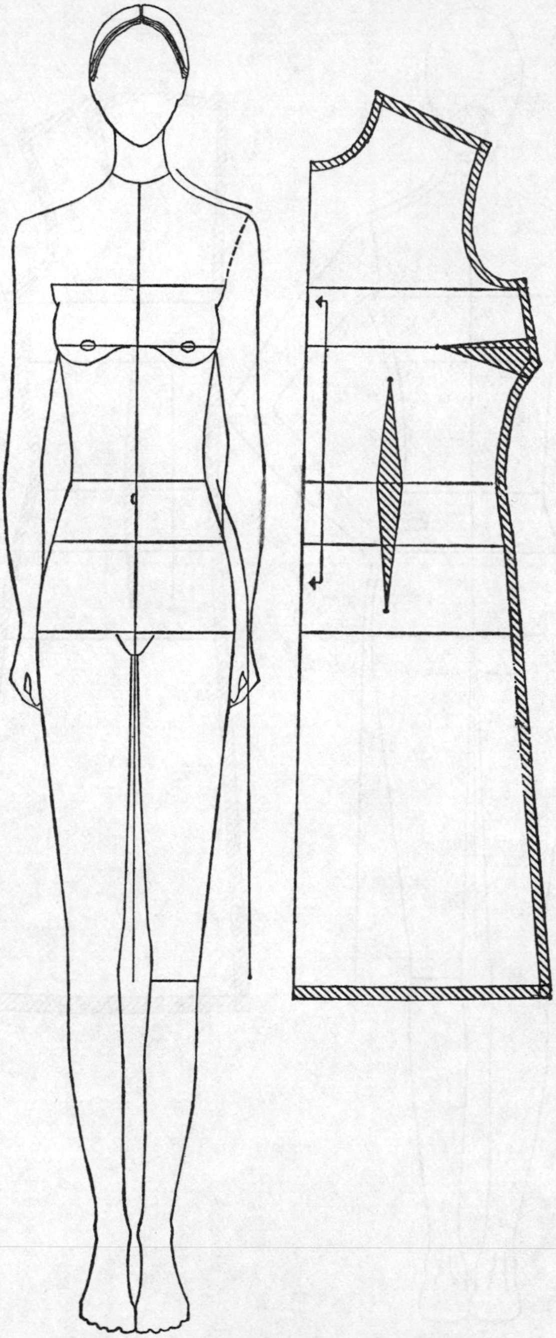

Fig. 13. Front of body and front pattern.

Fig. 14. Back of body and back pattern.

MEASUREMENT CHART

	cm / in
(1) Bust	..../....
(2) Waist	..../....
(3) Hips	..../....
(a) High	..../....
(b) Low	..../....
(c) Prominent thighs	..../....
(4) Back waist length	..../....
(5) Front waist length	..../....
(a) Centre back neck to bust point	..../....
(b) Bust to waist	..../....
(a) and (b) measurements combined give the front waist length	..../....
(c) Base of front neck to centre front waist	..../....
(6) Chest	..../....
(7) Across front	..../....
(8) Across back	..../....
(9) Neck	..../....
(10) Shoulder	..../....
(11) Bodice side seam	..../....
(12) Full length (waist to floor)	
(a) Front	..../....
(b) Side	..../....
(c) Back	..../....
(13) Arms	
(a) **Top**	..../....
(b) **Wrist**	..../....
(c) Outside length to elbow	..../....
(d) Outside length from elbow to wrist	..../....
(c) and (d) combined give the full outside length	..../....
(e) Under-arm length	..../....
(14) Legs	
(a) **Thigh**	..../....
(b) **Knee**	..../....
(c) **Calf**	..../....
(d) Outside leg length	..../....
(e) **Rise**	..../....
(f) Inside leg length–deduct (e) from (d)	..../....
Height	..../....
Size	..../....
Figure Type	....
Date	....

Silhouette

At the same time the silhouette of every design determines the extra allowance so that a pattern for a fitted garment has less, a semi-fitted has a little more ease and allowances are further increased for a loose-fitting garment. As this is calculated for all parts of the garment, and worked out proportionately, it is wise when buying the first pattern not to settle for a smaller size than recommended.

Sizing

Major commercial pattern companies have a uniform sizing system (not to be confused with wholesale sizes) and their patterns should not be at odds with each other in matters of size denominations. But, if in doubt, it is safer to opt for a slightly larger, rather than too small a pattern. Taking in seams at the fitting stage is a good deal easier than letting them out and there is, of course, a limit to how much you can let out seams. In due course your experience will allow for better discrimination between the variety of patterns available and you will settle for the one nearest to your figure.

There is still another aspect of ease which must be understood. While your size based on body measurement is constant for all types of clothes, pattern measurements must increase for every garment worn over another. A jacket, worn over a blouse and skirt, must allow for this. A coat worn over a suit must be large enough to fit over it comfortably. As the layers increase, so does the amount of ease and this in no way detracts from the principle of shape on any type of garment. A coat can be small or large, fitted, fully-flared, or boxy in shape or look, but its size denomination remains the same.

Personal Choice

Choose the pattern with the bust size nearest your own for dresses, coats, and blouses since this will give a better fit around the neckline, shoulder and armhole—the difficult fitting areas. Buy trouser and skirt patterns according to waist size and adjust the hip measurement if necessary. If your hip size is much larger in proportion than your waist, then the pattern should be bought to hip size. With combination patterns—coat, top, trousers and skirt—chose the bust size and adjust the waist and hip if necessary. When measurements fall between two sizes, choose the smaller sizing if you are small boned, the larger if you are large boned.

Look for designs which have few seams, darts or details such as pockets, collars, or buttonholes. Suitable fabrics are also suggested for each design and it is essential to check on these, as wrong fabrics would alter the design shape. On the back of the pattern envelope there is a description of the garment as well as a back view. It is most important to read this, since an easy-looking flared skirt with unpressed pleats may have concealed pockets, making it a more complicated pattern to work on for the first attempt.

The number of pattern pieces is also given and comparing it with similar designs can help you to find the simplest design to make up. A list of haberdashery needed (zips, sewing silk, etc.) is also given. Combination patterns with skirts, trousers, tops or jackets and coats, in one pattern-envelope are the best value. Children's patterns follow similar lines with special sizings for toddlers and children including chubbier ones.

Fashion Measurement

Professionally there is yet another way of measuring known as **fashion measurement**: this quite simply refers to the ever present question of how long the skirt, how deep the neckline and how narrow or wide the shoulder is in prevailing fashion trends.

It means, in practice, the gentle art of keeping the design in balance while shortening, narrowing, or lengthening. It is not, therefore, feasible to lop 20 cm (8 in) off the hem and trust you have a new short length, or add 30 cm (1 ft) and expect the result to be current fashion.

In high fashion, measurements are often carried to extremes to make way for change. The skirt is brought down to mid-calf, for example, in order to get everyone used to the idea that the mini has had its day, or the shoulders are widened to pave the way again for a padded look.

Adjusting Pattern to Figure

The variety of fashion designs and the diversity of design adaptations are too numerous to count, but adjustments to patterns to fit the individual figure are common to most.

Having taken a closer look at yourself, you will have gained a better appreciation of the complex structure of your body. The pattern can now be seen in relation to its contours and the reasons for seams and darts to accommodate your shape will seem less mysterious. Good patterns are positive statements of design and fit. They are constructed to comply with the human anatomy and the splendid articulation it is capable of. But we must realize and take note of the fact, that no two people are exactly alike, whether in build of body, appearance or any other form whatsoever. So some adjustments of patterns to allow for individual differences in basic figure types are inevitable. On the whole though, these should only be of a relatively minor nature and mainly consist of small additions to, or subtractions from girth and/or length measurements.

There is one rule however which must be obeyed: alterations to one part of a pattern invariably affect another and so **lengthening or shortening any given seam line must be accompanied by doing likewise to any other, which ultimately holds two separate parts together.** To give just one example, an addition to length of front shoulder requires an equal increase to back shoulder seam. Where facings and linings are affected by alterations to main parts of the pattern, do make sure that here, too, identical adjustments are made. Although really an elementary principle, this is often ignored or overlooked.

Irrespective of any type of design other than one consisting of one piece of fabric (not very often found), no single part of a garment is of any use on its own unless sewn to another at some position and all of them must be cut to fit together perfectly. At the same time, a pattern for a design consisting of numerous parts need not be frightening to any reader. After all, every garment when finally assembled has reverted from *x* number of oddly-shaped, separate pieces to one whole complete recognizable form, with clearly definable lines such as centre front, centre back and sides throughout the whole of a garment.

Anticipating chapter five, in which we suggest six basic garments, four of these will be used to illustrate likely adjustments on patterns (the same adjustment methods can apply equally to the two remaining garments):

(1) Skirt.
(2) Sleeveless shift dress.
(3) Jacket with sleeves.
(4) Trousers.

When the pattern has been removed from the envelope, smooth out any creases with a warm, dry iron. The accompanying instruction sheet repeats front and back views of the garment(s), alongside the pattern view. Each piece of pattern is distinctively marked for easy identification. Place body pattern pieces on a table with the side seams facing each other; the back on the left-hand side, front on the right-hand side; collar near the neckline; cuff near the sleeve; and facings close to where they are going to be sewn to. Remember that you are looking at half of the back or front piece (each to be cut twice).

Compare the *bust*, *waist* and *hip* measurements of the pattern with your own, by measuring from centre back to side seam and from side seam to centre front at the appropriate place. Make certain that seam allowances, pleats darts, overlaps and buttonwraps are not included. Double this measurement and you can now ascertain the exact amount of ease allowed on the pattern. These are usually quite generous and it is left to your discretion to decide if, by comparing your body measurements to those stated on the pattern envelope, increases or decreases are needed. Carry out the same comparison

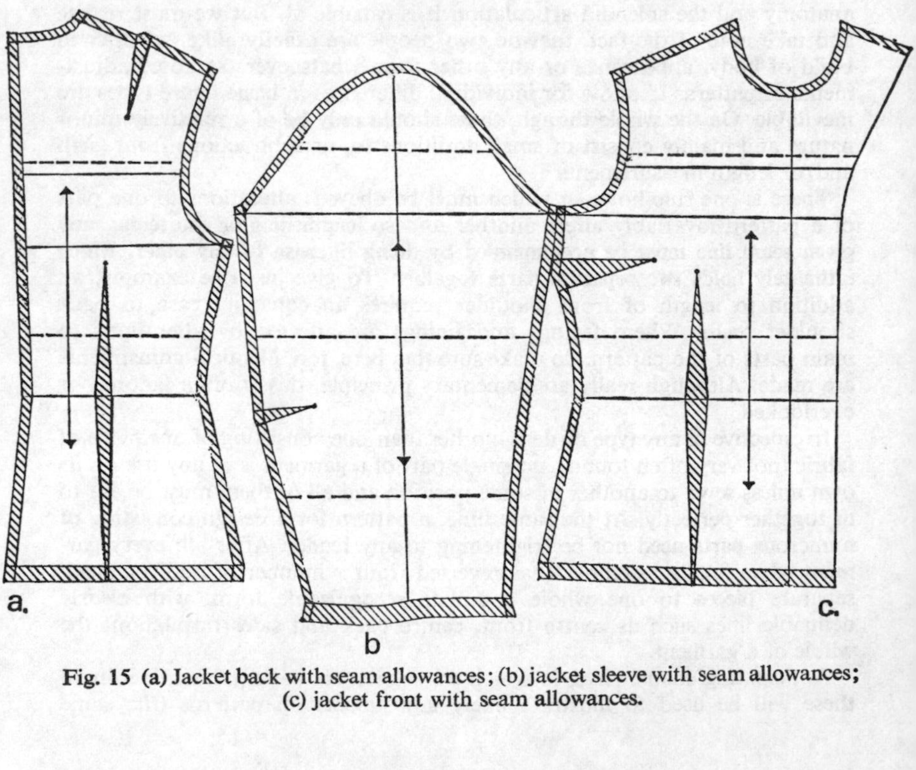

Fig. 15 (a) Jacket back with seam allowances; (b) jacket sleeve with seam allowances; (c) jacket front with seam allowances.

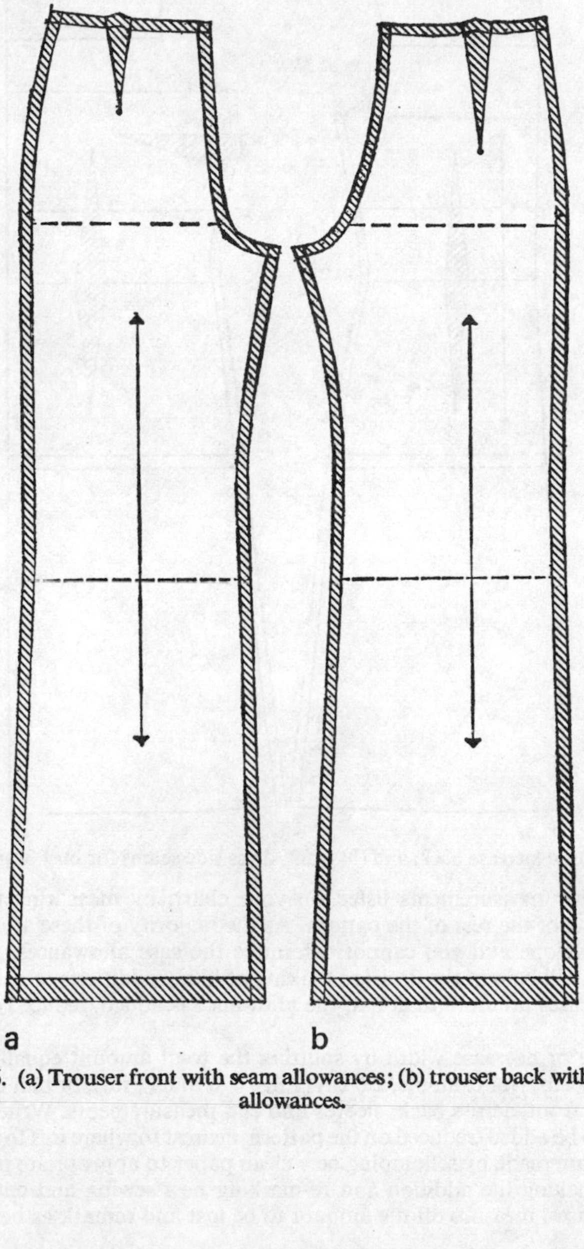

Fig. 16. (a) Trouser front with seam allowances; (b) trouser back with seam allowances.

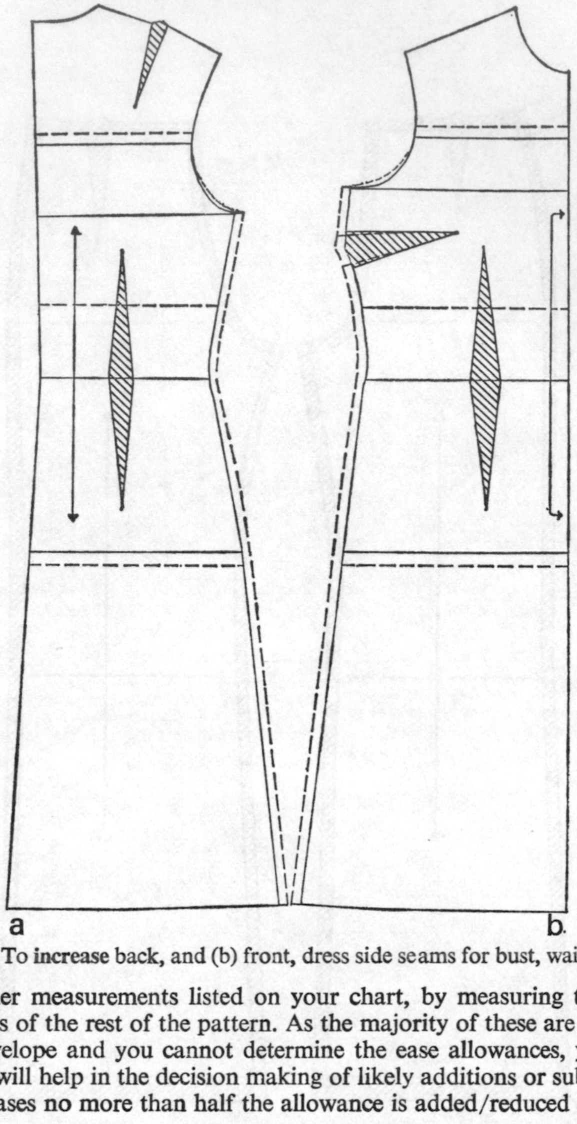

Fig. 17. (a) To increase back, and (b) front, dress side seams for bust, waist and hips.

for all other measurements listed on your chart, by measuring the appropriate parts of the rest of the pattern. As the majority of these are not stated on the envelope and you cannot determine the ease allowances, your commonsense will help in the decision making of likely additions or subtractions. (In most cases no more than half the allowance is added/reduced at the side seams.)

Increase or decrease width by splitting the total amount equally over the four side seams (for example, 2·5 cm (1 in) = 6 mm ($\frac{1}{4}$ in)), or half of the total for across front, across back, sleeves and cuff measurements. Write down the amount to be added/reduced on the pattern, nearest to where it is to take place. Increases are made by sellotaping new clean paper to appropriate parts of the pattern, making the addition and re-marking new sewing and cutting lines. For decreases, measure off the amount to be lost and remark as before.

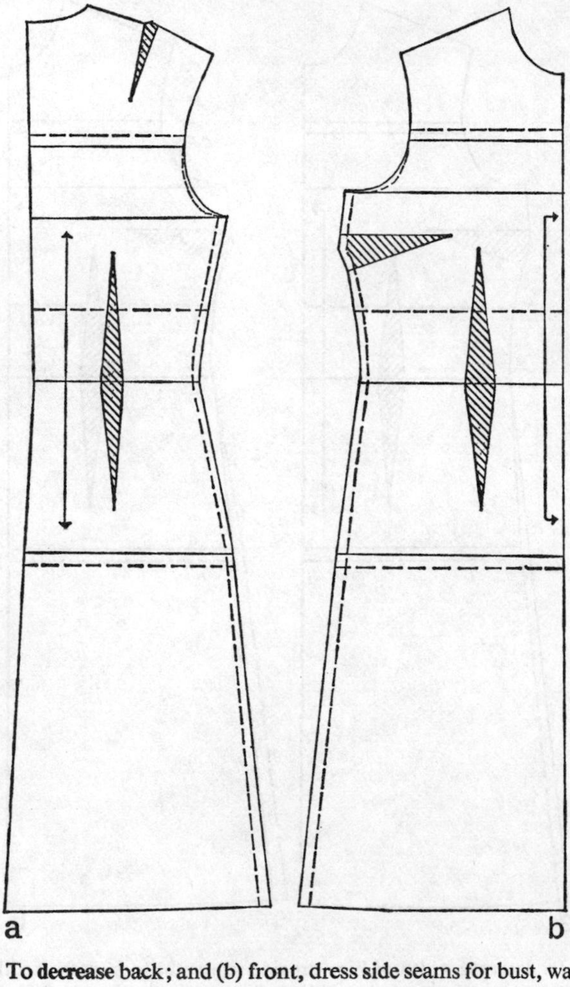

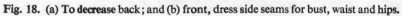

Fig. 18. (a) To decrease back; and (b) front, dress side seams for bust, waist and hips.

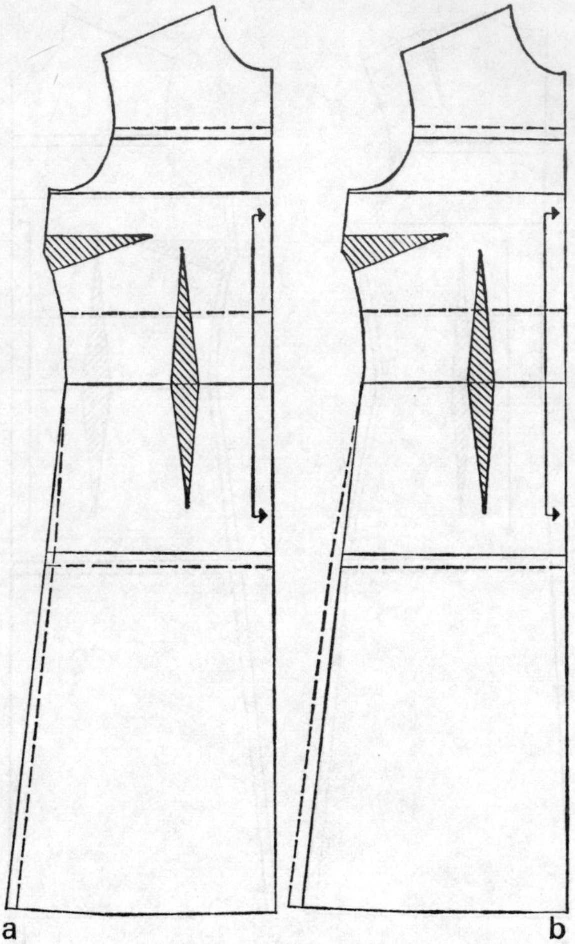

Fig. 19. (a) To decrease width of hips on side seam; (b) to increase width of hips on side seam.

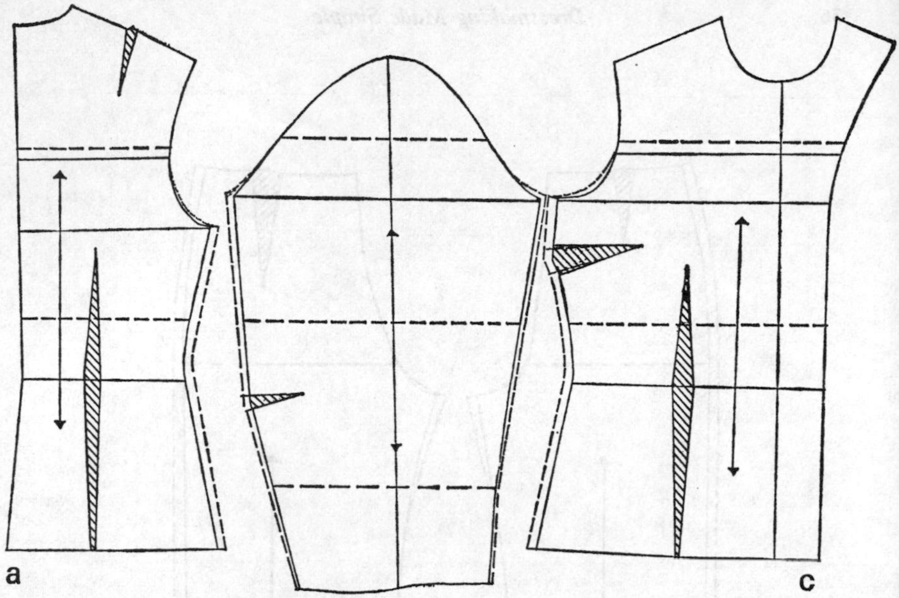

a b c

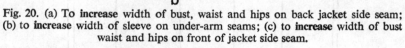

Fig. 20. (a) To increase width of bust, waist and hips on back jacket side seam; (b) to increase width of sleeve on under-arm seams; (c) to increase width of bust waist and hips on front of jacket side seam.

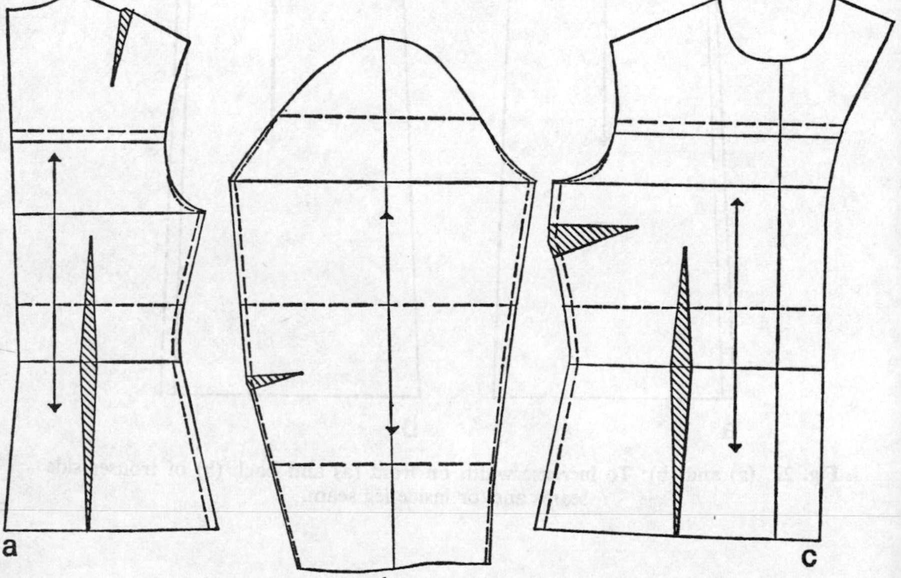

a b c

Fig. 21. (a), (b) and (c): To decrease width as for Fig. 20.

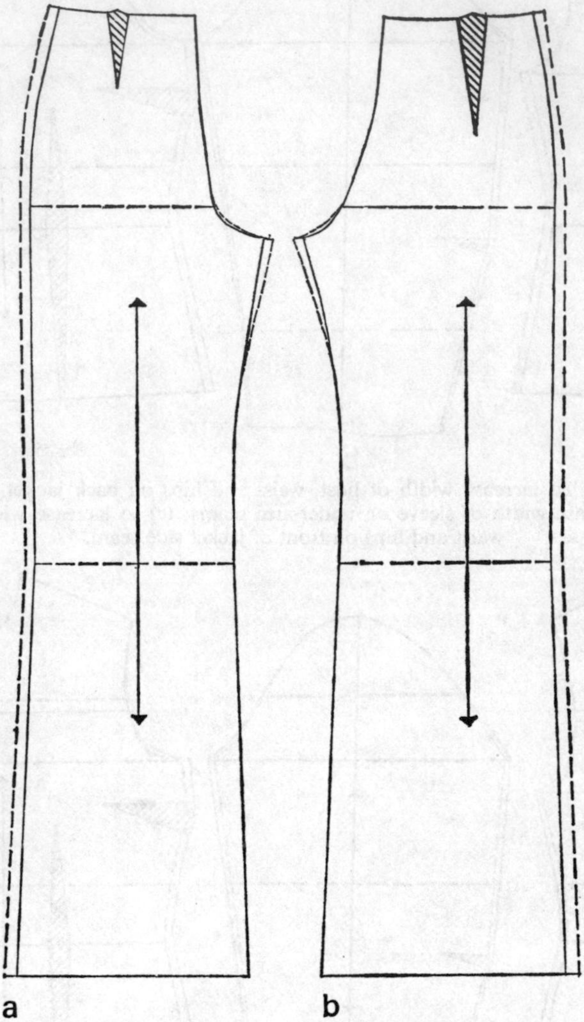

Fig. 22. (a) and (b): To increase width on front (a) and back (b) of trouser side seams and/or inside leg seam.

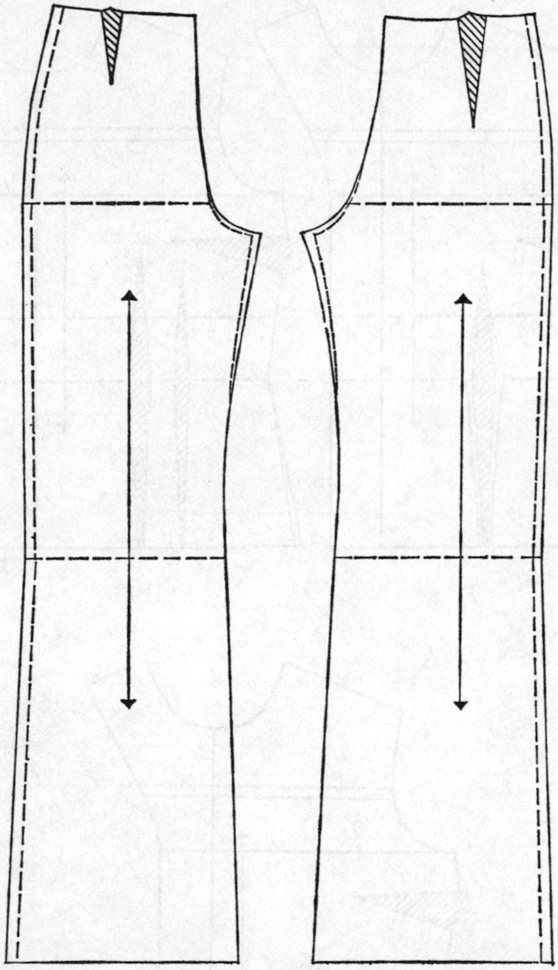

Fig. 23. (a) and (b): To **decrease** width as for Fig. 22.

When adjustments are necessary on only the bust, waist or hips, good use can also be made of darts as an additional aid towards good fit. Darts are used to create shape, technically known as **suppression**. Hence to suppress material from a prominent bust and/or hips to a small waist, requires a deep waist dart, whilst the reverse (large waist, small bust and/or hip) needs only a shallow one. Generally, when deviations from a standard set of measurements occur, adjust to individual measurements by increasing or decreasing the size (depth and length) of waist darts, or add a second dart for decreases.

Patterns are usually marked with special lines at the places most suitable

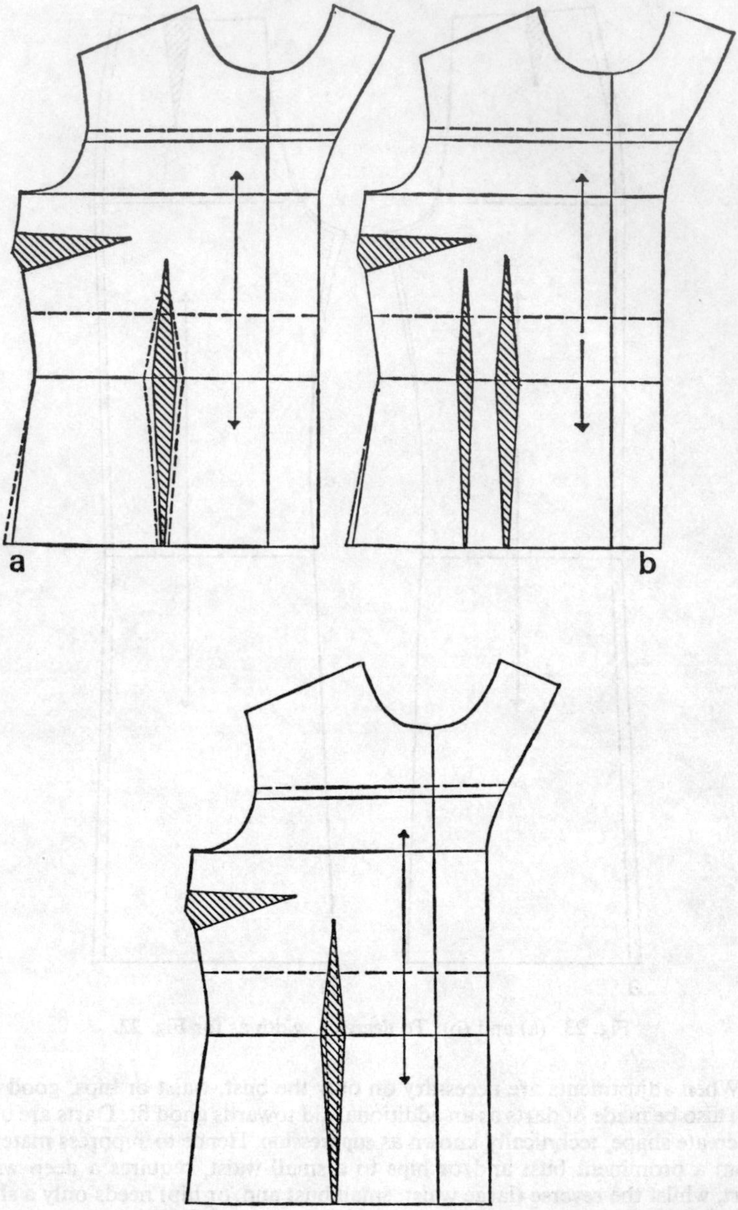

Fig. 24. (a) To increase depth of dart on front of jacket for a smaller waist/prominent bust; (b) second dart introduced to achieve the same result but spreading the increase more evenly if in excess of just a small amount; (c) to decrease dart for a larger waist.

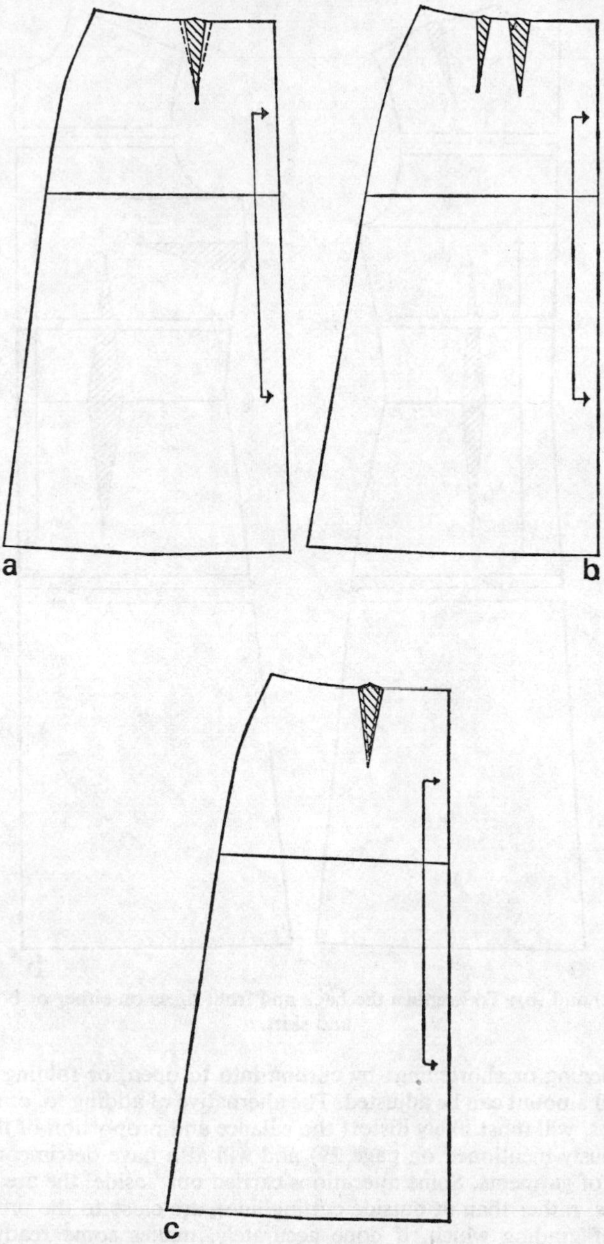

Fig. 25. (a) To increase dart on skirt for a smaller waist/prominent hips; (b) second dart introduced to achieve the same result. See Fig. 24 (b); (c) to decrease dart for a larger waist.

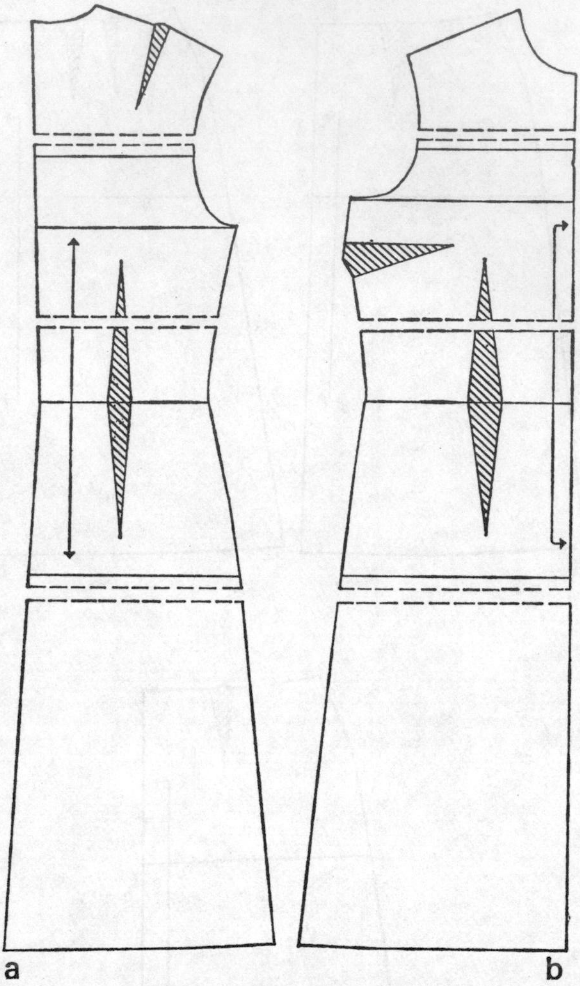

Fig. 26. (a) and (b): To **lengthen** the back and front dress on either or both bodice and skirt.

for lengthening or shortening: by cutting into to open, or folding to close, the desired amount can be adjusted. The alternative of adding to, or chopping off at hems, will most likely distort the balance and proportion of the design (as previously mentioned on page 29) and will also have detrimental effects on the fit of garments. Some alterations carried out 'inside' the areas of pattern pieces, rather than at outside cutting lines, are close to the professional method of grading which, if done accurately, makes some ready-to-wear garments so perfect in fit. On many designs, the spaces between a group of buttonholes and buttons may be affected by lengthening or shortening. Re-mark to ensure that spaces are equi-distant again.

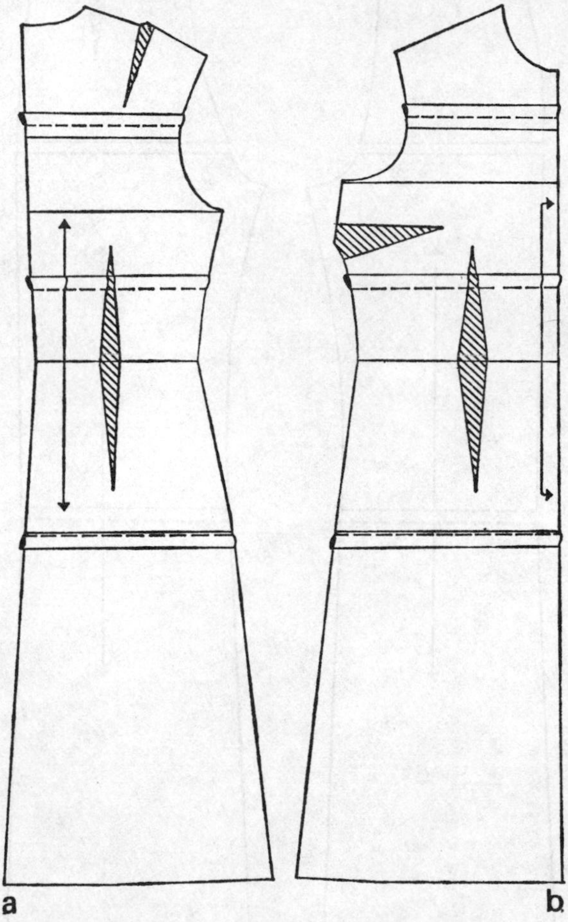

Fig. 27. (a) and (b): To shorten the back and front dress.

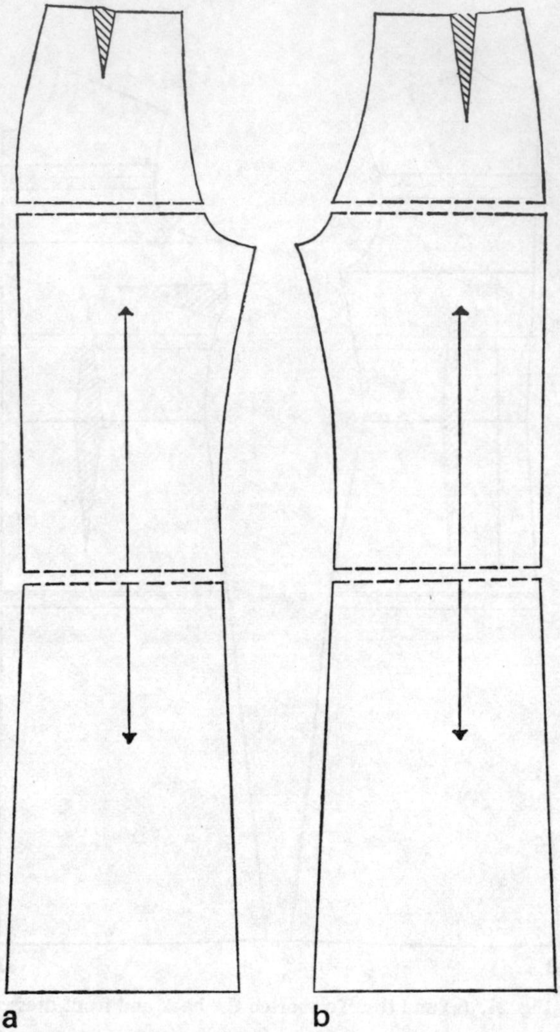

Fig. 28. (a) To lengthen the front; and (b) the back, of trousers from either or both waist to crutch—and crutch to hem.

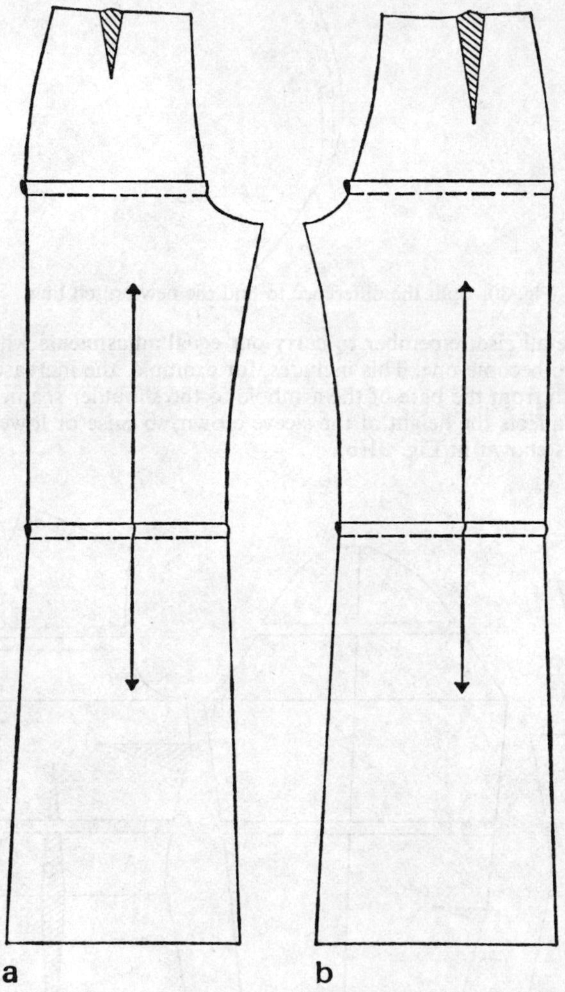

Fig. 29. (a) and (b): To shorten the trousers.

Fig. 30. Split the difference to find the new crutch line.

But above all else remember to carry out **equal adjustments** wherever two pieces join to become one. This includes, for example, the increase or reduction in length from the base of the armhole to the shoulder seam. Alteration to this area affects the height of the sleeve crown, so raise or lower it correspondingly as shown in Fig. 31(b).

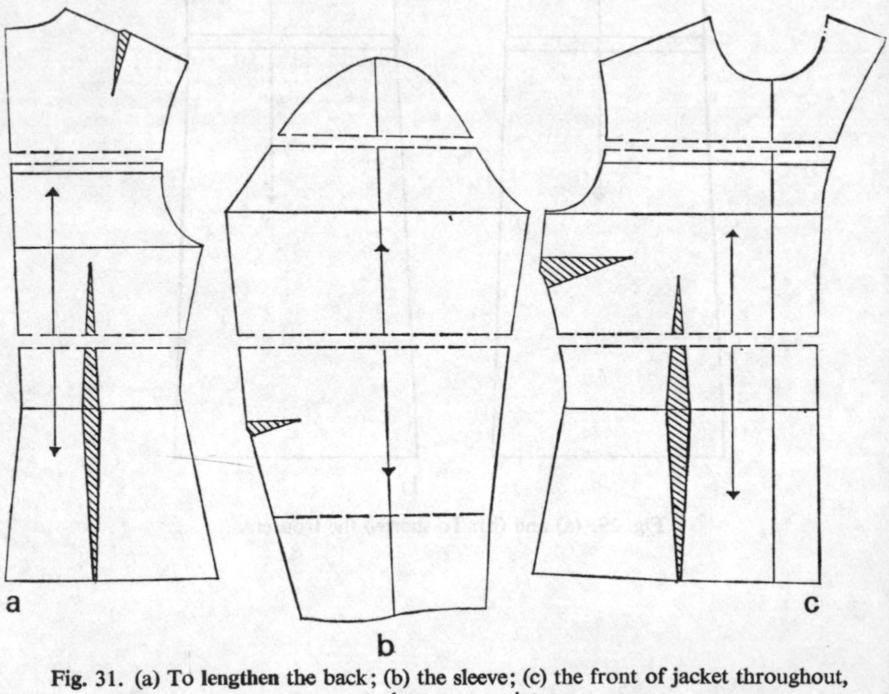

Fig. 31. (a) To lengthen the back; (b) the sleeve; (c) the front of jacket throughout, or where appropriate.

Measure all curved lines with tape in an upright, rather than flat, position. This way accurate readings can be taken. A flat tape moved along a curve increases the true amount between two given points.

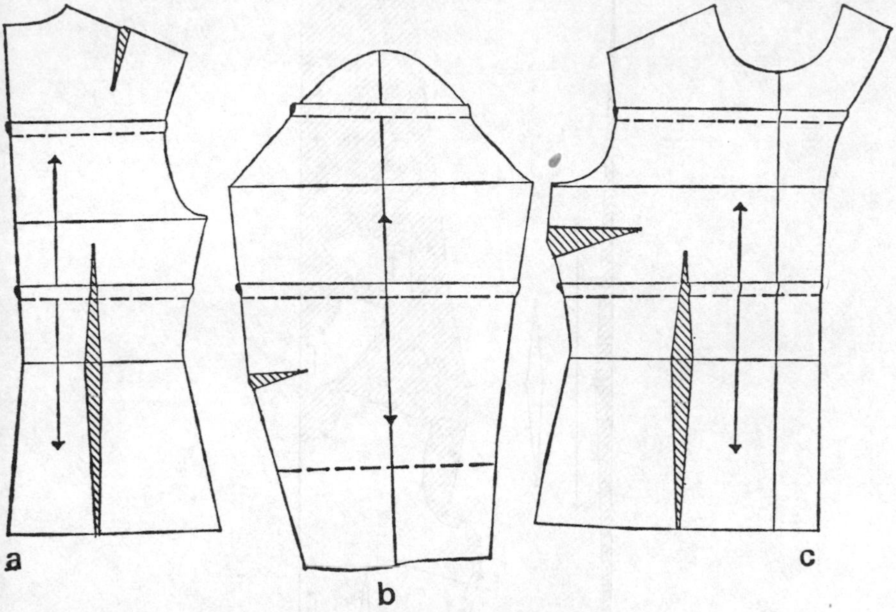

Fig. 32. (a), (b) and (c): To **shorten** jacket and sleeve.

Preparing Pattern for Layout on Fabric

Once again make sure that all creases on the pattern have been ironed out. Count all the pieces and check that none have got lost. Look out for instructions stating the number of each pattern piece to be cut. If you use a fabric with a right and wrong side, make absolutely certain that the two halves of all parts are paired—finding two left sleeves after cutting out, is not going to please you very much. Study grain markings on all pieces and never ignore them.

One of the instructions may read *Place on fold* and be sure to do so for, if you have not, this particular part of the garment is useless, as no seam allowance has been added and there are now two half pieces where one was meant.

Be sure to recognize specific markings for cutting lines, sewing (stitching) lines, notches as balance marks, seam allowances and marks denoting centre front and back, darts, buttonholes and pocket and button positions. Finally cut off all surplus paper on pattern, leaving clean lines for cutting. You may indeed feel anxious and impatient to get on with the cutting of your fabric, but minutes spent in good preparation of the pattern may save hours of frustrated sewing.

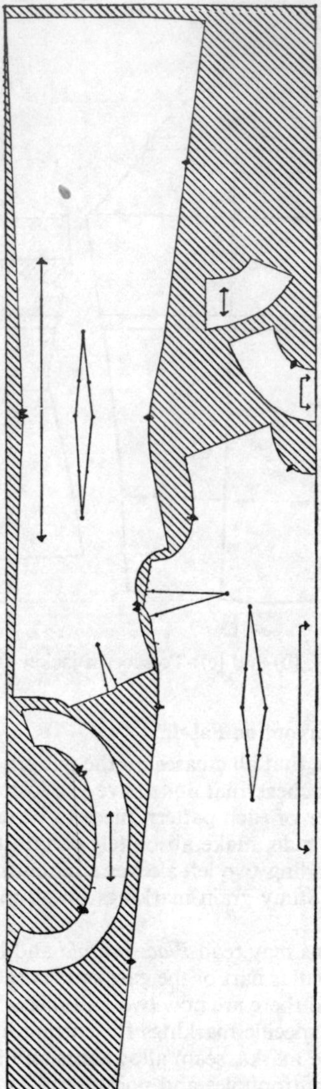

Fig. 33. Layout of dress pattern on narrow fabric.

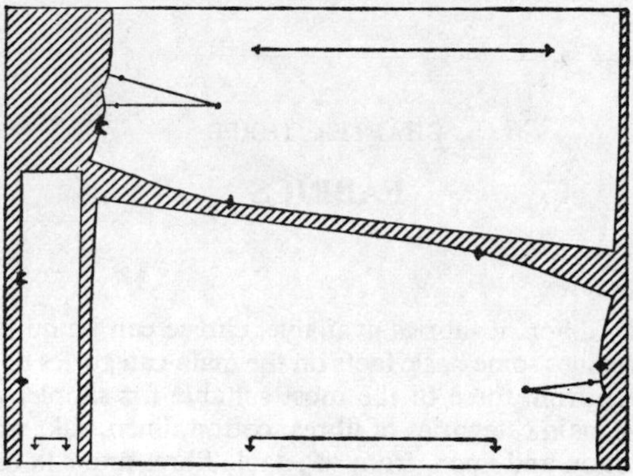

Fig. 34. Layout of skirt pattern on wide fabric.

CHAPTER THREE

FABRICS

Types of Fabrics

With so many different fabrics available, choice can be quite bewildering. This chapter provides some basic facts on the main categories of fabrics, and a selection is made from these of the most suitable for simpler making-up.

There are five main categories of fibres: cotton, linen, silk, wool, and manmade fibres. Cotton and linen, from vegetable fibres and silk and wool from animal fibres, are known as 'natural'. Manmade fibres are manufactured as the name implies, from a wide variety of chemicals and raw materials.

Good and Bad Points

Naturally to the Natural Fibres First

Cotton, from the seed pod of the cotton plant, is very absorbent, durable, lightweight, strong and even stronger when wet: it combines comfort with washability and smoothness. No bad points here, though it has a slight tendency to crease and is not warm enough in winter for some people. The good points, apart from those already mentioned, are that it is easy to make up, presses beautifully and does not stretch or distort when handled.

It blends with manmade fibres to give even greater crease resistance, drip-dry qualities and finishes. Among the many weights and types are poplin, sailcloth, denim, gingham, cotton gabardine, pique, seersucker, organdie, chintz, velveteen and corduroy.

Linen, from the flax plant, is another durable and absorbent fibre, with a lustrous finish. Very hard wearing but, unless it has a special finish, creases easily and frays, making it rather difficult for beginners to make up. Blended with manmade fibres it contributes absorbency, texture and strength and can be made crease resistant. Dress linen, terylene and linen, household textiles and upholstery fabrics, are among the best known linens.

Silk, spun from the cocoon of the silk worm, could well be labelled exquisite. It is lustrous, very strong, durable and springy, though very fine and delicate to handle. It has the added virtue of being warm in cold weather and cool in very hot climates. A fairly experienced hand is needed to make it up, and silk needs very special care and finish. A wide variety of weights include brocade, chiffon, crêpe, foulard (tie-silk), georgette, jersey, lace, organza, satin, shantung, velvet and faille.

Wool, there certainly is no substitute for—coming from the warm and woolly sheep the fibre is springy, durable, with good insulation, absorption and is crease and flame resistant. This warm and comfortable product makes up very well and is shrinkable, so it is excellent for tailoring where shape can be achieved with pressing. Some finishes on wool need special attention: when there is a surface texture, care must be taken so that it does not shine or mark, as described on page 52. Some of the many types of woollen fabrics include felt, flannel, gaberdine, jersey, melton, velour, serge, tweed, barathea and crêpe.

Man-made Fibres

Man-made fibres form two main groups, **cellulose** and **synthetic**. The first group includes rayon, acetate and triacetate. Although processed from wood pulp, a natural base, it is through chemistry that these fibres are obtained. The term 'synthetics' is used loosely for all man-made fibres, but in fact refers only to those chemically created—nylon, polyester and acrylic fibres, among many others. They certainly have many easy-care qualities such as being drip-dry, washable and crease-resistant but, on the other hand, do not handle as well as natural fabrics and can be harder to make up. When blended with naturals, a happier compromise is reached with the best qualities of the manmades and the texture and handle of the natural fabrics. The better known from the man-made groups, including some blends, are nylon, orlon, acrilan, dynel, rayon, courtelle, tricel, terylene, polyester, crimplene and vinyl.

The Fabric for the Garment

Beginners Please

Now that you have an idea of the tremendous variety of fabrics available and an outline of their qualities, the choice can be simplified. We recommend the best of these for ease in making-up, looks and to gain experience in handling fabric perhaps for the first time. From the cotton group choose denim, sailcloth, cotton gabardine or medium to heavy weight poplin and, if patterned, a small print only is advisable. They are easy to stitch, press well, will not distort or stretch in handling and so retain their shape. As they also do not fray too easily, ragged seams and hems are avoided. Look for crease-resist finishes and minimum care.

Wool, plain worsted flannel, closely woven tweed, or similar plain wool cloth all make up easily. As these are softer fabrics some may need shrinking, although most are pre-shrunk (more about this on page 51). The fabrics hang particularly well and plain grey flannel is an all-time classic, which looks expensive too. Tweed needs no further introduction, but remember it must be closely woven such as 'Donegal' or 'Herringbone', both of which are patterned weaves.

Jersey, the medium to heavier weight, double knit jersey, has the same qualities as woven wool but is stretchier as it is a knitted fabric. Even so it sews as easily as the others and is certainly one of the most comfortable materials to wear.

With all of these a good finish is easy to achieve, there are no headaches over initial preparation, which is so much more encouraging than a desperate fight with some springy velvet or saggy crêpe!

Some Fabric Terms

You will need to be well acquainted with some descriptions of fabrics and terms used which crop up regularly on pattern envelopes and in the instructions. The essential ones for beginners in particular, as they can affect fabric choice and making-up, will be explained here and a more comprehensive list is given in chapter fifteen.

Grain

Clothes cut correctly on the grain hang well and retain their shape, but what is 'grain'? Woven fabric has two sets of threads running at right angles to each other. The **warp** is the lengthwise grain, running vertically along the fabric and the **selvedge** is the finished edge lengthwise. The **weft** is the crosswise thread, running horizontally from selvedge to selvedge and called the crosswise grain.

Bias

Sometimes referred to confusingly as 'on the cross' is the diagonal of the fabric. The true bias is found when the fabric is folded in a triangle so that the

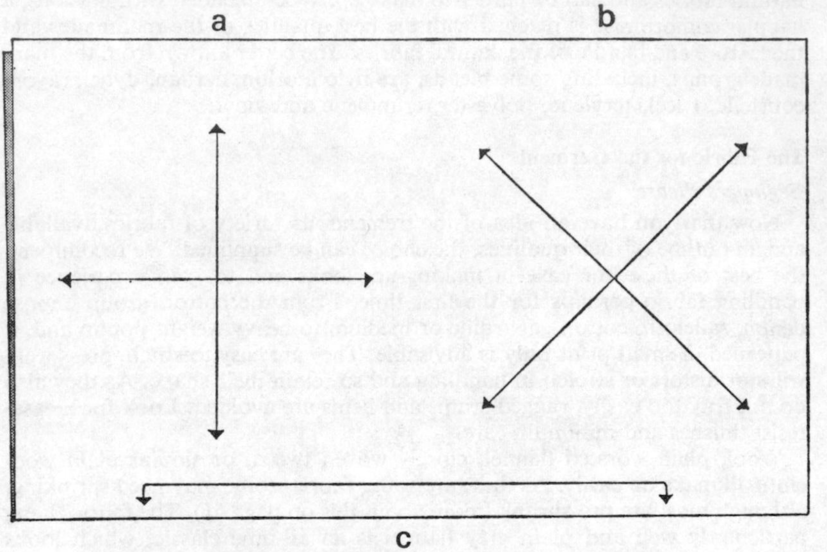

Fig. 35. (a) Straight grain; (b) bias grain; (c) fold of fabric.

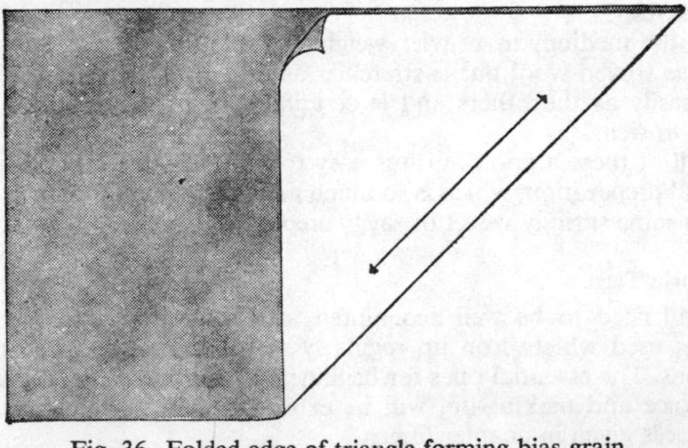

Fig. 36. Folded edge of triangle forming bias grain.

crosswise threads go in the same direction as the lengthwise threads and where they meet, at the folded edge of the triangle formed, is the **bias** with maximum stretch to the fabric.

Off-grain

This is when the lengthwise and crosswise threads are not at true right angles to each other or if there is a curve in the weave. This can be checked by seeing if the ends of the fabric have been cut or torn evenly. If they have not, make a tiny cut in the selvedge at the end, and pull a crosswise (weft) thread, even if it does not come out completely it will mark the grain with a line, which can be used as a guide for cutting, otherwise the garment will not hang well.

Bonded

This refers to two fabrics which have been sealed to become a single fabric. This is done for several reasons: woven and knit fabrics, or laces, are bonded to tricot knit or taffeta for self-lining; coating fabrics to interlining for warmth and shape retention; as well as bonding two fibres together to make one reversible fabric.

Laminated

Another term for a fabric that is joined to a backing of synthetic foam to provide insulation and warmth with little weight, which also keeps its shape and is crease resistant.

Nap

Some hairy or downy fibres are brought to the surface and then brushed or pressed flat to give a soft effect or sheen. This napping on woollens such as broadcloth, fleece, melton, doeskin (so called because of its suede like finish), reflect a different light in each direction, so all garment sections must be cut with this nap running in the same direction. These fabrics are among those prone to watermarking, dealt with on page 52.

Pile

These fabrics are woven with an extra set of looped yarns raised on the surface and clipped to stand up and form the rich surfaces of velvet, velour and velveteen. Corduroy velvet has fine to wide ribs or 'whales', or can be novelty patterned and textured. The same cutting problems exist for these as in the napped fabrics and for the same reasons, although there are some velvets produced which can be cut in both directions. Deep pile fabrics are very thick and usually made from manmade fibres to simulate fur.

These napped and pile fabrics are not suitable for beginners to work on, but they need explanation as they often appear in the pattern description and, if the terms are not understood, can cause confusion.

Pre-cutting Preparation of Fabric

Shrinking

This applies mainly to woollen goods and is the contraction of fabric after washing or dry-cleaning, or when fabric has not been fully shrunk by the manufacturer. Most fabrics are pre-shrunk, but this still allows for a three per cent reduction. To make a test, cut a small section of the material and trace its shape for accurate measurement. Then soak the material scrap in water, dry with a hot iron and measure against the tracing to see if there has been any reduction in size.

If further shrinking is necessary, try to make an ironing space as wide as possible to lay the fabric on—a kitchen table covered with an old clean piece of blanket or sheet is ideal. Lay the fabric right side down and thoroughly dampen a clean absorbent cloth (linen tea towels, or piece of sheeting) and lay it over the fabric. With a hot iron gently press, without sliding the iron as one would normally do, so that the heat goes right through without pushing or distorting the fabric. Continue pressing until all the fabric has been completely covered; a light press to dry off the top cloth should then be adequate.

Fabric Faults

Look out for faults and damages when buying fabrics. These may have occurred during weaving or knitting by the manufacturer and should be marked with strings, threads, tape or similar, on selvedges for easy identification. Shops will make an allowance on the length in compensation, but you can insist on a faultless length if you consider this allowance to be insufficient.

Sometimes creases are found in fabric lengths in the shops. Care should be taken in pressing these, as there is a possibility that they may have been made at the production stage, and would be nearly impossible to remove. Rare enough perhaps but, if this has happened and had not been noticeable in the store, the material should be returned to the manufacturer. With normal creasage, pressing under a damp cloth should be sufficient. On jersey fabrics, however, the fold is not always removable, in which case the pattern should be laid on the fabric so as to avoid the fold line.

Watermarks

These occur on fabrics with a surface as in blazer cloth, some flannels, fine wool such as doeskin and on pure silks. The marks may have been caused by sprinkled water or uneven pressing with a damp cloth, which leaves patches or spots when the fabric is dry. Apart from the fact that some of these should not have been damp pressed anyway, or at least on the wrong side under a cloth, the remedy is to steam or press all the fabric again under an evenly damp cloth. Do not put pressure on the iron; the idea is to steam the surface gently to revive the flattened or marked patches—The entire surface must be re-done otherwise a new set of marks would appear.

Labelling for Consumer Protection

With all these dreadful warnings, it would appear that choosing a fabric, which might or might not need special care depended on guesswork but, of course, careful labelling giving a description of the fibre content is required by law in this country. The labelling on care of fabrics also protects the consumer and the retailer. These labels state if the fabric is washable, crease resistant, dry-cleanable, non-iron and so on, so that its suitability for a particular design or easy handling can be evaluated (for details see pages 269 and 288).

Finish

A treatment applied to a fabric to add to its serviceability, to make its appearance more attractive as well as being more pleasant to handle. Finishes are applied to all fabrics, special finishes being added to counteract any undesirable feature in a fibre.

Special finishes available include: colourfast, crease/wrinkle resistant, drip-dry, durable press, mildew resistant, stain and spot resistant, shrinkage control, wash and wear, washable, waterproof and water repellent/resistant.

Choosing a Fabric for Lining

The purpose of a lining is to give body to a garment and help keep its shape. Its main purpose is to finish the inside, enclosing all the raw edges. Loosely woven and stretchy fabrics will retain their shape more readily and linings are essential in straight skirts to prevent seating. This type of lining is not meant to give shape to the garment, that is the purpose of an interlining or backing.

The lining should be firm, yet soft and pliable. Taffeta is the best for the firmer fabrics and different weights are available: rayon taffeta medium weight is ideal for all purposes; poult taffeta is heavier and more suitable for coats; and bemberg rayon is much finer and has the softness of silk, but is firm and good for dresses and skirts. Taffetas are available in other manmade fibres, which are washable and better for the washable top fabrics, whereas some rayons are not washable and others would have to be pressed damp. Lining crêpe is not advisable at this stage, as, although it has a pleasing handle, it is stretchier, more difficult for the novice to make up and is usually more expensive than the taffeta range.

These are some of the basic facts on fibres, which will help by categorizing them, to show why the fabrics suggested for the basic projects are the best choice.

A comprehensive list of fabrics, with notes on the care and handling of the more difficult ones will be found in chapter fifteen, with the more advanced dressmaking techniques (chapter fourteen) and the glossary of sewing and fabric terms (Appendix Two on page 283) will supply further information.

Fig. 37. (A) Small-print cotton top; (B) flannel trouser suit; (C) herringbone tweed jacket; (D) plain cotton sun dress and jump suit; (E) patterned wool jacket; (F) jersey battledress jacket with leather edging.

Fig. 38. (A) Flannel jacket with fur collar; (B) dogtooth wool jacket; (C) cotton gaberdine suits; (D) herringbone tweed jacket; (E) Cotton jacket, bra and trousers; (F) jersey jacket with knitted collar.

CHAPTER FOUR

HAND TOOLS AND EQUIPMENT

Apart from investing in a good sewing machine, if you do not own one already, most hand tools and items of equipment for dressmaking are not very expensive and are easily obtainable. As some are more essential than others, they are listed in two groups, (1) the most necessary ones and (2) those which are desirable, followed (on page 58) by a more detailed guide.

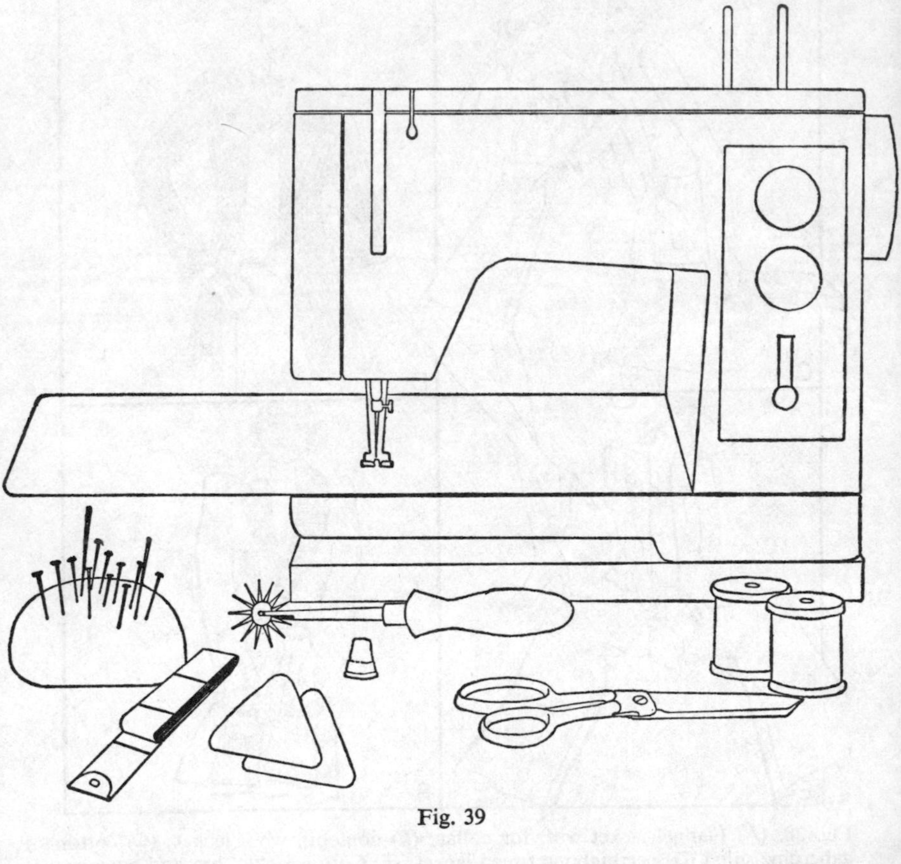

Fig. 39

Essential for	Desirable for
Machining	
(1) Sewing machine (Lockstitch)	(32) Silicone aerosol spray
(2) Bobbin case	Teflon presser foot
(3) Bobbins	
(4) Machine needles	
(5) Machine oil	
(6) Brush	
(7) Screwdriver	
Pressing	
(8) Electric iron	(33) Tailor's pressing cushion/pad
(9) Ironing board	(34) Tailor's pressing clapper
(10) Sleeve board	(35) Velvet board
(11) Damp rag/pressing cloth	
Cutting and Handsewing	
(12) Cutting shears	(36) Electric cutting shears
(13) Tape measure	(37) Cutting table/board
(14) Metre/yardstick	(38) Pinking shears
(15) Steel pins	(39) Pin cushion
(16) Tailor's chalk	(40) Wax chalk
(17) Ruler	(41) Set square
(18) Tracing wheel	(42) French curves
(19) Paper scissors	(43) Pattern notcher
(20) Pattern weights	(44) Stiletto
(21) Pencils	(45) Felt tip pens
(22) Rubber	(46) Magnet
(23) Plain, white, or tissue paper	(47) Seam ripper
(24) Sellotape	(48) Clippers
(25) Sewing needles	(49) Bodkin
(26) Small scissors	(50) Fashion templates
(27) Thimble	(51) Dressmaking tracing paper
Fitting	
(28) Dress stand	(52) Hem marker
Garment Care and Protection	
(29) Clothes brush	(53) Polythene bags
(30) Cleaning fluid—spirit, or aerosol stain remover	
(31) Coat hangers	

Essential Equipment

(1) *Sewing machine* (*Lockstitch*)

Brand names and makes of sewing machines are numerous. The basic principle of lockstitching is still the same since the invention well over one

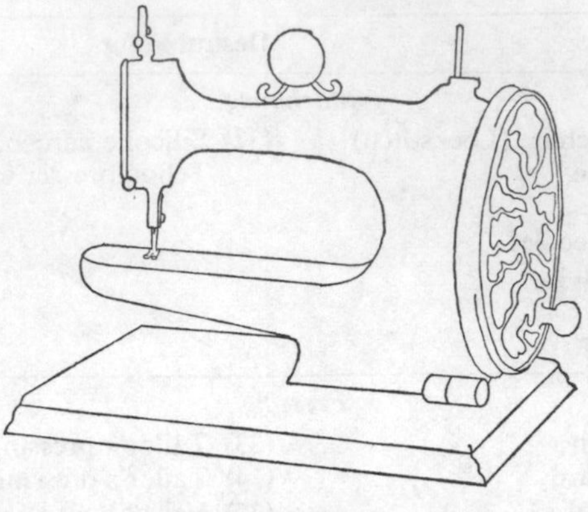

Fig. 40. 1870 Model.

hundred years ago and is common to all sewing machines. Modern precision-built machines are refined for better performance and are faster with less effort in use. Some domestic types are built with specific emphasis on taking a variety of attachments for decorative stitches, buttonholes, oversewing, embroidery, etc. The variety of these often determine the price of a machine rather than the performance as a straight Lockstitch. (See Care and use of the Lockstitch on page 64.)

(2) *Bobbin case*

A small round case, fitting underneath the plate, which holds the bobbin wound with sewing thread. This thread connects and 'locks' with the top thread passed through the needle. At least one spare is advisable. On some machines the bobbin case is a fixture and spares are unnecessary.

(3) *Bobbins*

Usually made of metal, bobbins are also available in transparent materials for easy identification of coloured threads. Keeping a reasonable number at hand, saves constant rewinding of the same or other coloured threads used.

(4) *Machine needles*

Match the size of needle to the thickness of fabric. Needles range in sizes from thin—low numbers, to thick—high numbers: No. 9 is a very fine needle for silk, chiffon and sheers; No. 11 is suitable for linen, cotton and rayons; No. 14 is a medium-weight needle used for denim, poplin, flannel and worsteds; No. 16 is used for thicker wools, such as some coatings; No. 18 is suitable for very thick wools such as coatings.

(5) *Machine oils*

Ordinary domestic oil in a suitable tube or can is adequate.

(6) *Brush*

A small brush for cleaning areas above the plate and below the bobbin is essential. An old tooth brush or small paint brush works well.

(7) *Screwdriver*

Check what sizes you need to fit the screws holding the needle, plate, etc.

(8) *Electric iron*

Use a medium weight iron, with heat control. Keep the base clean at all times, but when stained clean with steel wool pad or silicone aerosol spray, see (32).

(9) *Ironing board*

The normal domestic type is adequate—ideal when its height is adjustable. It must be free from wrinkles and creases on the underlay and cover, and should be firm and stable when in use.

(10) *Sleeve board*

Some are attachable to ironing boards, otherwise use a heavy type to prevent movement along the board. It is essential for all tubular shaped garments.

(11) *Damp rag/pressing cloth*

A plain white piece of cotton, approximately 1 m × 46 cm (39 × 18 in) is sufficient for cottons and similar fabrics, and soft canvas is best for wool. A pressing cloth can be obtained pre-treated, otherwise soak it in plain water overnight to extract any dressing on the fabric, or it will stick to the iron. Machine neaten all raw edges.

(12) *Cutting shears*

The best shears are 25–30 cm long (10–12 in) with two sizes of handle; one small for the thumb and one large for the fingers. Cut out with long, clean strokes and do not use these shears for anything but fabric (paper cutting will blunt them). Avoid dropping them for, if you do, they may need re-setting. Made of quality steel they will last a lifetime.

(13) *Tape measure*

Use a metric/imperial or metric tape measure only. Buy a good quality, non-stretch measure, preferably with solid metal ends.

(14) *Metre/Yardstick*

Use metric/imperial measures combined or metric only. It is obtainable in wood, perspex or metal and must be smooth for marking long lines on patterns. Use for levelling hem lines at fittings, unless a set square (41) is available or a hem marker is preferred (52).

(15) *Steel pins*

Be sure to use dressmaker steel pins with sharp points, as other pins bend easily. Sizes start at 2·5 cm–4·5 cm (1 in–1¾ in). Short pins are best for use on paper and thin fabrics and longer ones for heavier and thicker materials.

(16) *Tailor's chalk*

Use white tailor's chalk for marking out the pattern and the alterations at fitting stages. Test the chalk mark on a sample of fabric first to make certain it can easily be removed. When white chalk does not show up well on a fabric do not use coloured chalk, as it smudges and leaves permanent marks. A hard pencil, lightly applied on the wrong side of the fabric, is better than coloured chalk.

(17) *Ruler*

Metric and imperial measures combined or metric only, 30 cm (12 in) minimum, for marking short, straight lines on patterns and garments—the perspex type is best.

(18) *Tracing wheel*

Use for transferring marks from one part of pattern to another, from pattern to fabric or the reverse and from fabric to fabric. The type with a wooden handle and sharp spikes is recommended, as blunt, cheap ones require heavy pressure and leave marks difficult to see. If the table used is precious and you do not want it damaged, place a piece of hardboard between the table and tracing area, since the wheel leaves permanent marks.

(19) *Paper scissors*

Use fairly large scissors—paperhanger's scissors are ideal.

(20) *Pattern weights*

Any small, heavy, flat objects that are lying around are suitable, or they can be bought in specialist shops. Use for weighing down patterns when adjusting, tracing, or marking-in on fabric.

(21) *Pencils*

Use medium to hard, black and coloured pencils for easy identification of the adjustments/alterations on patterns. When drawing curved lines, let the pencil follow the movement of the wrist.

(22) *Rubber*

Any size or shape, but it must be clean.

(23) *Plain, white, or tissue paper*

Fine white, clean pattern or tissue paper for pattern adjustments.

(24) *Sellotape*

Additions to paper pattern with plain white or tissue paper are best held with sellotape for permanency, as pins fall out easily and damage the original pattern. It is also useful for removing dust, etc., from garments (see 29).

(25) *Sewing needles*

Needles are usually available in ten sizes from 10—short and thin, to 1—long and thick (average size 7–8 for general sewing, slightly larger for tacking). Within this range, sizes of needle eyes also vary from very small to large. The thickness of fabric and thread determine the size of needle. Unless the fabric is particularly delicate, avoid using very short needles as they are just a trifle difficult to work with, unless you are accustomed to using them.

(26) *Small scissors*

About 12·5 cm (5 in) long, with sharp, pointed ends for buttonholes, use for cutting off ends of threads, etc.—small surgical scissors are ideal.

(27) *Thimble*

The closed type is commonly used. Look for one with a magnetic head to catch stray pins. The tailor's open thimble is also available, but using it requires practice.

(28) *Dress stand*

A large variety of makes and types are available in shops and stores: stands are made of cardboard or wire and some are adjustable to accommodate varying figure types and to comply with a multitude of different body measurements. This is certainly an advantage, but on all of these stands you are restricted to only pinning the garment. If you contemplate trying your hand at simple toile making, or even if you do not, consider investing in a type of stand normally used by professionals, which is available in specialist shops. On these stands the base is covered with strong canvas with slight padding underneath to take pins. It is adjustable in height and rests on either a flat metal base or tripod with castors. Some have collapsible shoulders which is an asset when trying to get tight garments over it, but do not sacrifice a good shape for the sake of having a collapsible type. Settle for the stand nearest to your own measurements and if necessary slightly smaller (it can be padded out) rather than larger.

(29) *Clothes brush*

A clean brush for removal of dust and loose threads. For pile fabrics use sellotape, as dust, etc., will stick to it, and a brush will only spread it around.

(30) *Cleaning fluid—spirit or aerosol stain remover*

There are many commonly used types on the market. The fluid must be applied with a clean piece of cloth and always test first on a sample piece.

Accidents may happen. If you prick your finger with a needle or pin and bleed, and this soils your fabric, remove the blood stain in the following way. Cut off a length of white sewing cotton from the reel, roll it into a small ball, moisten, and dab the stain with it. Renew the cotton ball as often as necessary.

(31) *Coat hangers*

Keep garments being made on hangers at all times. On garments with shoulder seams, if they have not been joined, pin them together. Keep skirts and trousers on hangers with bars. Bundling garments up in any stage of making, produces unnecessary creases and loss of shape.

Desirable Equipment

(32) *Silicone aerosol spray*

This is used to maintain smooth surfaces on the machine, iron and scissors. It is *not* an alternative to oil for the moving parts of the machine.

(33) *Tailor's pressing cushion/pad*

Shaped parts of garments, i.e. those caused by seams or darts, should not be pressed on a flat surface: to maintain shape, place the shaped area over a cushion and then press.

(34) *Tailor's pressing clapper*

A smooth block of wood with a flat base, used for penetration and evaporation of steam immediately the pressing cloth has been removed from the first pressed section of the garment. 'Pat' with the clapper and leave it on the section for a short time.

(35) *Velvet board*

Velvet, not the easiest of fabrics to handle, cannot be pressed in the ordinary way. Wire needle boards made of stainless steel come:

(a) in strips wide enough for pressing seams;
(b) shaped to lay on sleeve boards; or
(c) large boards to cater for parts of garment other than seams or small areas.

They are relatively expensive and not absolutely essential: steaming velvet is often preferable to pressing.

(36) *Electric cutting shears*

Small battery operated shears can make cutting easier on the more difficult and thicker fabrics.

(37) *Cutting table/board*

The table should be high enough to work comfortably on in a standing position. A wooden surface is best, but remember that a tracing wheel leaves marks so, if necessary, protect the table by placing a board on top. Hardboard is very suitable and can easily be purchased in any required size.

(38) *Pinking shears*

Use in place of neatening or oversewing edges on the seams of lighter-weight fabrics, the zig-zag edge reduces fraying of seams. The medium size, around 18 cm (7 in), is recommended.

(39) *Pin cushion*

The wrist type is best and can easily be made by putting layers of soft pieces of material inside an outer cover, which is stitched together by hand. Then attach elastic to the two lower sides, so that it fits snugly around your wrist.

(40) *Wax chalk*

Use as white tailor's chalk (see 16). The wax melts under a hot iron and is, therefore, removed automatically. Is not suitable for many fabrics, so test first on a sample.

(41) *Set square*

A large set square is very useful for levelling hemlines and is essential for pattern lines at right angles—the perspex type is best.

(42) *French curves*

An aid for marking curved lines on pattern or garments, for example, necklines and armholes. Use either a transparent perspex type, or one made of rubber which bends to any desired shape.

(43) *Pattern notcher*

Used for marking seam allowances and balance marks on patterns.

(44) *Stiletto*

A wooden handle with a sharp, pointed end, which is used to punch holes on patterns for darts, pocket positions, etc.

(45) *Felt tip pens*

These work especially well on calico for modelling on the dress stand, but are also used for marking all types of lines on paper patterns. Black and coloured, thin ones help to distinguish one line from another.

(46) *Magnet*

Pins in boxes often get knocked over and so a magnet saves time (and temper) in clearing them up.

(47) *Seam ripper*

Unpicking stitches with a seam ripper is a faster method then using scissors.

(48) *Clippers*

An alternative to small scissors.

(49) Bodkin

This is a needle with a large eye and without a point. It is used to draw tape/elastic through narrow channels.

(50) *Fashion templates*

A prepared outline drawing of the human body, ready for the introduction of design lines—available in specialist shops.

(51) *Dressmaking tracing paper*

An aid for marking with the tracing wheel, from paper to paper, paper to fabric, or fabric to fabric. Great care is needed to ensure markings are transferred to wrong side of fabric. It is most suitable for use on smooth medium-weight fabrics such as cotton or rayon.

(52) *Hem marker*

Two main types are available for levelling hemlines: (a) the pin type and (b) powder or tailor's chalk. In most cases, the metre/yardstick, or set square is adequate.

(53) *Polythene bags*

Garments made over a period of time collect dust, so protect them at all times by keeping them under a cover.

Care and use of the Lockstitch

The variety of sewing machines available and in use makes it impossible to cover all types and to discuss in detail every aspect of care and maintenance here.

We have therefore selected one make, the **Bernina**, which covers most of the important elements by way of example. This machine is extremely versatile and serves most requirements admirably.

As far as all newly or recently acquired machines are concerned, the manuals supplied set out full instructions for care and maintenance. For the benefit of owners of both new and older types of lockstitch machines, and particularly for those without manuals, this section deals with basic information on the general use of sewing machines, partly based on the Bernina type.

When using a portable sewing machine do not place it too close to the edge of your table. Allow sufficient space for your left elbow to rest on the table, so that your arm is well supported. Sit exactly in front of the needle, leaning your body slightly forward.

Make sure that the motor is correctly connected for safety.

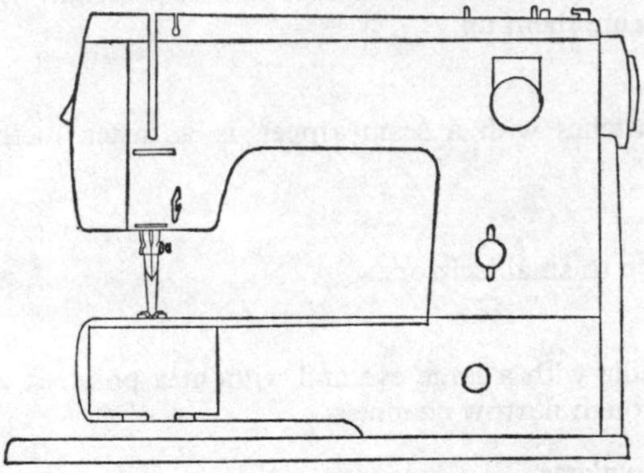

Fig. 41. Current model.

Always use the correct needle size and type suitable for the fabric. Never use a blunt, bent or hooked needle. Inspect the needle regularly. Some synthetic fabrics can blunt a needle during the course of sewing a single garment. A blunt needle can easily be detected by moving a fingernail against the point of the needle, when the machine is *not* in use.

Insert the needle either according to the manual supplied which is normally with the groove facing you, or on some machines, to the left side, push the needle up as high as it will go before securing it with the needle clamp screw. Loosen the screw for the needle insertion by a half turn only.

Always use suitable thread size and type, and the same thickness for top and in bobbin. The combined thickness of top and bottom thread should never exceed the thickness of the fabric being sewn.

Threading-up

Thread the needle with the presser foot in a raised position, otherwise there is too much pressure on the thread tension disc. Turn the handwheel, at the right side of the machine, towards you to bring the needle to its highest position.

To bring up the bottom thread, hold the needle thread loosely, turn the hand wheel to lower the needle into the needle hole of the plate and bring the needle up. Pull the needle thread slightly, and the bobbin thread will come up at the same time. Pass both threads under, and to the back of, the presser foot.

Sewing

Commence sewing by placing the fabric under the raised presser foot and needle. Line up the needle exactly on the seam line, but just a fraction below the cut edge of the fabric. Lower the foot, place your fingers on the thread ends, and turn the hand wheel until the needle is pinned to the fabric. By starting to sew with the needle already in the fabric, the moving parts of the machine are set at positions which cause least initial load on the motor. This releases the pressure on the first stitch, avoids the possibility of the thread breaking and also ensures that the fabric will not be pushed out of position by the lowered presser foot. Stitch for about 1 cm ($\frac{3}{8}$ in) and reverse stitch. Then using even pressure with the fingers of the right hand, guide the fabric slowly and evenly through the front of the presser foot without pushing or pulling the fabric, but holding it gently at the side and towards the back with the fingers (not the flat) of the left hand. Do not watch the needle, but keep an eye on the presser foot.

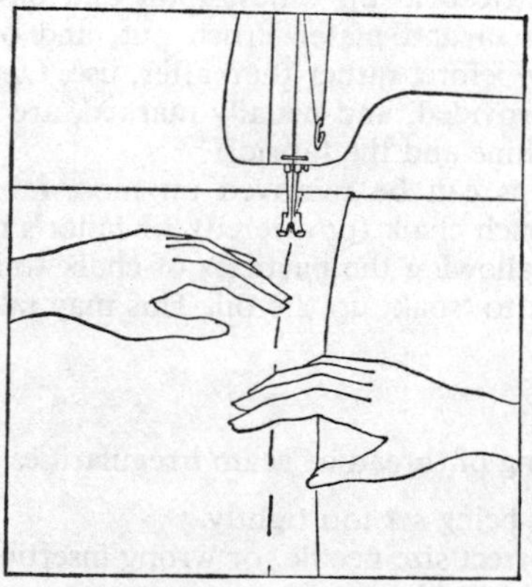

Fig. 42. Correct hand positioning.

At the end of a seamline, on stopping the machine, take the needle up to its highest position and raise the presser foot to release the top thread tension. Always remove the fabric to the rear of the machine and leave at least 5 cm (2 in) of thread before cutting it off.

To turn a sharp corner, do not attempt to machine this in one continuous movement. Instead, stop the machine at the end of the first sewing line, with the needle lowered into the fabric on the last stitch and so pinning the needle to the fabric. Lift the presser foot, turn the fabric to the second sewing line, lower the foot and carry on sewing.

Tension

Normally the tension should not need altering if accurately set at the beginning, with the exception of special sewing effects such as when top stitching you need to use thicker buttonhole twist/silk thread.

Incorrect tension causes uneven stitches or 'looping' in either top or bottom thread. If looping occurs at the back of the fabric, the top tension is faulty, if at the top of the fabric the bottom tension will need adjusting. Most tension problems are caused by:

(1) An incorrectly inserted or damaged needle.
(2) The use of incorrect thread on the fabric.
(3) The tension mark on the machine has been wrongly set.
(4) The bobbin tension is incorrect. Test this by removing the bobbin case. With the full bobbin left inside, hold the thread end and suspend the entire case. It should descend slowly and evenly, when the end of the thread is shaken gently. If it falls too quickly, or does not move at all, the tension spring will need adjusting by a slight turn of the small screw in the bobbin case. Turn it clockwise to tighten or anti-clockwise to loosen. Hold the bobbin case over a tray or table in case the screw comes out inadvertently, so that it can easily be found.

Cleaning and oiling

Keep the machine clean at all times. Fluff and pieces of thread collect around the bobbin area and plate. Brush out, and oil the working parts lightly and frequently before, rather than after, use. One or two drops of oil put into the points provided, and usually marked, are sufficient. Too much oil will stain the machine and the fabric.

Accidental oil stains can be removed on most fabrics by covering the stained area with French chalk (powdered), or tailor's chalk (scraped with a knife or blade), and allowing the particles of chalk to settle on the affected area. Leave the chalk to 'soak' up the oil. This may take some hours and is best done overnight.

Breaking of Thread

Continuous breaking of thread or seam irregularities may be caused by:

(1) Thread tension being set too tightly.
(2) Damaged, incorrect size needle, or wrong insertion of needle.
(3) Faulty (knotted/weak) thread.
(4) Fluff or pieces of thread around bobbin area and/or plate.

Attachments

The wide range of attachments available is equal to the variety of sewing machines. Many of these attachments are designed for advanced sewing processes. Among the many and most useful ones supplied with the Bernina and other well known makes, are: (1) **the zig-zag foot** and (2) the **zip foot.**

(1) The zig-zag foot is designed to allow the swing needle to sew in a variety of widths for decorative stitching and the finishing of seam edges. The needle

is set according to the width required. With the needle set in the centre position, this zig-zag foot also doubles up for straight stitching.

(2) The Bernina type zip foot has two 'cut-outs', to allow the needle to stitch to the left and right sides of the normal centre (**swing needle**). The zip is sewn in from one end on each side with the position once set to the left and once set to the right side.

The **half-foot** is designed to fit other types of machines and, as the name implies, with one half of the foot missing it can only get close enough to the zip teeth on one side at a time. In this case, the zip has to be sewn in from the top to the bottom on one side of the teeth, and from the bottom to the top on the other side.

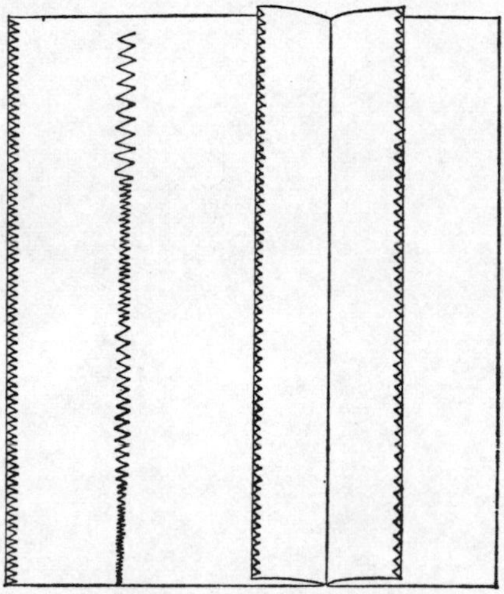

Fig. 43. Zig-zag stitches.

This attachment is also ideal for piping edges on garments or cording inserted into seams, when the ordinary presser foot does not lend itself for accurate stitching over and close to raised surfaces on the fabric.

a b c

Fig. 44. (a) Bernina Zip foot; (b) Bernina Zig-zag Presser foot; (c) half foot.

PART TWO: MAKING SIX SIMPLE GARMENTS

CHAPTER FIVE

SIX BASIC GARMENTS

Co-ordinating

One of the effects of changing attitudes in recent years has been the popularity of fashion co-ordinates and separates, with the opportunity to mix and match, style and colour. For this reason and for simplicity, we are introducing six basic garments equally suitable for adults and children. Readers can attempt to make these with confidence and they will lead on to many types of more advanced designs at a later stage. All six garments have common features in design and making-up procedures, which are built up progressively.

Similar shapes are used (as shown in Figs. 45–48, on pages 72–4) for:

(1) Skirt. Semi-flared, to any decided length.
(2) Trousers. Semi-flared, waist or hipster fitting.
(3) Shift dress. With or without sleeves, semi-flared.
(4) Jacket. } Semi-fitted, semi-flared, edge to edge cardigan
(5) Light weight coat. } style, single or double breasted or wrapover.
(6) Top/shirt. With or without sleeves, semi-fitted.

Illustrations of interchanging these garments, to form an extensive wardrobe, are given in Figs. 49–53. Other permutations are possible and can be increased by mixing fabrics and/or colour.

As the illustrations show, only five decorations are used at this stage:

(1) Plain patch pocket.
(2) Patch pocket with flap.
(3) Collars: (a) shirt and (b) collar with facing.
(4) Buttonholes.
(5) Top stitching.

It is suggested that these five decorations are also used in varying positions on different garments later on. They are intended as practice to achieve correct proportions by decoration.

Planning

By now readers will have organized the tools and equipment needed for dressmaking. They have become familiar with terms generally used, or at any rate can refer to them in the Glossary on page 283. Measurements have been taken and pattern size is known. Now planning becomes crucial.

Within the range of designs one to six initially (see pages 72–4) we recommend that readers make a plan for a basic wardrobe. For what use and when are the garments to be worn? To arrive at a final decision it is necessary to ask the following questions. Apart from the reasons described in page 3, for what purpose is the skirt, dress, or jacket to be used? Perhaps a summer

Fig. 45. (A) Skirt; (B) trousers.

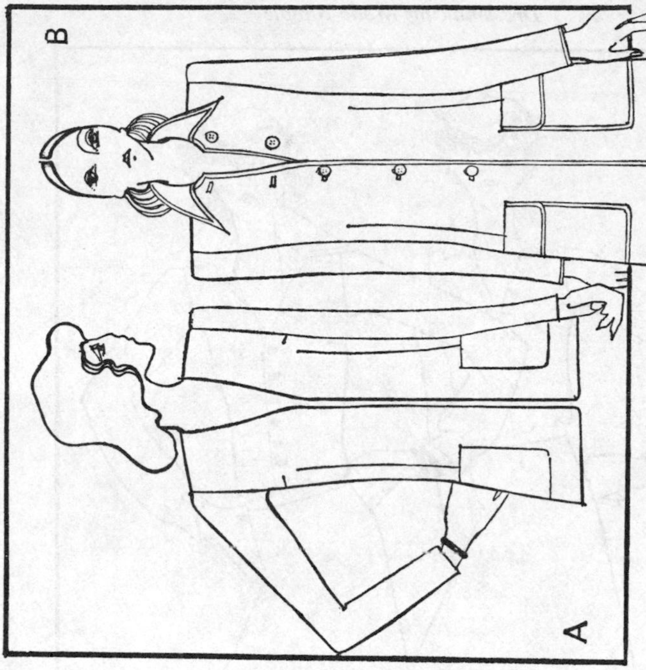

Fig. 47. (A) Jacket; (B) coat.

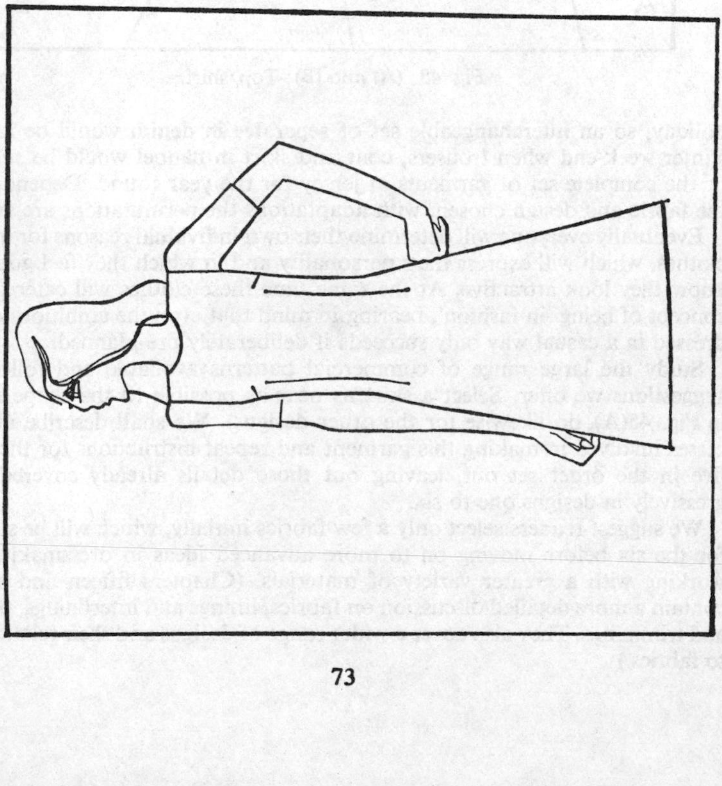

Fig. 46. Shift dress.

Fig. 48. (A) and (B): Top/shirt.

holiday, so an interchangeable set of separates in denim would be ideal; a winter week-end when trousers, coat and skirt in flannel would be suitable; or the complete set of garments in jersey for the year round. Depending on the fabric and design chosen, with adaptations the permutations are endless.

Eventually everyone will determine their own individual reasons for making clothes, which will express their personality and in which they feel good and know they look attractive. At the same time these clothes will cater for the concept of being 'in fashion', bearing in mind that even the ambition to look dressed in a casual way only succeeds if deliberately pre-planned.

Study the large range of commercial patterns available and follow the suggestions we offer. Select a skirt as near as possible to the shape shown in Fig. 45(A), do likewise for the other designs). We shall describe all processes involved in making this garment and repeat instructions for the other five in the order set out, leaving out those details already covered, progressively in designs one to six.

We suggest readers select only a few fabrics initially, which will be suitable for the six before moving on to more advanced ideas in dressmaking and working with a greater variety of materials. (Chapters fifteen and sixteen contain a more detailed discussion on fabrics, linings and interlinings, threads and trimmings. They also cover a wider range of designs and their relationship to fabrics.)

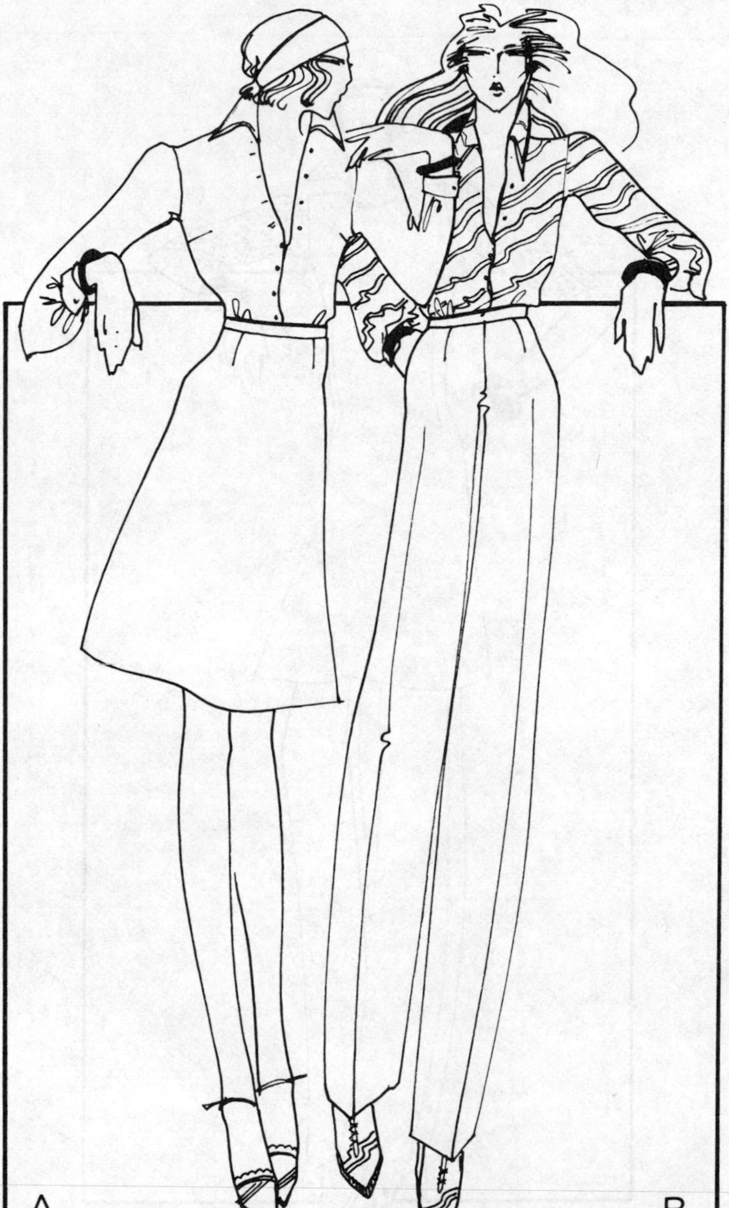

Fig. 49. (A) Skirt and shirt; (B) trousers and shirt.

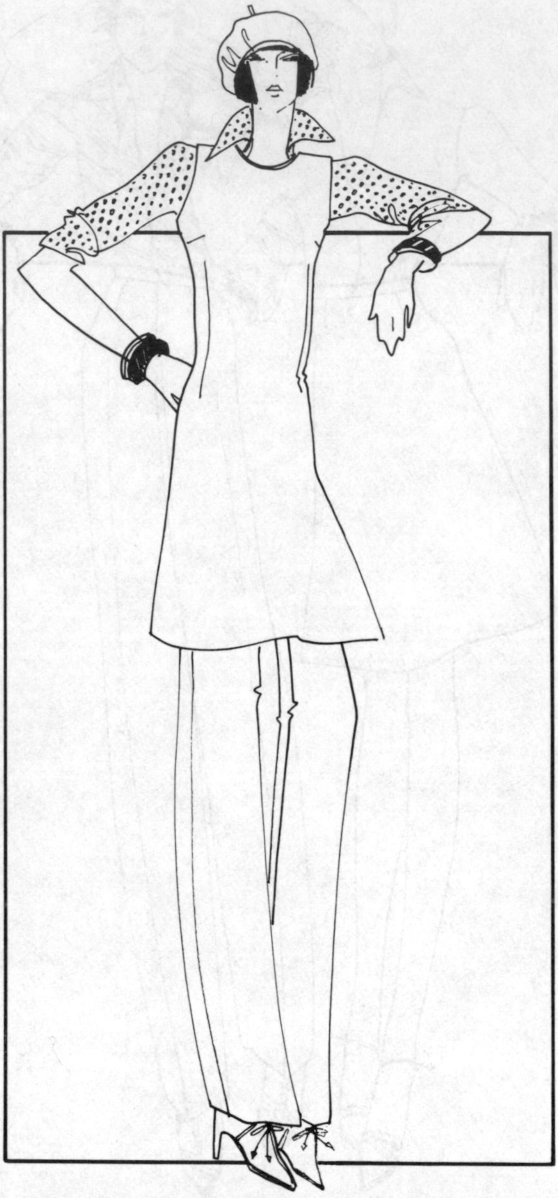

Fig. 50. Sleeveless shift dress over shirt and trousers.

Fig. 51. (A) Jacket over shift dress and shirt; (B) jacket over shirt and trousers.

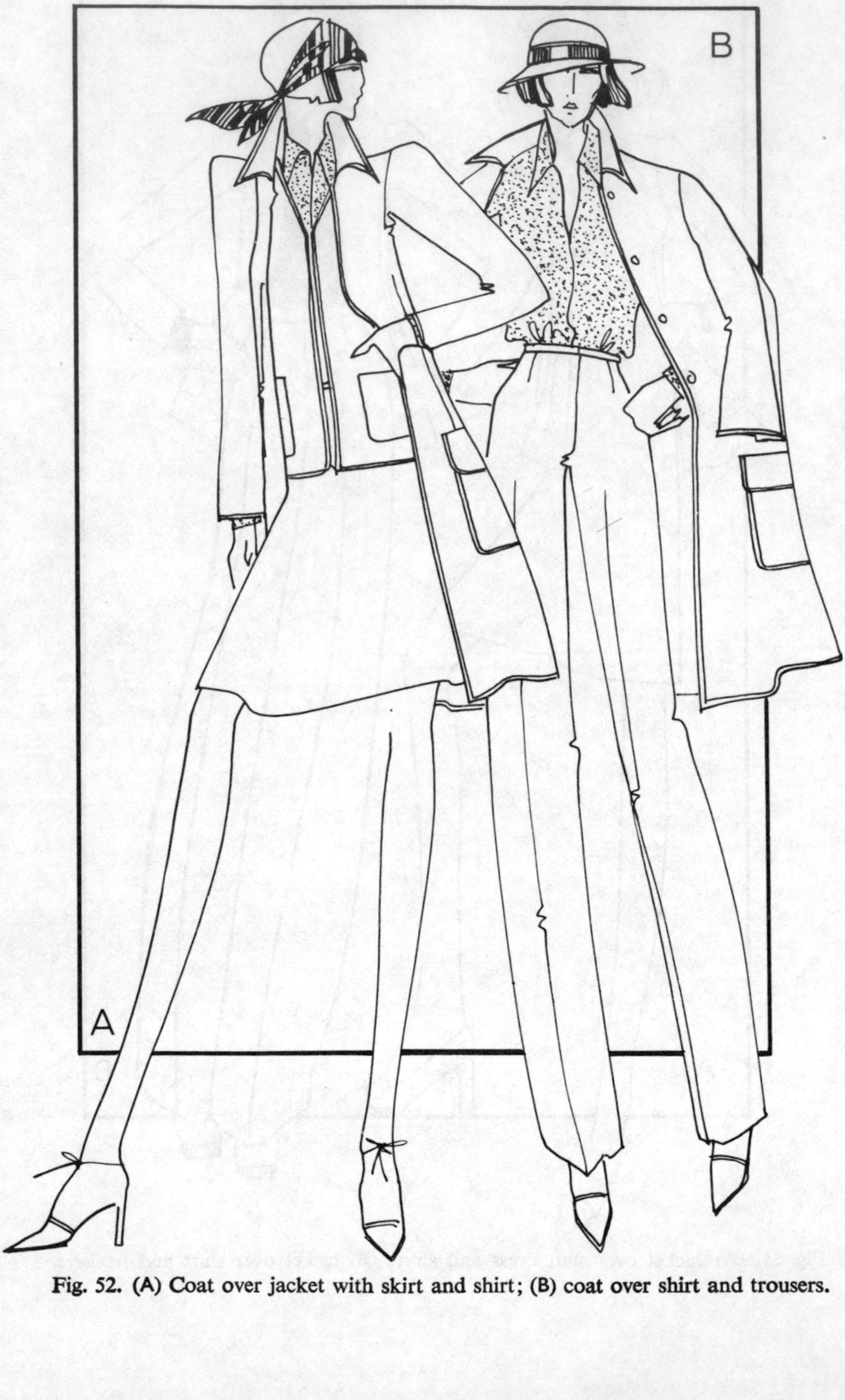

Fig. 52. (A) Coat over jacket with skirt and shirt; (B) coat over shirt and trousers.

Fig. 53. (A) Coat over shift/dress with top/shirt; (B) coat over jacket and trousers, with shirt.

The following, as mentioned on page 49, are ideal for our purposes. We list them again:

Woven wool: Plain worsted flannel
Plain closely woven tweed (Or similar fabric).
Woven cotton: Medium to heavy weight poplin
Sailcloth
Gabardine
Denim
(Small prints if patterned).

These fabrics are not difficult to handle, as the firm and close weave structure prevents undue stretching and retains shape. Large patterns should be avoided at this stage, as they require matching and make for less easier sewing.

Knitted wool: Medium to heavy double knit jersey.

In the case of wool jersey some stretch and give takes place, as a knitted fabric is meant to give, but it is still firm enough compared to loose-structure fabric. Although allowances over and above body measurements are smaller (as explained on page 27) jersey has a beautiful handle and feel. Its characteristics are most suitable for many designs and it is extremely versatile.

Having decided on the fabric and bought the required amount, select a matching lining if possible for the wool fabrics—plain light-weight taffeta is ideal. Our 'six' will look better if lined, as this helps them to retain their shape longer and they will also feel better in use.

A list of trimmings for each garment will precede making instructions. These trimmings must be at hand before you commence cutting out and making up.

CHAPTER SIX

THE FIRST DESIGN: THE SKIRT

In order to eliminate unnecessary repetition the processes for each section will be listed in groups and individually described, when appropriate, at the beginning of each design. These processes will follow through all the other designs, with new ones added where applicable. For example processes for seams, darts, hems, etc., for the skirt will be used throughout as basic methods and are good for all fabrics. Simultaneously, the hand sewing and other processes on practice pieces, as suggested, will help you to gain experience in handling fabrics.

Fig. 54

The Basic Skirt

The basic skirt is semi-flared, with two side seams and one centre back seam, with a zip opening set on the waistband. The method of putting the zip into the back seam is the same as for putting the zip into a side seam.

Now the pattern has been chosen, its measurements are checked (and adjusted if necessary), the fabric has been bought and the tools are ready.

Trimmings

The following trimmings are required:

(1) White/contrast coloured tacking cotton.
(2) Mercerized sewing thread (sylko type 40).If a perfect match is difficult

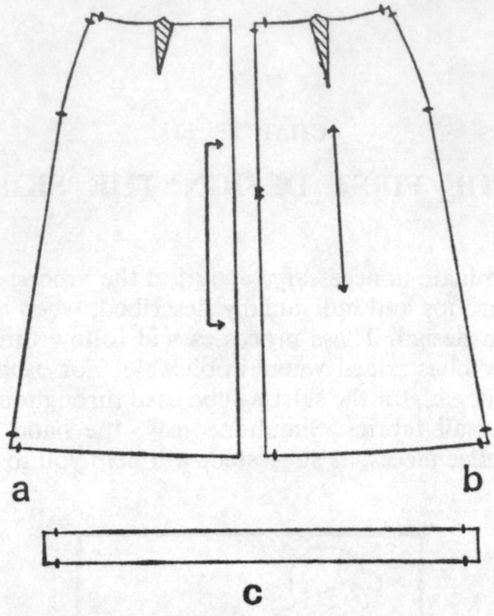

Fig. 55. Basic pattern shape: (a) front; (b) back; (c) waistband.

to obtain, choose a slightly darker colour which will work in well and is a better match than lighter colours.

(3) Skirt-weight zip fastener 20·5 cm (8 in) in length.
(4) Fusible interlining for the waistband (see interlinings on page 271).
(5) Skirt hooks and bars for the waistband, size 2.
(6) Tape or ribbon for loops.

Basic Hand Stitches

The five basic hand stitches (in order of use) are as follows:

Tailor Tacking
Tacking/Basting
Oversewing
Blindstitch
Slipstitch

Practice Piece

For a beginner, hand stitches, machine stitching and any new process should be worked out on a sample piece of fabric, before putting the garment together. This will save much time and unnecessary handling of the garment, as well as giving confidence and accuracy. A piece of fabric—the same weight and texture as the one you will be using, 25 cm (approximately 10 in square)—cut in half will be ideal.

Tailor Tacking

The first stitch needed is the marking stitch, called tailor tacking, which transfers pattern markings and balance marks from the pattern to the fabric.

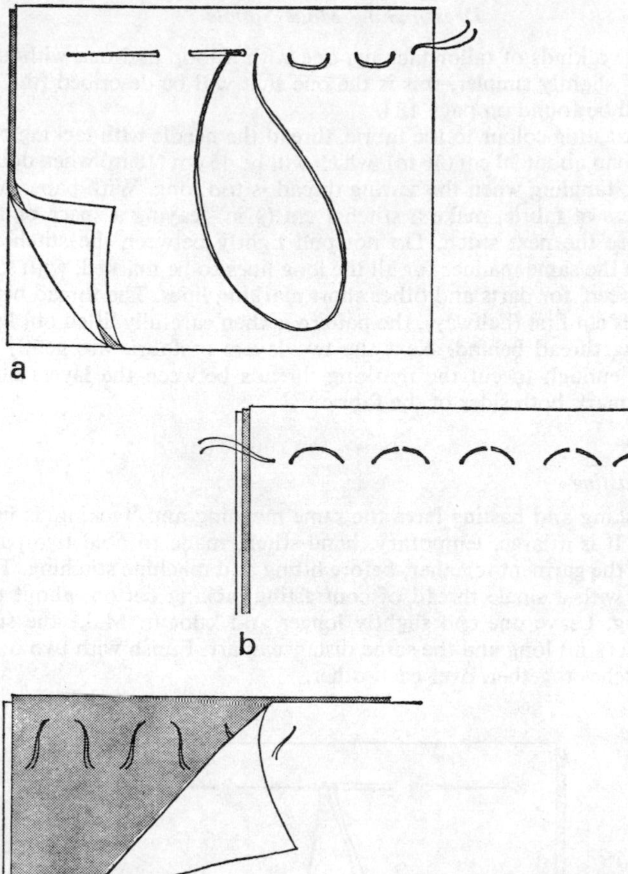

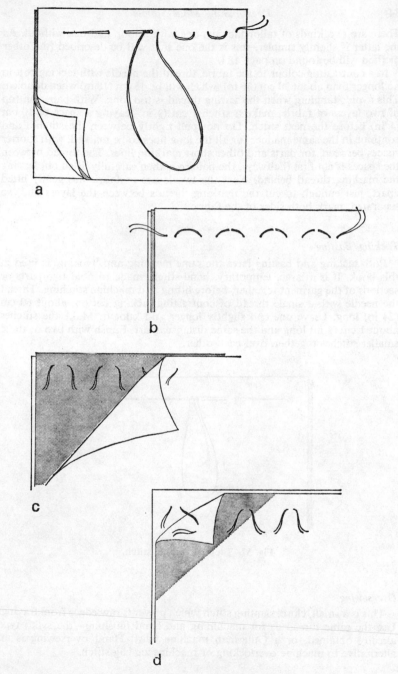

Fig. 56. (a), (b), (c) and (d): Tailor tacking.

There are two kinds of tailor tacking, one with a loop and one without. As the latter is slightly simpler, this is the one that will be described (the other method will be found on page 183.

In a contrasting colour to the fabric, thread the needle with tacking cotton no longer than about 90 cm (36 in), which will be 45 cm (18 in) when doubled. This avoids tangling when the sewing thread is too long. With paper on top of two layers of fabric, make a stitch 1 cm ($\frac{3}{8}$ in) leaving a space of 10 cm (4 in) before the next stitch. Do not pull tightly between the stitches and continue in the same manner for all the long lines to be marked, with shorter spaces between, for darts and other short marking lines. The thread between the spaces is cut first (halfway), the pattern is then carefully lifted off, leaving the marking thread behind. Next the two layers of fabric are gently lifted apart, just enough to cut the marking threads between the layers and, so separated, mark both sides of the fabric.

Tacking / Basting

Both tacking and basting have the same meaning and 'tacking' is used in this book. It is a large, temporary, hand stitch, made to hold two parts or sections of the garment together, before fitting and machine stitching. Thread the needle with a single thread of contrasting tacking cotton, about 60 cm (24 in) long. Leave one end slightly longer and knot it. Make the stitches about 1 cm ($\frac{3}{8}$ in) long and the same distance apart. Finish with two or three smaller stitches together, over each other.

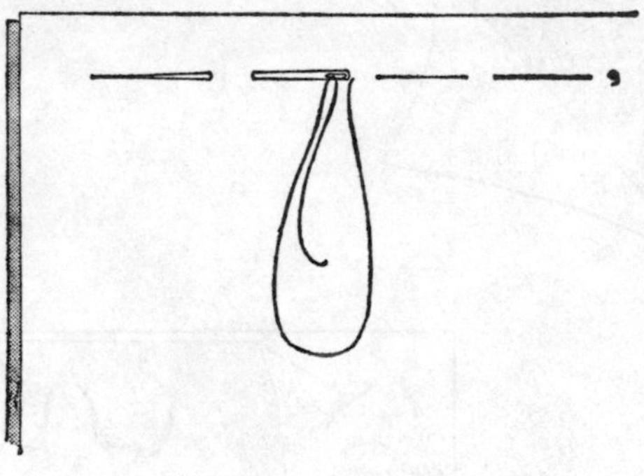

Fig. 57. Tacking/basting stitch.

Oversewing

This is a small, close, slanting stitch which prevents raw edges from fraying. Use the same thread as for machining and hand finishing—the sylko type already obtained, or a Guterman machine twist. Hand oversewing is an alternative to machine overlocking or machine zig zag stitch.

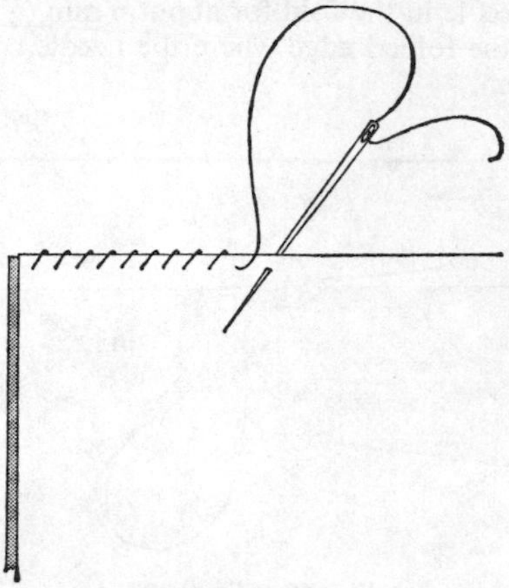

Fig. 58. Oversewing stitch.

Blindstitch

So called as it is practically invisible on right side of hems, even before pressing, it is made by tacking the hem up on a tacking line about 2 cm (¾ in) from the raw edge. The edge is then turned back fractionally and a very small stitch is taken on the hem allowance, with the next stitch made approximately 1 cm (⅜ in) further along, picking up one or two threads of fabric only, on the garment side. Do not pull tightly between stitches, just firmly enough to hold the two layers together.

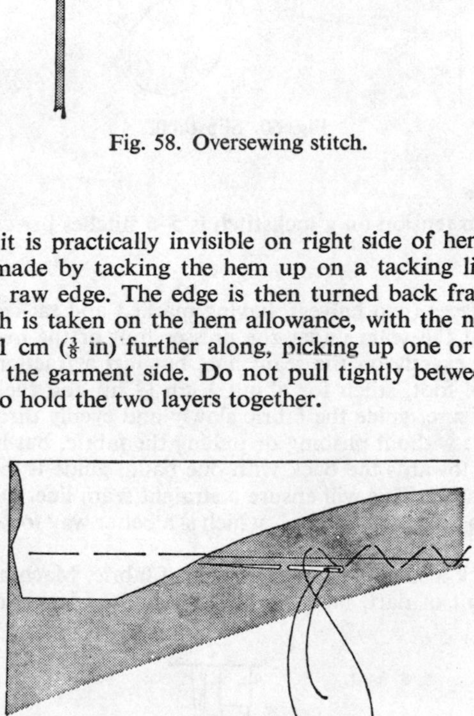

Fig. 59. Blindstitch.

Slipstitch

Another stitch holding two layers of fabric together, with one thread of material picked up on each side alternately, which is used for hems and waistbands with a turned-in folded edge. It is used here on the skirt to turn in the waistband on the inside, for the lining hem and for sewing the lining to the zip tape. Pick up a single thread of the material below the folded edge, then slip the needle in the fold for about 6 mm (¼ in). Pick up another single thread below the folded edge where the needle comes out and repeat for the rest of the hem.

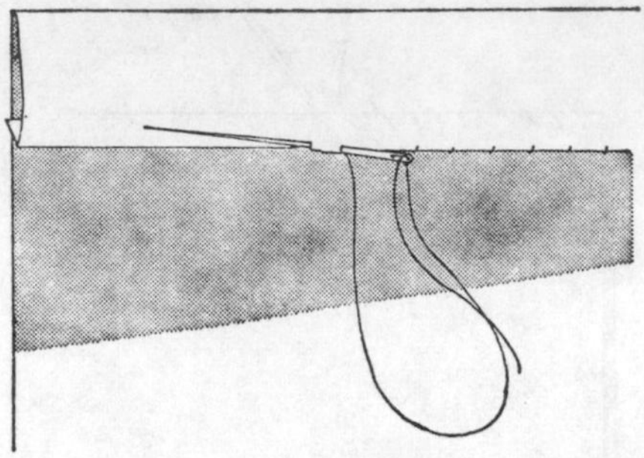

Fig. 60. Slipstitch.

Machine Stitches

The regulation tension on a lockstitch is 5–6 stitches per cm (⅜ in).

Practice Piece

On sample pieces (two halves), having marked and tacked a seam, place the beginning of the seam under the presser foot of the machine, with the needle lined up exactly on the seam line, but just a fraction below the cut edge. Lower the foot, stitch for about 1 cm (⅜ in) and then reverse stitch. Using even pressure, guide the fabric slowly and evenly through in front of the presser foot: without pushing or pulling the fabric, but holding it gently at the side and towards the back with one hand, guide it through the front with the other hand. This will ensure a straight seam line. Do not watch the needle, but keep an eye on the foot, which is a better way to keep the machine stitching on the sewing line.

Mark and tack a small dart on the piece of fabric. Machine from the wide end, to the point of dart, tapering off to make the last stitches exactly on

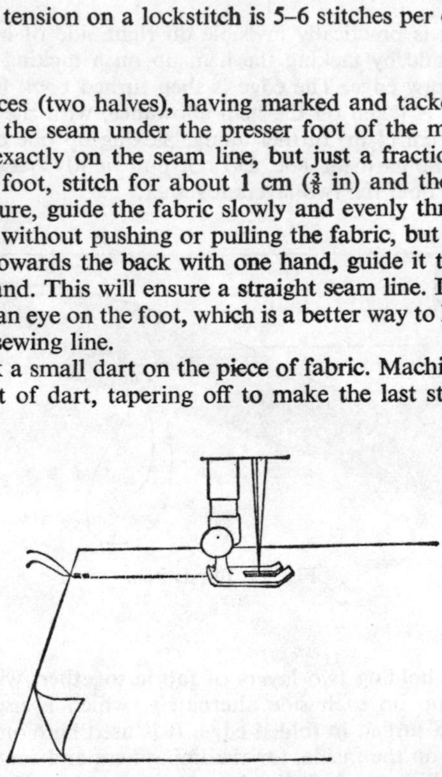

Fig. 61. Machine stitching.

the folded line. Leave the thread ends long enough to tie in a knot, without pulling which would pucker the end of the dart, before cutting off.

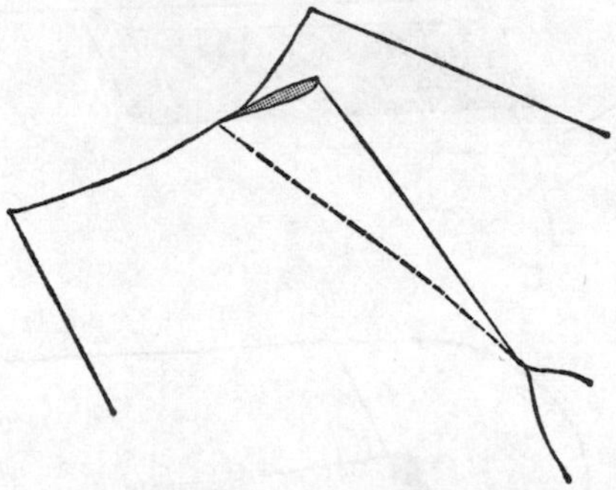

Fig. 62. Stitch dart.

Staystitch

A line of machine stitching on the curved or bias cutting lines of garments, between the cut edge and sewing lines and close to the latter, prevents stretching when working on fabrics. It is used, in this instance, at the waist seam and upper part of the side seam, at the hips of the skirt.

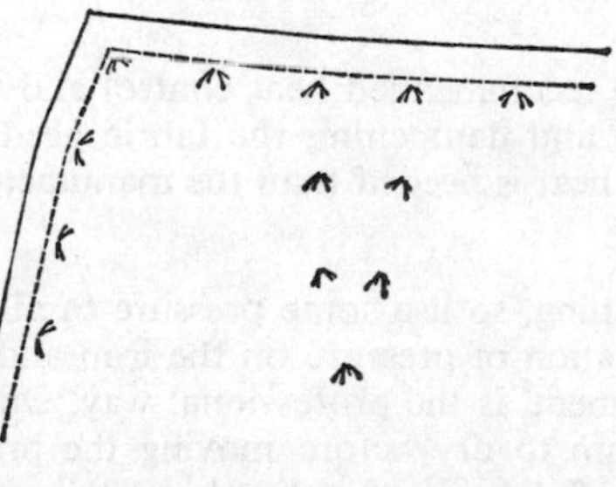

Fig. 63. Stay-stitching and marking thread.

Pressing

Under-pressing

As one process is completed, such as the seams or darts, under-pressing is most essential. Open the seams and flatten the darts by pressing on the wrong side of fabric (over a slightly damp cloth for woollen fabrics). On some fabrics, particularly softer wool, seam and dart impressions are apt to show on the right side. To avoid this, place a piece of thin narrow card between the seam allowances, darts and garment. Using a damp or even a dry cloth, when appropriate for some fabrics, prevents shine marks caused by the base of the iron on direct contact with the fabric. Shine marks are virtually irremovable, so taking care by using a cloth at all times is worth the effort. Press flat seams on the ironing or sleeve board and shaped parts over the tailor's pressing cushion/pad.

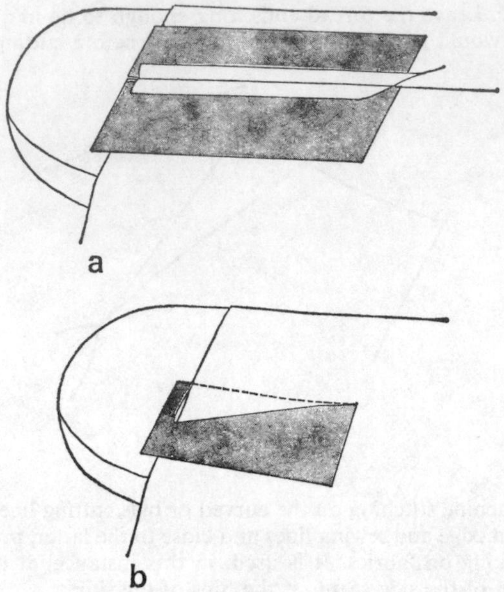

Fig. 64. (a) and (b): Place thin card between seam allowances, dart and garment.

Heat

Set the iron at the recommended heat control and test on a sample piece just how much heat and dampening the fabric needs. You may find that slightly more or less heat is needed than the manufacturer suggests.

Pressure

Pressing is not ironing, so use some pressure to allow heat and steam to penetrate. A combination of pressure on the iron and sliding it with a continuous lifting movement, is the professional way. On removal of the damp cloth, allow the steam to dry before moving the pressed section of skirt. 'Patting' it with the flat back of a brush or tailor's clapper hastens this process.

Iron Marks

The base of the iron will gradually stain. If these stains are not removed, the iron will stick and leave marks on the pressing cloth and these marks will easily transfer to the fabric (see page 59).

Processes in Order of Making-up

As previously mentioned on page 81 the list set out below is an outline of the processes involved in making-up a skirt, which is then followed by a detailed description of each stage.

Initial Processes (see page 89)

Fabric and Pattern Preparation: Layout of Fabric
Laying-out and Pinning the Pattern to Fabric

Cutting-out the Fabric, Lining and Interlining
Marking
Fusing the Interlining

First Steps to First Fitting (see page 91)
Staystitching
Pinning Cut-out Pieces and Darts
Tacking the Darts, Seams and Zip
Tacking the Waistband and Hem

First Fitting for Shape and Alterations (see page 92)

Final Assembling and Completion (see page 96)
Machining and Under-pressing the Darts and Seams
Inserting the Zip
Attaching Lining to Waist Seam
Waistband

Second Fitting (see page 98)
Adjustments and Final Machining

Hand Finishing (see page 98)
Seams
Waistband
Lining
Hem

Final Pressing (see page 99)

Initial Processes
Fabric and Pattern Preparation: Layout of Fabric

With your fabric checked for shrinkage and correct grain, fold it as described in the cutting layout accompanying the pattern instructions.

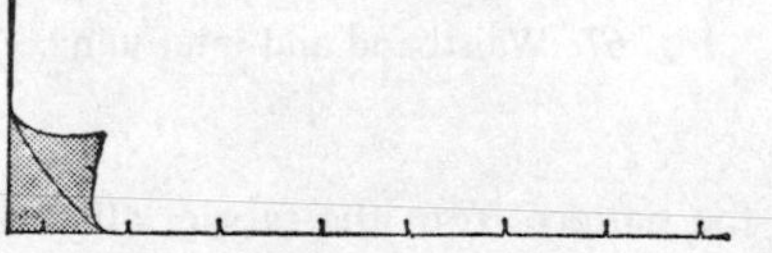

Fig. 65. Snip into selvedge.

Generally, if not already folded, fold it in half along the lengthwise grain with right sides facing, one selvedge on top of the other. If these selvedges are tight and pucker, release tension by snipping into them at regular intervals, which will allow the fabric to lie flat. Ensure that the fold is always on the grain.

Laying-out and Pinning the Pattern to Fabric

The pattern pieces are laid on the fabric according to the layout, as shown on the pattern envelope, placing pieces which lie on the folded edge first. Check very carefully that the straight grain lines on the pattern pieces correspond to the straight grain of the fabric. Place weights on the pattern pieces to hold them in position and pin paper to fabric, making sure that neither pattern nor fabric are pulled or distorted.

Cutting-out the Fabric, Lining and Interlining

Fabric. Cut with long even strokes, using shorter strokes for curved edges. Balance marks on commercial patterns are cut around, not into the seam,

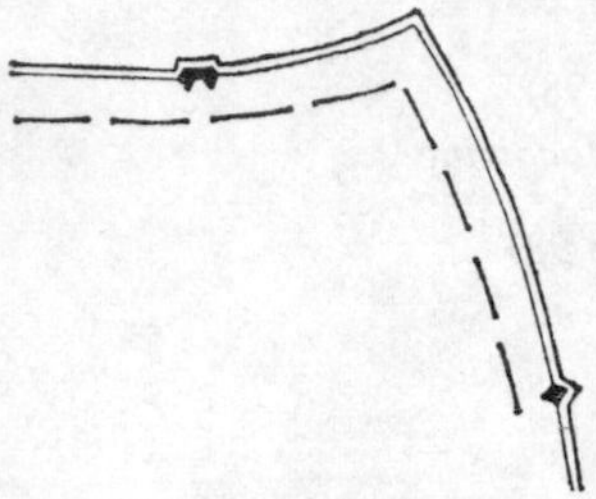

Fig. 66. Cut **around** balance marks.

otherwise this could lead to problems when letting seams out.

Lining. If the skirt is to be lined the lining is cut from the skirt pattern, with no alteration except that it is cut shorter, i.e. at the finished skirt hemline, and the waistband is not required. Apart from this, cutting is the same as for skirt in fabric.

Interlining. Cut the interlining for waistband without seam allowances.

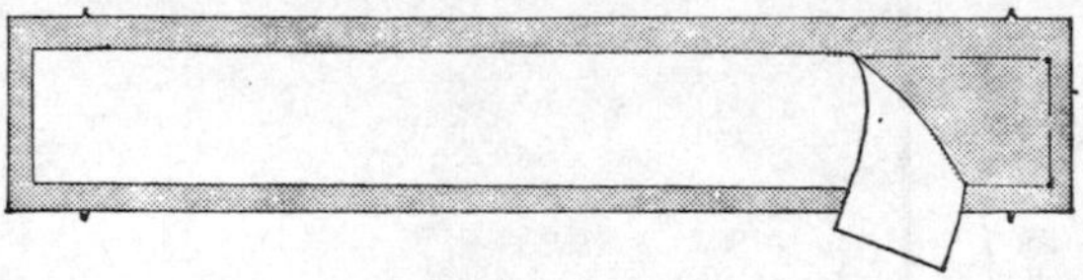

Fig. 67. Waistband and interlining.

Marking

Before removing the pattern from the fabric, all sewing and fitting lines must be marked with tailor tacking. On the skirt these lines are the side seams, darts, waist, hem, zip opening, centre back seam and waistband. After removing the pattern, additional tack lines to mark the centre front, and weft grain at hips, will be a help for the first fitting.

Fig. 68. Tackmarks for centre front, and weft grain.

Fusing the Interlining

Interlining, not to be confused with lining, gives body, strengthens and stiffens a part of a garment—in this case the waistband. The fusible—iron-on type—is easiest to apply. Match grade to weight of fabric and stiffness required (see page 271). Place the sticky side (with raised surface of gum (resin) substance) to the wrong side of the band up to, and just touching, the seam allowance. Press under a dry cloth, using pressure only, and *do not* slide or push the iron, which would wrinkle or twist the fabric and interlining. Press so that the entire surface is thoroughly covered and allow the heat to penetrate and fuse interlining to fabric. Do not handle the interlined part for a few minutes, until it has cooled.

First Steps to First Fitting

Always work with clean hands and protect the garment from getting grubby during the making-up process. Light coloured fabrics, especially white ones, should be kept (semi-wrapped) in an old, clean sheet or similar cover.

Keep all cut-out parts not being worked on in a neat pile. Work on one part or section at a time, to avoid confusion.

Staystitching

Staystitch the waistline and hip curve seams.

Pinning Cut-out Pieces and Darts

Matching sewing line tacks, fold and pin darts which should taper to a point. Pin the side seams next, matching the balance marks. Tack and prepare the lining in the same way.

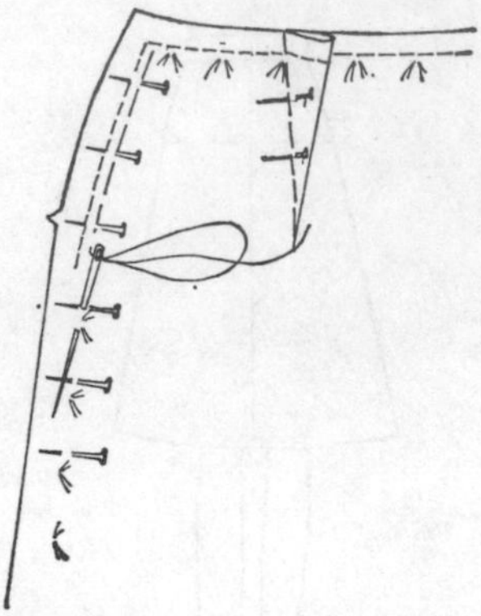

Fig. 69. Staystitch, pin, tack darts and seams.

Tacking the Darts, Seams and Zip

Tack darts and seams and lay the zip right side up inside the opening of the centre back seam (or left side seam) with the top of the tape ends at the waist cutting edge. Pin the right-hand seam allowance with the folded edge next to the zip teeth. Tack 3 mm ($\frac{1}{8}$ in) from this edge. Turn back and pin the left side seam allowance to where it just barely covers the right edge of the opening. Tack this lapping side 1 cm ($\frac{3}{8}$ in) from the folded edge.

Tacking the Waistband and Hem

Waistband. Before attending to the waistband, pin and tack lining to the inside waist, with seams of lining facing seam of skirt. Pin the waistband, right sides together to skirt waist, matching balance marks and darts and tack firmly.

Hem. Pin back the hem allowance and tack 2 cm ($\frac{3}{4}$ in) from cutting edge.

First Fitting for Shape and Alterations

Drastic alterations should not be necessary if care has been taken in carrying out all processes so far. Good fit is based on the following main aims:

(a) A snug, but comfortable fit at the waist.
(b) A smooth fit over hips allowing just sufficient ease for movement on this semi-flared skirt, will avoid seams splitting when sitting or bending down.
(c) A level hem.

It is important to appreciate that the hang of the skirt is controlled from the waist, which also affects the hemline. In other words, an uneven hemline may be corrected by alteration to the waist seam. So, in the first place, put the skirt on and check it vertically by casting an eye from waist to hem. If this is not even, it may well need lifting or dropping at the waist. Firm fabrics retain their shape and should not drop.

As soon as you have taken a look at the skirt, return to the waist and start fitting from top to bottom. Bear in mind that the varying thicknesses of fabrics may make a difference to girth measurements. The skirt made in

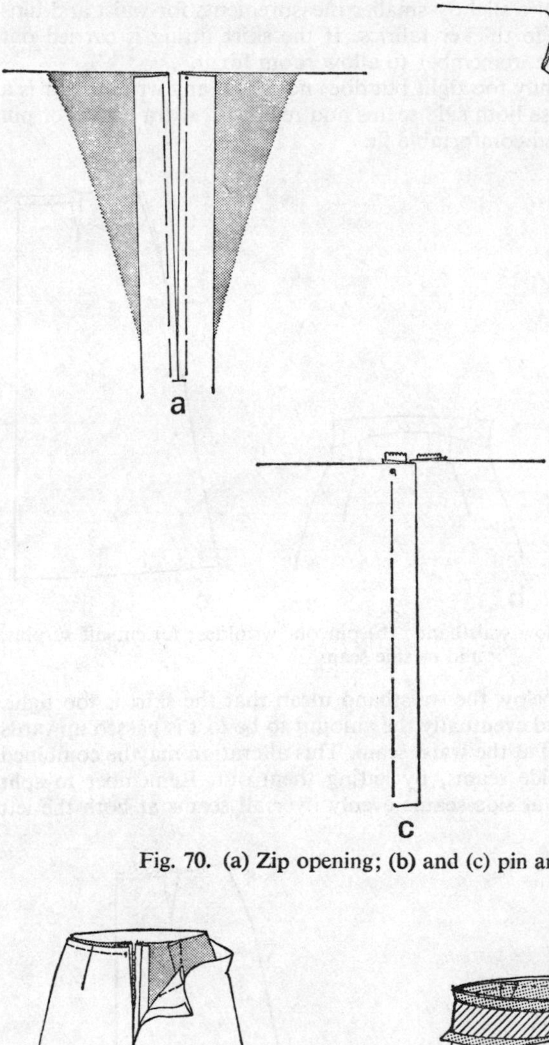

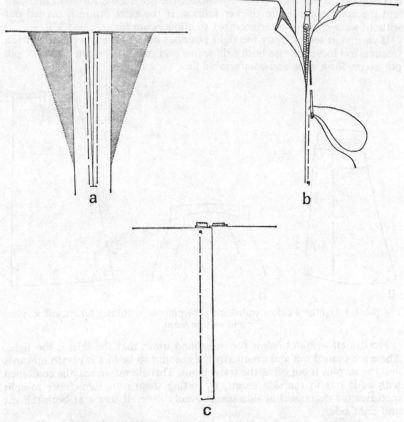

Fig. 70. (a) Zip opening; (b) and (c) pin and tack zip.

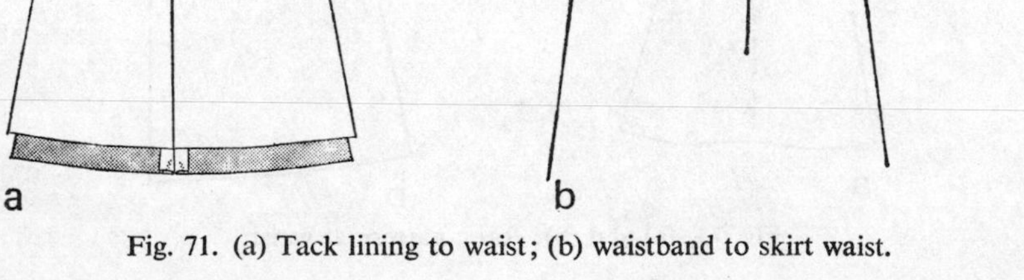

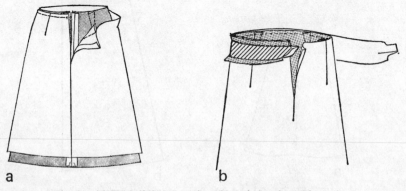

Fig. 71. (a) Tack lining to waist; (b) waistband to skirt waist.

a cotton fabric will require slightly smaller measurements for waist and hips and the reverse applies to thicker fabrics. If the skirt fitting is carried out without wearing a blouse, remember to allow room for it.

If your skirt feels slightly too tight but does not show any wrinkles, or is a fraction too loose, release both side seams and rejoin for extra width, or pin out excess for a snug and comfortable fit.

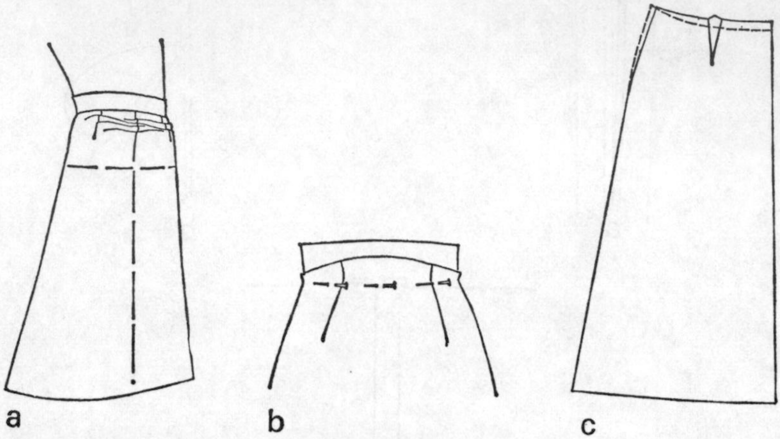

Fig. 72. (a) Tightness below waistband; (b) pin out wrinkles; (c) cut off surplus, add to side seam.

Horizontal wrinkles below the waistband mean that the skirt is too tight. These are pinned out and eventually the amount to be lost is passed upwards and the surplus is cut off at the waist seam. This alteration may be combined with additions to the side seams, by letting them out. Remember to split increases (or decreases) at side seams evenly over all seams at both the left and right side.

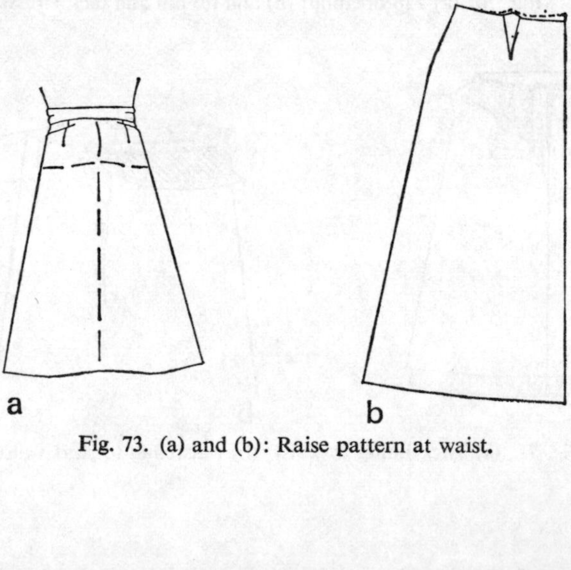

Fig. 73. (a) and (b): Raise pattern at waist.

Riding-up at the front is caused by a large abdomen, or at the back, by a large seat. Raise at the front/back waist of the pattern at centre, for additional length and taper the waist seam allowance to the original width at the sides.

Prominent hip bones may cause tightness at the sides of the front. If so, open the side seam at the waist and a section of the waistband, and release part of the dart, using the gained amount towards a second dart. Leave a

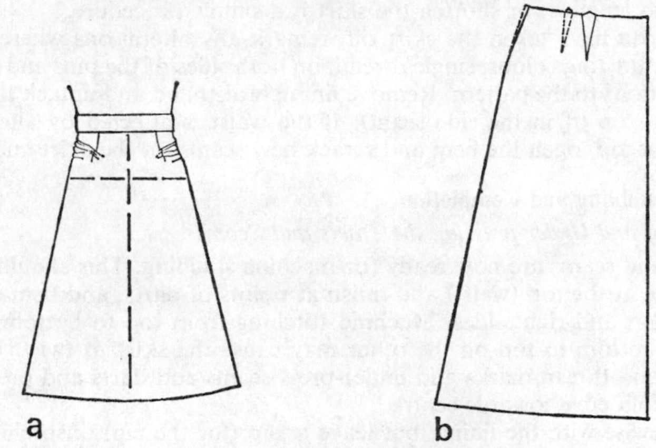

Fig. 74. (a) and (b): Add second dart.

space of 3·8 cm (1½ in) from the first one and pin out the second approximately 2–2·5 cm (¾–1 in) deep, in slanting direction to the most prominent part of the hip bone. Add the small amount lost by the additional dart to the front side seam and repin seam and waistband. The principle relating to the use of darts discussed in chapter two—Adjusting Pattern to Figure on

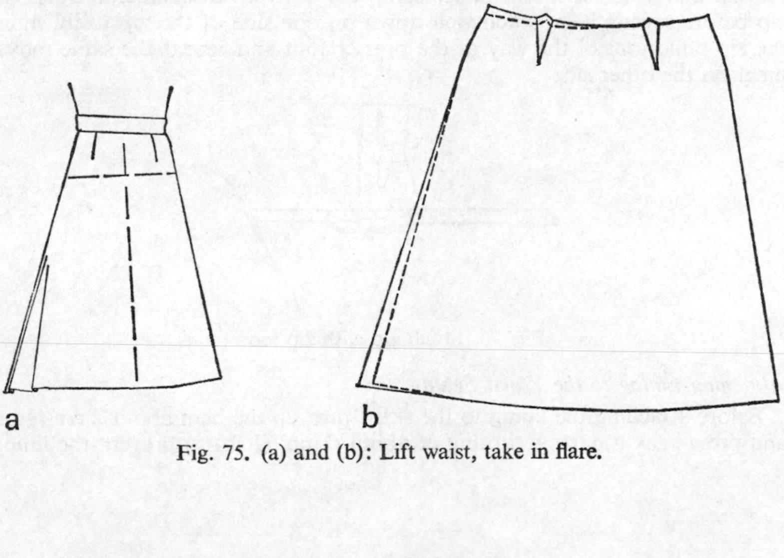

Fig. 75. (a) and (b): Lift waist, take in flare.

page 29—still holds good. A proportionally small waist and prominent hips equals a deep waist dart(s) or the reverse.

An uneven flare at the sides is either caused by fabric which has been cut off-grain (see page 50), or uneven hips. In both cases lift the waist to shorten the side seam, or drop to lengthen, the side seams at the waist.

Finally, attend to the hemline, ensuring that it is level, with the aid of metre/yardstick, set square or hem marker, by measuring from floor level up to the required length and mark it accordingly. Once the hem is level a decision to lengthen or shorten the skirt is a simple procedure.

When you have taken the skirt off, remark any alterations where pinned with a contrasting colour, single thread, on both sides of the pins and transfer the alterations to the pattern. Remove lining, waistband and untack the lower end of the zip (if in the side seam). If the waist is affected by alterations, remove the zip, open the hem and retack new seams on the skirt and lining.

Final Assembling and Completion

Machining and Under-pressing the Darts and Seams

Darts and seams are now ready for machine stitching. This should always commence at the top (waist) and finish at points of darts, and hem of skirt, on both left and right sides. Machine stitching from top to bottom on one side and bottom to top on the other may cause the skirt to twist. Remove all tacks and thread marks and under-press seams and darts and press darts with the fold edge towards centre.

Do likewise with the lining, but leave a gap (for the zip) unstitched. Raw edges on thin fabrics not hand oversewn can be machine neatened by turning seams back just under 6 mm (¼ in) and top stitching them from the wrong side, or can either be zig-zag stitched or **overlocked.** Most domestic machines are not capable of an overlocking stitch, but it is widely used in colleges and in industry.

Inserting the Zip

If the zip has been removed from side seam because of alterations, retack the zip and stitch it to the skirt, using the zip foot attachment. Open the zip before sewing it in, stitch well down on one side of the zip teeth, move the zip puller out of the way of the presser foot and repeat the same movement on the other side.

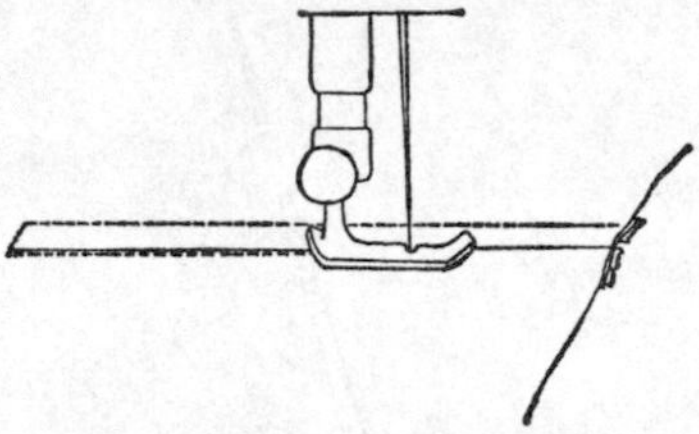

Fig. 76. Stitch zip with zip foot.

Attaching Lining to the Waist Seam

Before attaching the lining to the skirt, turn up the hem about 2 cm (¾ in) and press back a narrow turning of about 6 mm (¼ in) to prevent the lining fraying. Tack back the hem and slipstitch. After pressing, attach lining to the inside waistline of the skirt, wrong side of the lining to the wrong side of the skirt (seams of both facing) matching darts, seams and balance marks. Tack firmly in position.

Waistband

Before retacking the waistband to the skirt, which may have needed altering to fit a smaller or larger waist, the ends which will eventually lap-over to

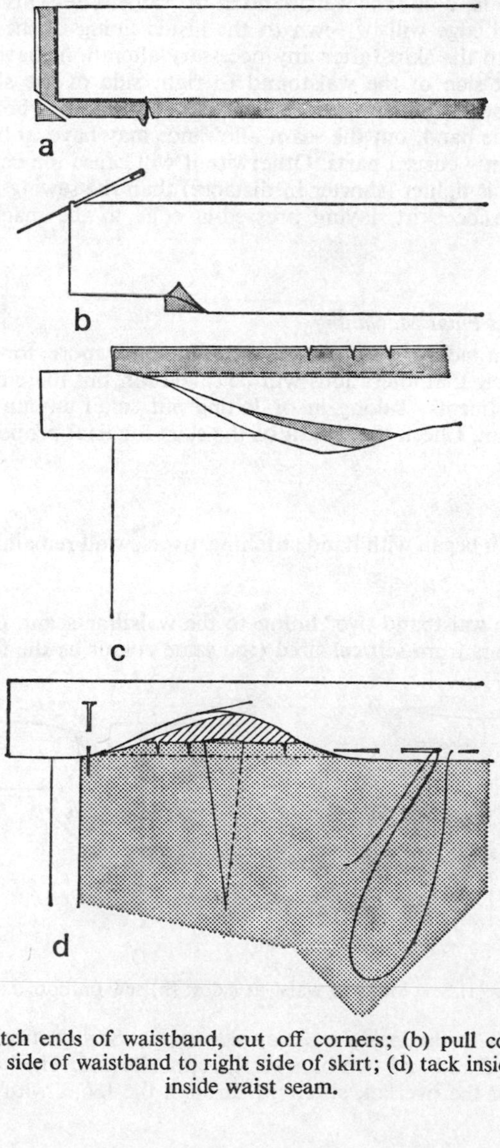

Fig. 77. (a) Stitch ends of waistband, cut off corners; (b) pull corners; (c) tack unpressed right side of waistband to right side of skirt; (d) tack inside waistband to inside waist seam.

fasten, are finished first. The waistband is folded in half, right sides together. Each end is then machine stitched across and up to the mark on the seam allowance, which joins the band to the skirt (see Fig. 77).

Next cut the corners off the seam allowances, to reduce bulk and to make neat corners when turned through. A small cut is also made at the ends of over and under wraps almost to the stitching line at the mark where it finishes. Then the ends are pulled through to the right side—the corners can be made sharper, by gently pulling them with a needle. Press the ends, and press *one* seam allowance in, along the waistband at the same time. This will save time later, when this edge will be sewn to the inside lining of the skirt. Retack the waistband to the skirt (after any necessary alterations have been made), unpressed right side of the waistband to right side of the skirt. Machine stitch on the tacked line. Do not press waist seam open, both seams face upward, into the band, but the seam allowance may have to be cut back or clipped on slightly curved parts. Otherwise it will cause the band to pucker, as the cut edge is tighter (shorter in distance) than the sewing line. Turn the band to the inside skirt, laying pressed-in edge to the machine line and tack down.

Second Fitting

Adjustments and Final Machining

With the hem tacked back slip on the skirt, once more, for a final fitting. It is now unlikely that alterations will be called for, but there may be a need for small adjustments. Taking in or letting out small amounts can still be easily carried out. Check the length of the skirt for final proportion.

Hand Finishing

Seams

Ending as you began with hand stitching, oversew all remaining raw edges.

Waistband

Slipstitch the waistband over lining to the waistline seam. Cut and make loops for hangers from **self-coloured** (the same colour as the fabric) tape or

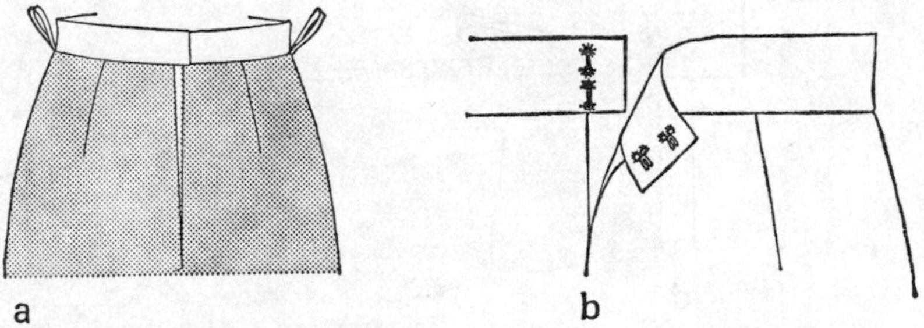

Fig. 78. (a) Sew loops to waist at sides; (b) sew on hooks and bars.

ribbon, and sew to the inside waist at side seams. Sew on two hooks to one end of the waistband and two bars to the opposite end. The hooks are sewn to the inside of the overlap, stitching through the loops with tightish overstitching, and a few stitches underneath the hook itself, which will keep it flat. The bars are sewn to the right side of the underlap, again stitching securely through the loops.

Lining

The lining is sewn down on each side of the zip, with small slipstitches to the zip tapes.

A few long stitches to form a bar, can be sewn at the hem of the lining at the seams, to join it to the skirt hem. This stops the lining from dragging up inside the skirt

Hem

Tack 1 cm ($\frac{3}{8}$ in) from the cut edge, then blindstitch.

Final Pressing

Final or 'top' pressing will give your skirt a crisp finished look. Good under-pressing has taken care of most of this process. All that remains is to press out any remaining creases and to cover parts such as the waistband, zip and hem which need a little extra attention. Remember to press over a pressing cloth, straight parts on the ironing board and shaped ones over a tailor's cushion/pad.

CHAPTER SEVEN

THE SECOND DESIGN: TROUSERS

Making the Trousers

The actual sewing processes for making the trousers are the same as for the skirt. The difference between the two is in the fitting and alterations to garment and pattern. Referring back to chapter two—'How to Take Measurements' (page 19) and 'Adjusting Patterns to Figure' (page 29)—will also help you to achieve a perfect fit.

One major point, is to make sure that the leg sections are clearly marked 'front' and 'back' on the cut out fabric, and the right side of the material is marked, when this is not obvious. Front and back trouser legs look very similar and when separated can easily be confused, resulting in a left front put to a right back, or even two front leg sections sewn together.

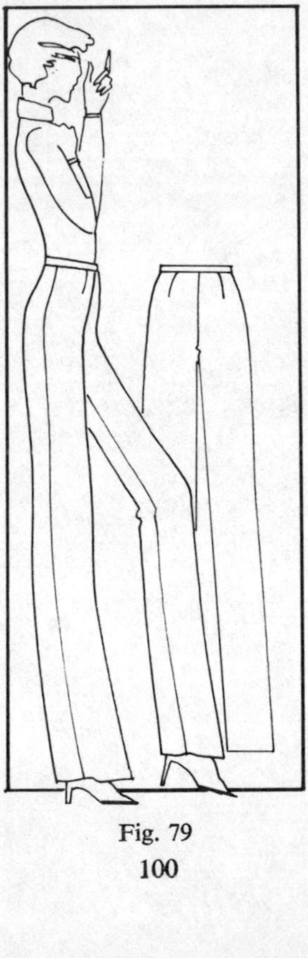

Fig. 79

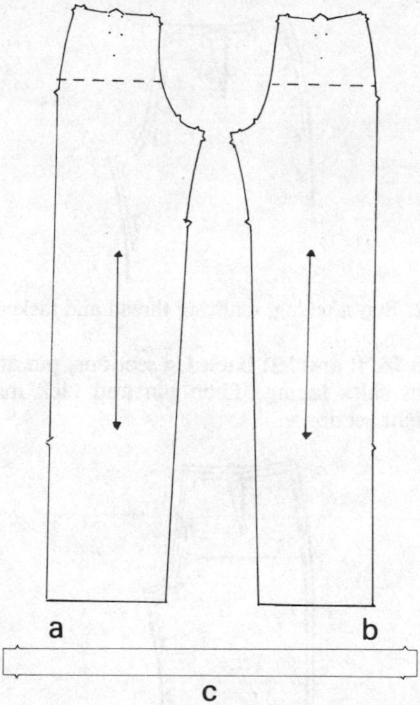

Fig. 80. Basic pattern shape: (a) front; (b) back leg; (c) waistband.

Trimmings

The same type of trimmings are used as for the skirt:

(1) White/contrast coloured tacking cotton.
(2) Mercerized sewing thread (sylko type 40).
(3) Skirt-weight zip fastener 20·5 cm (8 in) in length.
(4) Fusible interlining for the waistband.
(5) Hooks and bars for the waistband, size 2.

Initial Processes

After the pattern has been taken off, with seams and darts marked, fuse interlining to waistband, then staystitch the waist curve, crutch, top section of inside legs, and curved hip seams. Pin and tack darts.

Additional tack lines, placed horizontally at hip level, representing the straight weft grain, will be a help for the first fitting.

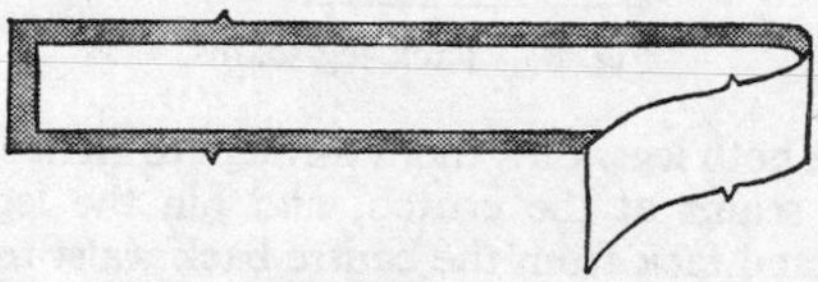

Fig. 81. Waistband and interlining.

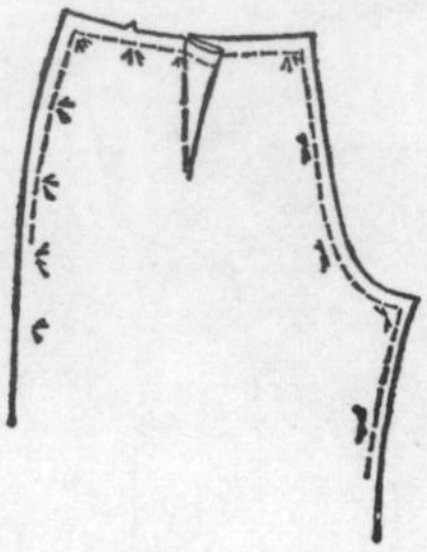

Fig. 82. Staystitching, marking thread and tacked dart.

Next take the left front and left back leg sections, pin and tack the outside leg seam first, right sides facing. Then pin and tack inside leg seam. Do likewise with the right sections.

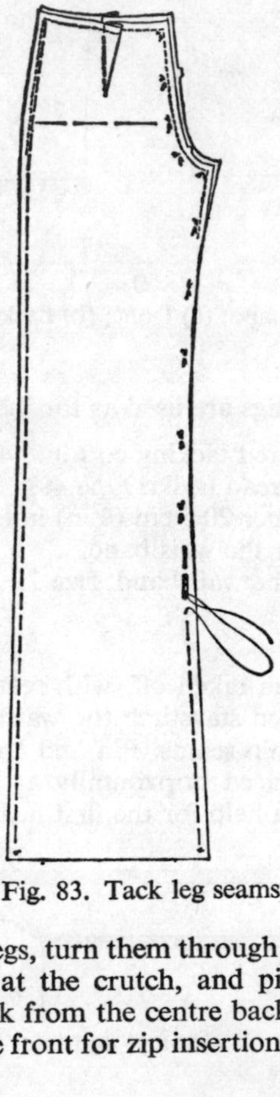

Fig. 83. Tack leg seams.

On completion of both legs, turn them through to right side, match notches and the inside leg seams at the crutch, and pin the legs together in this position. Then pin and tack from the centre back waist to crutch and to the opening mark on the centre front for zip insertion or, if this is at side, through to the front waist. The crutch seam is always stitched last, in the manner described, otherwise a good fit here will not be achieved.

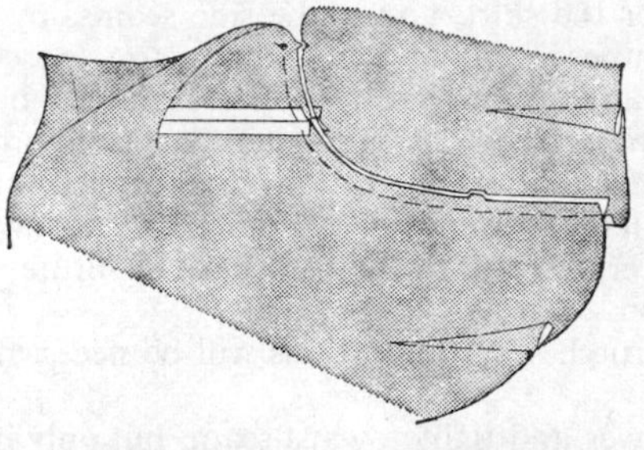

Fig. 84 Join legs together at the crutch seam.

Then:

(a) Pin and tack the zip, using same method described for the skirt.
(b) Pin and tack the waistband to waist seam, right sides together.
(c) Pin and tack leg hem allowances.

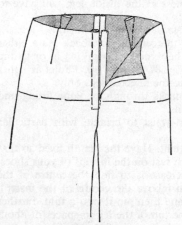

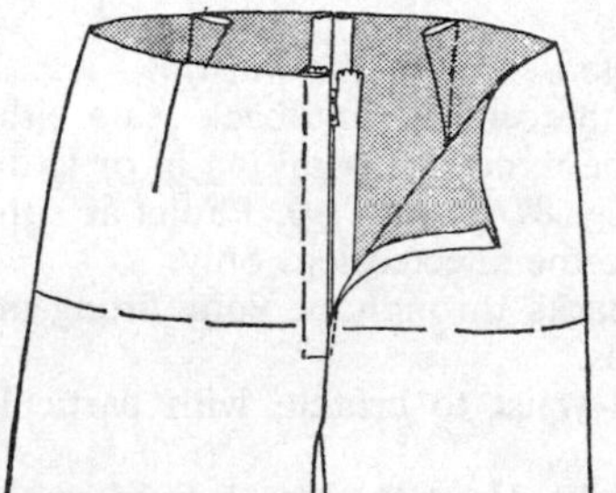

Fig. 85 Tack zip.

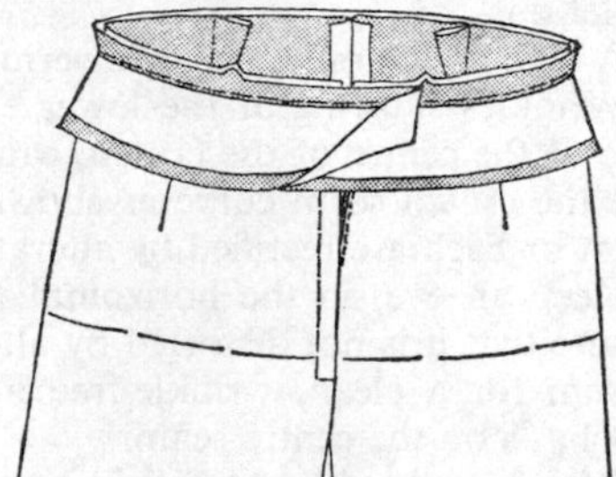

Fig. 86. Tack waistband to waist seam.

Fitting and Alterations

At first fitting aim for:

(a) A snug, but comfortable fit at the waist.
(b) A smooth fit over hips and seat, as tight as you like, but allowing sufficient ease for movement and no dragging wrinkles at crutch seam.
(c) Legs and side seams hanging plumb straight.

Wear the shoes which will go with your trousers, for without them the right length cannot be decided.

You will need assistance with this fitting.

Fitting the waist and hip area is very similar to that of the skirt. In both cases your individual body contours and the way you stand, which are unique to you, will determine the alterations needed.

As previously for the skirt, adjust the side seams, by taking in or letting out, for slight tightness or if fit is a fraction too loose, providing that no wrinkles show on any area of the trousers. Tightness below the waistband, which makes the trousers ride up is due to a large abdomen, seat, prominent hip bones, or uneven hips. Alterations are carried out as described on page 105, but—with the existence of an additional seam which joins the centre front, through the crutch and to the centre back—fitting trousers demands a little more attention.

Inside leg and crutch seam alterations will be necessary for the following faults.

A low crutch: lower and tighten waist seam, but only if *no bagginess shows* at the inside leg, just below the crutch. If it is baggy here take in the seam as shown in Fig. 87 (b). This alteration will automatically eliminate both bagginess and shorten the rise, so that raising the waist for a higher crutch is not always necessary.

If the crutch is not too low, and the inside leg is taken in, the crutch curve will need to be slightly lowered.

A high crutch, if combined with tightness at the inside leg, will have to be let out.

A **high crutch** only, needs lowering and loosening of the waist.

Wrinkles showing at the lower end of the centre front/back seam either side of the centre of the crutch, can also be removed by taking in or letting out the crutch seam curve as shown in Fig. 87 (f) and (g). Faults at either front or back are rectified by alterations to the affected legs only.

Keep an eye on the horizontal tack marks throughout your fitting and ensure that it is not distorted by alterations.

Aim for a clean, wrinkle-free fit from waist to crutch, with particular emphasis on the centre seam.

Both legs should now fall free and straight. Have the length fixed so that the hems at the centre of the front legs just rest on the insteps of your shoes. The best way to obtain the correct leg crease is to find the centre of the right front leg at the bottom of the hem (above the centre of the instep), hold it with your first finger and thumb and then pin it into a fold. Further pins are then placed gradually towards the top of the leg in spaces of about 9 cm (3½ in), in line with the grain. Replace pins, if the first attempt to achieve a straight fold fails and until it has been pinned at right angles to the hip grain mark. Do not try to pin the other trouser leg. You will find this crease when pressing, as described on page 108.

To increase/decrease the width at the hem let out, or pin in, equal amounts at both inside and outside leg seams.

Final Assembling and Completion

On completion of the fitting, mark carefully where alterations are to be made, in the same manner as for the skirt, and transfer the alterations to the pattern.

Tack the leg crease where pinned, and remove pins.

Even if no alterations need to be made before machining, remove the

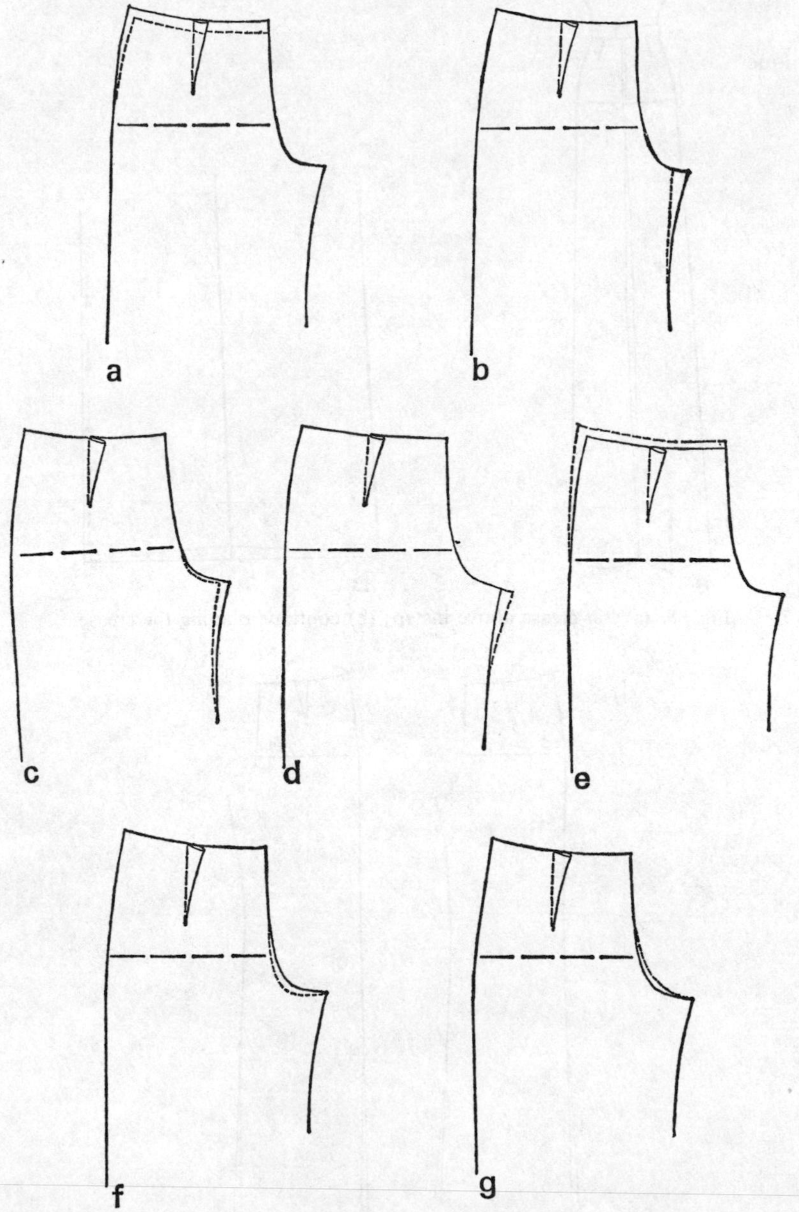

Fig. 87. (a) Lower waist seam and tighten waist; (b) take in inside leg seam; (c) inside leg taken in, lower crutch curve slightly; (d) let out inside leg seam; (e) raise waist seam and loosen waist; (f) take in; (g) let out crutch seam. (Broken lines represent alterations.)

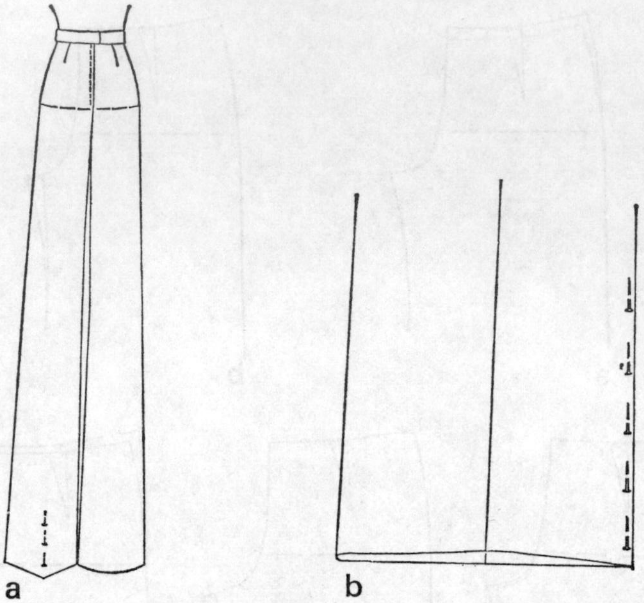

Fig. 88. (a) Pin crease above instep; (b) continue pinning the crease.

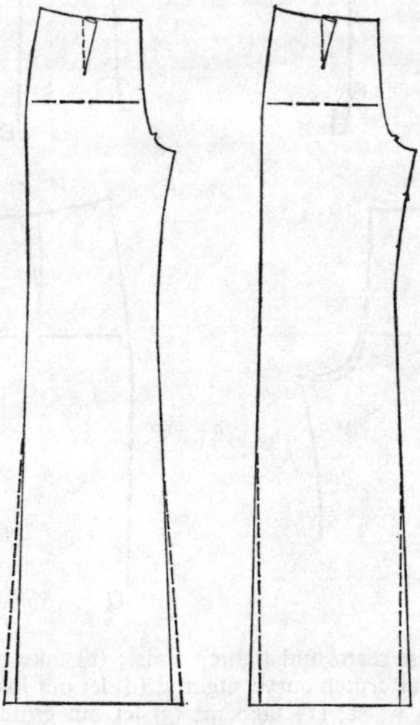

Fig. 89. Let out or take in equal amounts on both leg seams.

waistband and zip, and open the crutch seam and hems. To make the next step easier still, it is preferable to open the inside leg seam. This way machine stitching and under-pressing of side seams and darts now (the latter pressed towards the centre, facing each other) will be more efficient. Then the inside leg seams are machined, from top to bottom and under-pressed. If you cannot slide the legs over the ironing board, use the sleeve board instead.

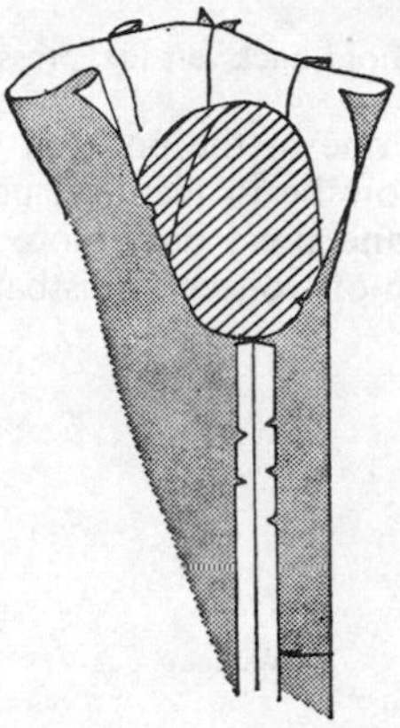

Fig. 90. Press seam on sleeve board.

Finish the side and inside leg seams with hand oversewing, overlocking or zig-zag stitch on woollens, or machine neaten on cottons.

Retack the crutch seam, following the pre-fitting method. To stitch, this needs a machine setting of about 8 stitches to 1 cm ($\frac{3}{8}$ in) or 20 stitches per in.

Ease the fabric carefully around the crutch curve, then machine stitch again over the same line to reinforce this seam.

Clip seam allowance on the curved, lower part of crutch every 2 cm ($\frac{3}{4}$ in), or cut back to 1 cm ($\frac{3}{8}$ in). Press seam open on a sleeve board or tailor's cushion/pad.

Reset the zip and machine stitch as skirt zip. Stitch final waistband ends as shown on page 97 and pin, tack and machine stitch the waistband to the waist seam of the trousers.

Re-tack hem allowances, slip the trousers on for a second fitting and check the right leg crease and length of legs before final pressing.

Finally after fitting, finish the waistband with slipstitch to waistband seam, sew on hooks to overwrap of band, bars to underwrap, see page 98. Finish raw edges of hems by oversewing, overlocking or zig-zag stitch for wool and machine neaten for cotton. Then blindstitch hems.

Final pressing is done for one leg at a time. Fold back the left leg towards the top of the trousers, as shown in Fig 91. Press the right leg, lightly at first, on the tacked front crease, remove the tacking cotton.

Smooth fabric from the front leg crease towards the back and press in this position.

Turn over to left leg, match inside leg seams of both legs from hem to crutch, which will give you the position of the crease. With the right leg

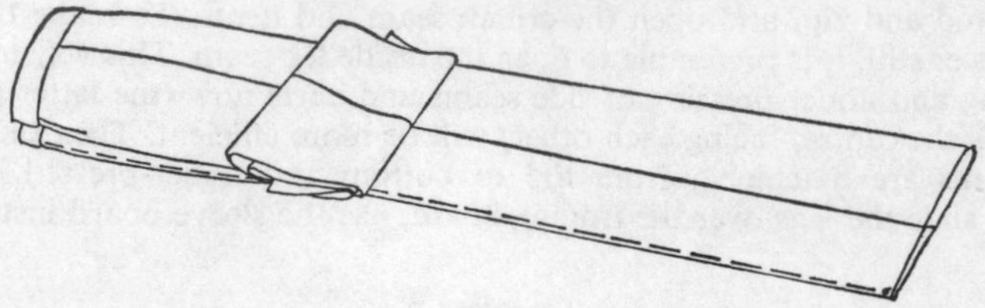

Fig. 91. Fold back left leg, press right leg.

folded back, press the left one in the position you have just found. Front and back creases should now be in identical positions on both legs. Place both legs together, check, and press once more on each side of the outside legs. Press the upper section of trousers, waistband, zip, on a sleeveboard or tailor's pad.

CHAPTER EIGHT

THE THIRD DESIGN: SHIFT DRESS

The Basic Dress

The dress is semi-fitted, semi-flared, with faced neckline, a zip opening in the centre back seam and set-in sleeves, or a sleeveless version with facing.

All stitches, seams, darts, zip insertion, hem and optional lining, are carried out using the same methods as for the skirt and trousers.

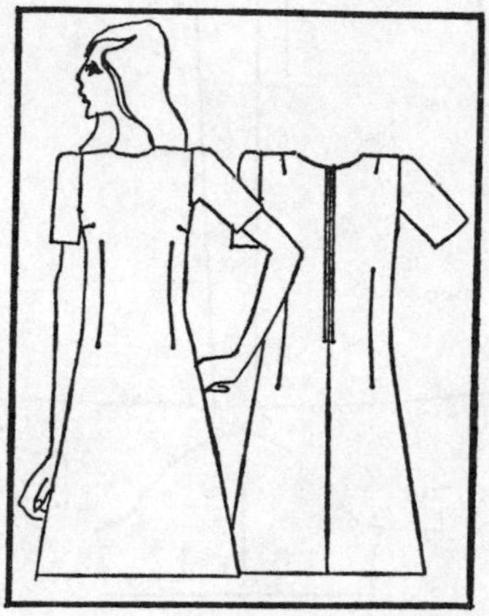

Fig. 92

New Processes

The two new processes are:

(a) The faced neckline (and armhole).
(b) The set-in sleeve.

Trimmings

The following trimmings are required:

(1) White/contrast coloured tacking cotton.
(2) Two reels of mercerized sewing thread (sylko type 40).
(3) Dress-weight zip fastener, 56 cm (22 in) in length.
(4) Lining (not including sleeves) optional.
(5) Fusible interlining for neck.
(6) Hook and bar for back neck opening, size 1.

Initial Processes

Having followed through similar working plans on the skirt and trousers

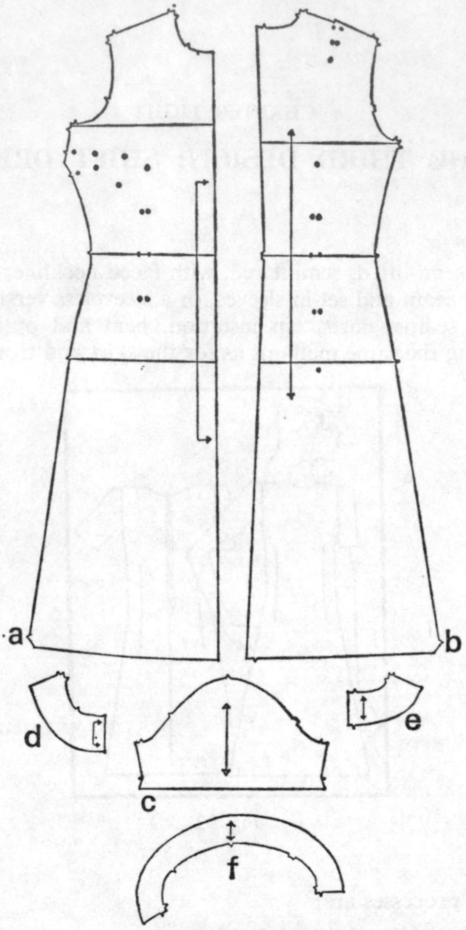

Fig. 93. Basic pattern shape: (a) front; (b) back; (c) sleeve; (d), (e) and (f) facings.

should make you feel confident about basic construction methods, e.g. stay-stitching, machining seams and darts. Now practice stitch a curve on two layers of fabric and turn the fabric to the right side to see that the finished edge has a good shape and lies flat.

If the garment is to be lined, cut the lining to the same shape as the dress, but shorter (as for the skirt, see page 90) and without sleeves.

Cut the interlining, using the neck facing pattern, but without seam allowances.

After marking, staystitch neck, armhole and hip curves, as these are liable to stretch. Fuse the interlining to the neck of garment, cut-edge of interlining placed to sewing lines of neck and shoulders.

Single-thread tack lines placed vertically at the centre front from the neck to the hem, through the centre of sleeves and horizontally across bust and hips, will be of great help at the fitting stage.

First, pin and tack all darts, then the centre back seam below the zip opening. Pin and tack the zip—leaving a small gap 6 mm ($\frac{1}{4}$ in) from the neck sewing line to the first zip teeth—followed by the shoulder seams, side seams, under-arm seam and lastly the hem.

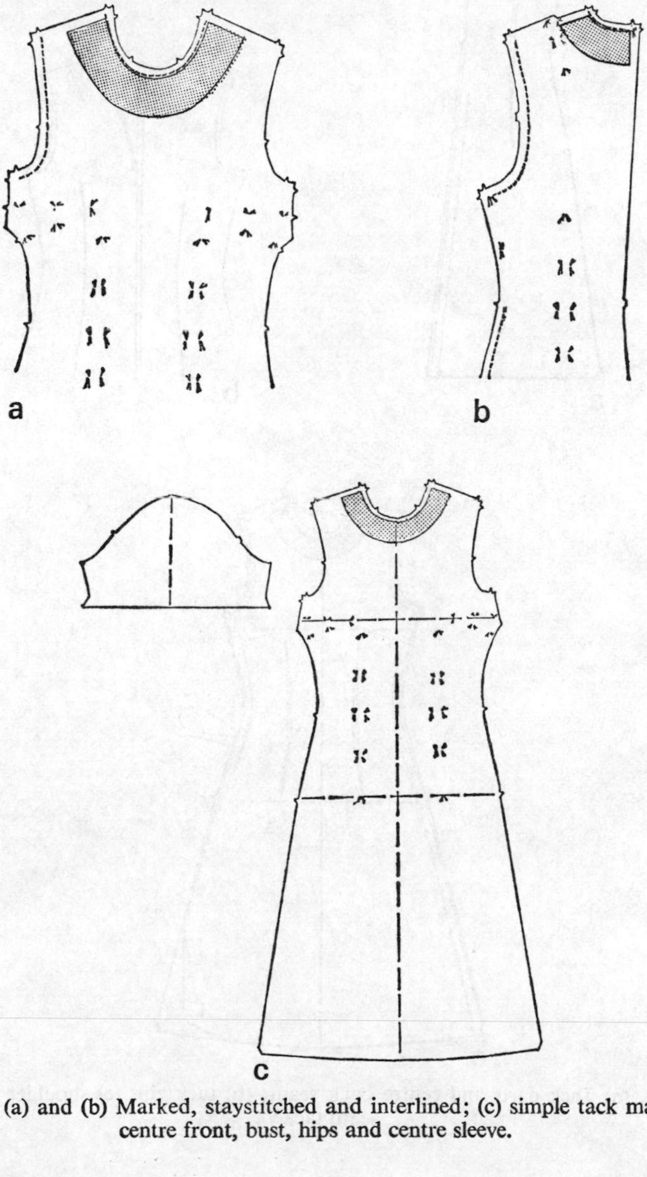

Fig. 94. (a) and (b) Marked, staystitched and interlined; (c) simple tack mark for centre front, bust, hips and centre sleeve.

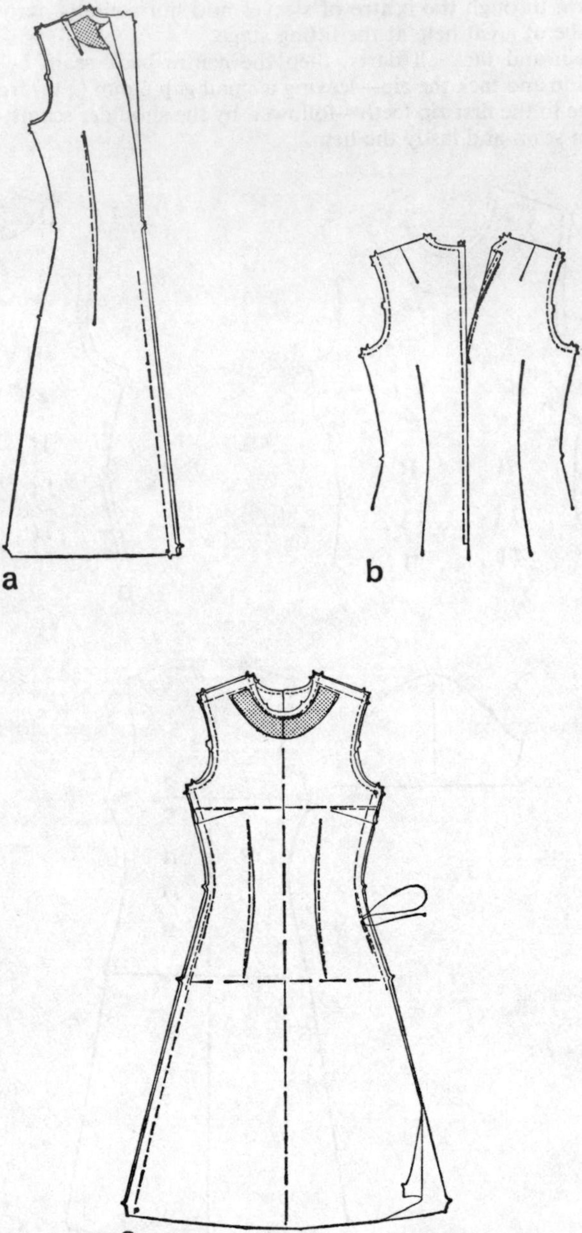

Fig. 95. (a) Tack darts and centre back seam; (b) tack zip; (c) shoulder and side seam tacked.

Do likewise with the lining, leaving upper part of the centre back seam open for the zip. With the wrong side of lining to wrong side of dress, pin and tack lining to neck and armholes of the dress.

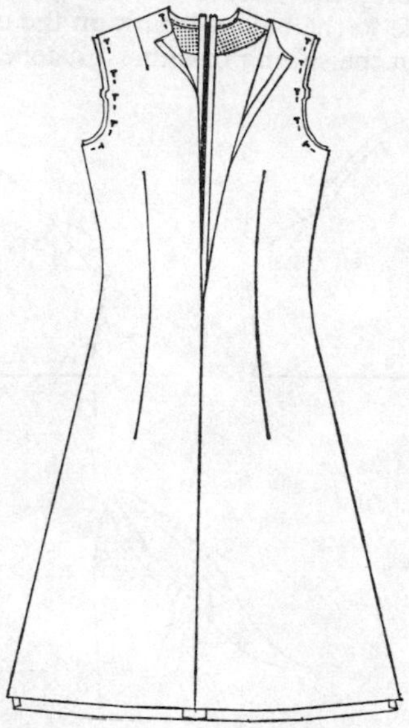

Fig. 96. Lining pinned and tacked to inside dress.

The Faced Neckline (and Armhole)

Next, the facings for front and back neck are joined, right sides together, at the shoulder seams. This is tacked to the neckline, right sides together, matching shoulder seams. Do not turn the facing to the inside of the neck until after the first fitting in case of alteration to the shape of the neck.

On a sleeveless dress join the armhole facings, matched to balance marks, and tack them to the armholes in the same manner as with the neck facings.

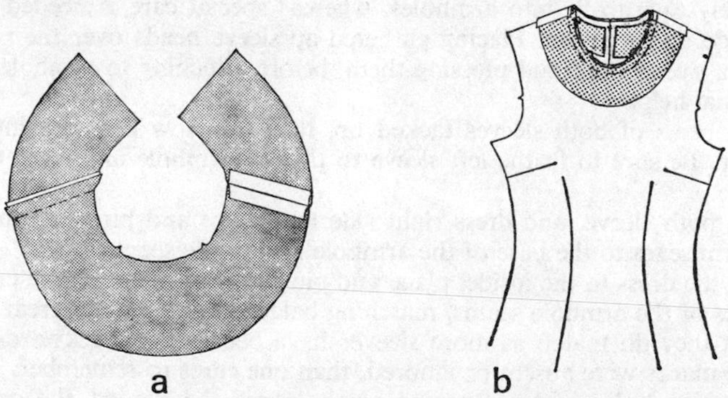

Fig. 97. (a) Join facings; (b) tack facing to neckline.

The Set-in Sleeve

The top of the sleeve, called the **head or crown**, is always larger than the armhole and must be 'eased-in' to allow for, and fit, the top of the arm and shoulder bone. Therefore, the sleeves need a gathering thread from the balance mark at one side to the balance mark on the other. This can be done with the largest stitch on the sewing machine. Fastened securely on one side,

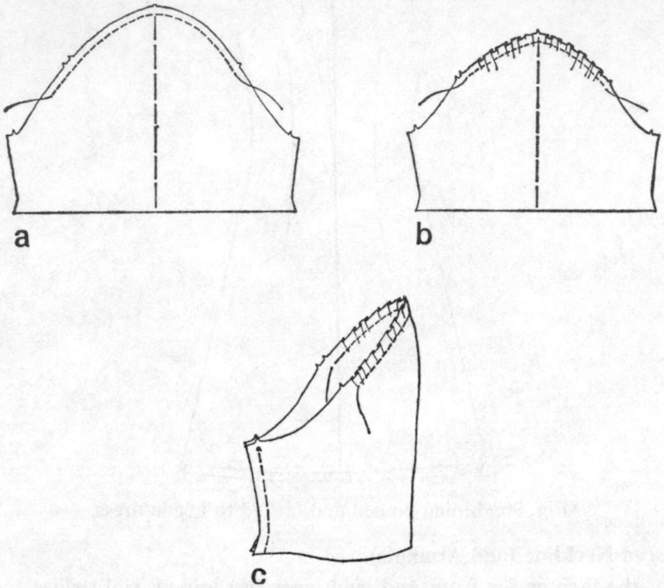

Fig. 98. (a) Sleeve head with gathering thread; (b) gathering thread drawn up; (c) gathered sleeve head and tacked underarm.

this thread is then drawn up to reduce the length of the crown to the circumference of the armhole and fastened on the other side. Spread the fullness evenly and avoid puckers or pleats. Sleeves made in woollen fabrics are comparatively easy to fit into armholes, whereas special care is needed if they are made up in cotton. Placing gathered-up sleeve heads over the rounded end of a sleeveboard and pressing them, before attaching to armholes, is an additional help.

With hems of both sleeves tacked up, they can now be fitted into each armhole. Be sure to fit the left sleeve to the left armhole and right to right armhole.

With both sleeve, and dress right side out, place and pin the top of the underarm seam to the base of the armhole at the side seam.

Turn the dress to the inside, place and pin the sides of the sleeve crown to the sides of the armhole seams, matching balance marks. Take great care to see that they do match as more sleeves have been set in backwards, when balance marks were absent or ignored, than one cares to remember.

With pins holding the sleeve to armhole pin the top of the crown to the shoulder seam. Now the sleeve is held to the armhole at the top sides,

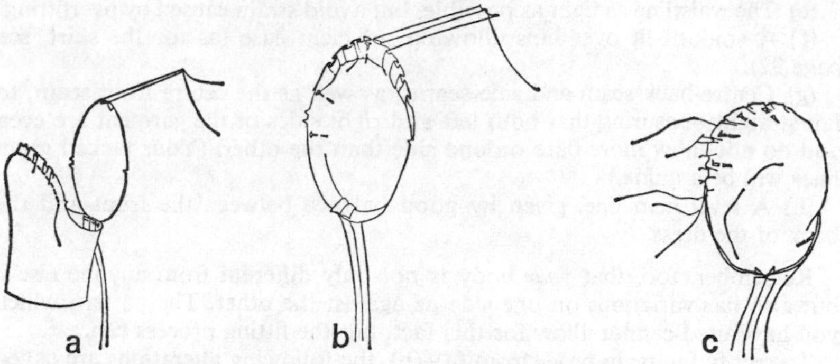

Fig. 99. (a) Underarm of sleeve pinned to bodice side seam; (b) sleeve pinned to armhole on the inside; (c) hold back top of sleeve over hand.

and the bottom and can be pinned (at right angles to seams) and tacked throughout. Remember to ease-in where the head is gathered and to avoid pleats or puckers. As an additional aid, the fullness can be spread and more easily distributed by holding the sleeve, as shown in Fig. 99(c).

Fitting and Alterations

To fit the shift dress remember to put on the same foundation garments you wore for taking measurements. Put on your most suitable shoes, make up to look your best and arrange your hair to leave the neck easily accessible for the fitting. Give yourself and your assistant ample time, so that the fitting can be carried out in a relaxed manner.

In as much as the hang of the skirt is controlled from the waist, the fit of the shift dress is determined first by the shoulders. Correct balance between the front and back of the dress depends on how well the shoulder seam is placed, no matter what length the design of the skirt. A hemline shorter at the front than at the back, or the reverse, may well require alteration to the shoulder seams, rather than lengthening at the hem. So apply the same rule as for the previous two garments and first cast your eye from top to bottom. Make a mental note of any obvious faults before getting on with the actual fitting. Success will come with patience.

Aim to have this garment free from wrinkles, without pull or strain on any parts in one direction or another. Bust and hips to fit tightly, but not to restrict movement. Working from top to bottom as before and make it your object to achieve:

(a) A well-shaped, comfortable neckline to lie smooth on the base of the neck, neither binding, nor too loose and gaping.

(b) Straight shoulder lines, of the correct length from the base of the neck at the sides, to the shoulder bones.

(c) Sleeves falling free, parallel to your body, comfortable below the arm pits—without unnecessary and unsightly bagginess.

Arms allowed to move freely, with adequate fabric across the front and the back of the bodice, between armholes on both sides.

(d) A smooth-fitting bustline, with darts placed in the correct positions.

(e) The waistline as tight as possible, but avoid strain caused by overfitting.

(f) A smooth fit over hips allowing sufficient ease (as for the skirt, see page 92).

(g) Centre-back seam and side seams, as well as the centre front seam, to fall straight—ensuring that both left and right sides of the garment are even and do not show more flare on one side than the other. (Your tacked grain lines will be a guide.)

(h) A level hem line, given by good balance between the front and the back of the dress.

Remember, too, that *your* body is not only different from anyone else's, but also has variations on one side as against the other. The pattern which you have used cannot allow for this fact, but the fitting process can.

To rectify faults, in order from (a)–(h), the following alterations are called for:

(a) Neckline too high, so lower, by pinning, as shown in Fig. 100.

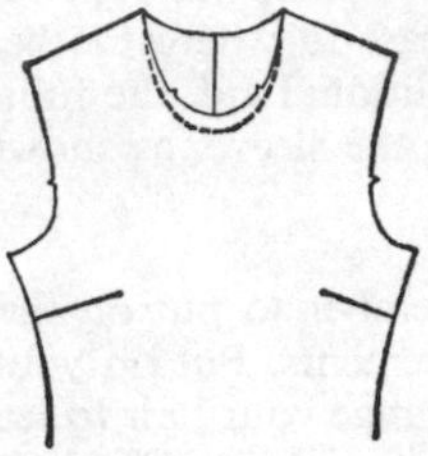

Fig. 100. Mark lower neckline.

A too-low neckline can be raised by reducing the seam allowance and see if taking in the shoulder seams at the neck will help.

(b) Excess fabric due to sloping shoulders: take in the shoulder seams and lower the armholes, as shown in Fig. 101(a).

Tightness from shoulder to bust caused by square shoulders is overcome by letting out shoulder seams and raising the armholes. This alteration may only be necessary for one side. Your shoulder bone structure also affects the length of the shoulder seam. Lengthen or shorten it to see that the sleeve crown fits to the end of the bone. Make sure that the top of the armhole at the shoulder seams retains a rounded shape after alterations.

(c) Crowns which are too short and so are dragging the sleeves up, need lengthening. Prominent shoulder bones may be the cause. In this event (as with all shoulder seam and armhole alterations) remove the sleeves and reset them, after letting out the sleeve seam at the crown.

Strain across the front or the back of the bodice between the armholes, which is causing tightness at sleeves. Let out the armhole seam where it is tight.

Excess fabric, horizontally between shoulders and bust at the front armholes is corrected by opening the shoulder seam and lifting the front shoulder only—from shoulder bone to nothing at the neck—or, if close to the bust, by increasing the depth of the under-arm bust dart by the amount of excess visible, and by as much as the front side seam can be lengthened upwards, to

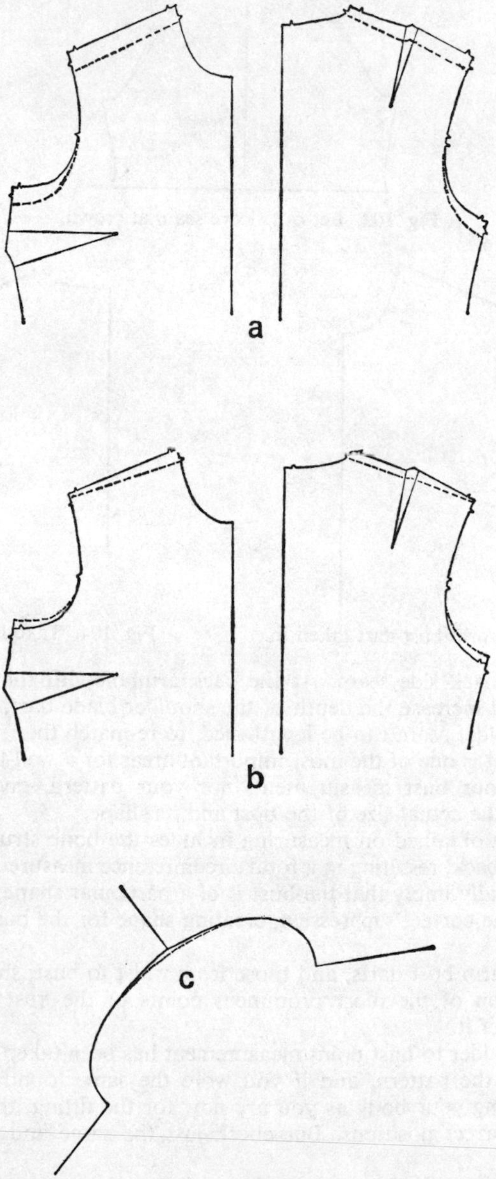

Fig. 101. (a) Alteration marking lines for lifted shoulder and lowered armhole; (b) raised armhole and shoulder let out; (c) keep rounded armhole shape.

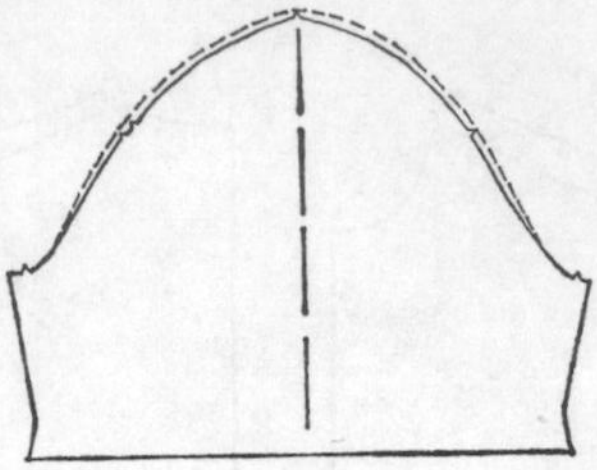

Fig. 102. Let out sleeve seam at crown.

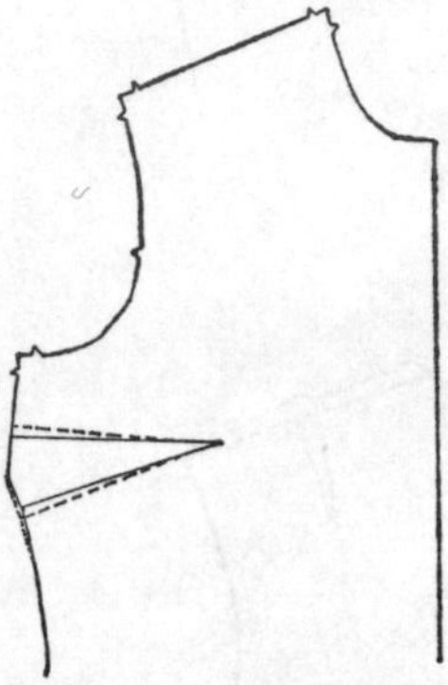

Fig. 103. Underarm bust dart taken in.

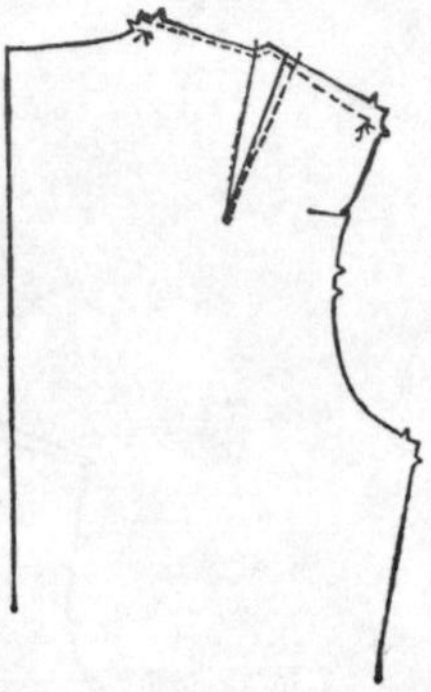

Fig. 104. Take in shoulder dart.

re-match the back side seam. At the back armholes lift the back-shoulder seam only and increase the depth of the shoulder blade dart, by as much as the back shoulder seam can be lengthened, to re-match the front.

(d) The bust is one of the most important areas for a well-fitting garment, but neither your bust measurement, nor your pattern, give an accurate indication of the actual size of the bust and its shape.

The reading obtained on measuring includes the bone structure and contours of your back, resulting in a total circumference measurement. This does not automatically imply that the bust is of a particular shape. So alterations to darts for the correct **suppression,** creating shape for the bust, may well be necessary.

The under-arm bust darts, and those from waist to bust, should be placed in the direction of the most prominent points of the bust and to within 2·5 cm (1 in) of it.

If your shoulder to bust point measurement has been taken accurately and checked with the pattern, and if you wore the same foundation garments when measuring your body as you are now for the fitting, the darts should be in their correct positions. But check just the same and adjust them if necessary.

Tightness across the bust may only need the releasing and letting out of the side seams, but alterations here affect the circumference of the sleeve head, as shown on Fig. 105. The under-arm seams will have to be adjusted accordingly.

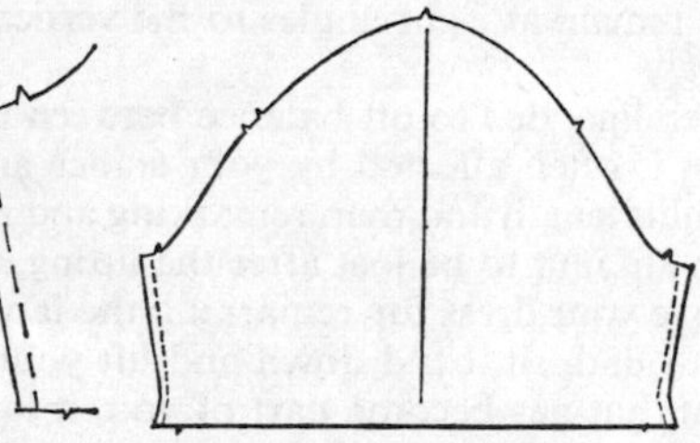

Fig. 105. Adjust underarm seam.

If after that wrinkles still show, the depth of the underarm darts should be increased and the loss of length on the front side seam made good, by as much as the seam allowance at the base of the armhole can be reduced.

(e) and (f) Side- and centre-back seams at the waist and hips can be adjusted by taking in or letting out small amounts, as previously described for the skirt on page 94. Equally, and in addition, waist darts can be increased or decreased. But beware of over fitting, which will result in unsightly wrinkles—those which look like soft folds, deep in the centre, but shallow at the ends (best observed on trousers between the knee and crutch when the leg is lifted with the knee bent) mean tightness, wherever they are. The direction in which these wrinkles show, indicates the area from which the tightness originates. Releasing seams at the point(s) mentioned, will eliminate this type of fault.

(g) Keep an eye on the tacked grain marks during the fitting. As long as

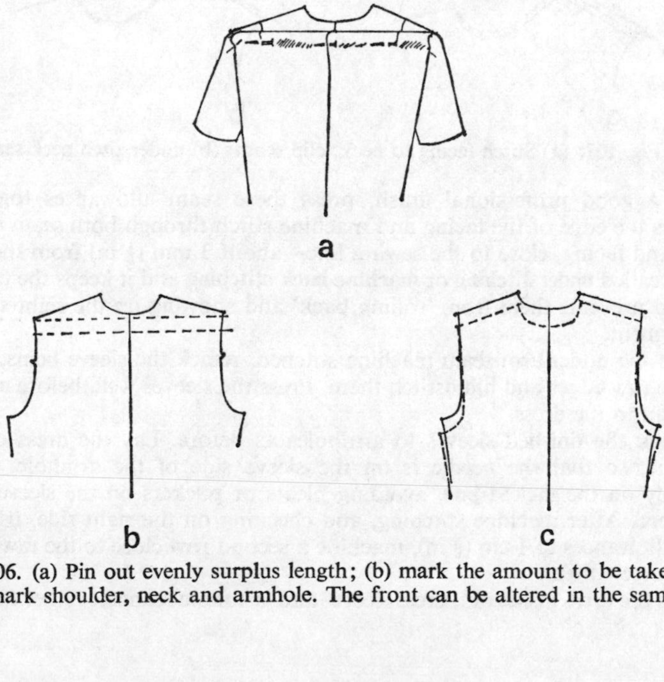

Fig. 106. (a) Pin out evenly surplus length; (b) mark the amount to be taken out; (c) remark shoulder, neck and armhole. The front can be altered in the same way.

the horizontal ones remain at right angles to the vertical, distortion will have been avoided.

(h) An uneven hemline, due to off balance between the front and the back section of the dress, is often affected by your stance and this is put right by pinning out the surplus length and then remarking and recutting the shoulders and neckline by the amount to be lost after the fitting, as shown on Fig. 106.

Before you remove your dress for remarking the fabric and pattern, apply a final test. Move around, sit, bend down and lift your arms. If the garment not only looks right, but has become part of you, it has passed the test with flying colours.

Final Assembling and Completion

When all the necessary alterations have been marked, remove the lining, facing, sleeves and zip. Transfer the alterations to the garment and pattern. As with the previous garments, all darts and seams on the garment and the lining are machine stitched and under-pressed, but leave the facings for joining to the neck, and sleeves to armholes, until later. Seam allowances are finished with oversewing, or machine neatening. The lining hem can also be finished at this stage.

With the garment machined, the zip reset, and the hem tacked for a second fitting, pin and retack the lining to the armholes and neck, wrong sides facing. Now machine stitch facings to neck (and armhole if sleeveless). Clip or cut back-seam allowances to allow the facings to lie flat, when they are turned to the wrong side.

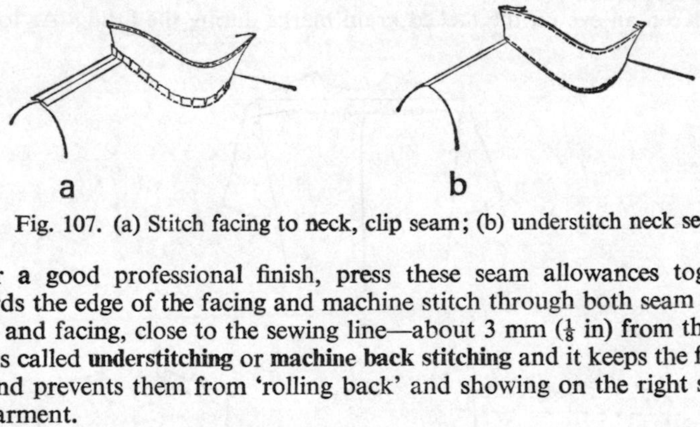

Fig. 107. (a) Stitch facing to neck, clip seam; (b) understitch neck seam.

For a good professional finish, press these seam allowances together, towards the edge of the facing and machine stitch through both seam allowances and facing, close to the sewing line—about 3 mm ($\frac{1}{8}$ in) from the line. This is called **understitching** or **machine back stitching** and it keeps the facings flat and prevents them from 'rolling back' and showing on the right side of the garment.

With the under-arm seam machine stitched, retack the sleeve hems, oversew the raw edges and blindstitch them. Press the sleeves well, before attaching them to the dress.

Retack the finished sleeves to armholes as before. Lay the dress on the machine, so that the needle is on the sleeve side of the armhole. Stitch carefully on the tacked line, avoiding pleats or puckers on the sleeve head as before. After machine stitching, and checking on the right side, trim the seam allowances to 1 cm ($\frac{3}{8}$ in), machine a second row close to the raw edges and oversew them.

With the dress inside out, press sleeve–and–armhole seams together towards the sleeves on the rounded end of the sleeve board. Press gently and do not push the iron too much as this causes stretching and loss of shape. The seam allowances on the neck facings at the centre back are turned in, and tacked to the zip tape. (Leave enough space between the facing and zip teeth to allow the zip puller to run freely.)

Sew the outside edges of the facings to the shoulder seams of the lining at each side (armhole facings if sleeveless to the shoulder and side seams).

Slip the dress on for second fitting and make final adjustments if necessary.

Finally, finish off the hem as described on page 85. (Catch lining hem to dress hem with a few hand stitches, to prevent the lining from riding up.)

Sew a hook and bar to the top of neck above the zip, in order to take the strain here.

Sew the centre back of the facings and lining to the zip tapes with slip-stitches.

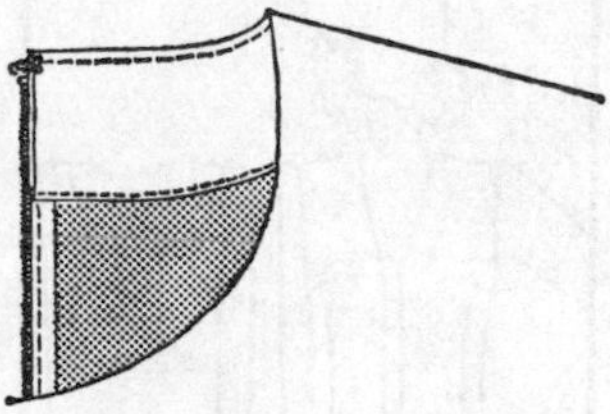

Fig. 108. Catch facing and lining to zip tape.

Remove all remaining marking and tacking threads.

Final pressing should now only consist of touching up, especially at the neckline, zip, and hem. Do not press these areas too heavily, otherwise impressions of the facings, etc., will show on the right side of the garment. Press sleeve heads over the rounded end of a sleeve board or small tailor's pad. The straight, flat skirt sections are best pressed over the ironing board on the wrong side of the garment, and all shaped areas over a tailor's cushion/pad, but **do not press any part without a pressing cloth.**

Careless pressing will flatten and destroy, whereas careful pressing will mould, retain and improve the shape, as built in by darts and seams.

Slight puckering may disappear if the seams are held taut when pressing, but do not stretch them and cause loss of shape.

CHAPTER NINE

THE FOURTH DESIGN: THE JACKET

The Jacket

Semi-fitted, semi-flared, edge to edge cardigan style, with faced fronts, set-in sleeves, patch pockets.

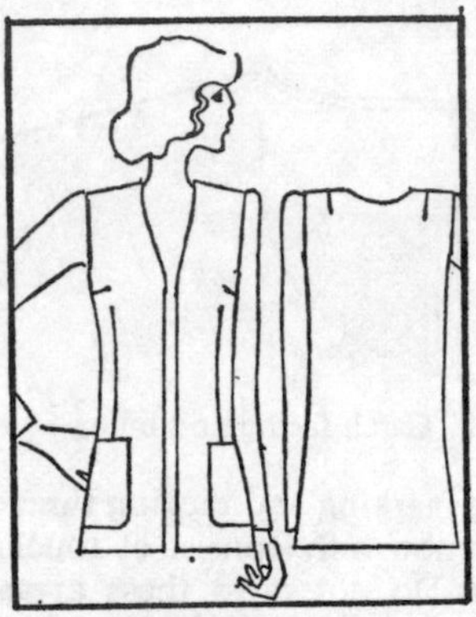

Fig. 109

New Processes

The new processes in this are:

(a) The felling stitch.
(b) The patch pocket.
(c) The jacket facings.
(d) Insertion of shoulder pads (optional).
(e) Hand-finished lining (optional).

Trimmings

The following trimmings are required:

(1) Tacking cotton and sewing thread as for the previous designs.
(2) Lining (optional).
(3) Fusible interlining for fronts, pockets and back neck.
(4) Shoulder pads (optional).

The Felling Stitch

This is a small hemming stitch used for hand finishing where machining is not possible, or where it would show to disadvantage. Used mainly to sew in linings to clothes.

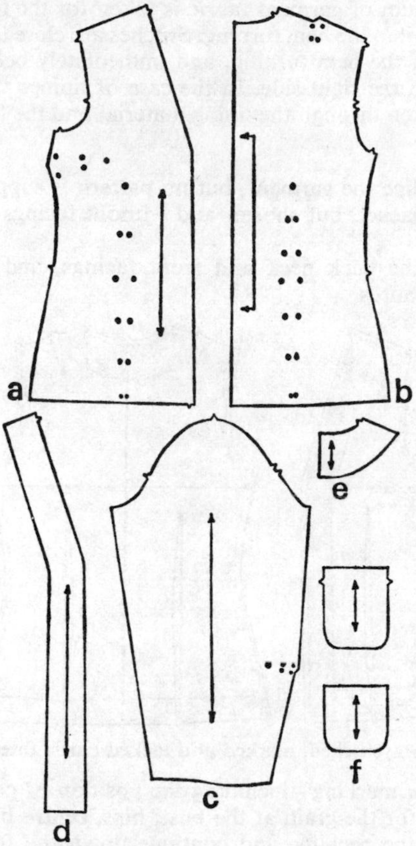

Fig. 110. Basic pattern shapes: (a) front; (b) back; (c) sleeve; (d), (e) and (f) facings and pockets.

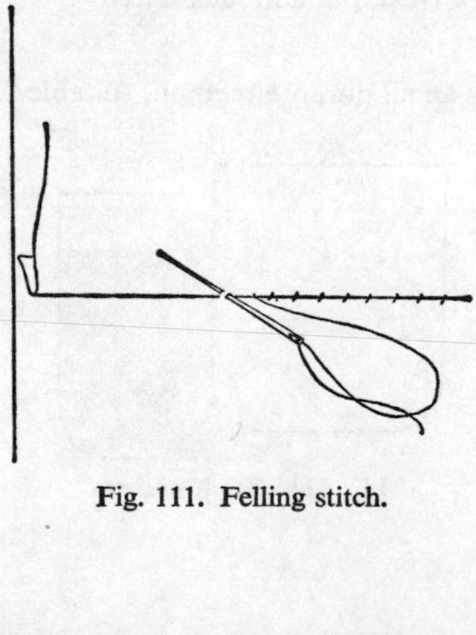

Fig. 111. Felling stitch.

A fractional amount of garment fabric is taken for the first stitch then an equally small amount in the hem turning. Stitches are close together and made on the very edge of the hem turning, and immediately below the hem, and should not show on the right side. In the case of linings this is easy, as the stitches are only taken through the lining material and the facing.

Initial Processes

If you decide to line the garment, but no pattern is supplied, cut it to the same shape as the jacket, but shorter and without facings (as for the dress and skirt).

Interlinings for the back neck and front facings, and pockets, are cut without seam allowances.

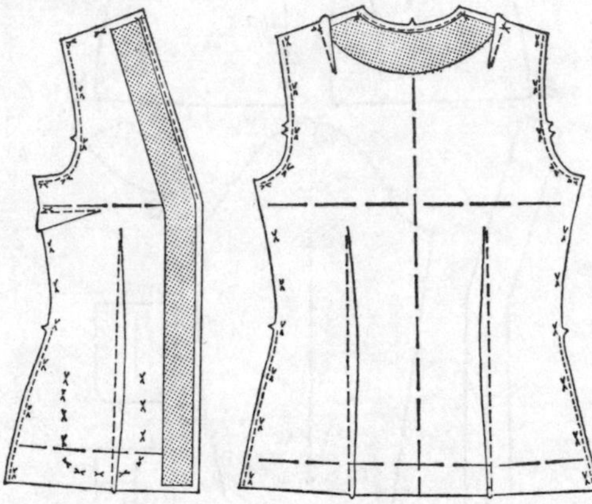

Fig. 112. Staystitched, marked and tacked darts, fused interlining.

On completion of marking—including the position of pockets and single-thread tack marks for the grain at the bust, hips, centre back and centre of sleeves—staystitch the neckline and continue down the fronts to the hem, which is most important as these must not stretch. Staystitch armholes and hip curve as before. Fuse the facing interlining to the wrong side of the garment (see Fig. 112). Next, pin and tack darts.

The Patch Pocket

The patch pocket is an all-purpose method, suitable for cotton or woollen fabrics.

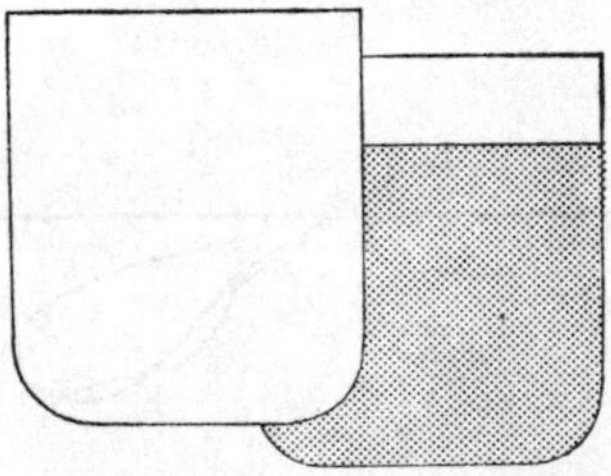

Fig. 113. Patch pocket.

The pockets are made up and then tacked to the jacket fronts, before the side and shoulder seams are joined: this is an easier and more accurate method of placing and attaching them to the fronts than it would be if the seams were joined first.

A practice pocket in a similar or the same fabric should be made first of all to gain experience in sewing corners and to achieve a uniform shape. Detailing on garments is most important and meant to be good—a careless, inaccurate finish on only one corner can ruin the effect of an otherwise well-finished garment.

The pocket, is cut with a facing in one, so the lined part will not show (see Fig. 114(a)).

The lining is cut to the same width as the pocket, but shorter, to meet the facing when folded back (see Fig. 114(b)). The edges of the facing and top of the lining need additions of seam allowances.

Interlining, cut and fused as shown in Fig. 114(c) eliminates unnecessary bulk in turnings. First mark and staystitch the pocket and then fuse the interlining to the wrong side of the pocket, exactly to the marking lines.

Stitch the pocket lining to the top of the pocket facing (right sides facing) leaving a gap in the centre of the seam of at least 6·5 cm (2½ in).

Fold over the pocket lining, right sides facing, so that all the edges meet (see Fig. 114(d)). Tack in this position and machine stitch all the way around the sides and lower edge. Use the edge of the interlining and staystitching as a guide.

Trim the seam allowances and top corners, and notch the curved lower edges, to ensure a neat, even shape on the curves when turned through to the right side.

Pull the pocket to its right side, through the gap left in the seam between the lining and the facing. Use a needle and gently pull out the top corners, to give them a sharp shape (see Fig. 114(f)). Smooth the curves at the bottom end, making sure that the lining does not 'roll', so that it shows on the right side. Sew up the gap in the seam (see Fig. 114(g)).

Tack the pocket all the way round, under-press, remove tacks and press again, to ensure that no impression of tacking is left (see Fig. 114(h)).

When the two pockets have been completed, they are ready for pinning and tacking to marking lines on the jacket fronts—before the side and shoulder seams are joined. Leave the pockets tacked only for the fitting, before attaching them permanently, in case alterations are made to the length of the jacket or the side seams, which would affect their placing (see Fig. 114(i)).

Proceed to pin and tack side, shoulder and under-arm seams. Put a gathering thread in each sleeve head, draw up, and spread the fullness evenly. Press on a sleeveboard.

The Jacket Facings

Join facings at the shoulder seam, right sides facing. (For an unlined version, machine neaten the outer edges of the facing to avoid over-handling at later stages.) Pin and tack at the front/back-neck facing to the jacket, right sides facing, and set in the sleeves identically to that method described, for the dress, on page 115.

If a lining is used, join the sections together in the same order as the jacket.

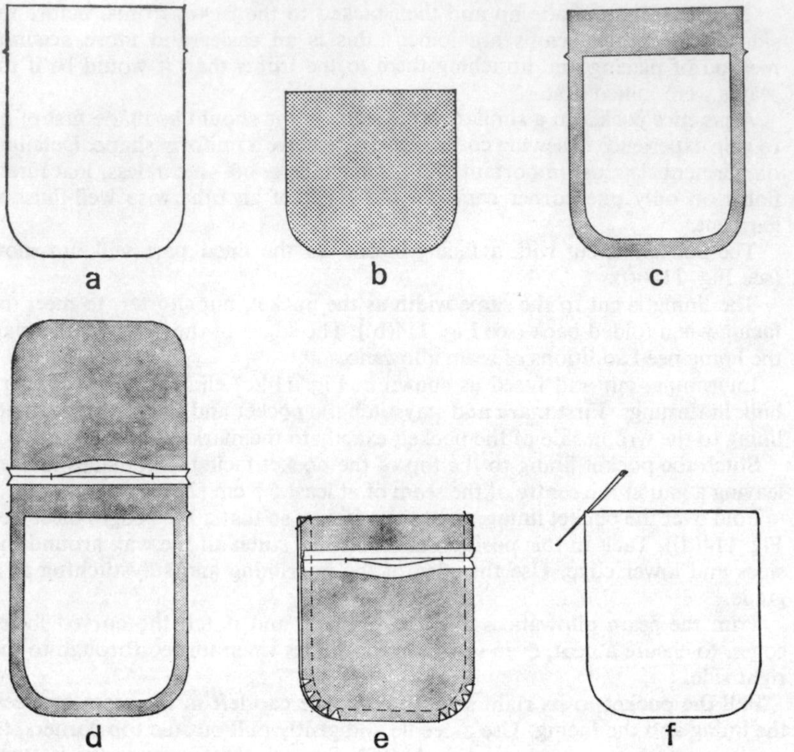

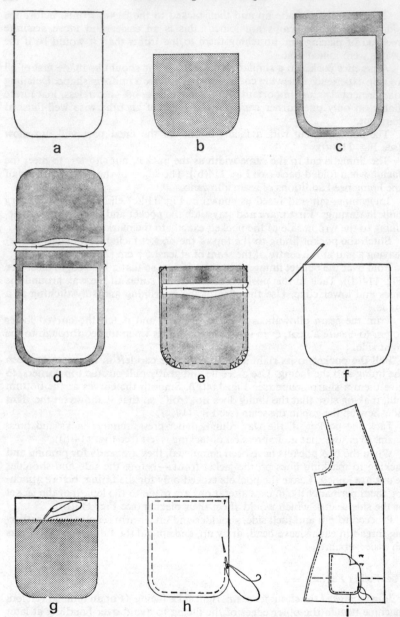

Fig. 114. (a) Pocket with facing cut in one; (b) lining; (c) interlining fused to wrong side of pocket; (d) and (e) gap left open, seam stitched and corners clipped; (f) pull out corners after turning through; (g) sew gap together; (h) tack pocket all the way round; (i) tack pocket to jacket.

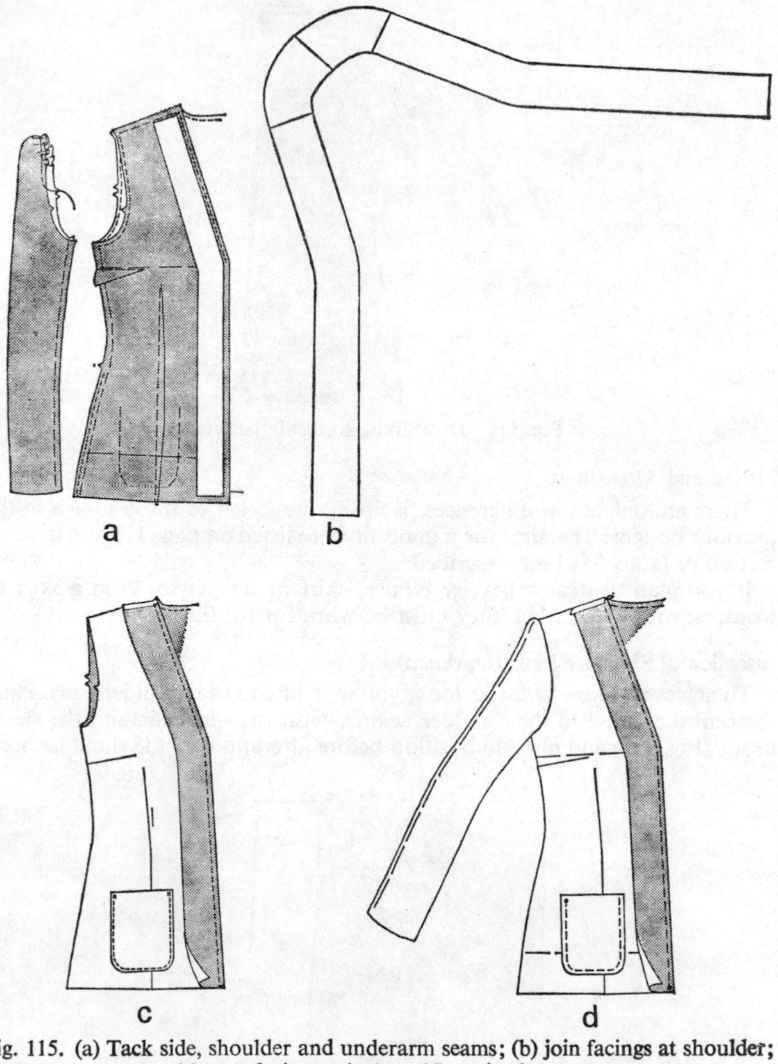

Fig. 115. (a) Tack side, shoulder and underarm seams; (b) join facings at shoulder; (c) tack facing to jacket; (d) set in sleeves.

Tack the hems of the jacket and sleeves. With the jacket turned inside out, place the wrong side of lining to the wrong side of jacket.

Pin the shoulder seams of both together to hold in position. Pin and tack the raw edges of the lining to the neck, front and the shoulder of jacket.

Pin and tack the hems, but allow the lining to be slightly longer from the shoulder to hem at the front and back, and also from the crown to hem of the sleeves. An otherwise tight lining will drag up the garment when it is turned back to the right side. You are now ready for the first fitting.

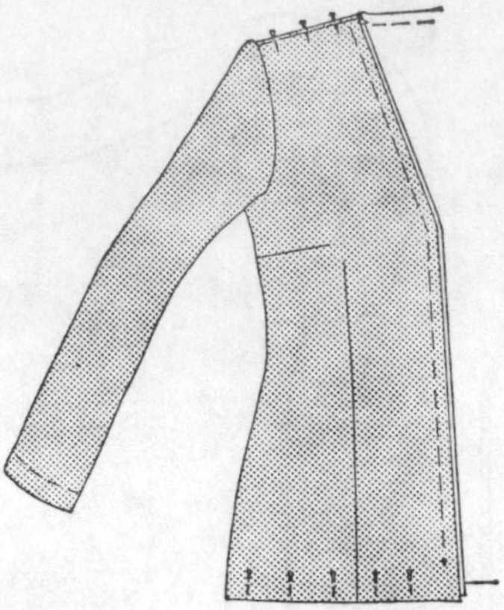

Fig. 116. Tack lining to inside jacket.

Fitting and Alterations

There are only a few differences in fitting the jacket to those shown in the previous designs. The aims for a good fit were listed on page 115 and the correction of faults has been described.

If you plan to wear a heavier blouse, shirt or jumper, or even a skirt or trousers, with your jacket, they must be worn for the fitting.

Insertion of Shoulder Pads (Optional)

To achieve a more 'tailored' look, you may like to use shoulder pads. Place the centre of these to the shoulder seams, with the wide side into the sleeve heads (Fig. 117) and pin into position before alterations to the shoulder area.

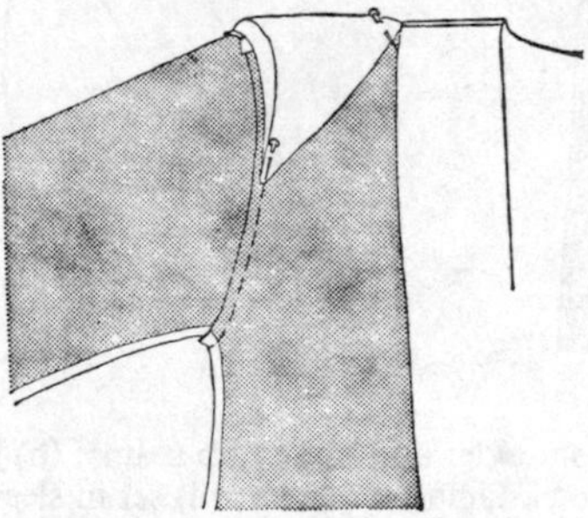

Fig. 117. Pin shoulder pad.

When standing still, the front opening should be edge-to-edge as designed and not show gaps below the *V* of the neckline.

A commonly found fault is the fronts falling away to expose a widening gap at the lower part of jacket, towards the hemline. If this does occur, one way is to lift the front shoulder seams (to nothing at shoulder bone) until the centre front edges meet (Fig. 118(a)).

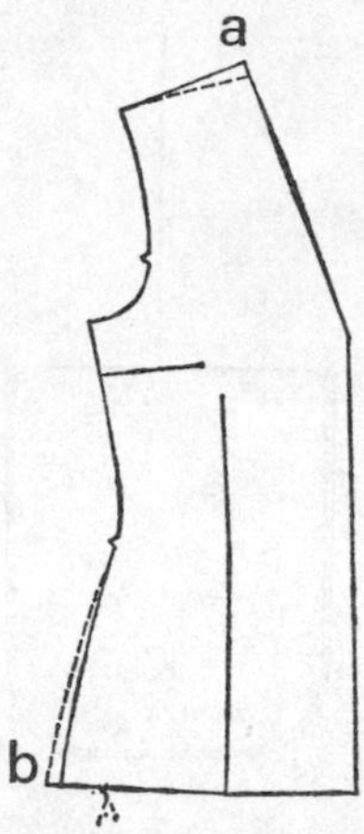

Fig. 118. (a) Lift front shoulder seam; (b) let out side seam.

This alteration *may* cause tightness at the hip side seams, and the front will need to be released and added to Fig. 118(b).

Ensure that the tacked grain marks are not distorted and that the bust and hip lines remain at right angles to the centre-back and front edges.

Shortening or lengthening the jacket is likely to affect the positioning of pockets, so raise or lower them accordingly.

Check for a level hemline and make sure that the lining does not cause strain to any parts of the garment.

Final Assembling and Completion

In preparation for a second try-on, mark alterations, remove the lining and open the seams. Remark, recut and transfer any alterations to the fabric and pattern. Machine stitch the darts and under-press. Stitch the pockets to the final position on the jacket fronts either by:

(a) Machine stitching on right side, close to the pocket edges. Backstitch securely at the top corners (Fig. 119(a)); or

(b) Handsewing with very small stitches—just taking in the edges of the pockets and one or two threads of the jacket fabric.

Now join the shoulder and side seams, and also the facings, to the back-neck and front edges.

Press the seams open, but facing seams together towards the front edges. Then:

Under-stitch the facings. Turn, tack and press them to the inside Pin, tack and sew in the sleeves and press on sleeveboard, as for the dress (see page 121).

Place shoulder pads with the pointed end to the centre of shoulder seam, and the wide edge level with the edge of the armhole seam allowance, or even a fraction beyond. Pin in this position and handsew (with a firm but not-too-tight tacking stitch) the armhole seam allowance to the shoulder pads as shown in Fig. 120(b). Turn the pointed end back by about 1 cm ($\frac{3}{8}$ in) and catch the pads to the shoulder seam with a few loose stitches.

Blindstitch hems on the sleeves and jacket (check that hem allowances are

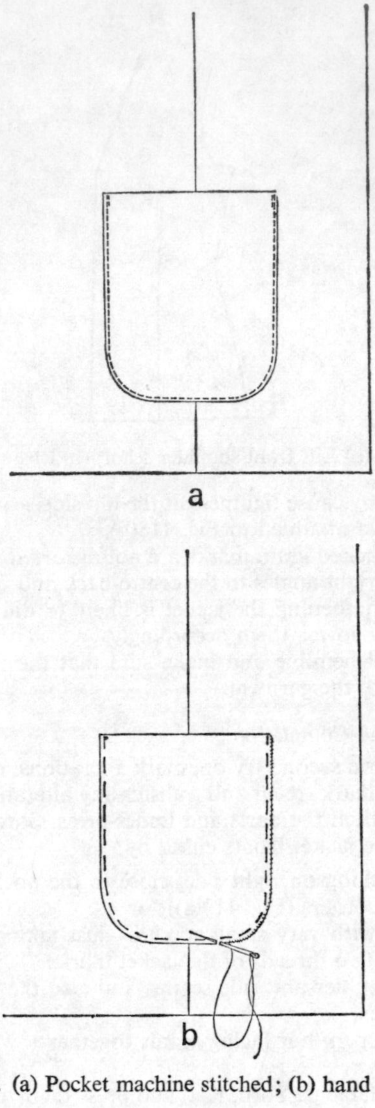

Fig. 119. (a) Pocket machine stitched; (b) hand stitched.

even in width) and then the facings to the inside jacket, with loose stitches to avoid sewing impressions on the right side. Finish the bottom of the facings over the jacket hem, slightly short of the finished edge with felling stitch making sure that facing is not sewn tight lengthwise. Remove all tack marks (see Fig. 120(c)).

Press the jacket well all over, before re-inserting the lining. You may like to slip on the garment at this stage, before completion, in case there are any minor adjustments.

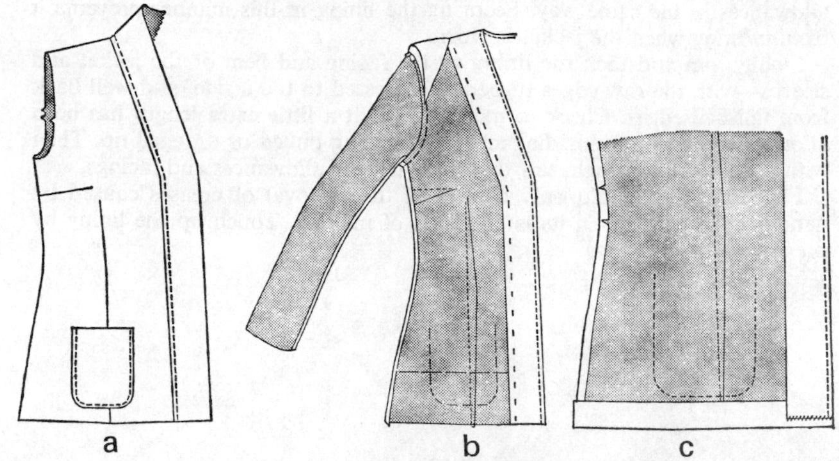

Fig. 120. (a) Understitch facing; (b) turn facing to inside; (c) sew facing to seam.

Hand-finished Linings

With the lining machined stitched and pressed, turn the jacket inside out and put the wrong side of the lining to the wrong side of jacket, preferably on a dress stand.

Pin to, and hold back, the lining at the shoulder seams. Sew the inside lining shoulder-seam allowances to the jacket shoulder-seam allowances, with loose stitches. Start from the front neck edge, pass over the shoulder pads, or through to the end of the seam allowances if no pads have been used and fasten off securely.

Match up the side seams and attach the lining to the jacket at the seam

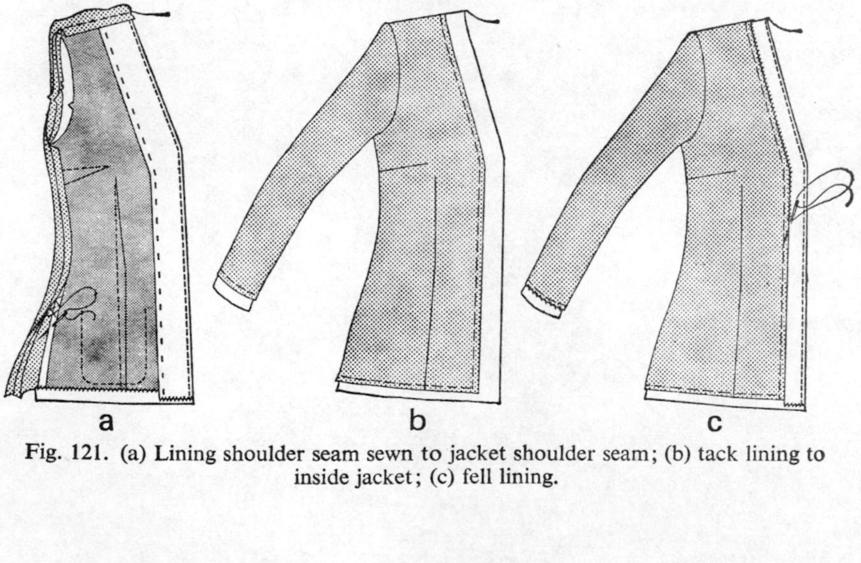

Fig. 121. (a) Lining shoulder seam sewn to jacket shoulder seam; (b) tack lining to inside jacket; (c) fell lining.

allowances in the same way. Securing the lining in this manner prevents it from twisting when the jacket is worn.

Finally, pin and tack the lining to the facing and hem of the jacket and sleeves—with the raw edges turned and pressed to the inside, and well back from finished edges. Check to make sure that a little extra length has been allowed, so as to prevent the jacket from being pulled or dragged up. Then with a small felling stitch, sew the lining to hem allowances and facings.

Final pressing should only consist of the removal of creases caused by handling the garment in its later stages of making. Touch up the lining by pressing lightly.

CHAPTER TEN

THE FIFTH DESIGN: THE SOFT COAT

The Soft Coat

This classic-shaped coat incorporates the basic methods of making-up suitable for most coats.

It is semi-fitted with the button and buttonhole and single-breasted front fastening, which, when joined at the neck to the collar, set in with facings forms a small rever and is worn open at the neck. It has a centre back seam, set-in sleeves and large patch pockets with flaps. The decoration introduced in addition, is top-stitching on pockets, collar and edges.

Fig. 122

The size and number of buttons may vary according to the pattern chosen. The actual buttonhole described is a piped one made from two folded strips of the same fabric, which is suitable for most coat type fabrics and buttons.

New Processes

The new processes are:

(a) The pockets and flaps.
(b) Top-stitching.
(c) Piped buttonholes.
(d) The collar with facing.

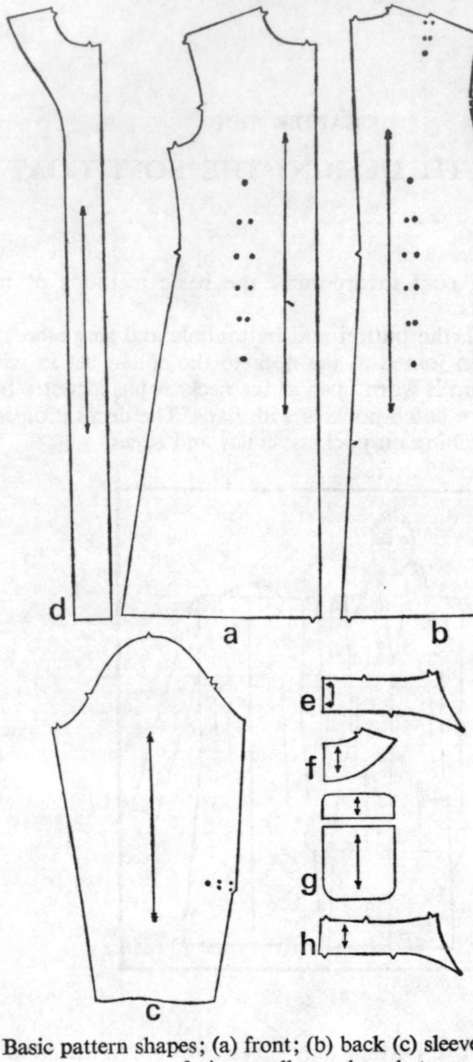

Fig. 123. Basic pattern shapes; (a) front; (b) back (c) sleeve; (d), (e) (f), (g) and (h) facings, collar and pocket.

Trimmings

The following trimmings are required:

(1) Tacking cotton and sewing thread as for all previous designs.
(2) Lining.
(3) Fusible interlining—heavy weight for fronts, collar and pockets.
(4) Buttons (including spare ones).
(5) Silk thread for top-stitching (optional).
(6) Shoulder pads.

Initial Processes

The previous processes listed in chapter nine are identical to those used for the coat up to and including the making of pockets, which on the coat have in addition, flaps and top-stitching.

With the marked and separated sections ready, staystitch all curved edges, fuse the interlinings to the fronts, back neck, pockets and flaps and under collar (once again all cut without seam allowances). Cut the collar interfacing

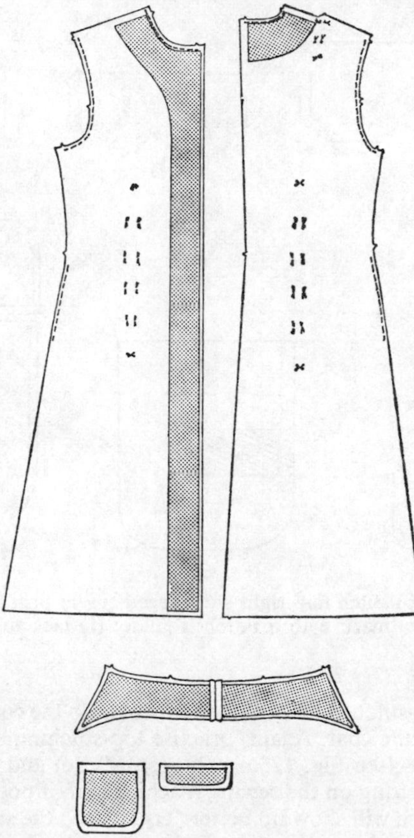

Fig. 124. Interlining fused to coat, under collar and pocket.

on the same grain as the under collar in fabric and, if cut in two sections, interline before joining the centre seam. Check to see that the buttonhole and pocket markings show on the right sides of the garments fronts.

Staystitch all curved edges, pin and tack darts and join facings at the shoulder seam.

The Pockets and Flaps

As in the case of the jacket the pockets are made before the side and shoulder seams are joined. The pockets are completed in the same way as described on page 125, with the addition of a flap. The flap is lined either in self (same) fabric if it is thin enough, or in lining on bulkier woollen materials. The lining piece is sewn to the interlined top flap, right sides together, leaving a gap along the top edge to pull the flap through to the right side. Trim the seam allowances, notch curves, turn through and sew the edges of the gap together by hand. Tack these edges, under-press, remove tacks and press again.

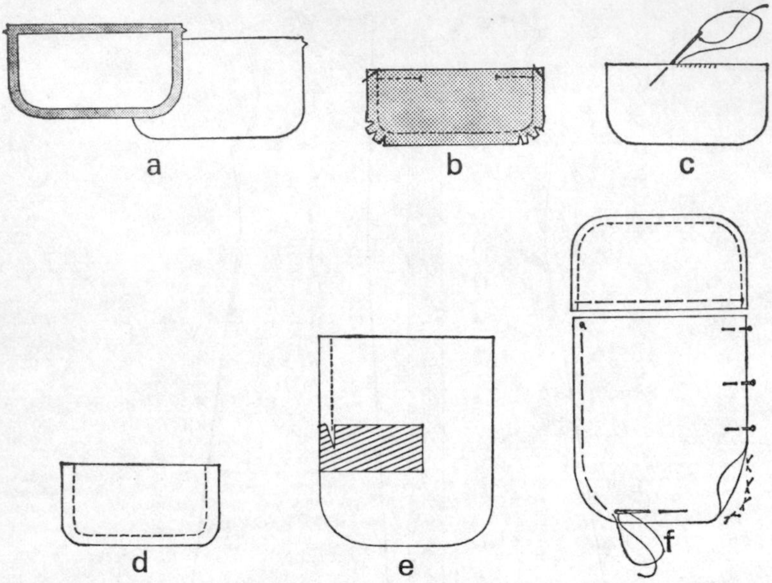

Fig. 125. (a) Flap; (b) stitch flap right sides together; (c) turn through, stitch gap; (d) top stitch; (e) mark with a notched guide; (f) tack to marking lines.

Top-stitching

The flaps are top-stitched before setting them onto the coat and the pockets are top-stitched to the coat. Again, practise top-stitching before working on the flaps themselves (see Fig. 125(a), (b), (c), (d), (e) and (f)).

Use the largest setting on the sewing machine and, if possible, a top-stitching silk thread which will show up better. Try to keep the stitching exactly the same level in distance from the edges. This will need a little practice. A small marker in cardboard can be a help here, in addition to an accurate tack line, to check the machining as you go along.

Top-stitch the sides and lower edge of the flaps, and pin and tack the pockets and flaps to the marking lines on the coat fronts, so that they are ready for final attaching after the fitting.

Piped Buttonholes

The next step is to make the buttonholes. As with all new processes, samples worked out before will make it all the easier and lead to better results on the actual garment. This applies especially to the making of buttonholes, and more than one should be practised to ensure that they are all identical in shape and size and placed in one line equi-distant from the edge.

The buttonholes are marked to finish at the centre front. A further allowance, approximately the width of the button to the edge of the coat, should be made. This space between the end of the buttonhole and the edge is called the button 'wrap'. Buttonholes cannot be placed closer to the right-front edge than this, otherwise the button wrap is lost and the buttons are off centre when fastened.

On the sample piece of fabric, mark two or three buttonholes, as shown on Fig. 126(a).

The size of holes must always be slightly larger—3 mm (⅛ in)—than the

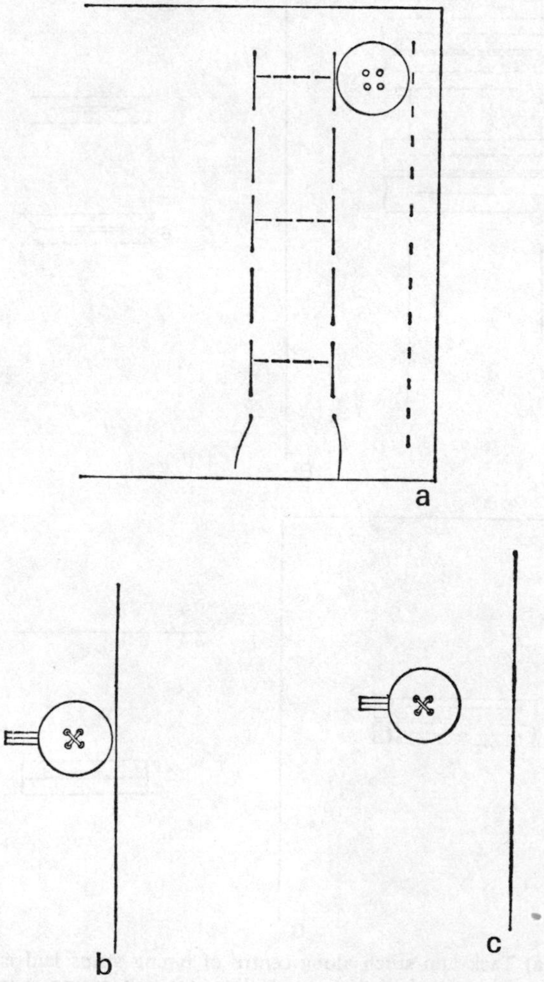

Fig. 126. (a) Buttonhole placing; (b) wrong placing; (c) correct placing.

diameter of the buttons, to allow the buttons to pass through easily and without causing strain to the holes.

Tack vertical lines each end of the buttonholes as well as horizontal lines. This will enable you to see where to place, start and finish the piping strips.

Make the piping for the buttonholes by cutting two rectangular pieces of

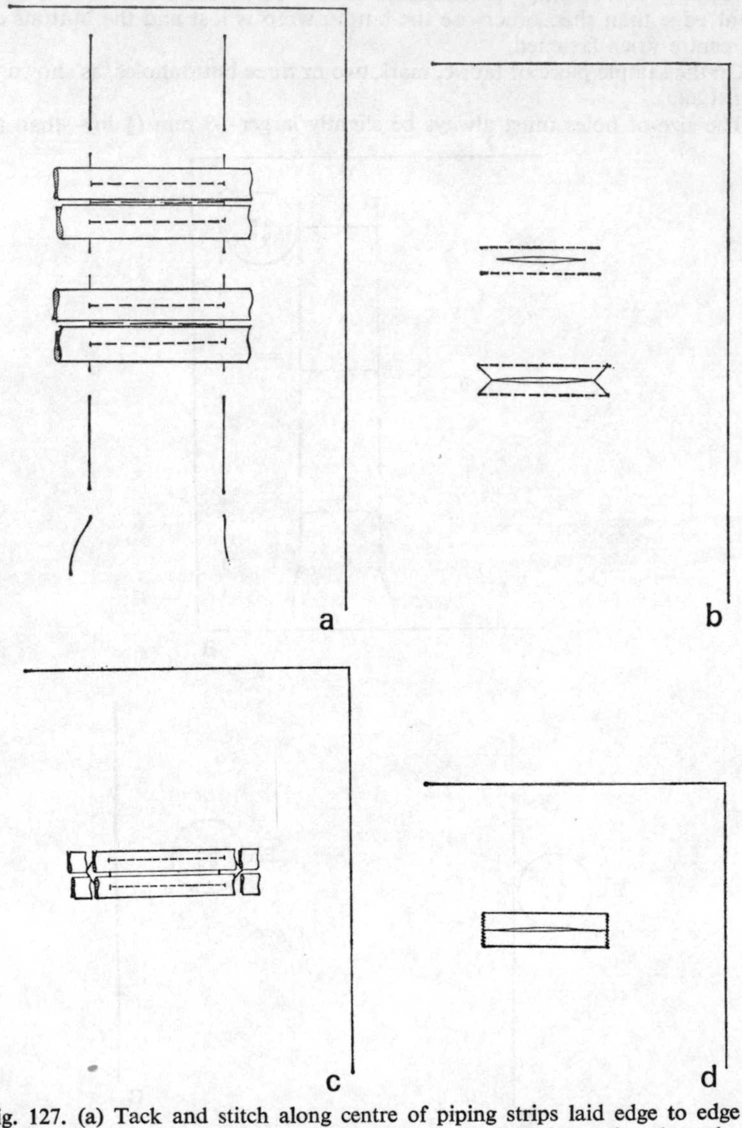

Fig. 127. (a) Tack and stitch along centre of piping strips laid edge to edge on marking line; (b) cut along buttonhole line; (c) pull piping strips through; (d) finish ends.

fabric on the straight grain, about 2 cm (¾ in) wide by the diameter of the button plus 2 cm (¾ in) long. Fold the strips in half lengthwise, wrong sides facing, then tack exactly along the centre of each strip.

This tack line must be exactly in the middle, otherwise the finished buttonhole sides will be uneven.

Now lay the **raw edges** of both strips to meet right on the tacked buttonhole line, on the **right** side of the fabric. The ends of piping strips should extend 1 cm (⅜ in) each side of the vertical tack lines. Pin, then tack the piping strips in position, on the centre tack of strips (see Fig. 127(a).

Machine stitch along this line on each side between vertical tacks on either side. Finish off each end securely.

Turn the fabric to the other side, and with small, sharp scissors cut along the buttonhole line to within 6 mm (¼ in) of each end.

Then cut into each corner just to the line of stitching. This must be done carefully and accurately, otherwise a neat finish of the buttonholes will not be possible (see Fig. 127(b)).

Now pull the piping strips through, so that all raw edges are on the wrong side of the garment (see Fig. 127(c)).

The small triangular pieces formed at each end are turned to the back when the piping is in position, and with the garment fabric folded back, sewn to the piping strips.

Under-press and remove all tack marks.

Before marking the buttonholes on the coat front, check to see that the markings are clearly visible and accurately placed on the **right** side of the **right** front.

With the pockets tacked in place, and buttonholes made, the side and shoulder seams can now be tacked together. For ease in handling, prepare sleeves as for the jacket, but do not set-in until the collar has been joined to the neckline.

The Collar with Facing

Tack the top collar (right side facing the right side of the under collar) on the outside edges, leaving the neck edge open.

Machine, taking one stitch across the collar points. This makes for neater corners when the collar is turned to the right side.

Trim seam allowances, especially at corners. Turn collar to the right side, pull out corners so that both are quite even and of good shape. Tack and under-press, making sure that the outside-edge seam does not show on the right side of the top collar. Tack the raw neck edges together with largish stitches.

The collar is then top-stitched in the same way as the pocket flap, on the outer edge and sides, at the same stitching distance from the finished edges.

Pin and tack the collar to the neck edge of the coat, matching balance marks, under collar side to right side of coat. Start at the centre back and pin/tack to either side at fronts.

Lay the facing right side down over the collar and tack, matching front and back of neck edges.

To turn the facing back to its final position for the fitting, it may be necessary to clip neck-seam allowances in one or two places.

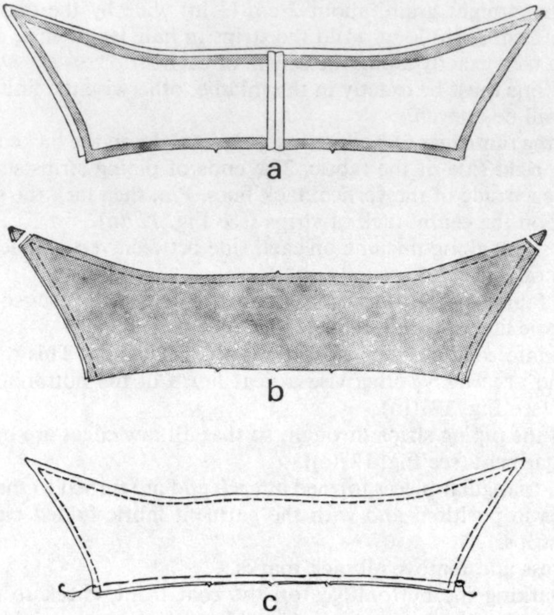

Fig. 128. (a) and (b) Stitch collar; (c) top stitch on right side.

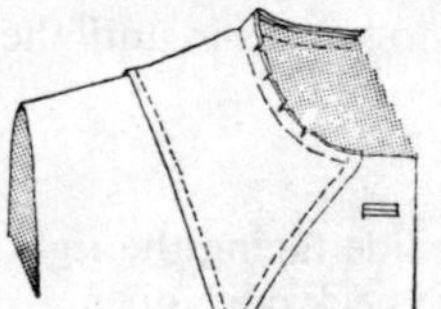

Fig. 129. Tack collar to neck edge.

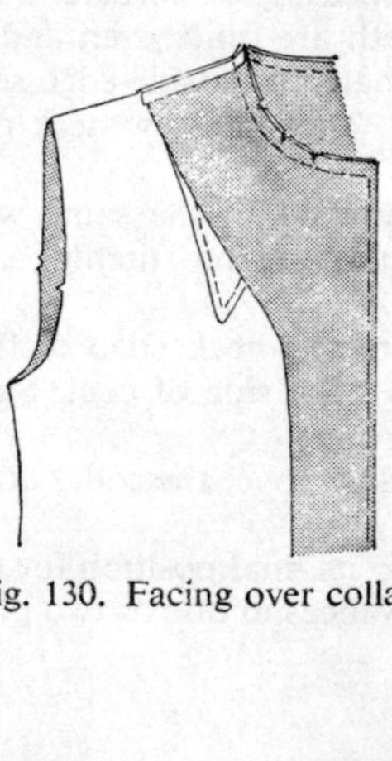

Fig. 130. Facing over collar.

With curves staystitched and interlined, an otherwise easily stretched neckline will keep its shape.

Set in the sleeves, pin and tack in the same way as previously. Place and pin shoulder pads, with the centre of pads to shoulder seams and extended to the edges of the armhole/sleeve crown seam allowances.

Tack the hems of the coat, sleeves and facings.

Prepare the lining with the hem tacked up, as it will not be sewn to hem of coat. Turn the coat inside out, put it on a dress stand if possible and attach the lining, in preparation for the fitting.

Fitting and Alterations

If your previous fitting for the jacket has been successful, you have by now mastered most of the problems which may arise. Whether you plan to wear your coat over a jacket, or not, is of great importance from a fitting point of view. If you are, you must of course allow sufficient room for a comfortably fitting coat.

Once again, the shoulder area is of prime importance. The correct positioning of the shoulder seams controlling the 'hang' of the garment, determine the balance and attention to this point must be the first step in fitting.

As the buttons are not yet sewn on, wrap the fronts over by the width of the button wrap and pin one side to the other at buttonholes. Check that you have a true vertical edge from neck to hem, and that both left and right fronts are even in length. Pin, or chalk mark the edge of the buttonhole side on the left front. When the coat is opened check that the distance from the edge to the mark is even throughout. Place pins into the button positions directly underneath the buttonholes.

Check the collar, see that it is wrinkle free and even on both sides. Turn the back of the collar up, it should fit just as well as turned down, you may even like it better that way. The pockets are an integral part of the design and must be well positioned in relation to the proportion of the whole garment. But they are functional, too, so put your hands in them and 'feel' that you can use them in comfort.

Final Assembling and Completion

As before, mark alterations, remove lining, open seams, remark (recut) and transfer to fabric and pattern. Machine stitch darts and under-press.

With the pockets firmly tacked in final position, top-stitch them to the coat, the same distance from the edges as on the flaps. Finish off the ends of stitching, at the pocket openings, securely. Lay the flaps right side down with the straight edges just above the pocket tops, tack and machine close to edges (no more than 6 mm ($\frac{1}{4}$ in) and fasten ends securely. Turn flaps down, press and make a few firm hand stitches at the top corners, to keep the flaps neat and in a flat position.

Rejoin shoulder- and centre side back seams (and under-arm sleeve seam if alteration has taken place) and press.

Pin and tack the collar to the neckline as previously in preparation for the fitting, then lay the facings right side down to the coat and over the collar. Ensure that all balance marks meet exactly. Pin and tack in this position from the centre-back neck to each side of the front-neck edge, and centre-front edges if the facings are not cut in one with the front sections.

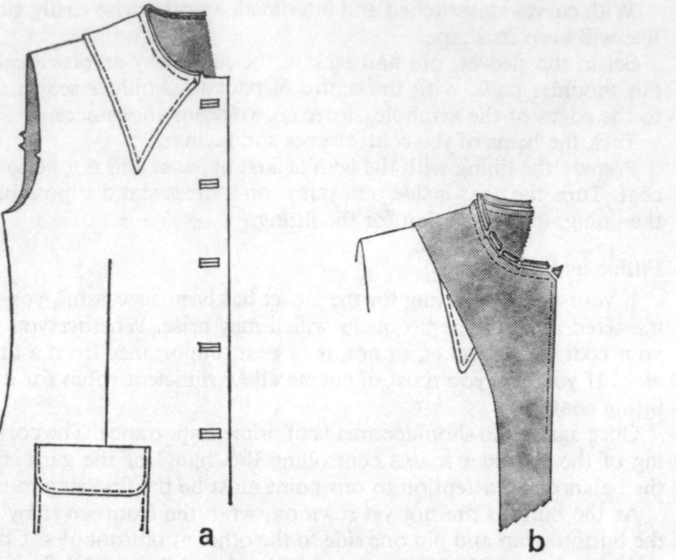

Fig. 131. (a) Top stitch pockets, (b) re-tack collar.

Machine stitch, trim seams and corners. Under-stitch through the facing and collar seams at the back neck to keep the collar firmly set in this position.

Turn back the facings to the inside of the coat, tack and press them.

To finish the buttonholes, mark the wrong side of the holes on the facing

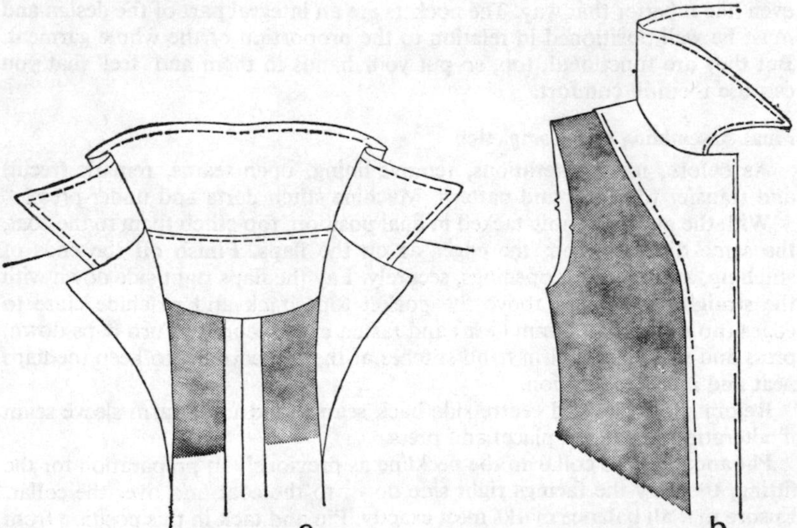

Fig. 132. (a) Understitch; (b) turn facing to inside.

side. Cut along the centre length of the buttonholes, then turn in the raw edges to make an oval shaped opening. With small felling stitches, neatly hem the turned in edges to the back of the buttonhole piping, without showing stitches on the right side of the garment.

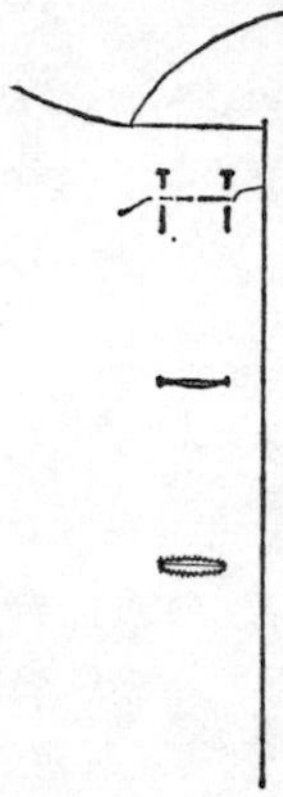

Fig. 133. Finish buttonholes.

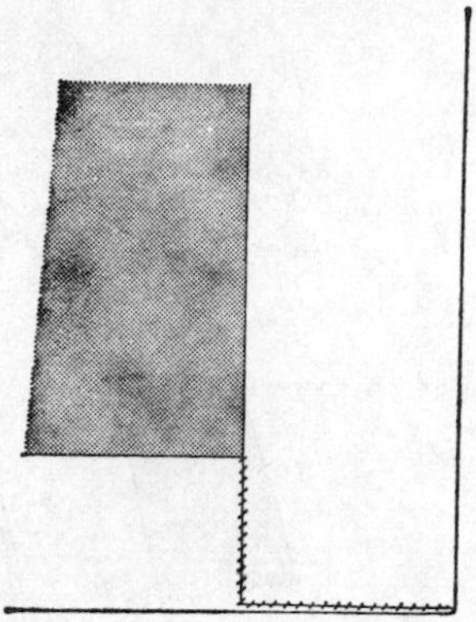

Fig. 134. Fell facing to hem.

Set the sleeves into the armholes and press on a sleeveboard (seams towards the armholes).

Sew in the shoulder pads as previously described for the jacket on page 129.

Blindstitch sleeve and coat hems, and edges of facings, to the coat with loose stitches.

Finish the bottom of the facings with felling stitches. Top-stitch sleeve and front edges, as for the collar and pockets if desired.

Remove the tack marks and press the coat well before sewing in the lining.

Try on the coat again before the last stage of lining it.

The prepared lining, sewn together, the hem turned up and stitched, and all of it well pressed, is placed to the coat which has been turned inside out.

As for the jacket, sew shoulder and side-seam allowances of the lining to those of the coat.

Press in a narrow turning to the wrong side of the lining edges at the back neck and through to the hem, as well as on the sleeve hems.

Pin and tack the edges to facings and sleeve hems as shown, and sew back with felling stitches.

The two separate hems (lining and coat) can be held together at the centre back and side seams with loose stitches to form a bar or small chain about 4 cm (just over $1\frac{1}{2}$ in) long, which prevents the lining from being dragged up in wear.

Sew on the buttons where previously pinned. Some buttons have holes to sew through and others have a **moulded shank** on the back to allow for the thickness of the fabric on the buttonhole side and to prevent tightness between buttons and holes when fastened. For a button with no moulded shank, depending on the thickness of the fabric, leave the sewing threads at least 3 mm ($\frac{1}{8}$ in) long between the fabric and buttons and twist the last few threads

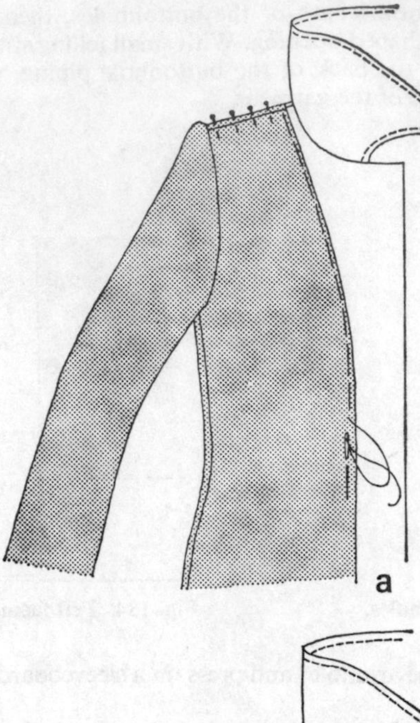

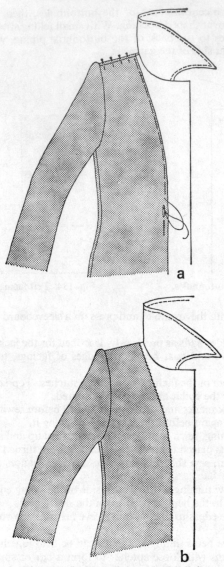

Fig. 135. (a) Tack lining; (b) fell lining.

around those holding the buttons to the coat. For both types of button, finish off by passing the needle once or twice through the shanks and through the loops formed by these threads. The buttons will then be allowed to move freely over the buttonholes. (See Fig. 256.)

Do not overpress the finished garment. Light touching up should be all that is necessary.

CHAPTER ELEVEN

THE SIXTH DESIGN: THE SHIRT

The Shirt

This, the last of our six basic garments, is a classic shirt shape, with the collar set onto a band and the sleeves gathered into cuffs. Those of our readers who prefer a sleeveless version, can make the shirt with faced armholes as described for the shift dress in chapter eight.

Fig. 136

New Processes

The new processes are:

(a) Shirt collar on band (stand)
(b) Cuffed sleeve with faced opening
(c) Hand-worked buttonholes

Trimmings

The following trimmings are required:

(1) Tacking cotton and sewing thread.
(2) Lightweight interlining (for a washable fabric use a suitable interlining).
(3) Small shirt buttons (including spare ones).

Initial Processes

Once again, the initial processes as previously listed, apply to this garment up to and including the staystitching. Then the new processes are incorporated.

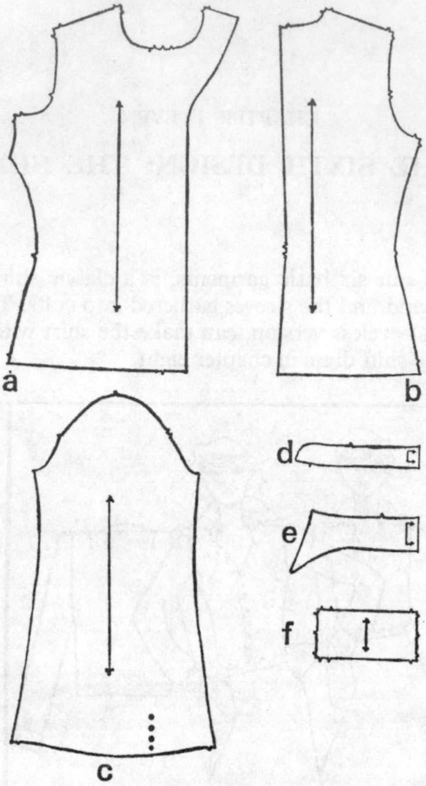

Fig. 137. Basic pattern shape: (a) front; (b) back; (c) sleeve; (d), (e) and (f) collar and cuff.

On conclusion of the fitting and alterations, the remaining processes are identical to those for all previous designs, except for making the buttonholes which completes the sequence in making this garment.

The sections of the shirt to be interlined are:

(1) The button wrap on centre fronts.

(2) The under collar—for a soft roll of the collar—or both top and under collar if you prefer a very stiff effect.

(3) The collar band on one side.

(4) The cuffs on one side.

Staystitch all curves in the usual manner, and then turn the front facing back to the inside and tack it to the neck edge and to the front of the shirt.

Shirt Collar on Band (Stand)

First, lay the top collar to the under collar right sides together, then tack and machine stitch the outer line of the edges, taking one stitch across the points.

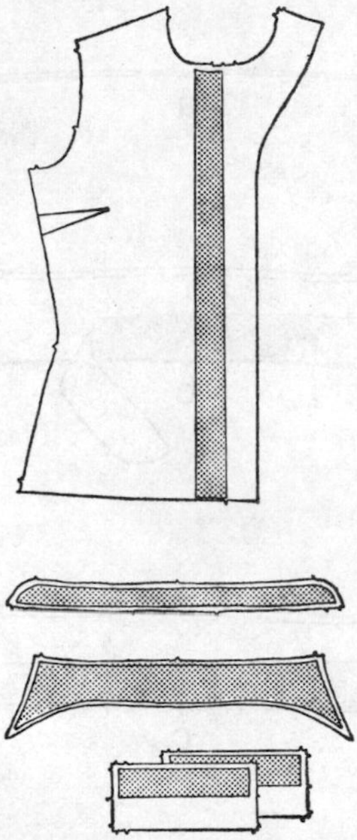

Fig. 138. Interlined button stand, collar and cuffs.

Trim seam allowances, especially at corners. Turn the collar to the right side and pull out the corners evenly. Tack and under-press.

Lay and pin the interlined section of the band right side down to the open edge of the interlined under collar, right sides together. Place and pin the second band section exactly on top of this on the other side, with the right side down to the top collar.

Pin, tack and then machine stitch along this edge and through the collar, making sure that both ends are even, and the same in distance on each side from the top collar ends. The neck edge of the band is left open (see Fig. 139(a), (b) and (c)).

Trim the seam allowance and clip the rounded ends, to make neat curves and to eliminate excess bulk in this seam.

Turn the band to the right side, tack, under-press, and press in the seam allowance on the band/top collar-side, for easier handsewing to the neck on the inside of the shirt later on.

The other section of the band is pinned and tacked to the outside neck edge, right sides together, and matching the shirt front edges exactly. (To ensure this tack the collar from the centre back to either side of the front, rather than in one series of stitches from one side to the other.) Now machine stitch this seam and trim and clip the seam allowances.

Finally, pin and tack the pressed-in edge of the band to the neck seam on the inside of the shirt and sew it to the neck with felling stitches.

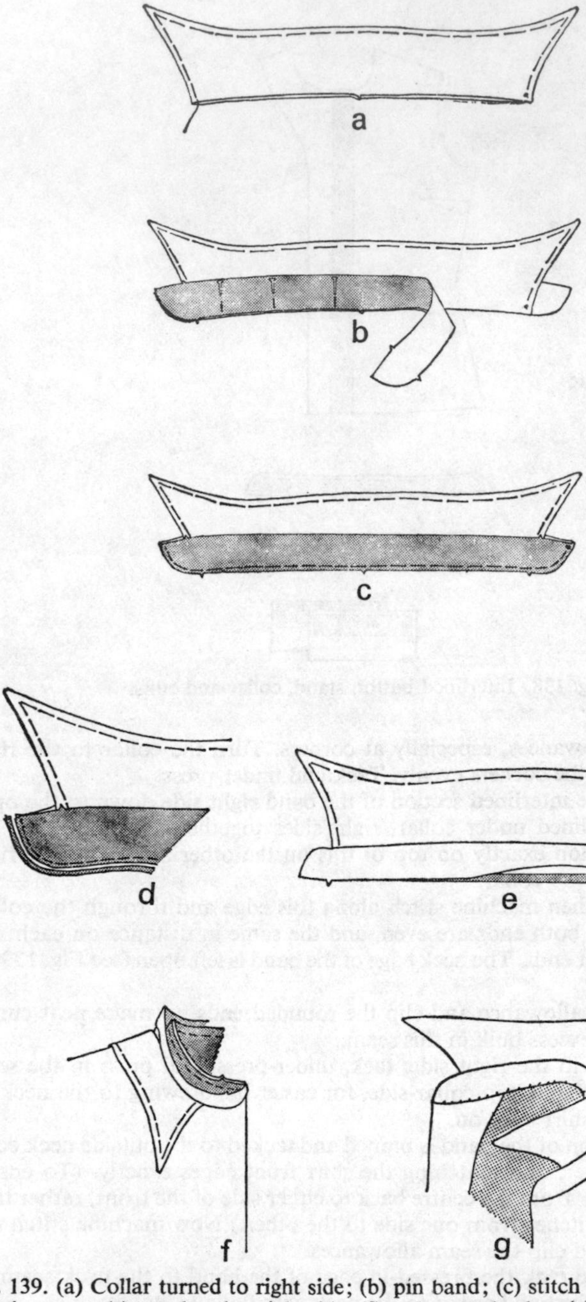

Fig. 139. (a) Collar turned to right side; (b) pin band; (c) stitch band to right side; (d) trim seam; (e) turn band to right side; (f) tack to neck edge; (g) fell to inside neck.

Cuffed Sleeve with Faced Opening

To prepare the cuffs, fold them over into two equal halves, right sides facing. Machine stitch both ends, trim seam allowances and top corners, and turn through to the right side. Tack and under-press. Press in the seam allowance on the interlined side of the cuff.

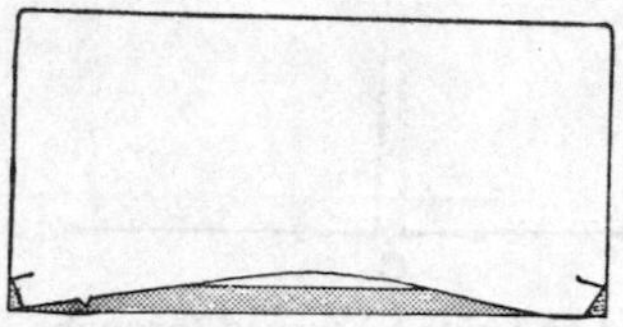

Fig. 140. Cuff turned to right side.

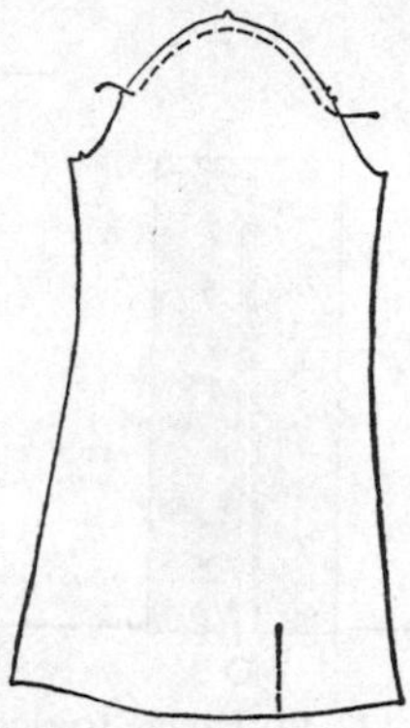

Fig. 141. Sleeve head gathering thread.

Run in a gathering thread around the top of the sleeve heads to ease in the fullness (as described on page 114) and under-press.

Each marked cuff opening is faced with a small piece of the fabric, cut about 6·5 (2½ in) wide by the length of the opening plus 2 cm (¾ in). Tack this facing to the opening mark, the centre of the facing piece in line with the opening mark, right side to right side of the sleeve.

Turn the sleeve to the wrong side where the marked line is uncovered and still visible, stitch along each side of the mark, 3 mm (⅛ in) from it and tapering to one stitch across the point at the end. Cut into the line of the opening, turn the facing through to the inside, tack and under-press. Then machine stitch again, close to the edges of the opening to strengthen it.

The raw edges of the facings should be oversewn and lightly caught to the sleeves.

Now put a gathered thread into the lower edges of the sleeves, draw them up to fit the cuffs and fasten off. Then machine the under-arm sleeve seams.

Place each of the unpressed edges of the cuffs to the gathered edges of the sleeves, right sides together: the ends of the cuffs to match the sleeve openings. Pin and tack cuffs to the sleeves along these edges, then turn the rest of the cuffs to the inside of the sleeves and tack the pressed-in seam allowance of each cuff to the inside seam line of the sleeves. enclosing the raw edges completely.

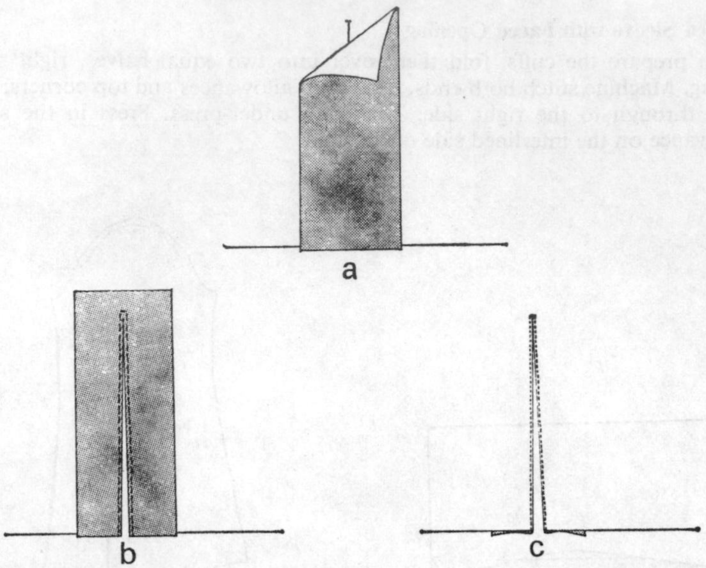

Fig. 142. (a) Facing to right side; (b) stitched and cut; (c) turned through.

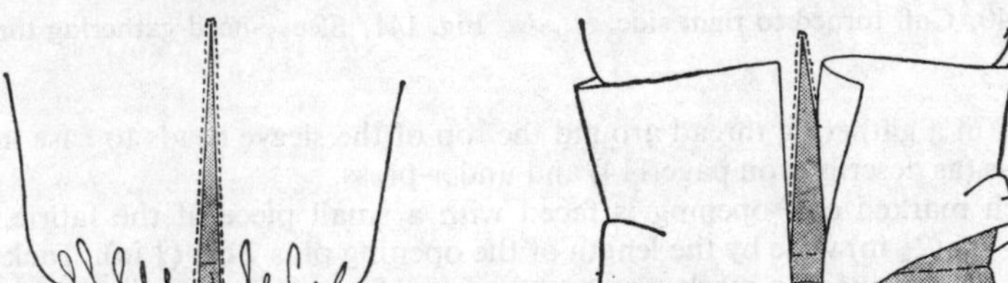

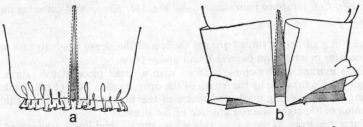

Fig. 143. (a) Gather lower edge of sleeve; (b) tack cuff to sleeve edge.

Pin and tack sleeves into armholes, and check that the cuff openings lie towards the back of the wrists, in line with your little fingers. Lastly pin and tack the hem allowance before the fitting.

Fitting and Alterations

By now you will know what to look for at the fitting stage, and be able to carry out any necessary alterations. But pay special attention to the length of sleeves and ensure that the gathered, lower parts create the right amount of 'pouch effect' over the cuffs, which are an important feature of this design and, therefore, should not be hidden by the sleeves. If these are too long, have the excess length pinned out and cut the surplus off at the bottom of the sleeves after the fitting.

Mark the buttonhole positions by pinning these on the front of the shirt vertically, and those on the collar band and cuffs horizontally.

Check that both sides of the front are even in length, and pin the button wraps, one on top of the other.

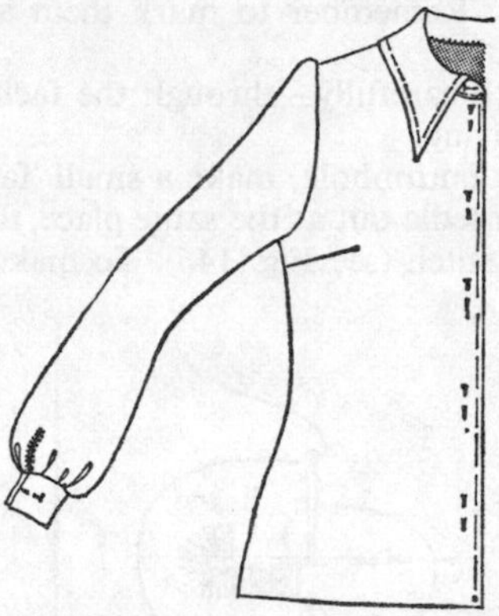

Fig. 144. Mark button-hole position.

Final Assembling and Completion

When the alterations have been marked and transferred, machine and under-press darts and seams in the normal manner. Oversew/neaten all raw edges. With sleeves taken out of the armholes, remove the tacks from the inside of the cuffs. Machine stitch the cuffs to the sleeves, as tacked, replace the inside cuffs and hem these to the cuff seams with felling stitches. Reset the sleeves and sew them in as described on page 120.

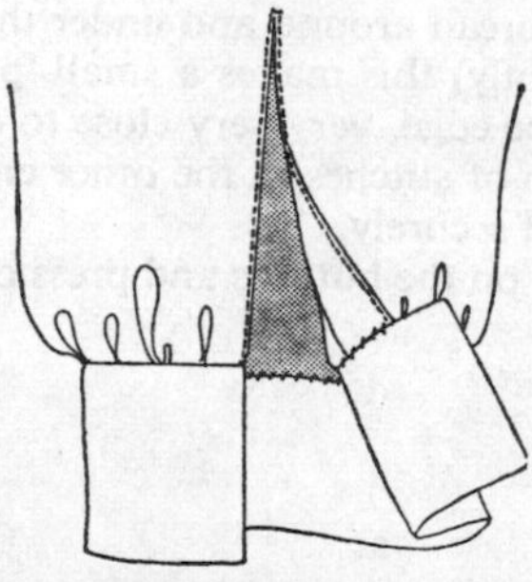

Fig. 145. Finish cuff.

The hem of the shirt can be blindstitched by hand. Alternatively, you can make two rows of machine stitching on a narrow turned-in hem. Remember to sew the lower edge of the front facings over the hem.

You will want to try on the shirt again just to make sure all is well and to make minor adjustments if necessary. After that, make sure all tack marks are removed and then press the garment.

Hand-worked Buttonholes

The 'worked' buttonhole can be made with the appropriate attachment on some sewing machines. Here, we describe the worked type made by hand.

First, ensure that the buttonholes are accurately marked on the relevant sections of the garment. Remember to mark them a little longer than the diameter of the buttons.

Cut the marked length carefully—through the facing—and oversew both raw edges to prevent fraying.

At one end of the cut buttonhole, make a small 'fan' of stitches, by oversewing and bringing the needle out at the same place, then continue along one edge with a buttonhole stitch (see Fig. 146). To make this, bring the needle

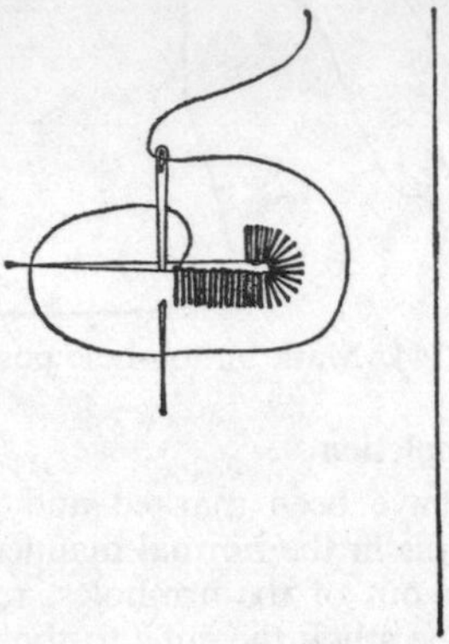

Fig. 146. Hand-worked buttonhole.

from the inside of the buttonhole, through the fabric, about 3 mm (⅛ in) from the edge, with the thread around and under the needle as it comes out, when pulled (not too tightly) this makes a small 'purl' on the edge. Repeat these stitches, all along the edge, very very close to each other, and the same length. Make another fan of stitches at the other end, and buttonhole stitch the other edge. Fasten off securely.

Last, but not least, sew on the buttons and press out any remaining creases on the garment.

PART THREE: FURTHER AND ADVANCED TECHNIQUES

CHAPTER TWELVE

DESIGN AND PATTERN ADAPTATIONS OF COMMERCIAL PATTERNS

Adjustments of patterns to figure and adaptations for good fit of garments have been described in some depth in chapter two. Together with the guidelines on fitting, much ground has been covered in this aspect of dressmaking.

When buying patterns, the choice of designs is so large that it would seem unwise to attempt major adaptations, both from a point of view of style and fit. Minor ones however, such as the lengthening or shortening of sleeves and skirts as part of design and proportion, as well as the changing of necklines, the adding of revers, or the adaptation of their shapes, are more common and desirable.

In this chapter we use our six basic garments once more, to illustrate by way of examples, some adaptations of the designs and their respective patterns.

Fig. 147 show three varying skirt lengths (A) (B) (C) and the addition of a knife pleat. Shorten or lengthen from the original pattern as shown in Fig. 148(a) (b) (c).

V-shaped design lines in Fig. 149(B), are an addition to the plain trousers in (A), which are shortened in (C). See Fig. 151 for pattern.

In Fig. 151 the original shift dress (A) has a lower neckline, an increase in length (B), and additional adaptations in (C), by a further increase in length, long set in sleeves, a *V*-neckline, and darts joined and followed through to the hemline. See Fig. 152 for patterns.

In Fig. 153 the long sleeves on the jacket in (A) become short ones in (B), while (C) shows revers added to the front of jacket, as shown in Fig. 154.

The coat design used in chapter ten is adapted for varying lengths in Fig. 155(A), (B) and (C), the latter also has an addition of revers, as shown in Fig. 156.

The long sleeves of the shirt in Fig. 157(A) are adapted to short sleeves with cuffs in (B), and the shirt worn outside the skirt has a tie belt, and yoke seam line in (C) (see also Fig. 158).

Fig. 147

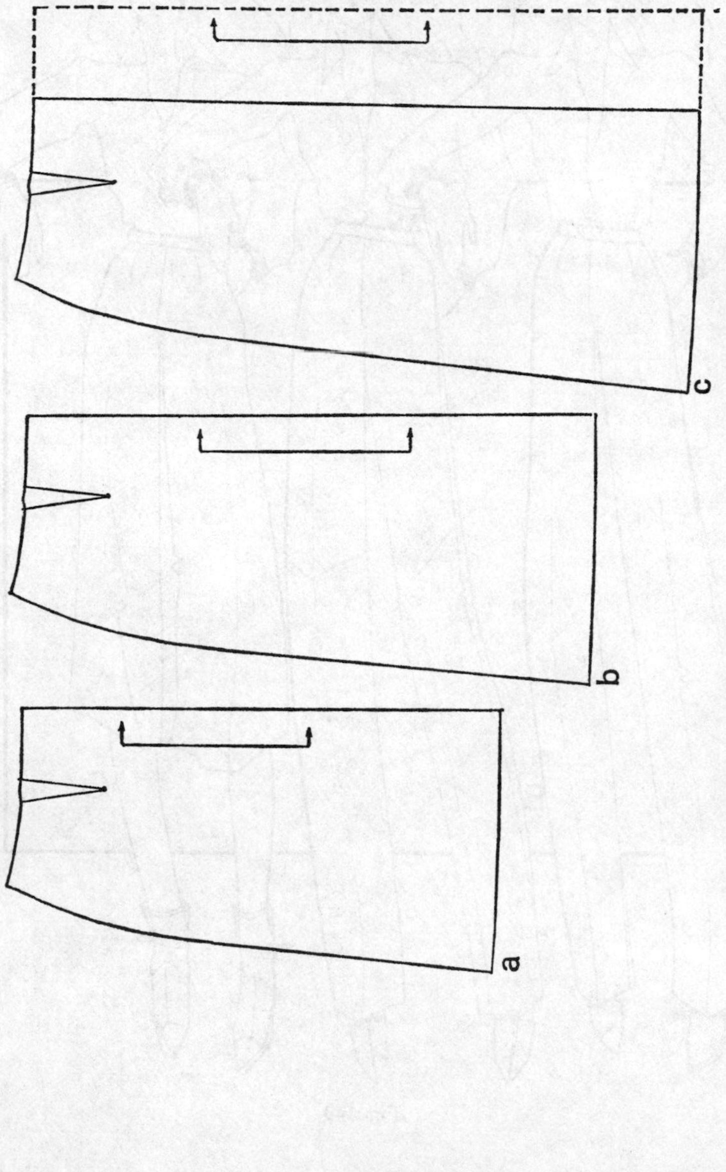

Fig. 148. (a), (b) and (c): Lengthen skirt as shown, fold centre front to fold of new (broken) line on each side, to form an inverted pleat for design (C).

Fig. 149

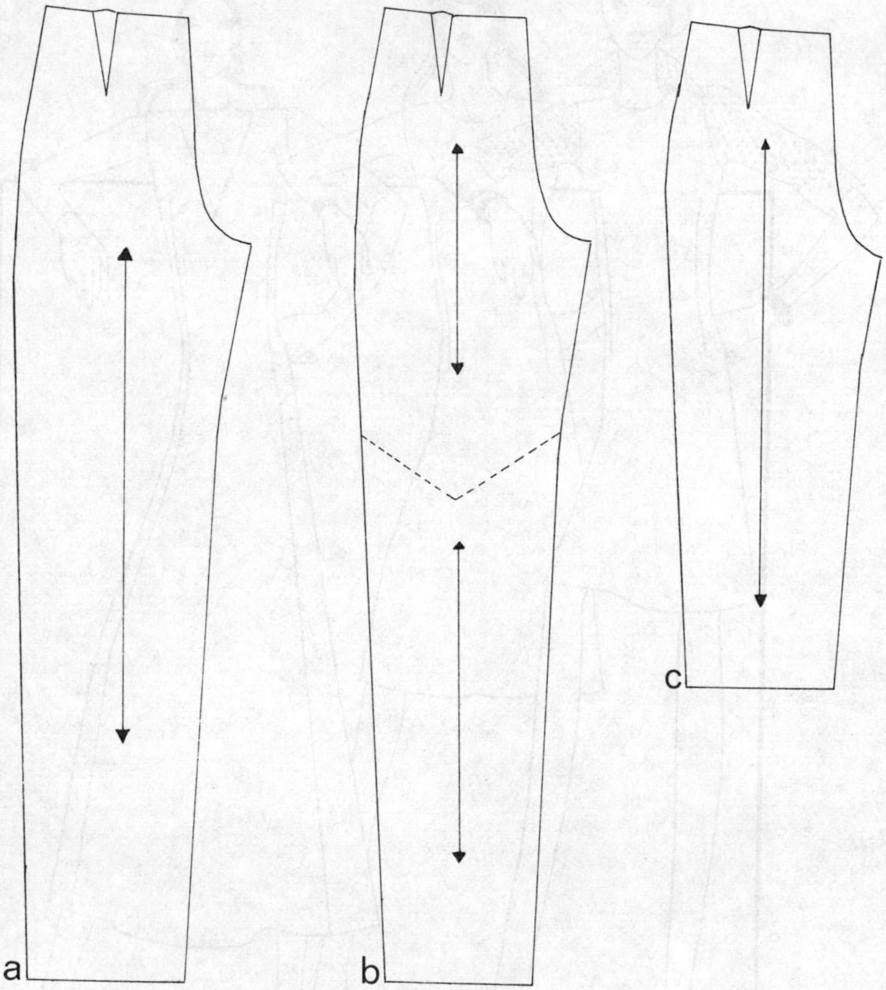

Fig. 150. (a), (b) and (c): Cut through design line for (B) add seam allowances on each side. Shorten trousers as shown for design (C).

Fig. 151

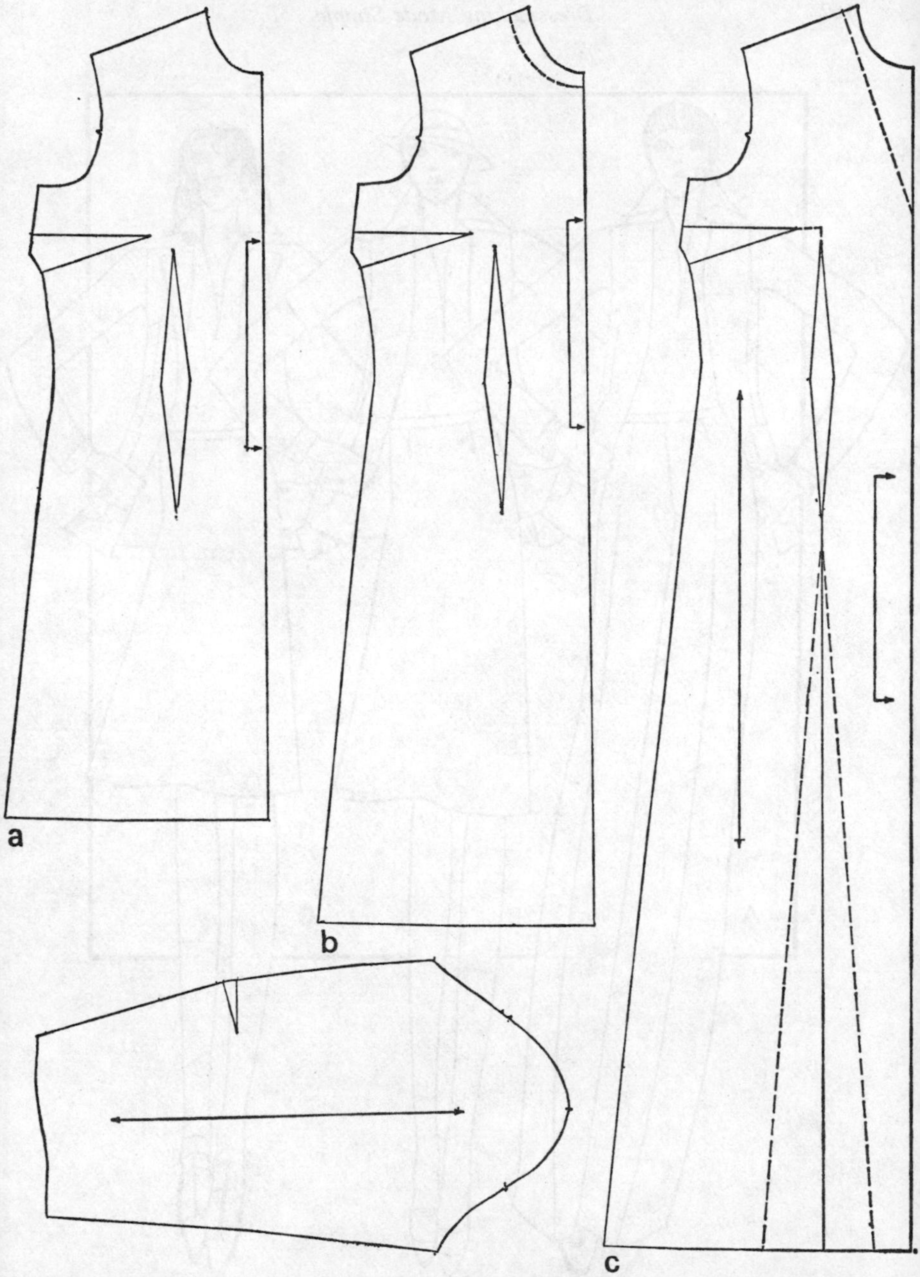

Fig. 152. (a), (b) and (c): Lengthen dress as shown for design (C), join bust dart to waist dart, and continue into seam as shown by broken lines. These are crossed over at either side from the solid centre line. The front panel is separated from the side panel, forming a flare when sewn together. After separation add seam allowances on on each side of new seam.

Fig. 153

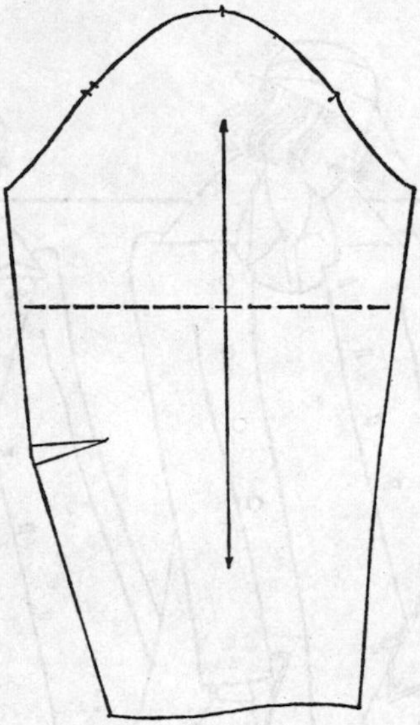

b

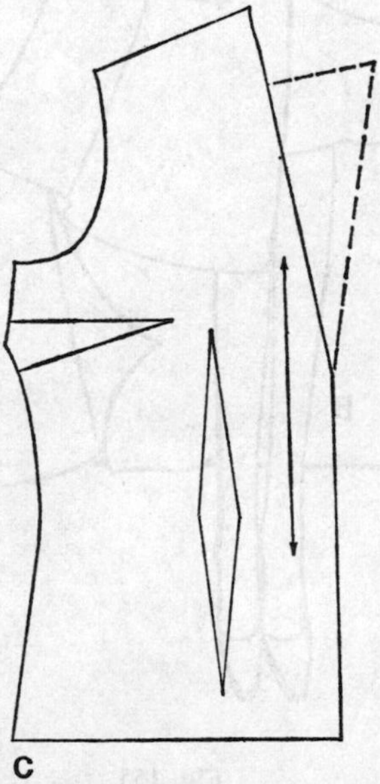

c

Fig. 154. (b) and (c): Shorten sleeve and add hem, for design (B). Add rever for design (C).

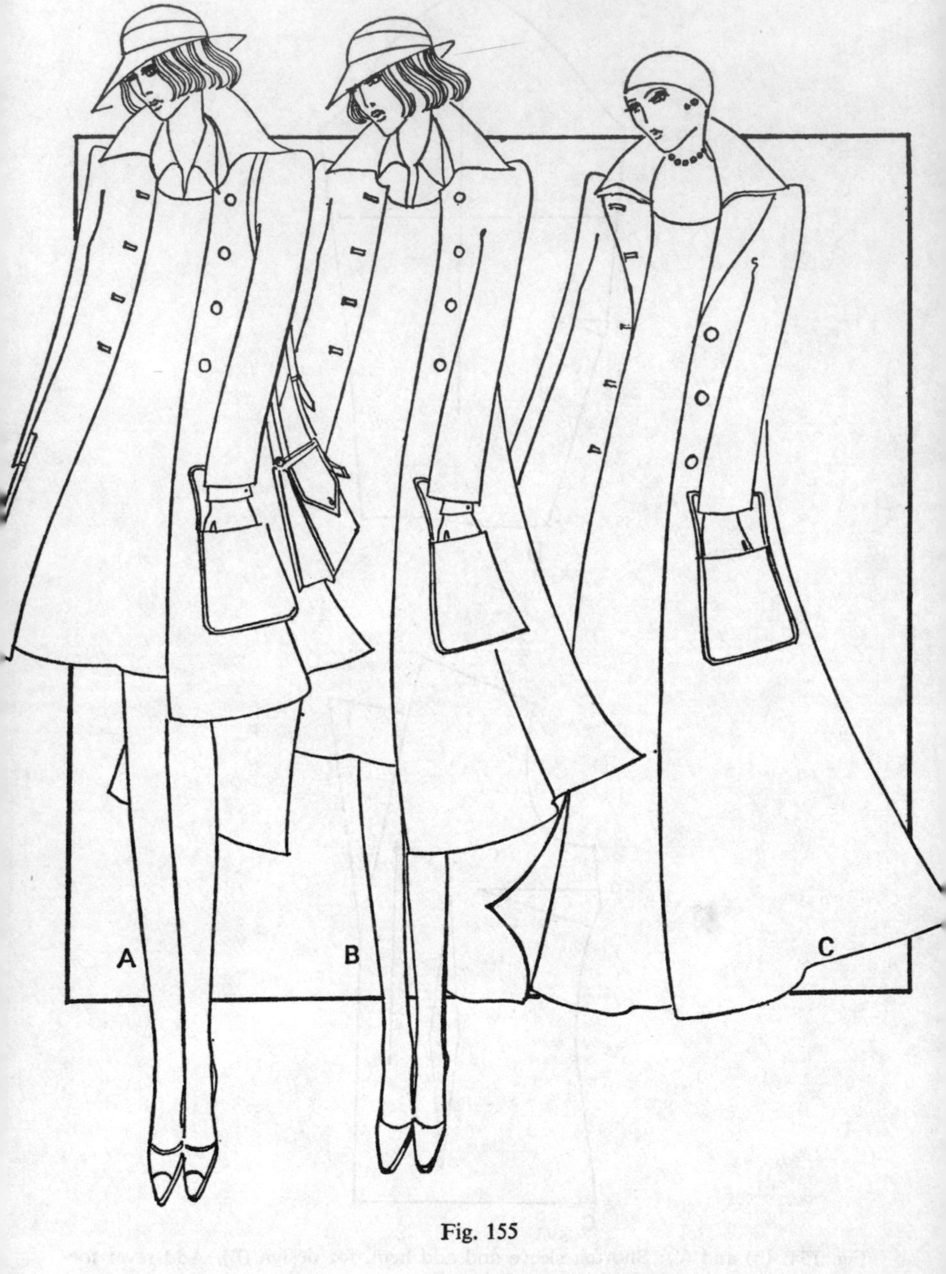

Fig. 155

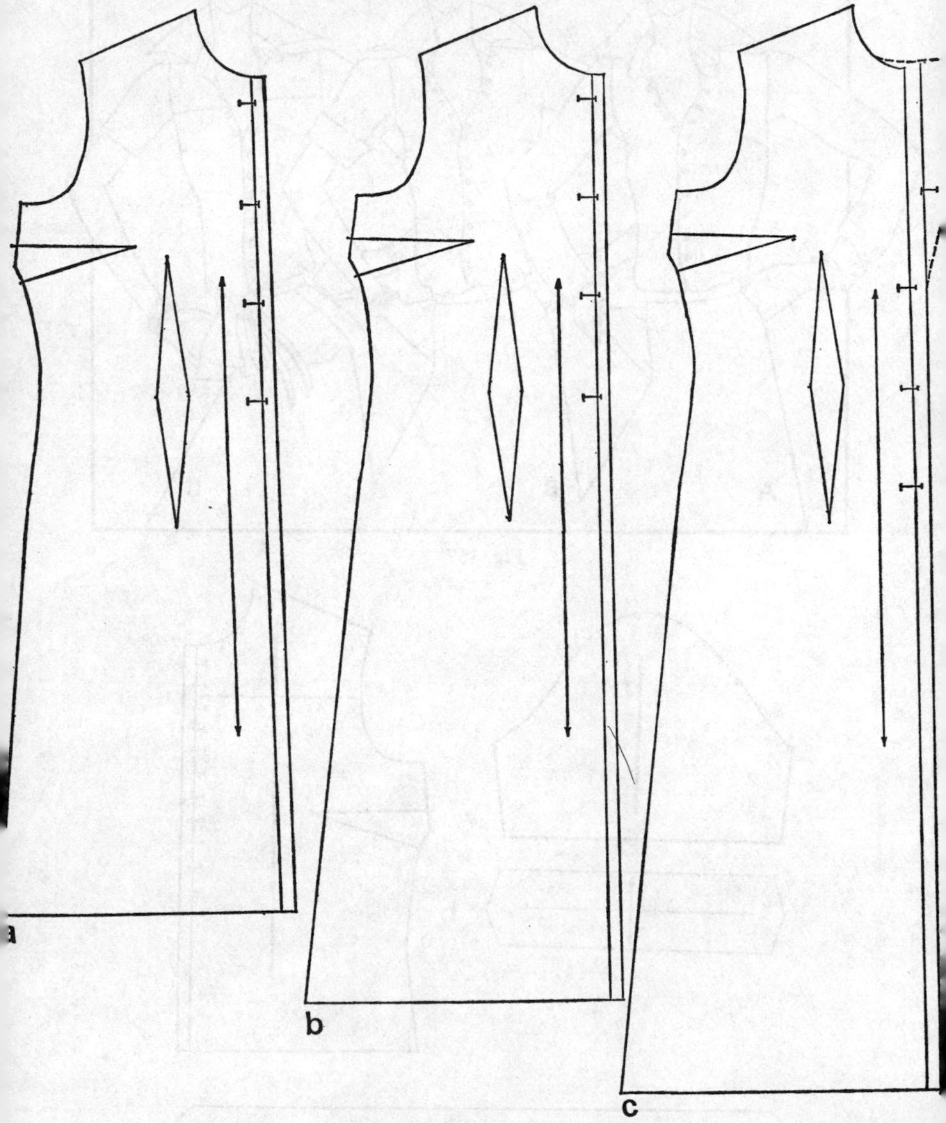

Fig. 156. (a), (b) and (c): Lengthen coat and add rever for design (C).

Fig. 157

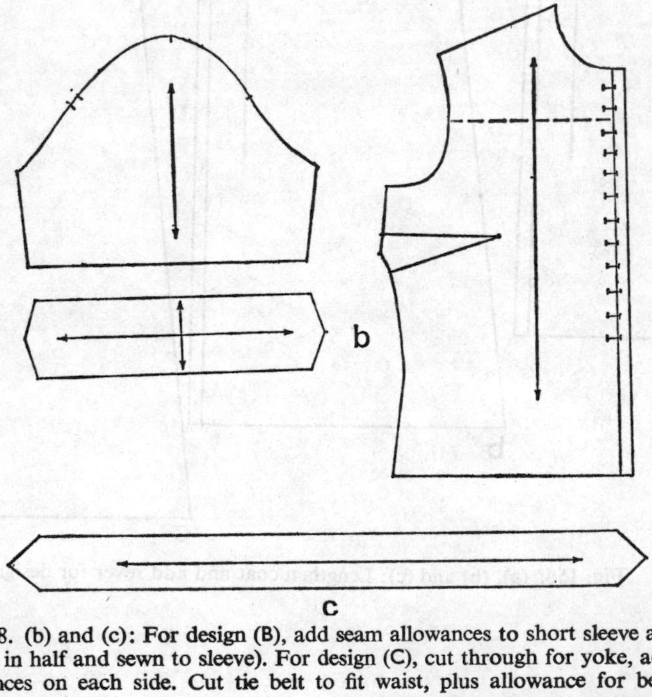

Fig. 158. (b) and (c): For design (B), add seam allowances to short sleeve and cuff, (folded in half and sewn to sleeve). For design (C), cut through for yoke, add seam allowances on each side. Cut tie belt to fit waist, plus allowance for belt ends.

CHAPTER THIRTEEN

FIGURE TYPES

Proportion and Balance

The *Oxford English Dictionary* defines proportion as *due relation of one thing to another or between parts of a thing*, or to put it another way, it balances one part with another and relates all parts to the whole.

In the context of this book, proportion affects both the human body and the garments with which we clothe and decorate it. The fact that the miraculous structure of the body is such that no two are exactly alike, determines our attitude when aiming to achieve designs of pleasing proportions. Silhouette and shape, their well-balanced division (used as a technical term **balance** also describes the correct joining of parts of a garment (see the Glossary on page 283) by design lines and decoration), all play vital parts and must be related to each other.

Figure types vary from the normal average one—based on a perfect or near perfect relationship between height, girth and weight—in many ways. Abnormal or irregular types range from short and slight build, to tall, stout and heavily-boned structured ones. Figures of average, short or tall height are additionally divided by an unequal distribution of weight in proportion to height and this weight may also be disproportionately spread on either top or lower parts of the body. Stance—erect, sway back or stooping, or with round shoulders—increases the variety of figure types and proportion of the design must be adapted to suit each individual type.

Silhouette Shape

Fig. 159

Primarily, fashion decrees silhouettes which prove popular at given times But, simultaneously, the selection from a range of shapes can be exploited by all figure types to advantage. This, together with a good use of fabric, skilful cutting, fitting and dressmaking will achieve satisfaction, no matter which figure type we have.

Fig. 159 shows examples of varying shapes ranging from slim, small and straight to semi-full, full and long and combinations.

As a general and simple rule, choice of shapes for irregular figures should be

Fig. 160. (A) Large skirt and small top for coat.

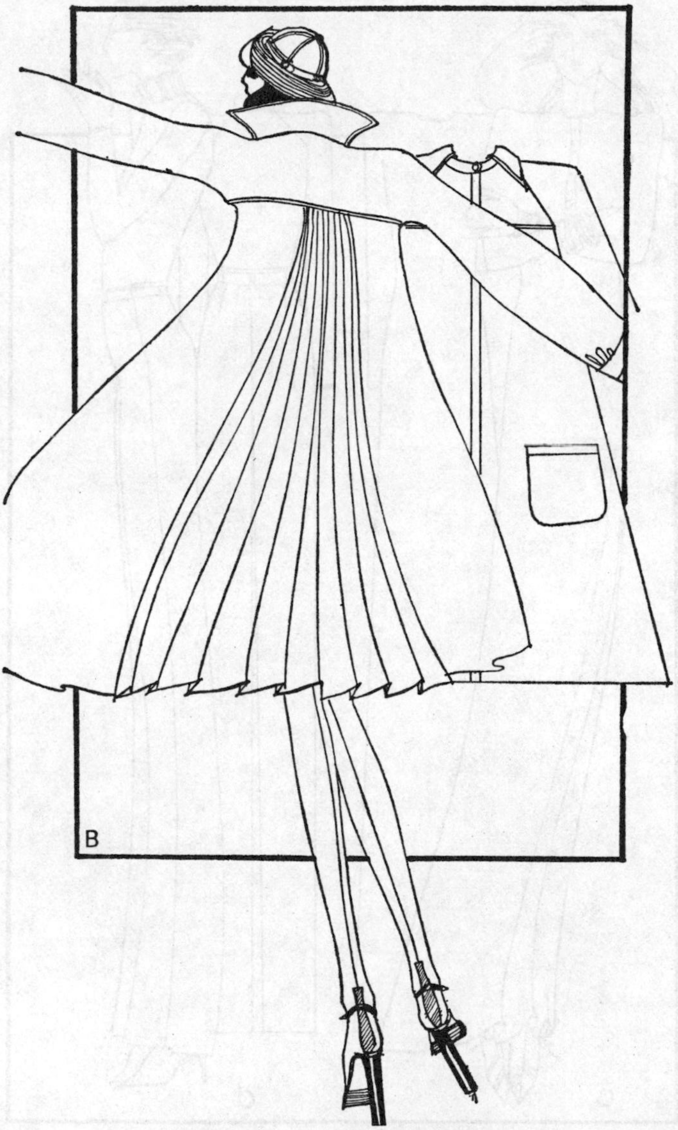

Fig. 161. (B) Pleats increase full shape of coat.

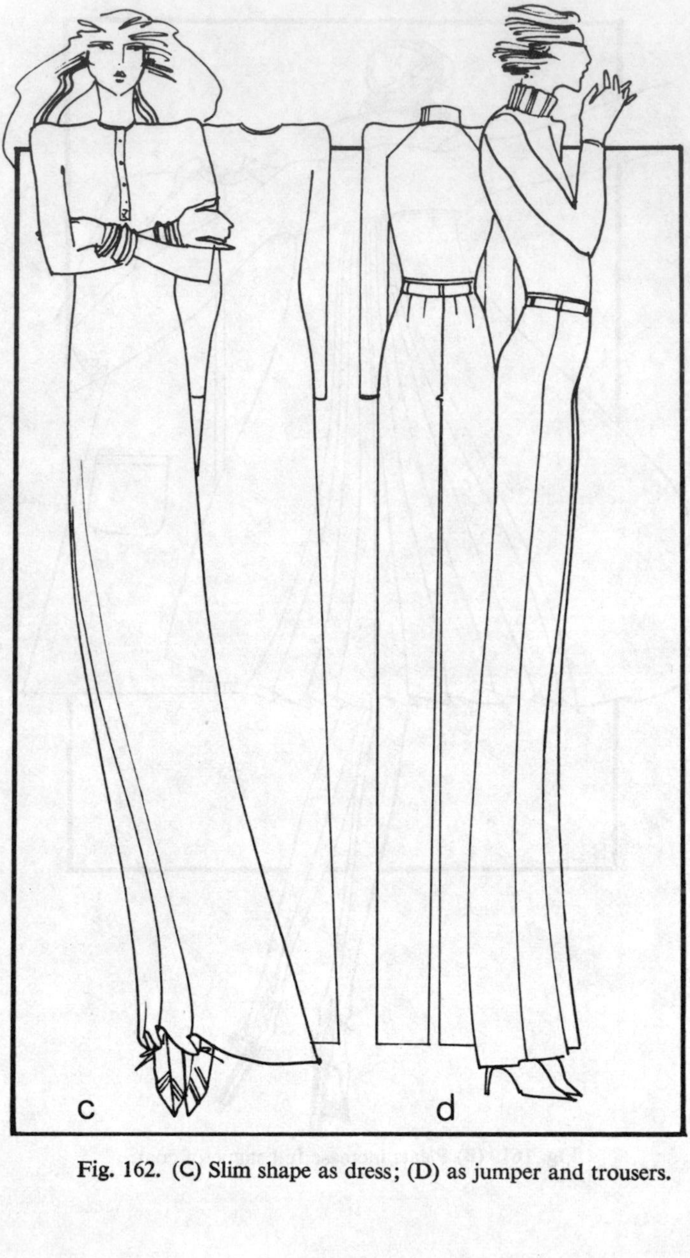

Fig. 162. (C) Slim shape as dress; (D) as jumper and trousers.

based on the aim to draw the eye from those areas, which are less in proportion to the rest of the body and emphasising those parts which are in proportion.

The silhouette of the short, full coats (B) and (E) are shown in contrast to the slim, close-fitting shapes in (C) and (D), while the full-skirted long coat with a small top (A) demonstrates the reverse effect by the fitted skirt and large top (F).

Fig. 163. (E) Full shape as raglan-sleeved coat.

Fig. 164. (F) Full-length close fitting skirt, full jacket.

Divisions by Design Lines

This principle can be extended to both design lines and decorations, acting as dividers. Lines, in both shape and direction, whether straight and hard, or curved and soft, short or long, thin or thick, continuous or broken, placed vertically, horizontally or in oblique position, control the balance of garments, and their visual effects depend on the prominence with which they are used. Often unequal divisions by design lines and/or decorations, rather than equal halves, produce pleasing proportion.

Fig. 165

Fig. 166. (A) Long seams from shoulder yoke; (B) zig-zag lines forming inset.

Fig. 167. (C) Curved seams forming insets on bodice and skirt.

Fig. 168. (D) Zig-zag seams top-stitched for decoration; (E) yoke and angled seams top-stitched.

Fig. 169. (F) Vertical seams incorporating pleats for fullness in skirt.

Within the range of silhouettes, Fig. 165 shows some examples of interesting design lines, introduced to focus additional attention for pleasing eye appeal. Figs. 166–9 also show the combined use of seams as design lines placed in varying directions and positions, attracting the attention of the eye and complementing the silhouette. For example, the yoke and the oblique—vertical seams joined together in (A) emphasize the upper parts of the jacket, while the zig-zag and vertical lines on the skirt in (B) stress the lower part of the garment. Acknowledging that the scope and variety of choice of design lines for figure types of good proportion is greater, does not imply that less care and attention for good proportion is demanded. Badly placed seams will reduce the attractiveness of any design, or even ruin it.

Division by Decoration

The trimming of garments with lace, fur, leather, braid, flowers, belts, bows, pockets, as shown in Fig. 170 and many other decorations, can considerably enhance the basic shape of clothes. But, as already mentioned they, too act as dividers and draw the attention of the eye onto the decorated sections of the garment—collars, neck and waistlines, sleeves and hems and other parts so treated, dominate the total look.

Fig. 170

This chapter and the illustrations in particular, aim to bring about an understanding of the wide range of design details available, and to encourage our readers to make full use of them. Experimenting with all kinds of ideas, with the help of some offered in chapter fourteen, will be far more enjoyable than the acceptance of restrictions imposed by dated rules.

Fig. 171. (A) Lace or flower applique.

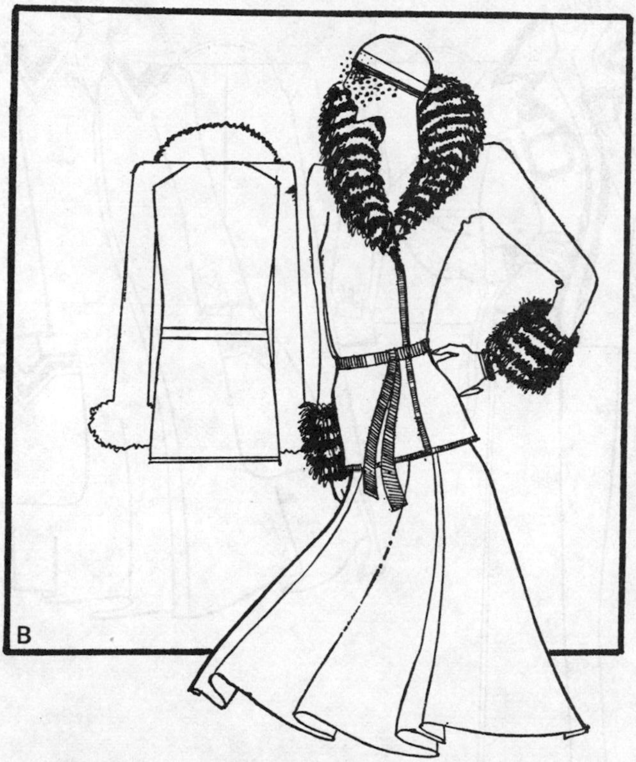

Fig. 172. (B) Fur collar and cuffs.

Fig. 173. (C) Leather edging; (D) braid or leather applique.

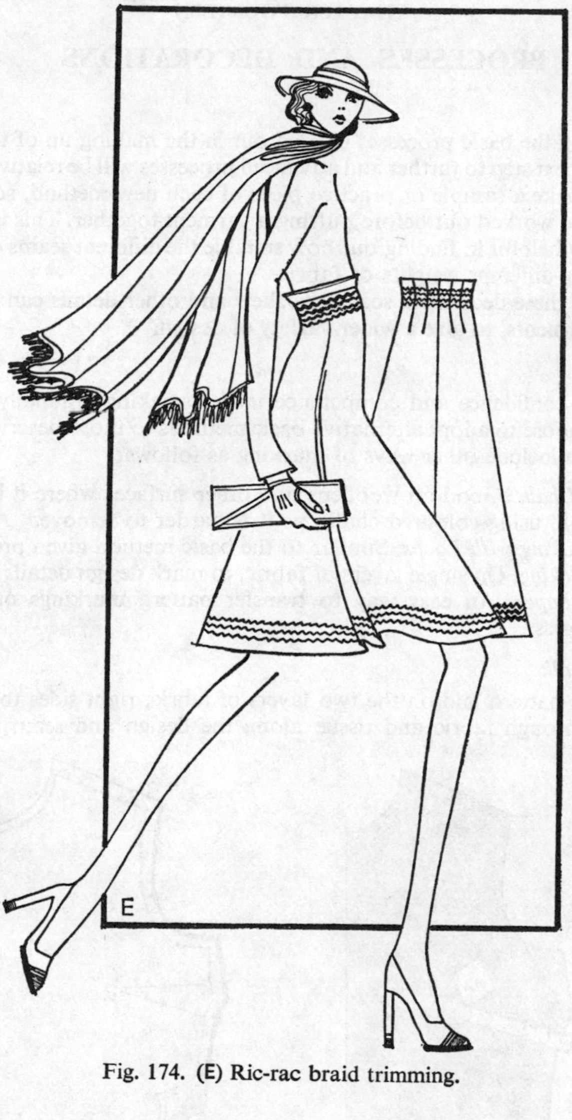

Fig. 174. (E) Ric-rac braid trimming.

CHAPTER FOURTEEN

PROCESSES AND DECORATIONS

Following the basic processes carried out in the making up of the six garments, the next step to further and advanced processes will be relatively simple.

Again, make a sample or practice piece of each new method, so any difficulty can be worked out before putting a garment together. This is of course particularly helpful in finding out how suitable the different seams or pockets, etc., are for different weights of fabric.

Many of these decorative seams, pockets and other details can be applied to basic garments, to give a wider variety of design.

Marking

As your confidence and competence in dressmaking gradually increases, you may choose to adopt alternative basic methods to those described in Part Two. These include other ways of marking as follows:

Tailor's Chalk. Good on woollens and other surfaces where it brushes off easily. Avoid using coloured chalk, as it is harder to remove.

Tailor tacking with Loops. Similar to the basic method given previously.

Trace Tacking. On single layers of fabric, to mark design detail.

Tracing Paper. An easy way to transfer pattern markings on firm but thinner fabrics.

Tailor's Chalk

With the pattern laid on the two layers of fabric, right sides together, pin carefully through fabric and tissue along the design and seam lines to be

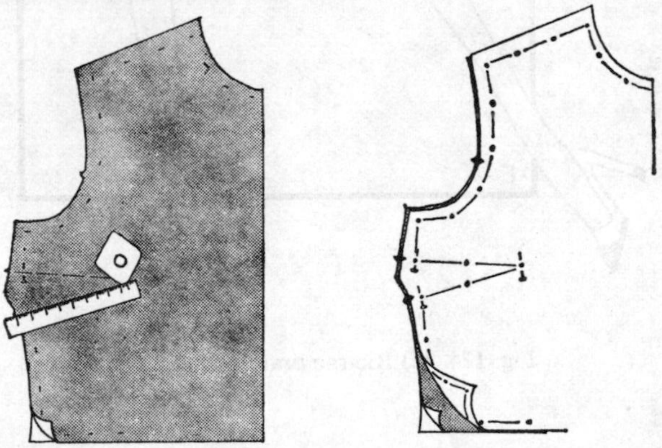

a b

Fig. 175. (a) Tailor's chalk; (b) pin and chalk on other side.

marked. After all the lines have been pinned, turn the fabric over, to the side without the pattern and chalk mark where the pins show. Use a ruler to draw the straight dart and seam lines. After this side has been marked turn the fabric back, and gently remove the pattern without taking the pins away. Now mark this side in line with the pins, just as for the other side, and remove the pins.

Tailor Tacking and Loop

This is almost the same as the method given in page 83, except there is an additional loop, which makes it less easy for the tack mark to fall out. Using double tacking cotton, make a stitch about 1 cm ($\frac{3}{8}$ in) long, leaving a 2 cm ($\frac{3}{4}$ in) loose end. Then, take another stitch, but do not pull it to lie flat, leaving it long enough to form a loop of about 4 cm ($1\frac{5}{8}$ in). Repeat and finish with a 2 cm ($\frac{3}{4}$ in) loose end on completion of marking line.

Cut through the top of the loop and, when marking is finished, lift the pattern off carefully as before. Then, lifting the fabric layers fractionally apart, cut through the cotton between them.

When tailor tacking on chalk marks without a pattern, it is not necessary to cut through the loops before lifting the fabric layers apart.

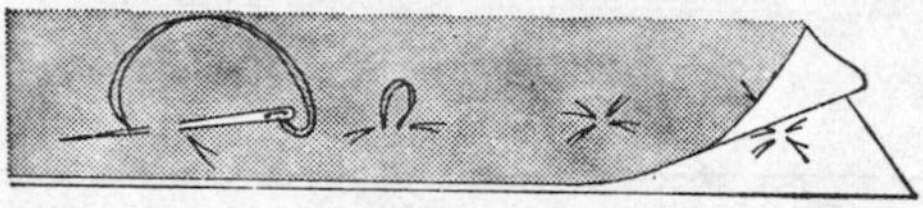

Fig. 176. Tailor tacking.

Trace Tacking

This is a single line of plain tacking stitches to outline design detail, as previously for centre front and grain positions on single layers of fabric. A single thread with a knotted end is used and stitches about 2 cm ($\frac{3}{4}$ in) long are adequate.

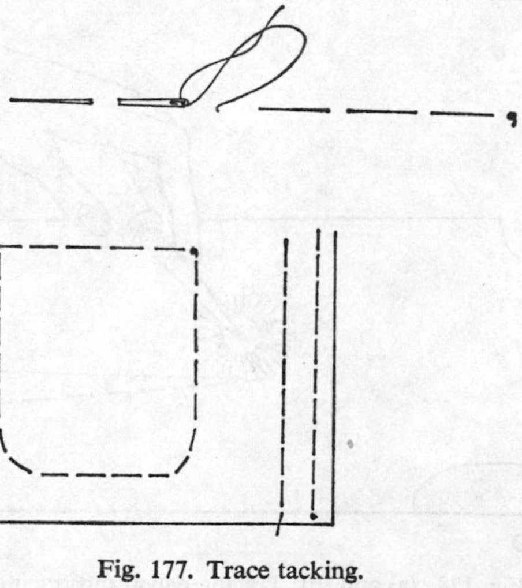

Fig. 177. Trace tacking.

Tracing Paper

For this you need dressmaker tracing paper and a tracing wheel. Use paper a shade darker or lighter than the fabric to be marked, and test on a scrap of material before to see how visible the line will be and how much pressure to use.

The tracing paper is laid with the coated side down to the wrong side of the fabric, with the pattern laid on top. (A layer of cardboard is essential underneath, unless you are using a cutting board, as the wheel will leave marks on a finished surface.)

Mark by following the lines of the pattern, rolling the wheel away from you. For straight lines use a ruler as a guide for the wheel. Two layers of

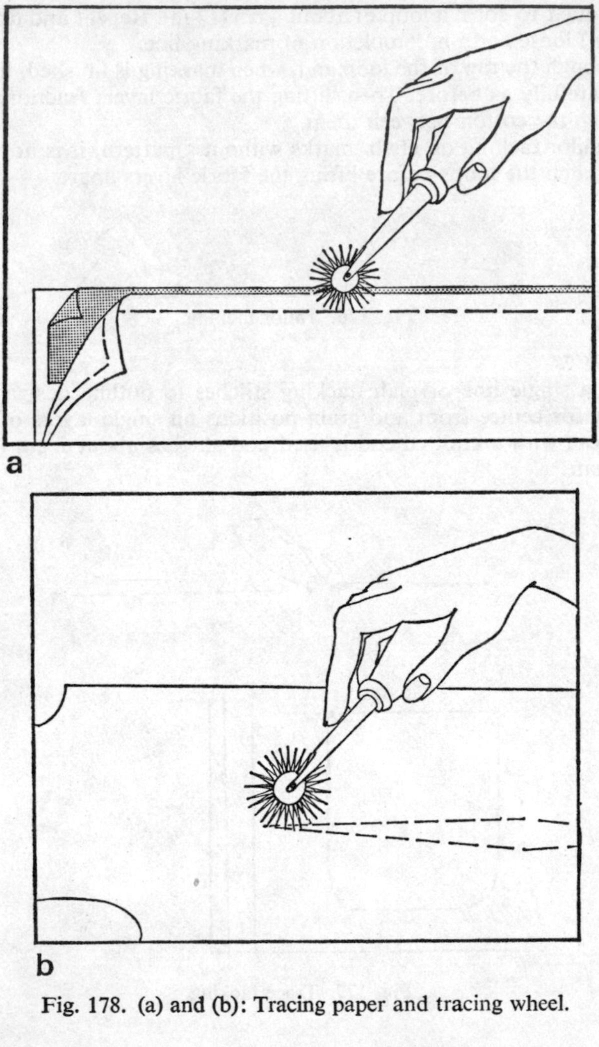

Fig. 178. (a) and (b): Tracing paper and tracing wheel.

fabric can be marked, which will of course have their right sides together with the pattern laid on top. The fabric must be thin and firm to do this, as more pressure is needed to mark through all the layers.

Basic Hand Stitches

All good dressmaking begins and ends with handsewing. Some of the following stitches have already been described but for easy reference we list them again with their particular uses.

Tacking/Basting

This is a long temporary stitch to hold sections of fabric together prior to machining or fitting. It is also used to indicate design lines or balance marks. Use contrast colour thread and make stitches about 1 cm ($\frac{3}{8}$ in) long.

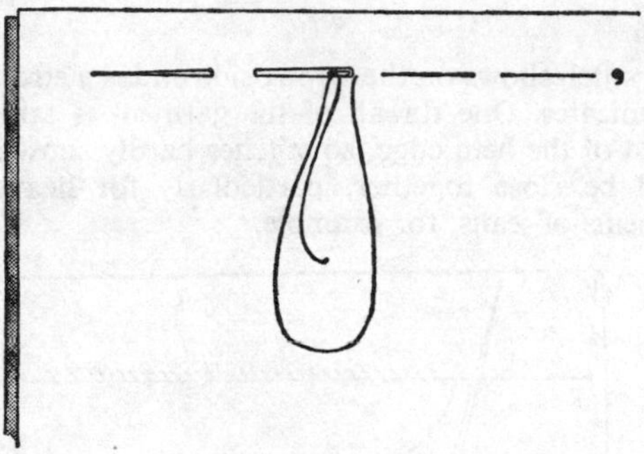

Fig. 179. Tacking/basting.

Diagonal Tacking/Basting

Another tacking stitch which holds several layers together firmly, to keep interlinings, facings and linings in place for fittings. It is a diagonal stitch on the upper side and straight on the other side.

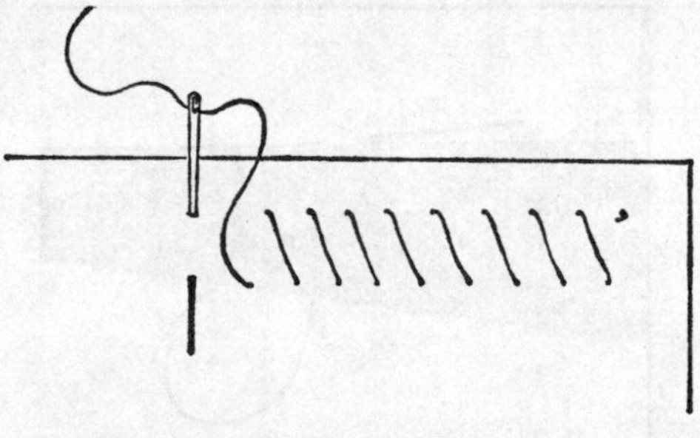

Fig. 180. Diagonal tacking/basting.

Running Stitch

This is a very small, simple, hand stitch used for gathering material, or easing in fullness. It can be used as a seam where there is no strain on the fabric, particularly on very sheer fabrics when a very tiny stitch is made. In principle, several small stitches are made by passing the needle through the fabric several times at once, then the needle is pulled through. For gathering, a stitch of 3 mm ($\frac{1}{8}$ in) is average and use a smaller stitch for a seam.

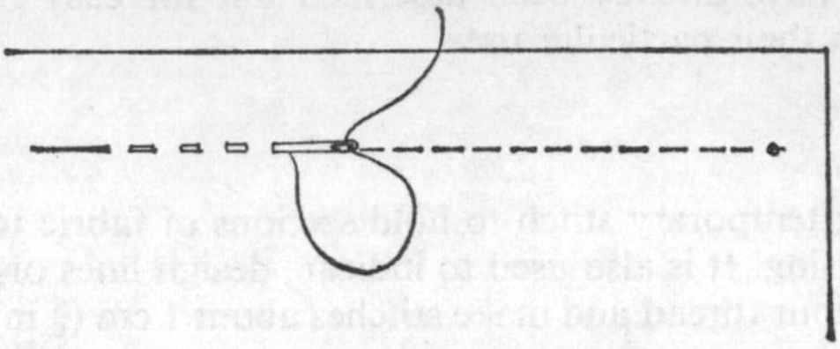

Fig. 181. Running stitch.

Hemming Stitch

This slanting stitch shows on the wrong side and is a strong stitch for hems as the name indicates. One thread of the garment is taken, then the next through the fold of the hem edge, so stitches hardly show on the right side. Stitches should be close together, particularly for heavy cotton fabrics, sheetings and hems of jeans, for example.

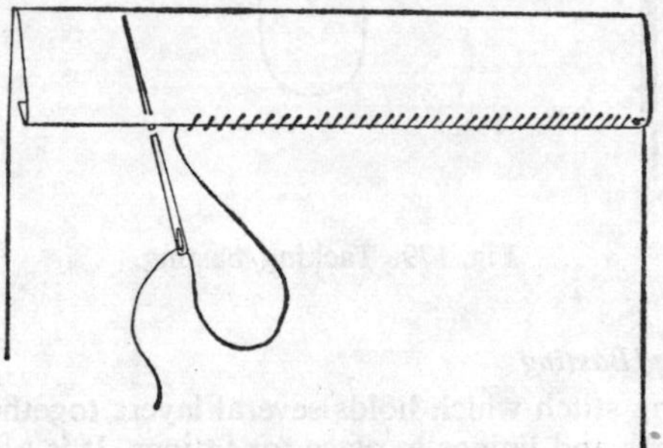

Fig. 182. Hemming.

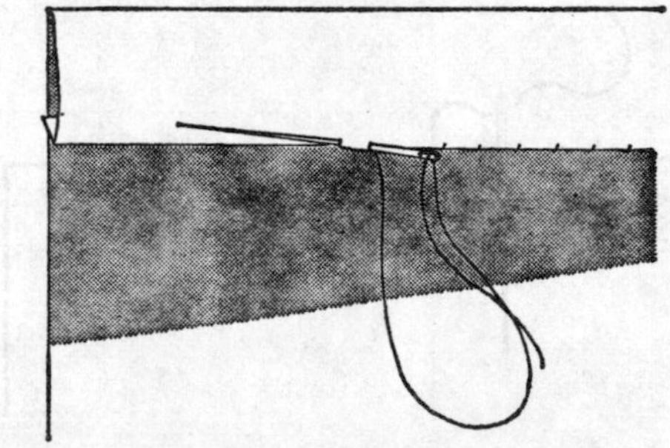

Fig. 183. Slipstitch.

Slipstitch

A similar method although not quite as strong as hemming stitch, but stitches do not show on the right side which makes it a good stitch for thin fabrics with a turned-in hem edge. The stitch is a thread taken on the garment fabric just below the hem turning, the next is through the fold of the hem along its edge, about 1 cm ($\frac{3}{8}$ in) long.

Felling Stitch

A tiny version of the hem stitch. Used to sew in linings or collar seams, where it is impossible to machine. Stitches must now show, but they are very strong. A minute stitch is taken through the very edge of the hem fold, and one thread below stitches are very close together.

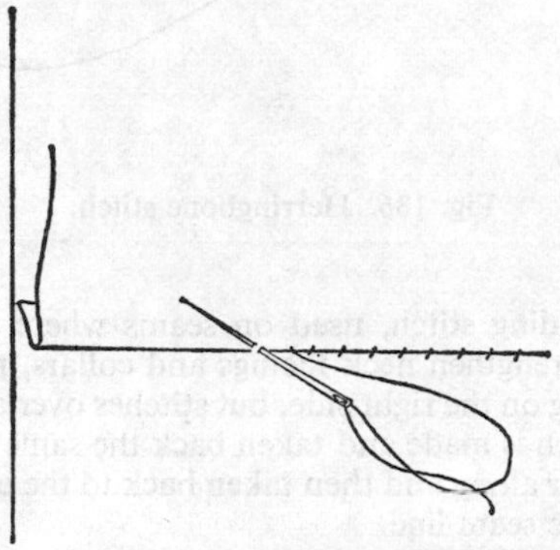

Fig. 184. Felling stitch.

Blindstitch

The best general stitch to hold down turnings, hems and facings, as it holds but does not pull or show the hem ridge on the right side. The turning edge to be hemmed is folded back a little way, and one thread taken on garment side and another through the turning leaving about 1 cm ($\frac{3}{8}$ in) between the stitches. The thread is never pulled tightly, just enough to hold the layers together. Used on nearly all fabrics successfully.

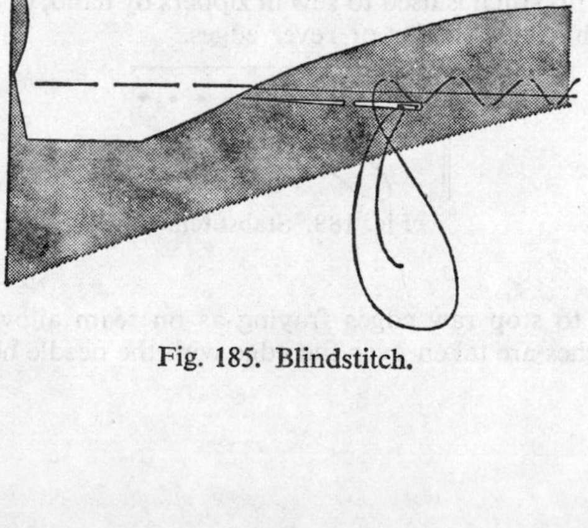

Fig. 185. Blindstitch.

Herringbone/Catch Stitch

Another good stitch to hold raw edges of hems, facings and interfacings. In this case the edge does not have to have a special finish, as the stitch itself prevents excessive fraying and is quite secure. Working from left to right a smallish stitch is taken through the fabric from right to left, then take one or two threads in the under fabric from right to left, the stitches will cross each other as you go along. An average of about 1 cm ($\frac{3}{8}$ in) again, between the stitches. This too is a stitch which can be used on most fabrics.

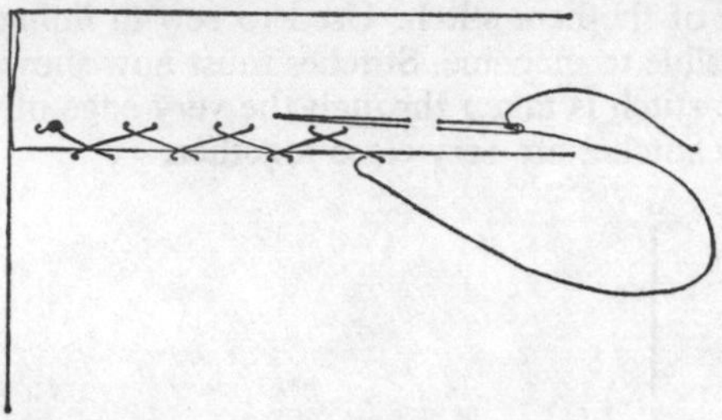

Fig. 186. Herringbone stitch.

Backstitch

This is a firm holding stitch, used on seams where it is not possible to machine stitch, to strengthen neck facings and collars, pockets, etc. It looks like machine stitching on the right side, but stitches overlap on the wrong side. A small running stitch is made and taken back the same distance. The needle is brought out further along and then taken back to the end of this first stitch. Repeat this along the seam line.

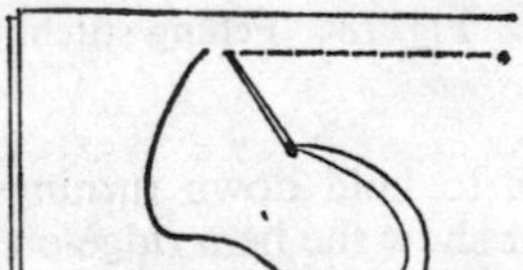

Fig. 187. Backstitch.

Stabstitch

A variation of the backstitch. The needle is taken back only a fraction, almost in the same place, in fact, then the next stitch only a few threads further along. This stitch is used to sew in zippers by hand, or can be used as a decorative stitch around collar or rever edges.

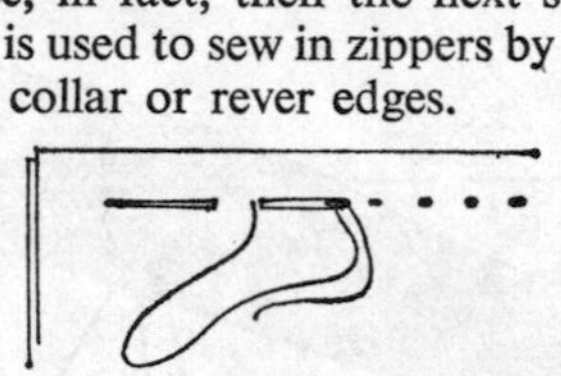

Fig. 188. Stabstitch.

Oversewing

This is used to stop raw edges fraying as on seam allowances and hem edges. The stitches are taken over the edge with the needle held in a slanting position. Stitches are fairly close together and should be the same size for a neat effect.

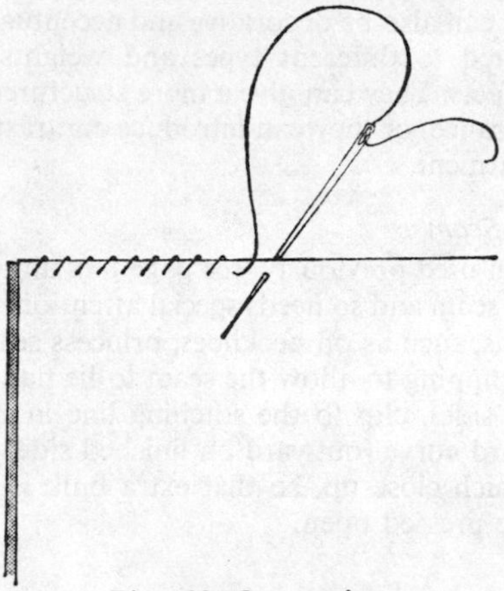

Fig. 189. Oversewing.

Blanket Stitch

This can be used as a finish for raw edges too, as well as being a decorative stitch. Working from left to right bring the needle out at the edge of the fabric, hold the thread down under the needle and draw the needle through the loop that has formed. Keep the stitches an even size. The edge will have a chain loop effect to it. This is the same stitch used over several threads to make a **bar tack.**

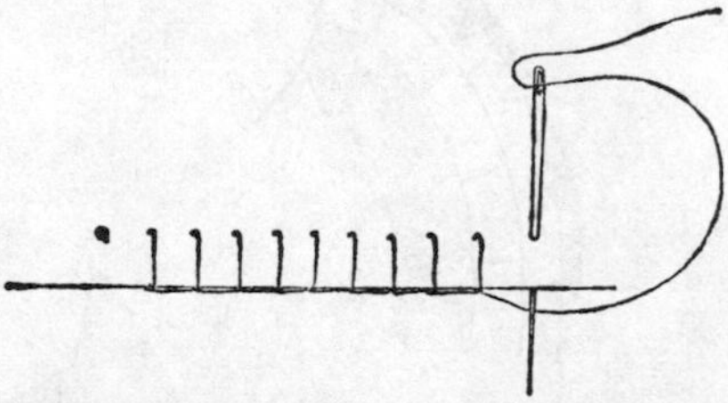

Fig. 190. Blanket stitch.

Whipstitch

This is a small slanting stitch made on two edges which have to be sewn together, without the stitch showing. This is used frequently when joining lace, or very sheer fabric edges. Again only one or two threads are taken each side and a very small seam or hem allowance is needed.

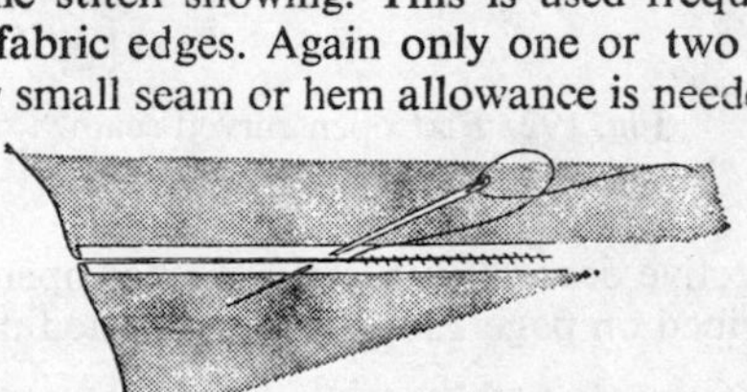

Fig. 191. Whipstitch.

Seams

Seams are the way to join two sections of a garment together, and so are functional, but they can also be decorative and accentuate design lines. Some are particularly suited to different types and weights of fabric, and can produce different effects. They can give a more structured or sculptured look, a sharp, crisp appearance, or they can introduce contrast material and colour into the made up garment.

Flat Open (Curved) Seam

The flat open seam used previously (see page 86), although basically simple can also be a curved seam and so needs special attention.

Most curved seams, such as on necklines, princess seam lines and Kimono sleeve seams, need clipping to allow the seam to lie flat. On an inward curve (inward on finished side), clip to the stitching line in spaces of about 1 cm ($\frac{3}{8}$ in). On an outward curve (outward on finished side) make notches to the line of stitching, which close up, so that extra bulk is eliminated when the seam allowances are pressed open.

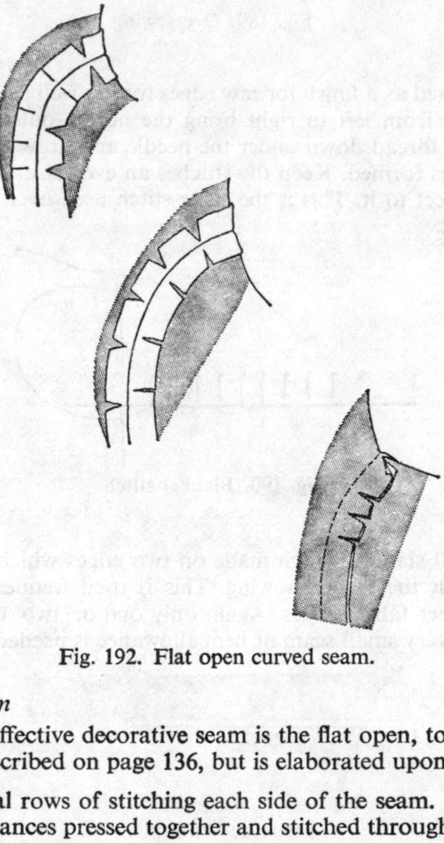

Fig. 192. Flat open curved seam.

Top-Stitched Seam

A simple and effective decorative seam is the flat open, top-stitched seam. This has been described on page 136, but is elaborated upon here:

(1) With several rows of stitching each side of the seam.
(2) Seam allowances pressed together and stitched through the allowances.

(3) A narrow padding strip placed each side of seam under the allowances and stitched through to give a padded effect.

Top-stitching silk used with a slightly larger needle on the machine and, of course, a larger stitch setting, looks best for plain top-stitching.

(4) The zig-zag stitch, too, can look interesting on denim type fabrics, such as a double row in a contrasting colour.

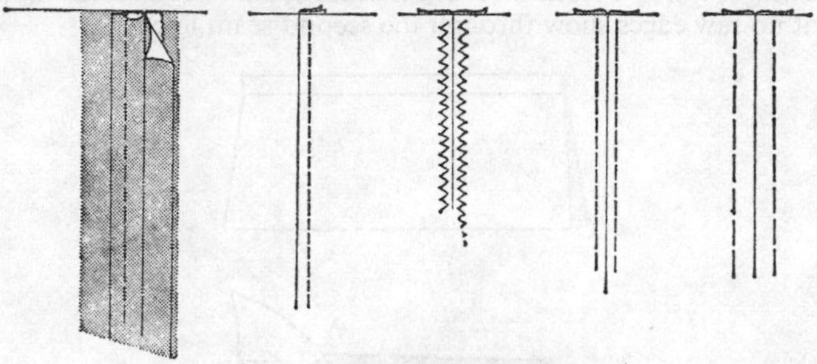

Fig. 193. Top-stitched seams.

Flat Fell Seam

This is a very strong seam, as it is double stitched. Ideal for denim and similar cotton fabrics, used on jeans, sportswear, leather and vinyl clothes and could be used to advantage on the garments suggested in Part Two. This seam can be made on either side of the fabric, but gives more emphasis used on the right side.

Make a flat open seam, but with *wrong* sides of fabric together. Underpress, then trim one seam allowance to 6 mm ($\frac{1}{4}$ in). Press in a narrow turning on the other seam allowance and fold over this pressed edge to cover the trimmed seam. Tack down and machine stitch on the edge of the turning.

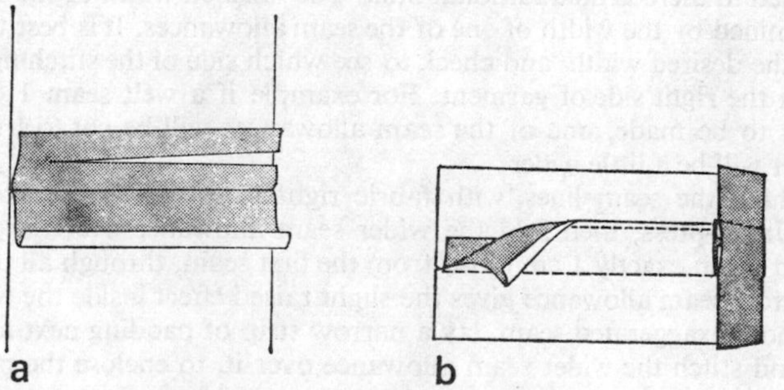

Fig. 194. (a) and (b) Flat fell seam.

French Seam

This one is for all very fine fabrics, where a seam allowance should be minimal, and for all lightweight fabrics which need a lot of washing, such as lingerie, children's clothes and nightwear.

It is a very narrow seam, also stitched twice, so is strong and no raw edges are visible.

Again make a seam with the wrong sides of fabric together, but a very narrow seam 3 mm (⅛ in) is best. If this is found difficult to sew, it can be stitched with a wide allowance and then trimmed down.

Under-press and turn the fabric so the right sides are together. Press with the seam allowances inside, seam line exactly on the folded edge and tack and stitch another seam line to enclose the raw edges of the first seam to just under 6 mm (¼ in). It is essential that the seam should be as narrow as possible and that no raw edges show through the second seam line.

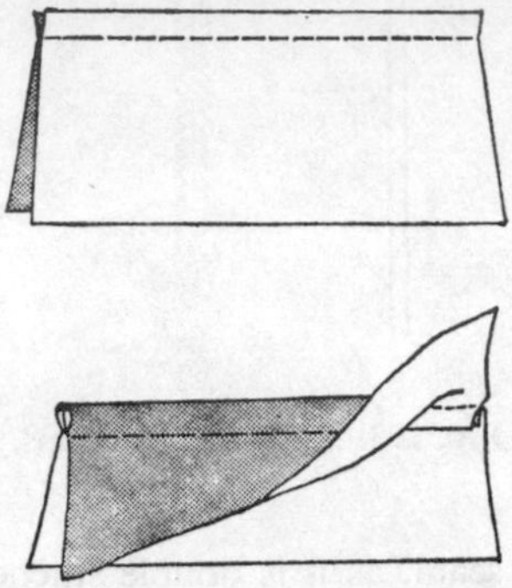

Fig. 195. French seam.

Welt or Raised Seam

This is an important seam, used widely in tailored clothes. It accentuates design lines, can give a sculptured (structured) look and is especially effective on plain surface woollens or tweeds with very small designs. Its advantage is that it can be used on quite thick fabrics, so it makes a good coat seam. It looks very like the reverse side of flat fell seam, but as the seam allowance is not turned in there is no additional bulk. The finished width of the welt seam is determined by the width of one of the seam allowances. It is best to cut this first to the desired width, and check to see which side of the stitching line will show on the right side of garment. For example if a welt seam 1 cm (⅜ in) width is to be made, one of the seam allowances will be cut to 1 cm (⅜ in), the other will be a little wider.

Matching the seam lines, with fabric right sides together, make a plain seam. Under-press, then fold the wider seam allowance over the narrower one, and stitch exactly 1 cm (⅜ in) from the first seam, through all the layers. The narrow seam allowance gives the slight raised effect inside the wider one. For a more exaggerated seam, lay a narrow strip of padding next to the first seam, and stitch the wider seam allowance over it, to enclose the padding.

Lap Seam

Another good seam, especially for thick fabrics or leather, but workable on most medium-to-heavy fabrics. Very easy to make and most effective on coat or jacket shapes, as it is a bulkier looking seam with a tuck-like fold which is the lap. When cutting, extra fabric is allowed on that side of the seam which laps over the other.

The seam is marked on the overlapping piece of fabric, as well as on a line

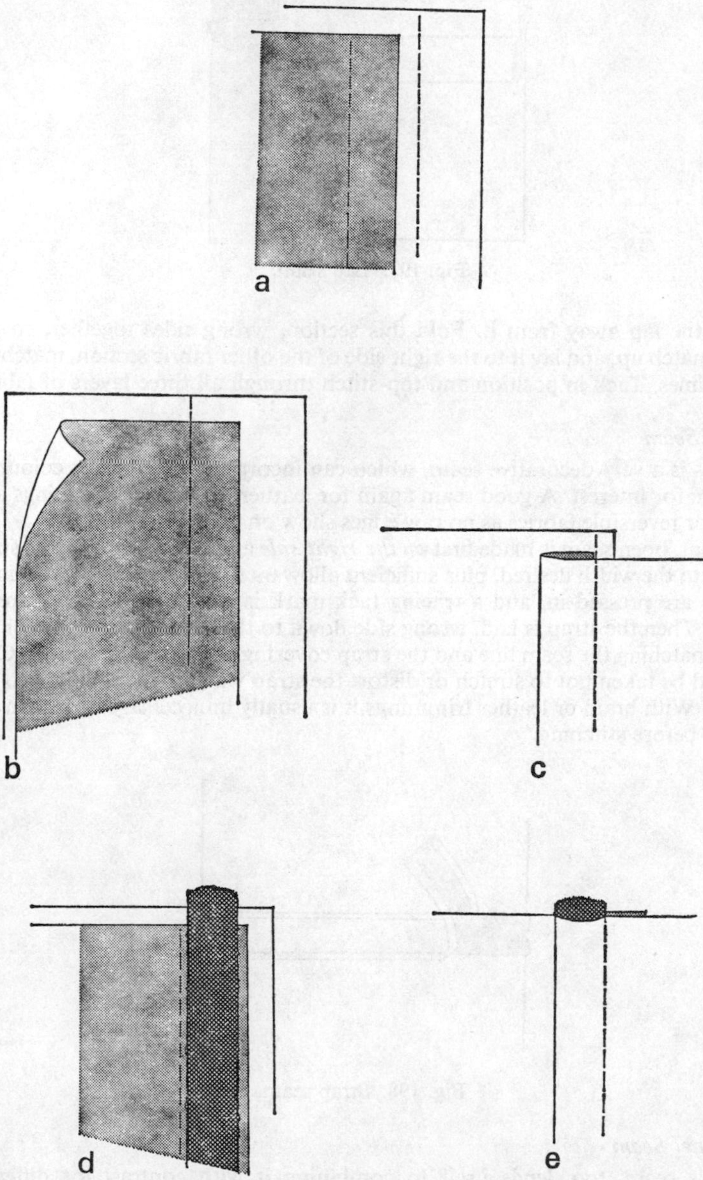

Fig. 196. (a), (b) and (c) Welt seam; (d) and (e) padded welt seam.

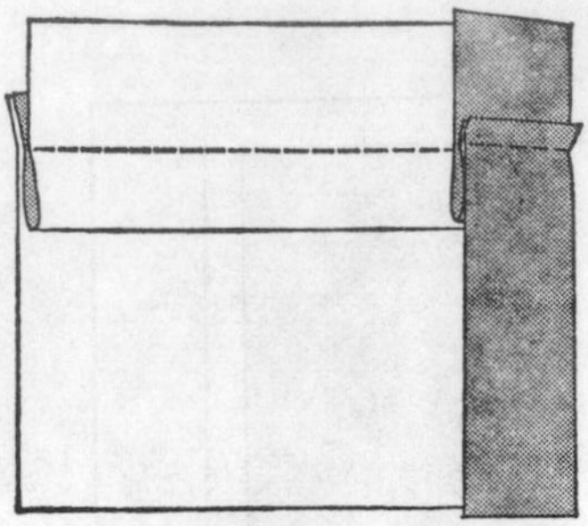

Fig. 197. Lap seam.

twice the lap away from it. Fold this section, wrong sides together, so the lines match up, and lay it to the right side of the other fabric section, matching seam lines. Tack in position and top-stitch through all three layers of fabric.

Strap Seam

This is a very decorative seam, which can incorporate a contrast colour or texture for interest. A good seam again for leather, or leather trimmings and also for reversible fabrics as no raw edges show on the wrong side.

A flat, open seam is made first *on the right side* and pressed open. The strap is cut to the width desired, plus sufficient allowance to make narrow turnings. These are pressed in, and a tracing tack mark is made along the centre of strap. Then the strap is laid, wrong side down to the seam—the centre-length tack matching the seam line and the strap covering the seam allowances. Care should be taken not to stretch or distort the strap when top-stitching it to the seam. With braid or leather trimmings it is usually unnecessary to turn in the edges before stitching.

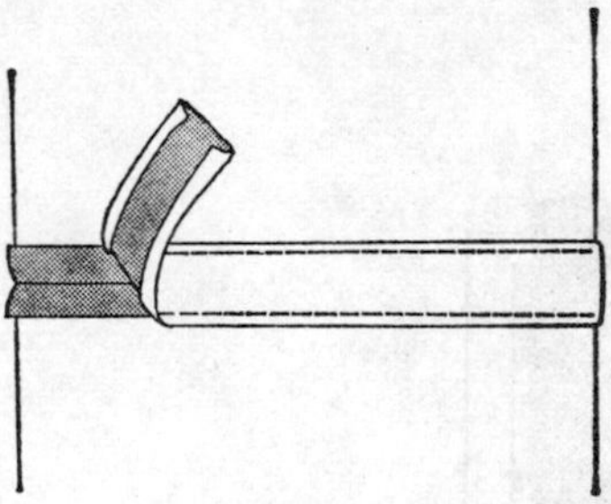

Fig. 198. Strap seam.

Channel Seam

This seam, too, lends itself to combining it with contrast, or different textural trimmings. It can be successfully used on most fabrics which are fairly firm, such as gabardine, flannel, heavy cottons and tweeds.

On the two sections to be joined, the seam allowances are pressed to the inside. The fabric for the underlaying 'channel' strip is cut so that it is slightly wider than the seam allowances together, plus the amount that will show through the gap. This will vary according to the design but it is just as effective, if the two sections meet, as the contrast shows through in a more subtle manner. A trace tacking line is made along the centre of the channel strip. The two sections to be joined are laid on the strip, with the folded edges of the fabric meeting the centre-tack line on the strip or, for a wider gap, the same distance each side from the centre. Tack in position and top-stitch through the fabric and strip, from the fold edge, 6 mm ($\frac{1}{4}$ in) or more depending on the thickness of the fabric.

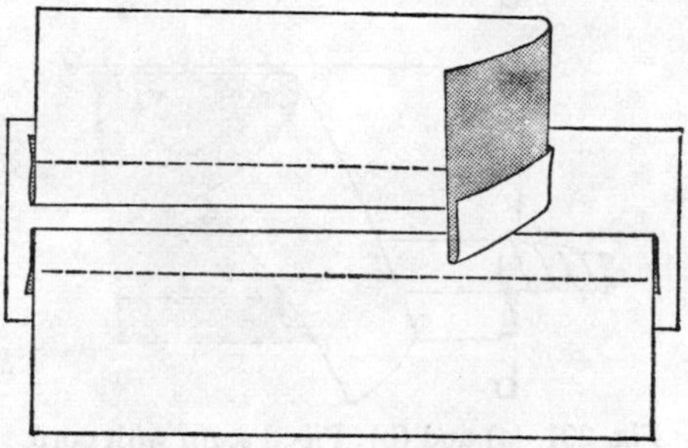

Fig. 199. Channel seam.

Piped Seam

This decorative edging for seams, as with the previous two seams, can introduce colour and contrast very effectively. It can be used on fairly fine fabrics too. Piped with a cord it gives a firmer, rounder edge; or with plain bias strips, a softer look. For a piped seam without a cord, fold a bias strip along the centre, right side out, and tack the piping together, marking off the area which will show. Lay the piping to the seam-fitting line on the right side of one section. Match the tacked fitting lines, with the raw edges facing the same way as the seam allowances on the main section of fabric. Lay the other sections of fabric right side to right side, seam allowances together and seam-fitting lines matching. Stitch together through all layers and press one section of fabric to face the opposite way.

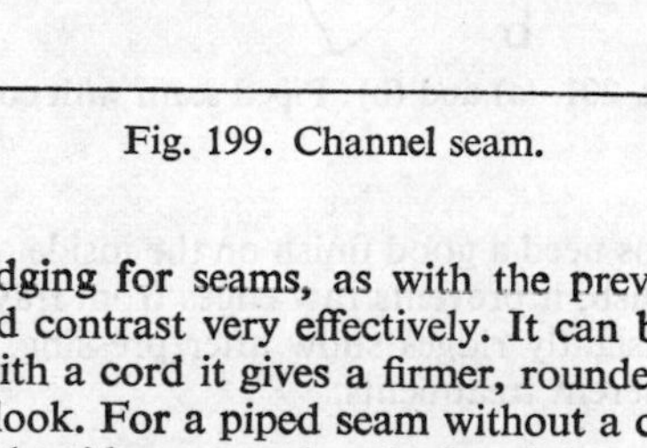

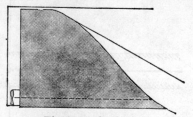

Fig. 200. Piped seam.

Piped Seam with Cord

First, a narrow cord is inserted into the piping material. Lay the cord along the centre of the piping on the wrong side of fabric. Fold over the piping to enclose the cord, and tack as close as possible to the cord itself, with a reasonable seam allowance left. Lay the corded piping to the fitting line on fabric just as the plain piping was done, and tack the other sections of fabric on top as before. The difference now is that it is sewn together with the zip foot attachment. This allows the stitching to be right next to the piping, making the corded edge neat and firm.

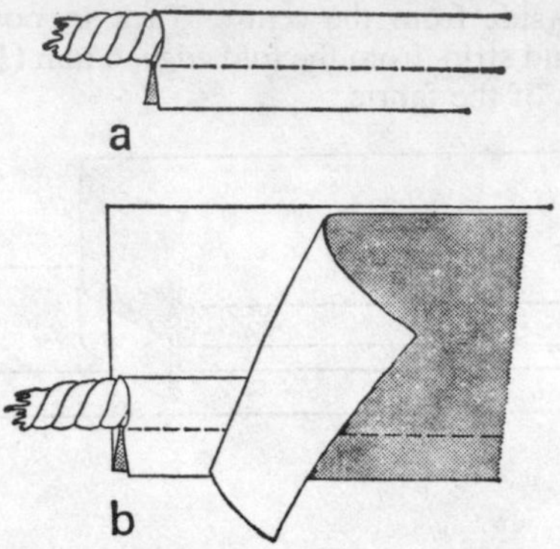

Fig. 201. (a) and (b): Piped seam with cord.

Seam Finishes

All well made seams need a good finish on the inside. Apart from the clean appearance of the finish, it prevents raw edges from fraying and, trimmed to an equal size, no unsightly ridges show after pressing. Various fabrics and garments call for different treatments.

Oversewn

An all-purpose finish for most seams, except lingerie and children's wear, which generally have french seams and so need no finishing. Stitches must be even, the size determined by the thickness of the fabric. Very thick, loosely-

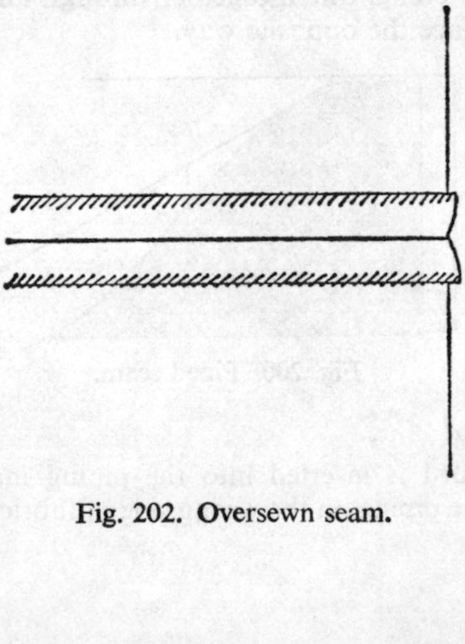

Fig. 202. Oversewn seam.

woven types, often need oversewing before seams are stitched together, as they fray very quickly: oversewing beforehand, helps to keep the correct seam allowance.

Machine neatened Seam Edge

This is a narrow turning on the seam allowance, which is edge stitched. Best for cotton and some rayon fabrics, as it usually gives too thick an edge on other materials and would be bulky and show when the garment is pressed.

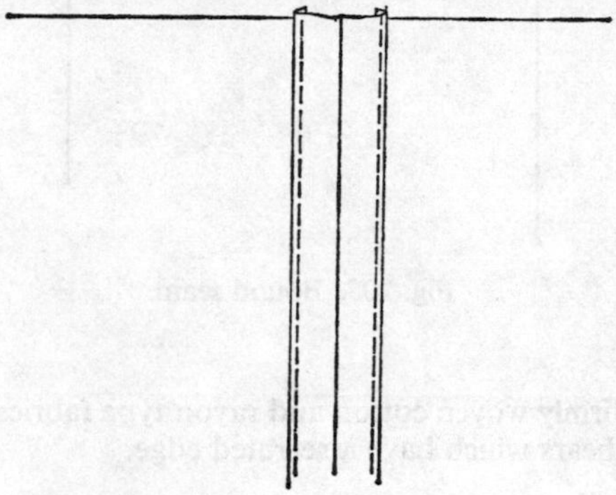

Fig. 203. Machine neatened seam.

Zig-zag Machine Stitch

The nearest domestic equivalent to an industrial stitch, good on most types of fabric (see page 67).

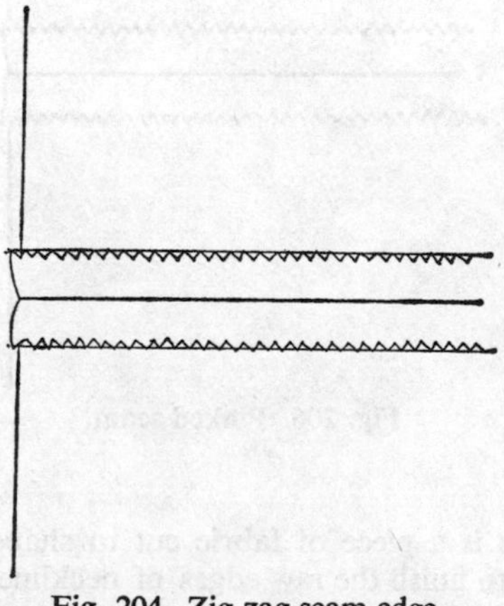

Fig. 204. Zig-zag seam edge.

Bound Seam

These are seams with a binding stitched over the edge of turnings. Mostly used on unlined jackets or coats, as it can be a little too heavy for lighter fabrics and may also hold the seam too tightly.

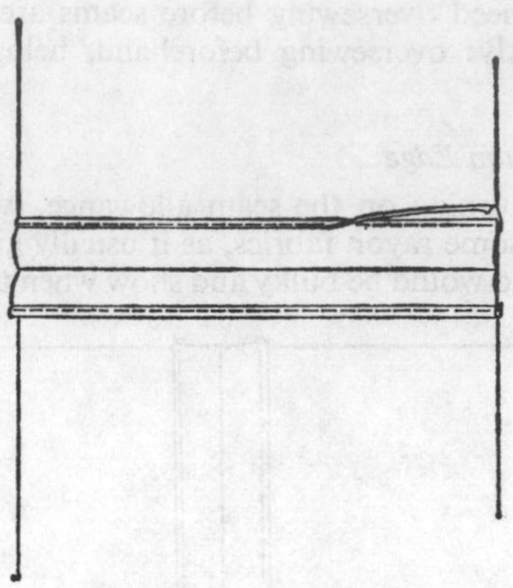

Fig. 205. Bound seam.

Pinked Seam

Only used on firmly woven cotton and rayon type fabrics and is made with special pinking shears which have a serrated edge.

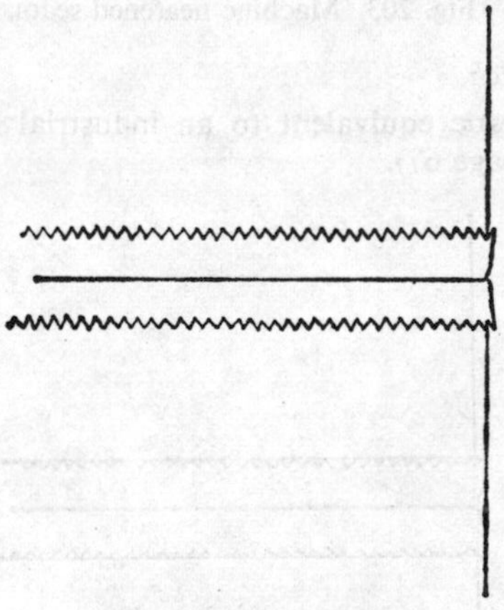

Fig. 206. Pinked seam.

Facings

In most cases this is a piece of fabric cut to shape and on the straight grain and is applied to finish the raw edges of necklines, armholes or openings in a garment.

The basic methods of applying facings have already been described in Part Two. It includes the faced slit opening on sleeves, on page 150, which is one example of the use of facings not cut to the exact shape of the main edge to be finished. Facings are also used to finish raw edges on wrapover skirts, shaped necklines, scalloped or pointed edges, false hems, and almost any raw edge, in fact, where a plain turn-back hem cannot be made. They also give added support to shaped edges. Facings can also be interlined.

The method of attaching a facing does not vary very much, but making for the different shapes needs some explanation.

The professional looking facing should be flat along the edge and not roll to show the seam on the right side. All curved or bias edges, loosely woven or stretchy fabrics should be staystitched first, of course, and the interlining pressed or sewn to the inside of garment before the facing is laid on.

Faced Slit Neckline

With the armhole and neck facing described on page 113, the faced slit-opening neckline is as simple, but an often recurring mistake is for the opening to be cut before the facing is attached.

The facing is cut to fit the neckline, with an additional tab to cover adequately the length of the proposed slit. Finish the outer edge of the facing with zig-zag stitch, machine edge, or oversewing. Mark the slit with a trace tacking, on garment and facing, staystitch and interface the wrong side of neck and slit mark. Lay facing right side to right side of garment, tack and then machine stitch on seam lines. When the slit mark is reached, stitch a little under 1 cm ($\frac{3}{8}$ in) at the neck edge tapering to one stitch across the end of slit mark, and then back on the other side to the neck.

Trim and clip the neckline, cut along the slit marking to the stitching lines, turn facing to the inside and under-stitch the neck edge as far as possible. Then finish rest with hand stitching around the end of the slit. Press and catch loose edge of facing to the garment or top-stitch.

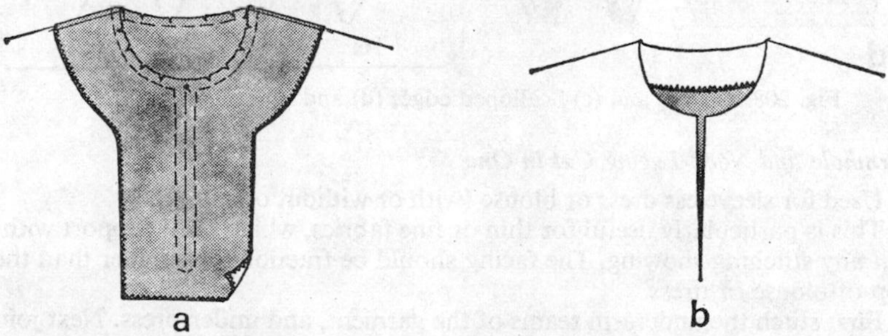

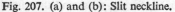

Fig. 207. (a) and (b): Slit neckline.

Facing Scalloped, or Pointed Hems and Edges

The scallops are marked on the garment and facing, but **not** cut. The facing is laid right side to right side of hem, matching scallop markings. Again the interfacing, on all but sheer fabrics where it might show to disadvantage, helps to improve the shape but if a very soft look is aimed for do not interface.

Stitch on the first scallop line, taking one stitch across where the next scallop begins, then cut around scallop leaving small seam allowances. Notch the curves and clip to the stitching line between the scallops, right up to the one stitch across. Cutting the shape afterwards prevents stretching, or distortion of shape. Turn the facing through to the inside, and understitch the facing and scallop seam allowances, to make a neat smooth edge.

The same method applies to a pointed edge. Points are cut after stitching—one stitch across each end of points, makes for a neat finish without puckering.

Other hem facings are described in the section dealing with hems on page 205.

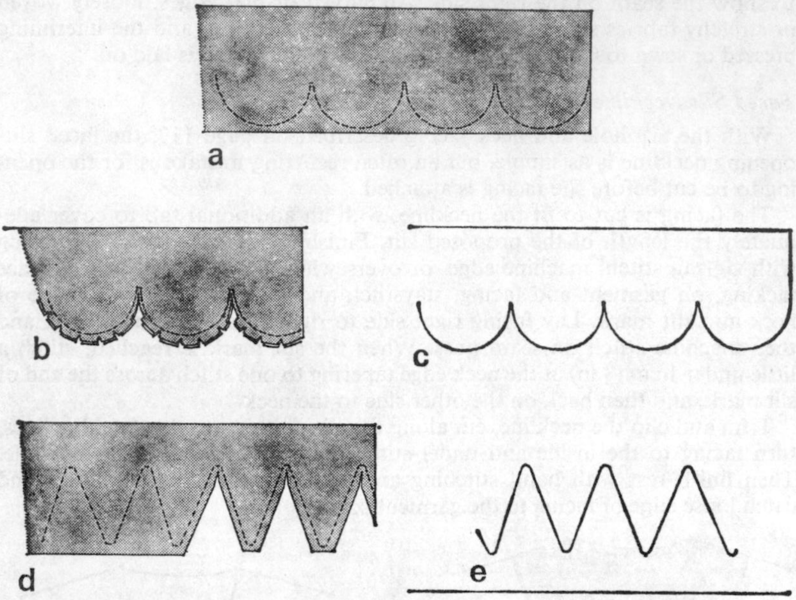

Fig. 208. (a), (b) and (c) Scalloped edge; (d) and (e) pointed edge.

Armhole and Neck Facing Cut in One

Used for sleeveless dress or blouse (with or without opening).

This is particularly useful for thin or fine fabrics, which need support without any stitching showing. The facing should be fractionally smaller than the top of blouse or dress.

First stitch the underarm seams of the garment, and under-press. Next join the underarm seams of the facing, press and then finish off the lower edge of facing, but leave shoulder seams open. Then, matching balance marks, stitch the facing right sides together to the garment around the neck and armholes. Trim and clip the seam.

Pull the facing through to the inside of the garment, through the open shoulder seams. Stitch the garment shoulder seam, press, then fold the shoulder seam of the facing over the garment seam and handsew together. When completed no raw edges show.

Grown-on Facings

Facings can be 'grown-on'. This is when the facing, say for example on a jacket or blouse front opening, is cut in one with the main part of garment, and then turned back on a fold line, as mentioned on page 146.

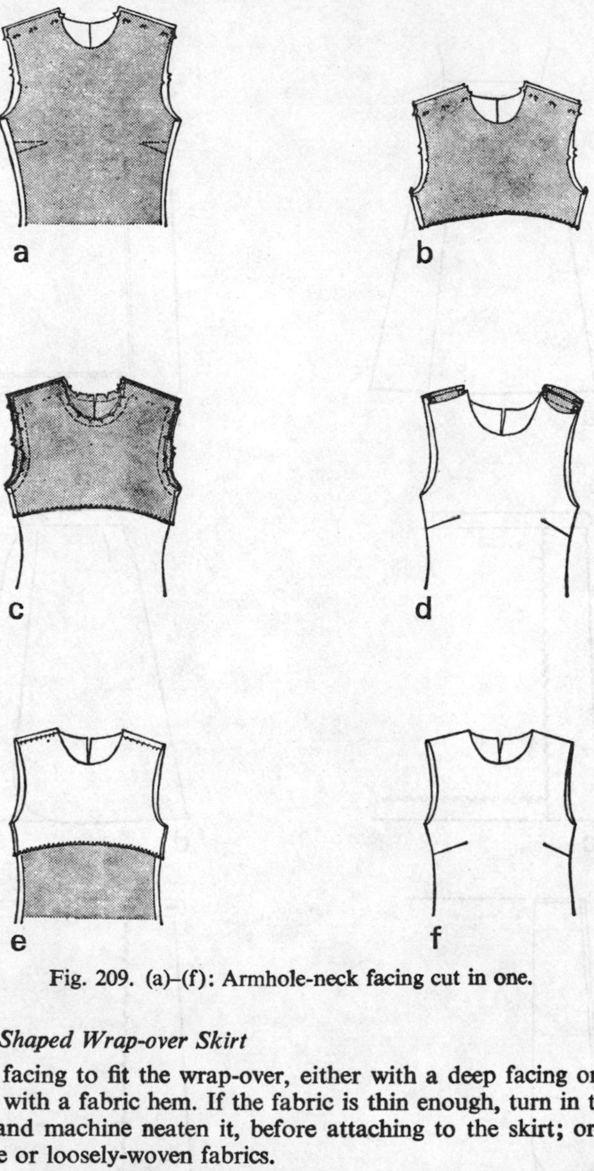

Fig. 209. (a)–(f): Armhole-neck facing cut in one.

Facing on Shaped Wrap-over Skirt

Cut the facing to fit the wrap-over, either with a deep facing or a band, cut in one with a fabric hem. If the fabric is thin enough, turn in the loose, raw edge and machine neaten it, before attaching to the skirt; or oversew on frayable or loosely-woven fabrics.

Machine stitch the facing to the seam line, trim and notch seam allowances on curved seams, clip corners on straight ones. Understitch whenever possible, turn facing to inside and press, rolling the seam to the inside if not already understitched.

Hand stitch loose, facing edges to the inside of the skirt, or bind with bias binding, particularly if the skirt is unlined.

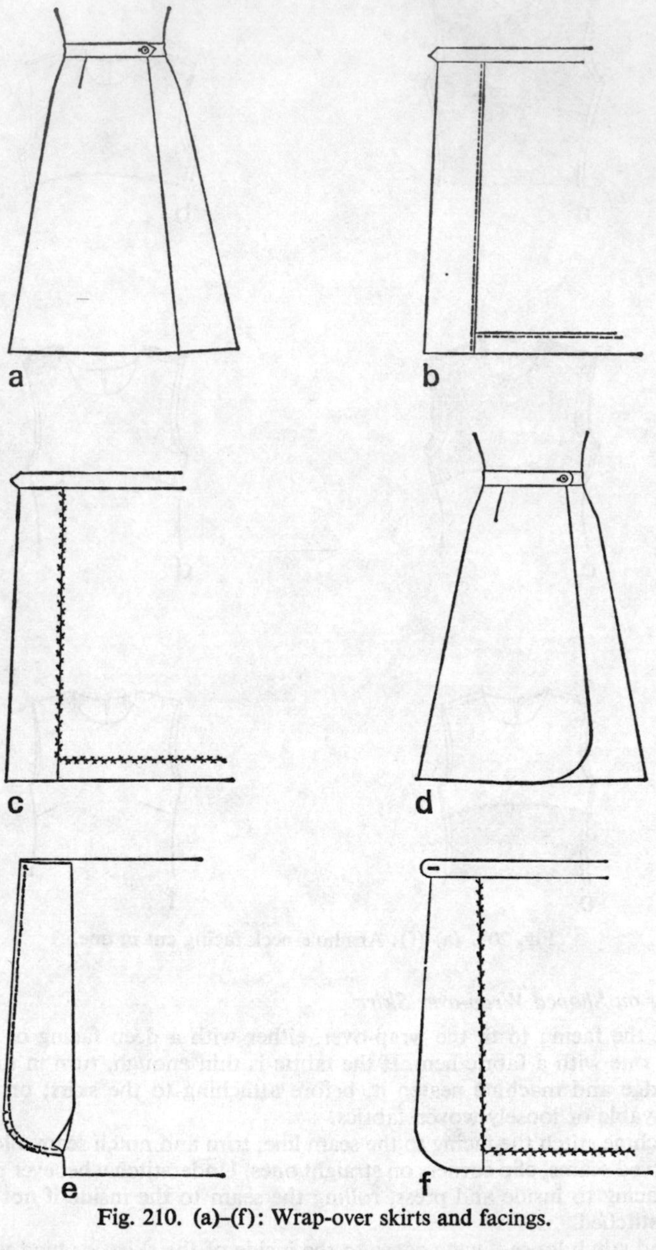

Fig. 210. (a)–(f): Wrap-over skirts and facings.

Decorative Facings

Finally, facings can also be used very simply as decoration, by sewing to the inside and turning them out to the right side. The edges are turned in and finished neatly and the facings can be top-stitched or handsewn to the outside of the garment.

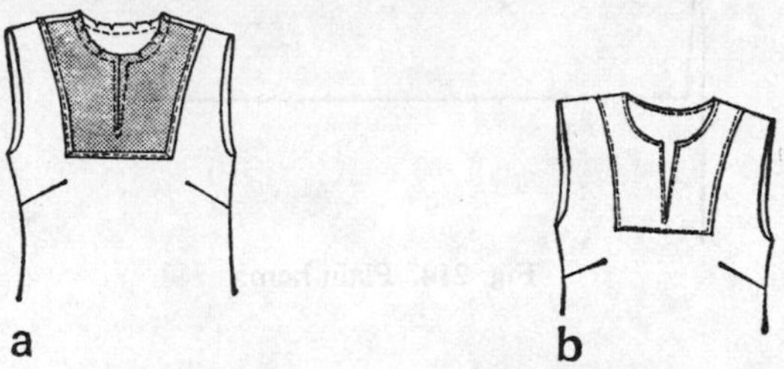

Fig. 211. (a) and (b): Reversed (decorative) facing.

Hems

As with most processes there are several methods, depending on the kind of fabric and type of garment. On all garments any slight fullness is caught in tiny pleats or tucks and evenly distributed.

Blindstitched Hem

The oversewn or zig-zagged raw edge and blindstitched hem is good for most types, as it holds the hem turning flat, so there is less possibility of a ridge or excess bulk showing on the right side.

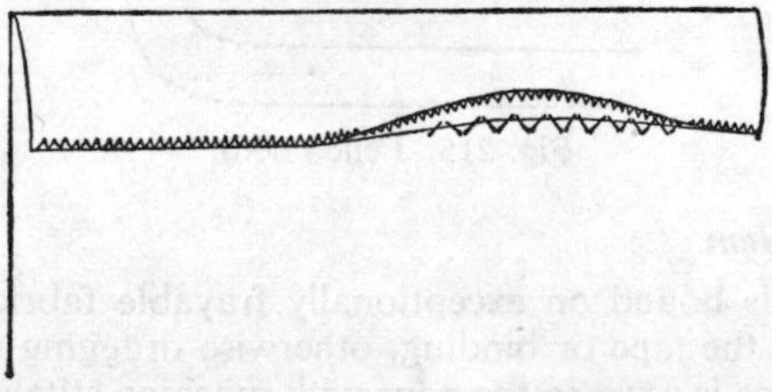

Fig. 212. Blindstitched hem.

Herringbone Hem

Turned up in the same way as the blindstitched hem, except that the raw edge does not have to be neatened first. The under-stitch of the herringbone is made through a thread or two of the fabric, the top stitch through the hem turning alone. A good hem again for most types of fabric.

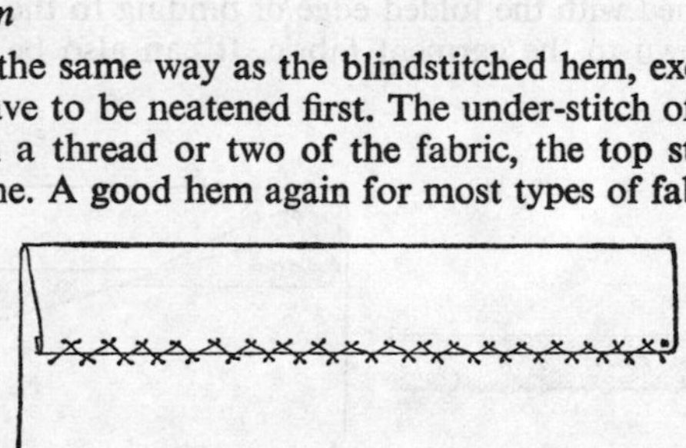

Fig. 213. Herringboned hem.

Plain Hem

This is mostly used now for detail finishing, on small hems on shirt sleeve openings, household linens or garments which have a lot of wear and washing, such as nightwear, overalls, etc.

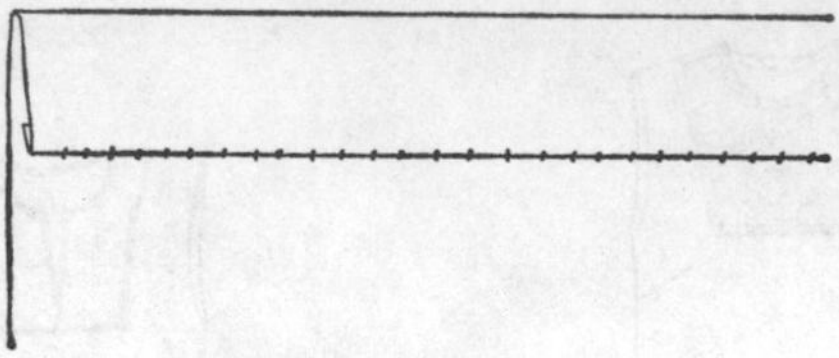

Fig. 214. Plain hem.

Felled Hem

A hem for linings and fine detail, on collars and handsewn pockets.

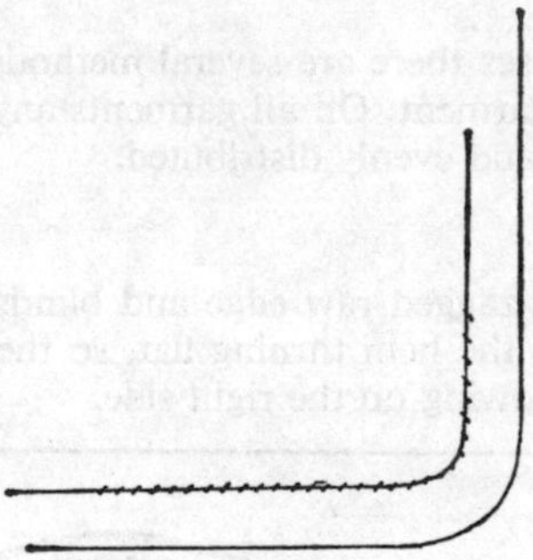

Fig. 215. Felled hem.

Taped or Bound Hem

The raw edge is bound on exceptionally frayable fabrics. Care must be taken not to pull the tape or binding, otherwise dragging will occur on the right side. The tape is sewn to the edge with machine stitching and the loose edge of tape is blindstitched to the garment fabric. Bias bound hems have the binding stitched with the folded edge of binding to the hem turning and the other fold sewn to the garment fabric. It can also be machined to the

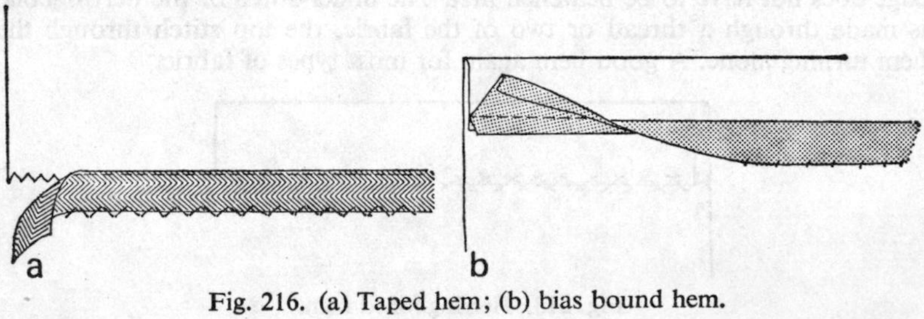

Fig. 216. (a) Taped hem; (b) bias bound hem.

edge to encase it totally and then slipstitched to the garment. This can cause a slight stretching on some fabrics.

Faced Hem

Sometimes called a false hem, this is made either when insufficient fabric has been allowed for a hem, or when it has to be let down. It is also a good way to finish a shaped hem.

Wide bias binding can be used, or a bias strip made from self or lining fabric, cut on the bias, and joined as shown in Fig. 217. The wide bias is sewn right sides together to the hem edge, pressed open and then the narrow hem fold on facing bias is slipstitched down.

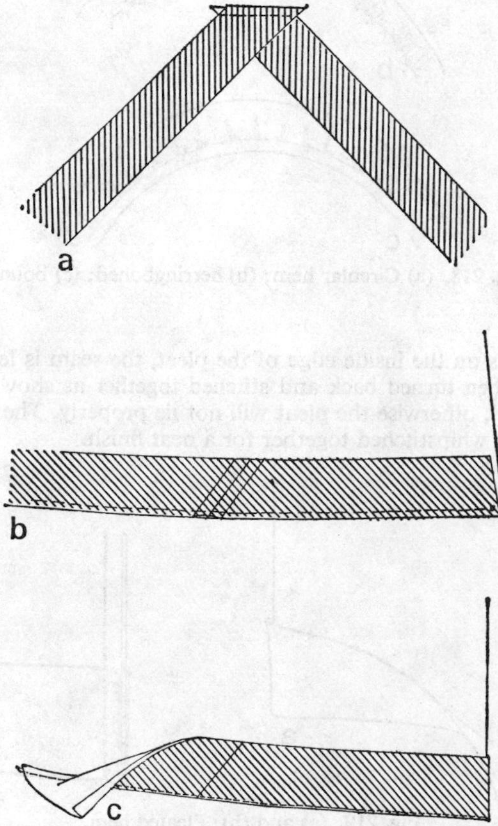

Fig. 217. (a) Bias strips joined; (b) sewn to hem edge; (c) slipstitched to fabric.

Circular Hem

This can be blindstitched, herringboned or bound. In all cases it must have the fullness evenly distributed and tacked in position, so as not to have uneven lumps in the turning. The turning allowance itself should only be about 2 cm (¾ in). A tack line along the hem edge, as well as near the turning, helps to make a better hem.

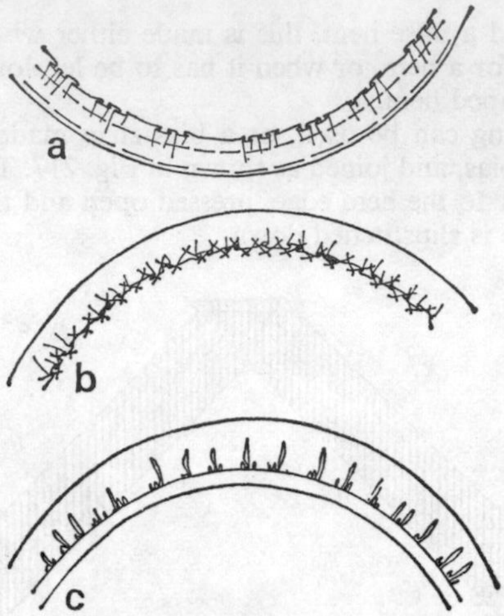

Fig. 218. (a) Circular hem; (b) herringboned; (c) bound.

Pleated Hem

If the seam is on the inside edge of the pleat, the seam is left open in the hem turning, then turned back and stitched together as shown in Fig. 219. This is essential, otherwise the pleat will not lie properly. The four layers at the hem can be whipstitched together for a neat finish.

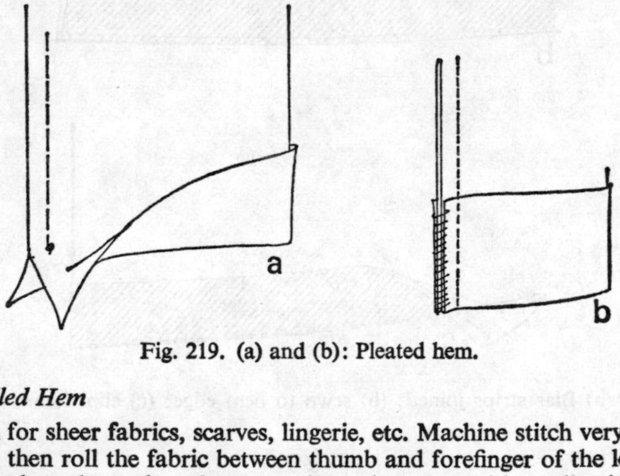

Fig. 219. (a) and (b): Pleated hem.

Hand-rolled Hem

A hem for sheer fabrics, scarves, lingerie, etc. Machine stitch very close to the edge, then roll the fabric between thumb and forefinger of the left hand, several inches along the edge at a time, then sew with a slipstitch, or a whipstitch.

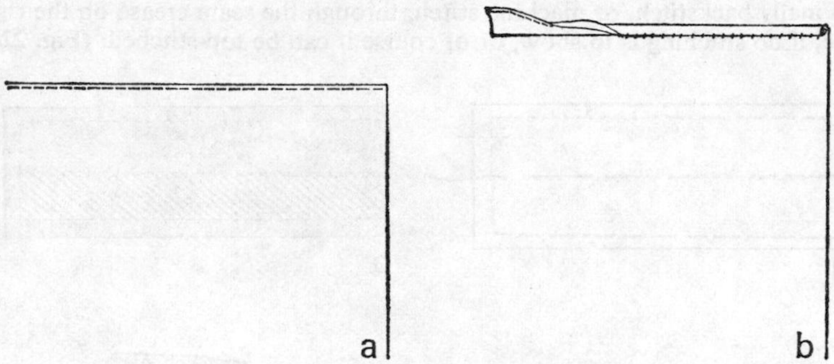

a b

Fig. 220. (a) and (b): Hand-rolled hem.

Waistbands

One simple way of making and sewing on a waistband has been explained on page 97, here are other ways of making and attaching waistbands to skirts and trousers.

Top-Stitched

Using a similar method but with a machine finish instead of handsewing it to the inside, the waistband is stitched first to the inside of the seam, right side of band to the inside of the skirt or trouser waist. Then it is turned to the outside and top-stitched to the waist seam on the right side. (Fig. 221.)

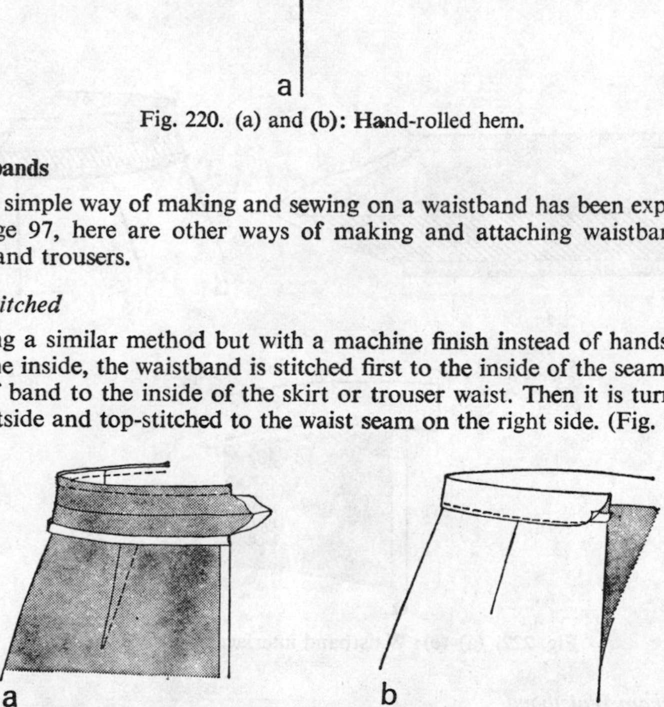

a b

Fig. 221. (a) and (b): Waistband topstitched.

Waistband Interfaced with Canvas

This method is used on thicker fabrics. On the waistband piece, the seam allowances and the centre fold line are marked. An interfacing piece of canvas is cut to the finished size of the waistband. Tack this to the band on the wrong side, with one edge to the centre fold line, and lightly stitch this to the band fabric or machine stitch 3 mm ($\frac{1}{8}$ in) from the centre line through the canvas. Finish the ends of the band as on page 97 and also neaten the seam allowance on the canvassed side of the band, which will be left loose and not turned in, to make less bulk at the waist.

Stitch the waistband with the unfaced side, right side to right side of waist, turn band to inside, and tack to the waist seam inside, leaving the neatened edge just below the seam.

Finally backstitch, or machine stitch, through the seam crease on the right side, if no stitching is to show, or of course it can be top-stitched. (Fig. 222.)

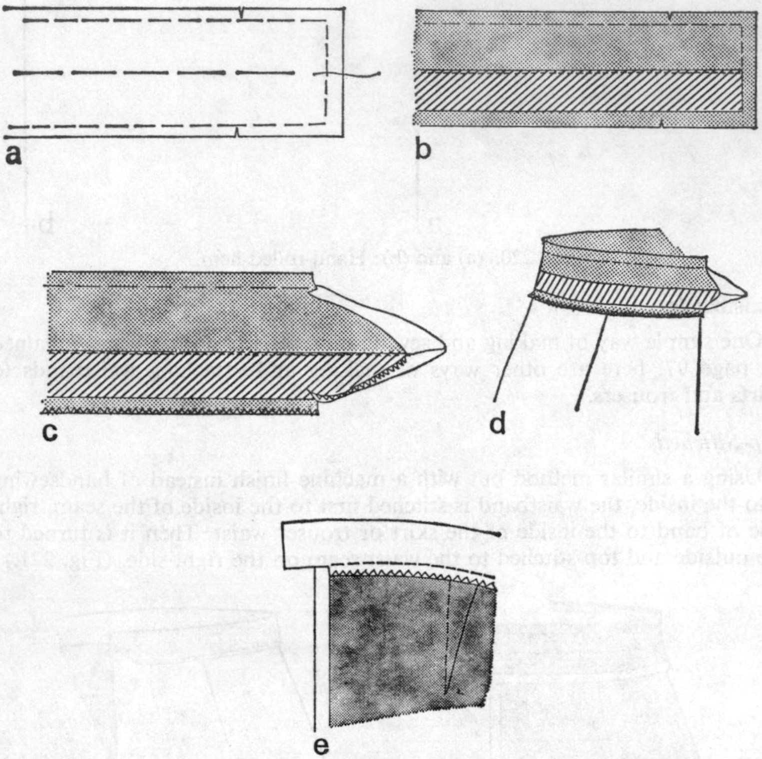

Fig. 222. (a)–(e): Waistband interfaced with canvas.

Petersham Waistband

This is a neat and easy to apply finish, suitable for a skirt where no waistband needs to show, or on thin fabrics.

Petersham can be bought already curved or, if not, straight petersham can be gently stretched along one edge to make a slight curve. This is done by pressing the band under a damp cloth with a warm iron. This curve helps as it sits well in the natural waist curve.

Lay the unstretched or smaller curved edge of the band to the waist seam, the other edge away from the skirt. Turn in the ends and edge stitch the band to the waist seam. Clip the fabric seam allowance. Turn the band to the inside and press, so the band does not show on the right side. An additional row of machine stitching can be made at the top through the fabric and band, on the right side.

With the band edges meeting edge-to-edge, hooks and eyes can be sewn on. (Fig. 223.)

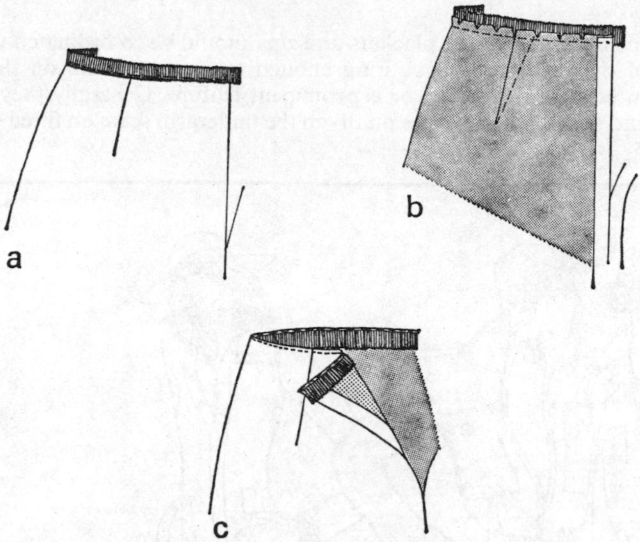

Fig. 223. (a), (b) and (c): Petersham waistband.

Waistband Finishes

More ways to finish the ends of a self-fabric band.

With a buttonhole. If this is a bound type, it must be made before the ends are sewn together.

Curved or tab ends. The tab point is stitched, right sides together as a plain end. The point and sides are trimmed and then turned through. A curved end is stitched and the curve is carefully notched so the end will be even and smooth. (Fig. 224.)

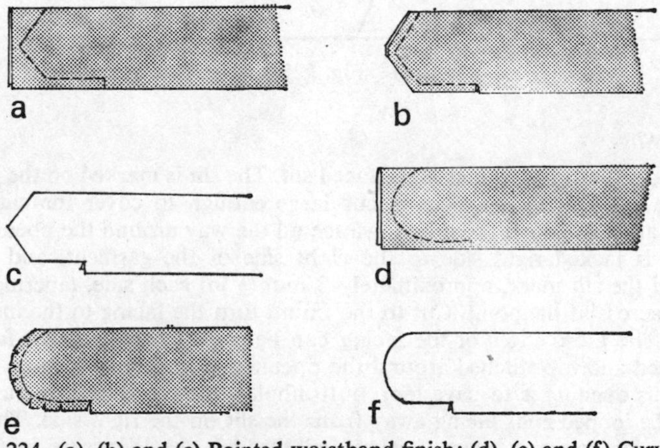

Fig. 224. (a), (b) and (c) Pointed waistband finish; (d), (e) and (f) Curved waistband finish.

Openings

The openings, fastenings, plackets and zips should be co-ordinated with the design of the garment, and be long enough to prevent strain on the ends. They can be nearly invisible, or a prominent feature. Generally they are on sleeves and necks, but are occasionally in the underarm seam on fitted clothes.

Fig. 225.

Faced Slit

The simplest of openings is the **faced slit.** The slit is marked on the garment or sleeve and a facing piece is cut large enough to cover the slit length. Leave at least 3·8 cm (1½ in) allowance all the way around the opening. The facing is tacked right side to the right side of the garment, and stitched around the slit mark, approximately 3 mm (⅛ in) each side, tapering to one stitch across at the point. Cut to the point, turn the facing to the inside and press. The loose edges of the facing can be sewn to the garment fabric, or neatened and top-stitched around the opening. (Fig. 226.)

If this opening is to have loop buttonholes, these can be made and sewn with the looped ends facing away from the slit on the right side. The facing is sewn on top and when it is turned through the loops are in position. (Fig. 227.)

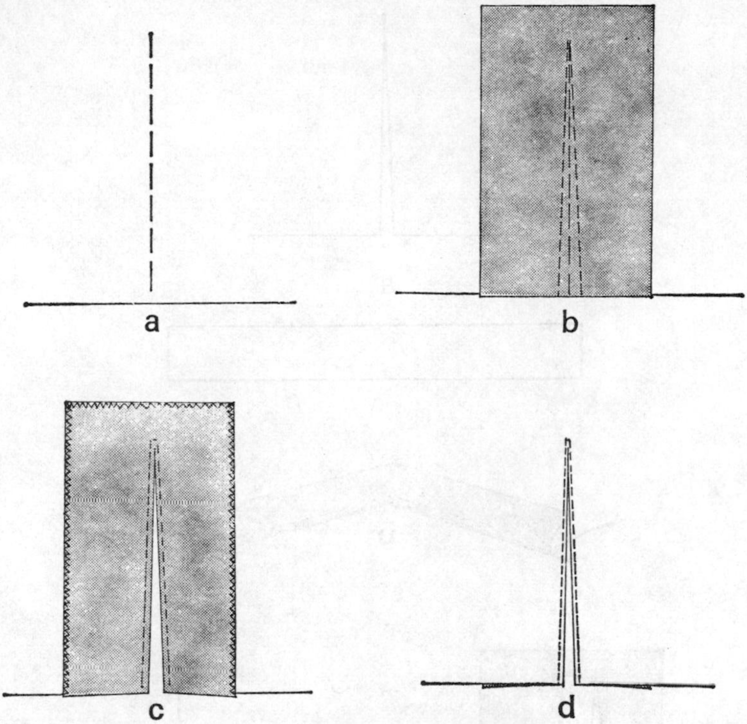

Fig. 226. (a)–(d): Faced slit opening.

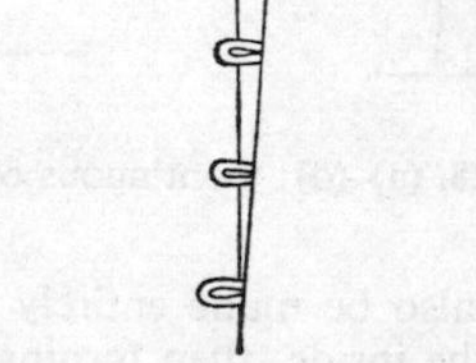

Fig. 227. Loop buttonholes.

Continuous Opening

This time the slit is cut first. A piece of fabric is cut, preferably on the bias, twice the length of the opening and about 3·5 cm (1⅜ in) wide. The slit is opened out and the strip laid along it, right sides together, and stitched, easing it over the point of the slit. Next, the strip is turned to the inside and a narrow hem turned in on it and then hemmed to the seam line.

The finished opening is pressed, so that the strip is folded inside, overlapping the underneath. (Fig. 228.)

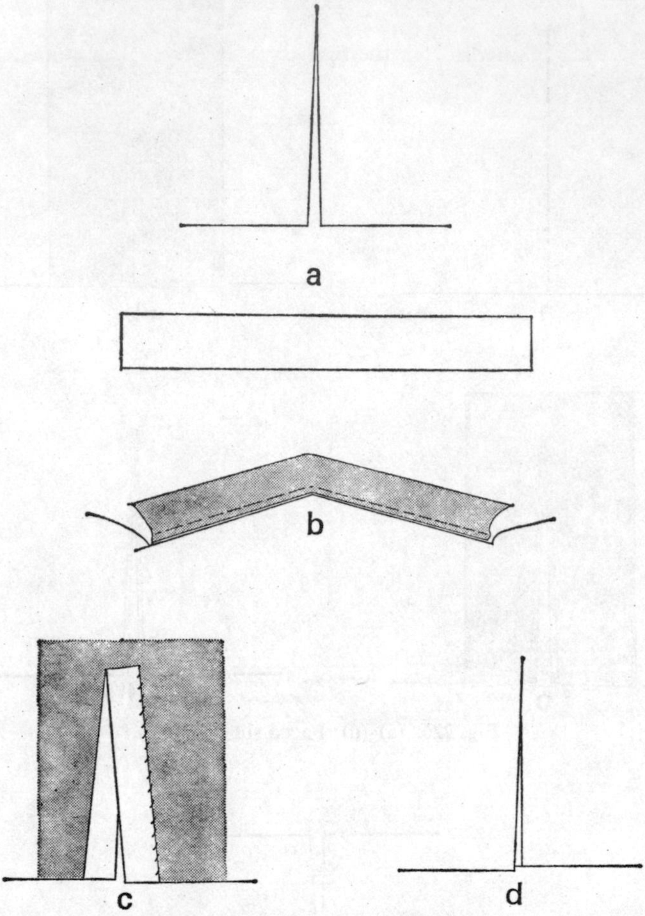

Fig. 228. (a)–(d): Continuous opening.

This same opening can also be made entirely with machine stitching, by stitching the strip first to the inside, then turning it to the outside and edge stitching it to the seam line.

Simple Tab Opening for Sleeves

Cut the opening. Cut a strip for a tab, 4 cm (1⅝ in) wide and at least 2 cm (¾ in) longer than the opening. Press in 1 cm (⅜ in) at one end and along one side of the strip.

On the underwrap side of the slit, make a very narrow hem. Lay the unpressed edge of the tab piece, right side down to the inside of the unstitched edge of the slit, the pressed end to the top of slit. Stitch this the length of the opening, then turn it to the right side and tack the pressed edge to the slit seam, making the tab end at the top neat and flat, overlapping the end of the opening and concealing it. Stitch along this tacked edge and around the tab end, easing in the fullness where the tab is pulled through at the top, or make a tiny pleat. (Fig. 229.)

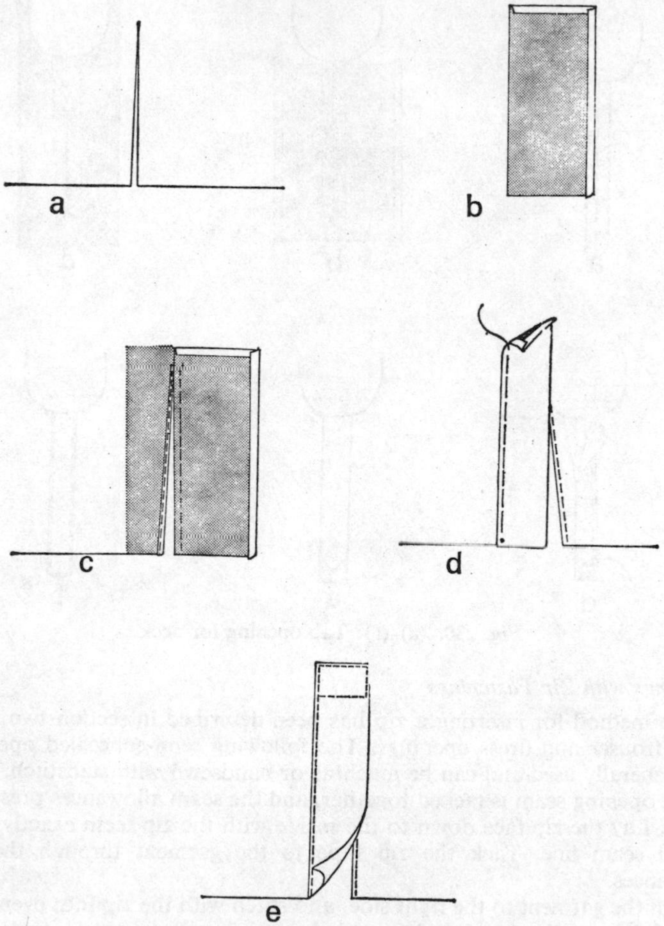

Fig. 229. (a)–(e): Tab opening for sleeve.

Tab for a Neck Opening

Cut two tab pieces, approximately 6 cm ($2\frac{3}{8}$ in) wide and 4 cm ($1\frac{5}{8}$ in) longer than the opening to be made. Stitch these each side of the marked opening, right sides to the right side of the garment, with a seam allowance of 1 cm ($\frac{3}{8}$ in).

Cut the opening, to within 1 cm ($\frac{3}{8}$ in) of the end, where it is clipped right into the corners of the stitching. The tabs are then turned through to the inside, again a seam allowance of 1 cm is turned in along each edge and sewn to the inside seam line of opening. The overlapping tab end is left on the right side, turned in neatly and stitched across the end, or shaped to a point, and top-stitched. (Fig. 230.)

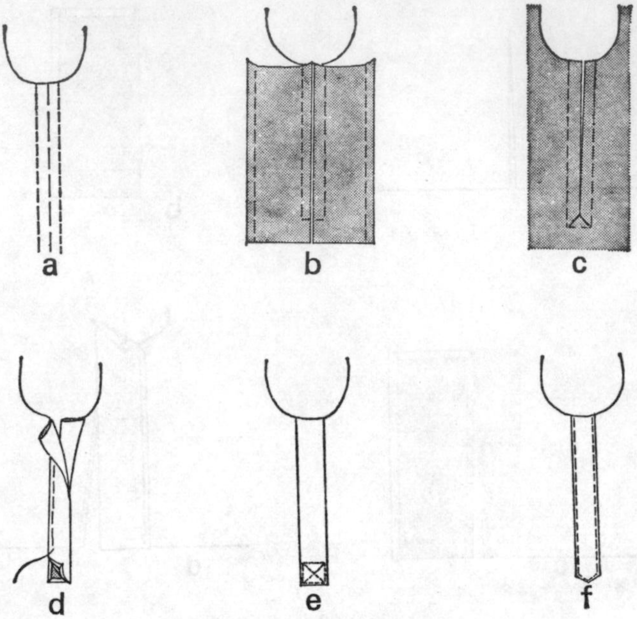

Fig. 230. (a)–(f): Tab opening for neck.

Openings with Zip Fastenings

One method for inserting a zip has been described in section two for the skirt, trouser and dress openings. The following semi-concealed opening is also generally used and can be machine or handsewn with stabstitch.

The opening seam is tacked together, and the seam allowances pressed flat inside. Lay the zip face down to the inside with the zip teeth exactly on the tacked seam line. Tack the zip tape to the garment through the seam allowances.

Turn the garment to the right side, and stitch with the zip foot evenly each side of the seam and across the end below the lower stop, press and remove the tack from the seam.

Alternatively the zip can be sewn with a stabstitch, which is better on the very fine, soft fabrics, or where machine stitching should not be visible. (Fig. 231.)

Inserting a zip in a fly front opening is a little more complicated as there are facing pieces sewn as well. On the trouser opening these are curved to fit the crutch seam, and special curved trouser zips are obtainable. For a straight fly opening a normal zip is suitable. Apart from the curved seam which must be clipped, the setting in is the same for both types.

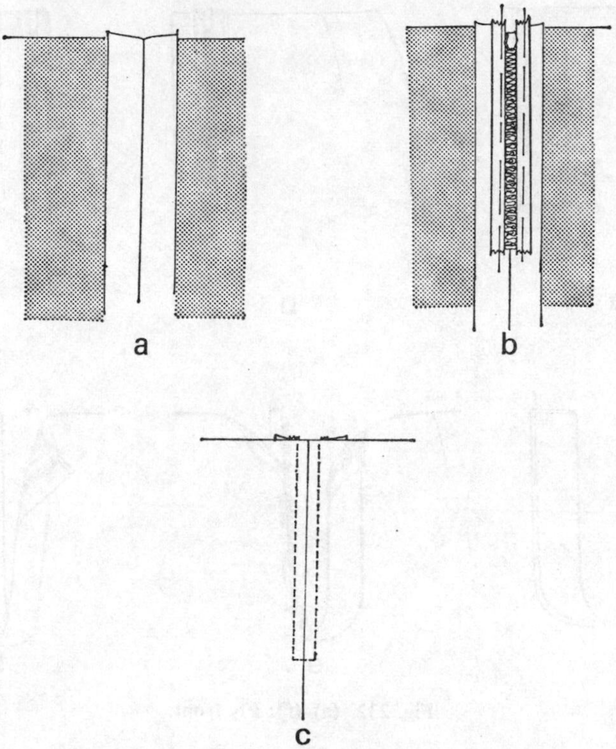

Fig. 231. (a), (b) and (c): Semi-concealed opening.

First stitch the shaped facing to the right side of the opening, clip and press the seam. Make the fly shield for the other side which is made from two facing pieces shaped like the one already stitched to the opening.

Lay the zip right side down on the faced side of the opening with one zip tape edge to the seam line, and the other towards the raw edge of facing.

Stitch this side of the tape, using the zip foot close to the zip teeth, and stitch again the same side but on the edge of the tape.

Turn the facing to the inside, tack and stitch it down, leaving the unstitched side of zip tape free.

Press in the other side of the opening, tack it over the free edge of the zip next to the teeth. Tack the fly shield behind this matching all the seam edges inside. Stitch through all the layers. Clip lower end of the seam, and make a few stitches in the same place at the end of the opening to strengthen. (Fig. 232.)

Pockets

These fall into three main groups.

(1) The patch pocket, with or without flap, which is set on the garment.

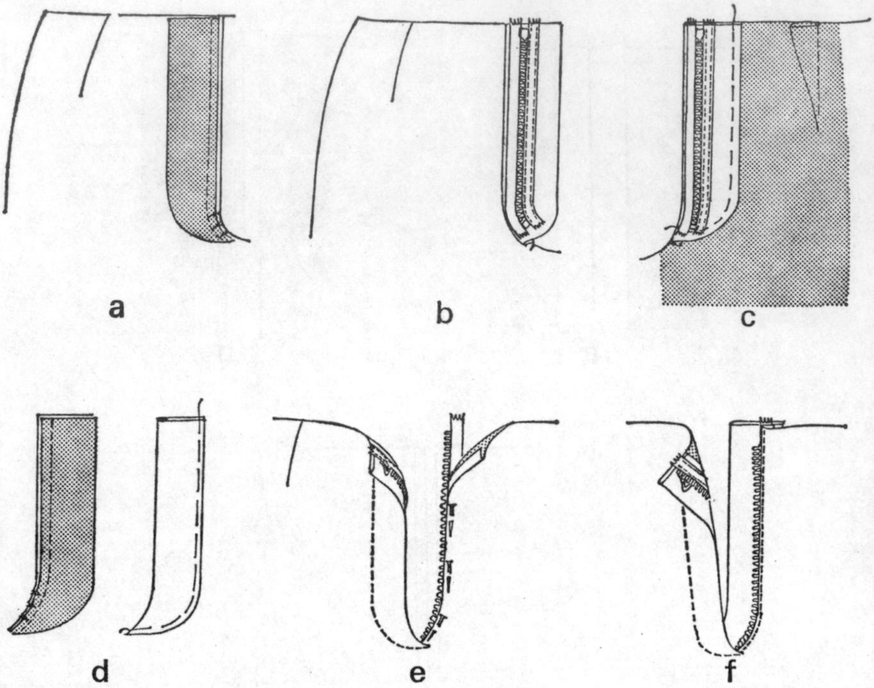

Fig. 232. (a)–(f): Fly front.

(2) The set-in pocket which has a special opening of one kind or another made in the garment.

(3) The pocket incorporated into a seam. As pockets are important decorations great care should be taken in placing and making them, so that they are well integrated in the design.

Pocket shapes and sizes can vary enormously but, as a general guide for size, top pockets are usually smaller than lower pockets.

Sizes generally vary for pockets on dresses, jackets, etc., from 9–15 cm (3½–6 in) and large patch pockets on coats and skirts from 20·5–25·5 cm (8–10 in).

Patch Pocket with Flap Cut in One

This is a simple variation of the basic patch pocket described on page 125. Interface the pocket on the wrong side, cut a facing to the shape of the flap plus 3·8 cm (1½ in) below the fold line. Machine stitch the flap facing to pocket, right sides together. Turn to the inside, under-press and tack back the turnings of the pocket. Herringbone stitch the raw edge of the flap on the inside. Hand stitch or top-stitch to garment.

To introduce further detail, the edges could be bound with contrast fabric or braid, or top-stitched in a contrasting coloured thread. (Fig. 234.)

Fig. 233

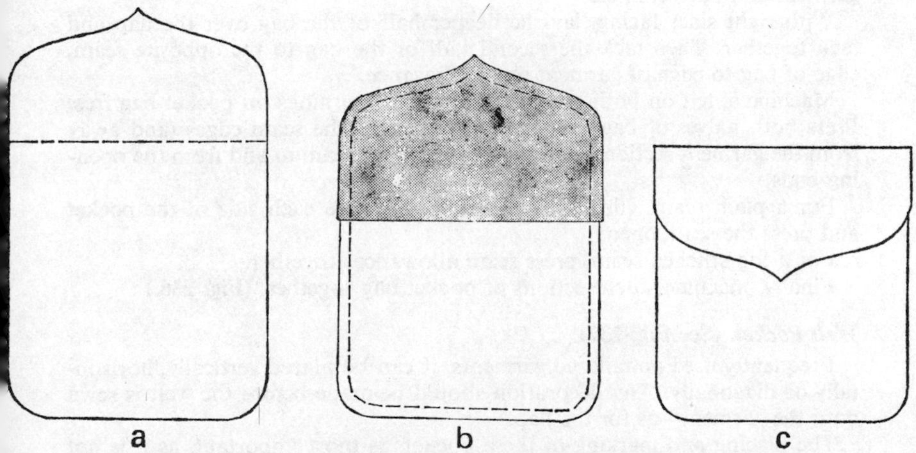

a b c

Fig. 234. (a), (b) and (c): Patch pocket with flap cut in one.

Pocket Set-in Seam (Concealed)

One of the easiest to make, it is often used on many types of garments.

Mark the pocket opening on both sides of the seam (use the widest part of your hand as a guide for width).

Cut a pocket bag with seam allowances in lining, or self fabric if it is a thinnish type, slightly longer than the opening (use your hand again to find the right depth).

Lay the two halves of the bag—raw edges level with edges of seam allowances—right sides together, and machine stitch to seam allowances (between seam line and seam-allowance edges of garments).

Press both halves of the pocket bag towards the seam edges and away from the garment sections, then place the garment seams right sides together and join up to, and from, the pocket-end markings, thus leaving a gap to form the opening.

Clip one side of seam allowances, above and below the pocket opening. Press the garment-seam allowances open and stitch the sections of the pocket bag together. Strengthen each end of the opening with small hand stitches. (Fig. 235.)

Pocket Set-in Seam, with a Flap. (See Fig. 236)

A similar method to the above is used for a seam pocket with a flap, which can be varied with top-stitching, buttonhole or other decorations, though all are made on the flap before and it is sewn into the seam of the garment.

Cut a pocket bag, one half deeper (by the width of the seam allowance) and slightly longer than the opening.

Cut flap pieces with seam allowances, interline on wrong side and machine stitch together. (Identical to the pocket flap on the coat design on page 136.) Turn through, press and, if it is to be decorated, do so now.

Mark the pocket opening on both seams of garment.

Lay the flap, unstitched edge between opening marks right sides together and level with the seam allowance edge of garment. Tack in position on the garment and flap seam line.

With right sides facing, lay the deeper half of the bag over the flap and tack together. Then tack the second half of the bag to the opposite seam, edge of bag to edge of garment seam allowance.

Machine stitch on both sections, leaving the turnings on pocket bag free. Press both halves of bag (not the flap) towards the seam edges (and away from the garment sections) and join the garment seam to and from the opening ends.

For a plain seam, clip into one seam allowance each side of the pocket and press the seam open.

For a top-stitched seam, press seam allowances together.

Finally, machine stitch sections of pocket bag together. (Fig. 236.)

Welt Pocket. (See Fig. 237)

Frequently used on tailored garments, it can be placed vertically, horizontally or diagonally. Any decoration should be made before the welt is sewn onto the garment—as for the flap.

The placing and marking of these pockets is most important, as it is not

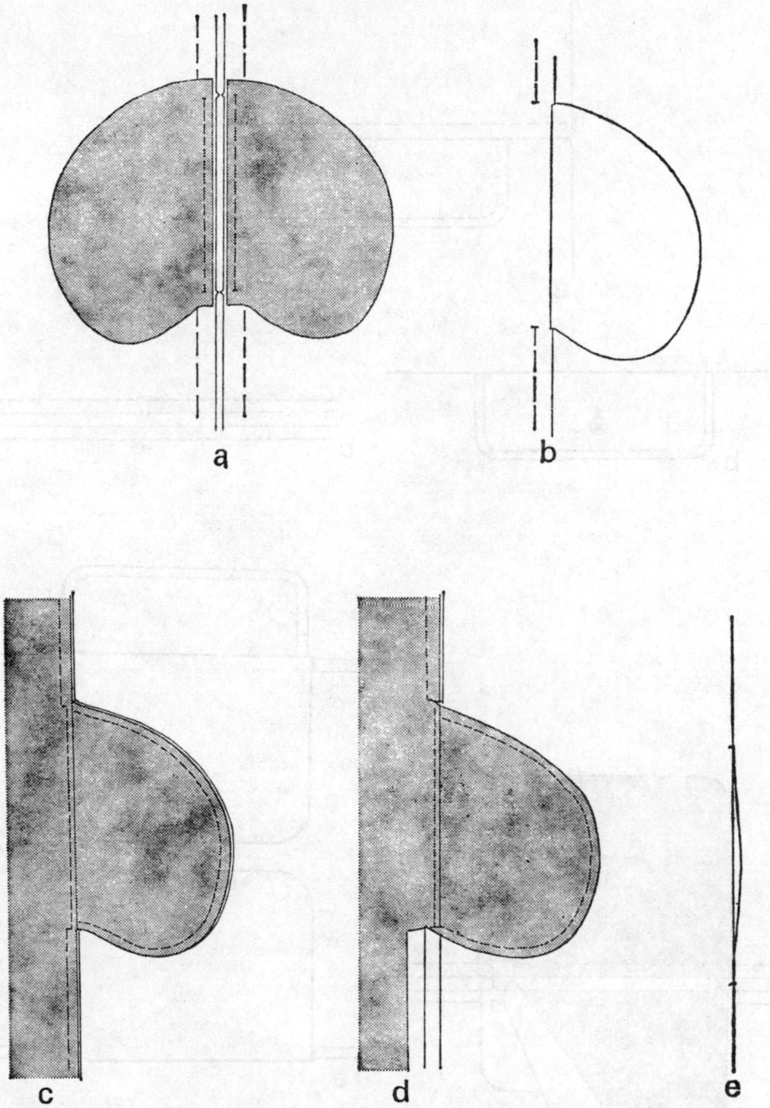

Fig. 235. (a)–(e): Pocket set in seam.

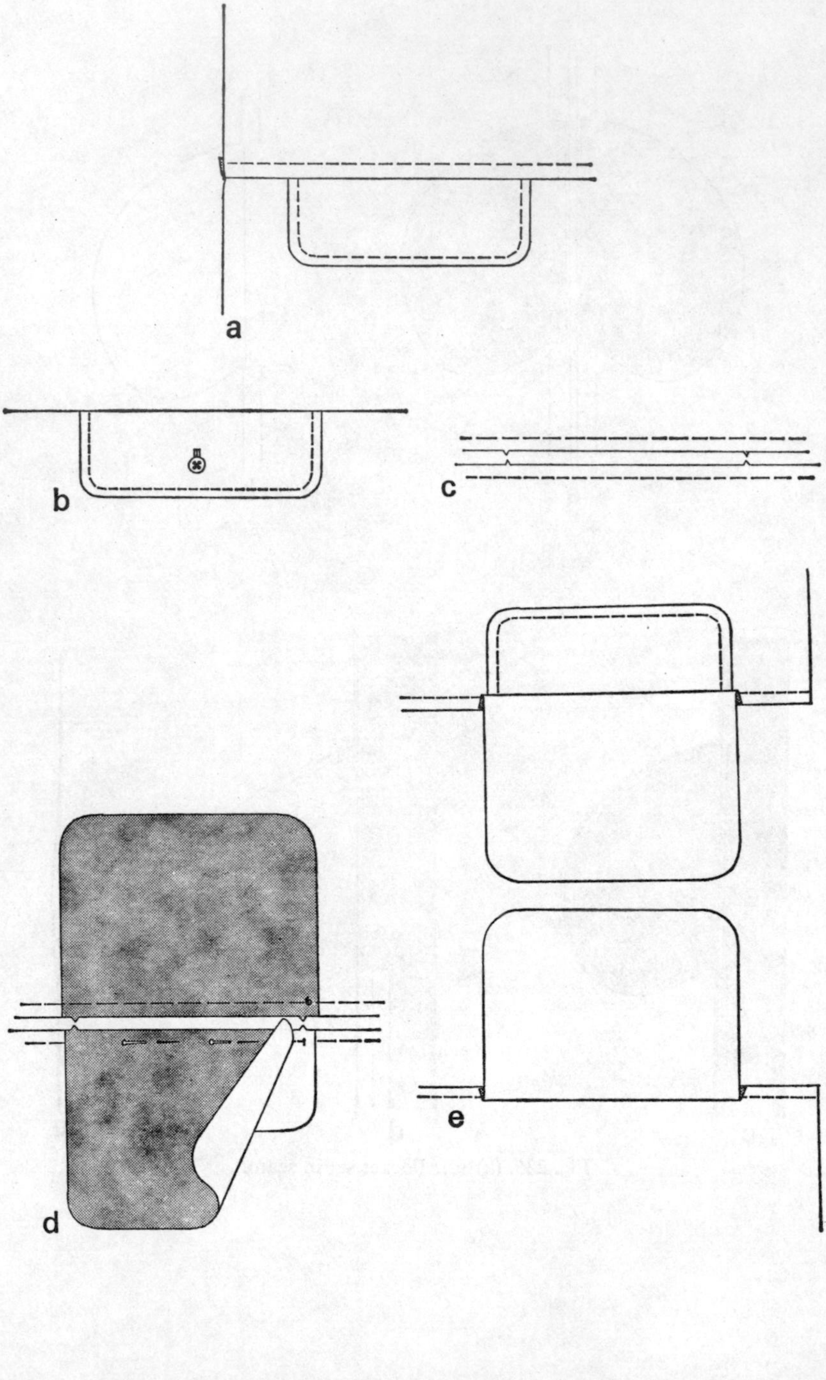
a
b
c
d
e

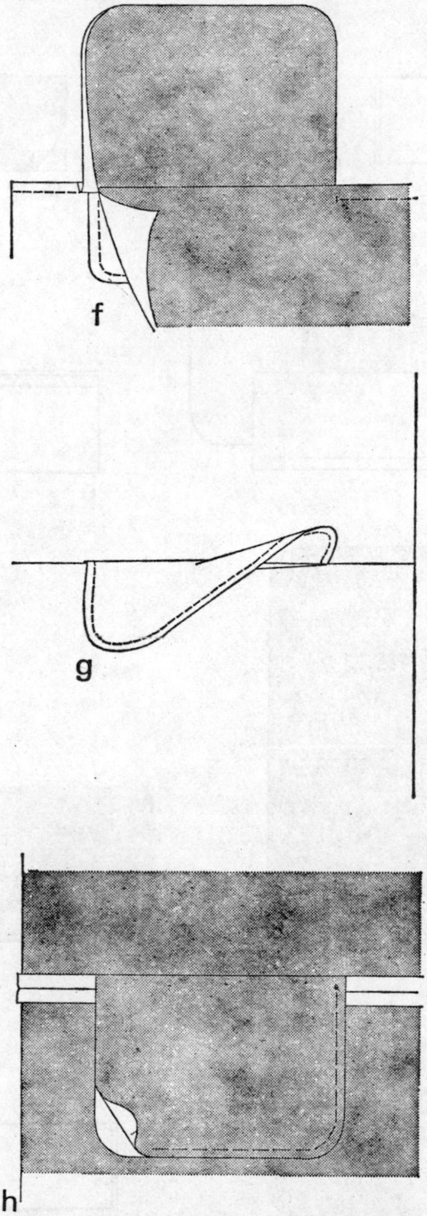

Fig. 236. (a)–(h): Pocket with flap set in seam.

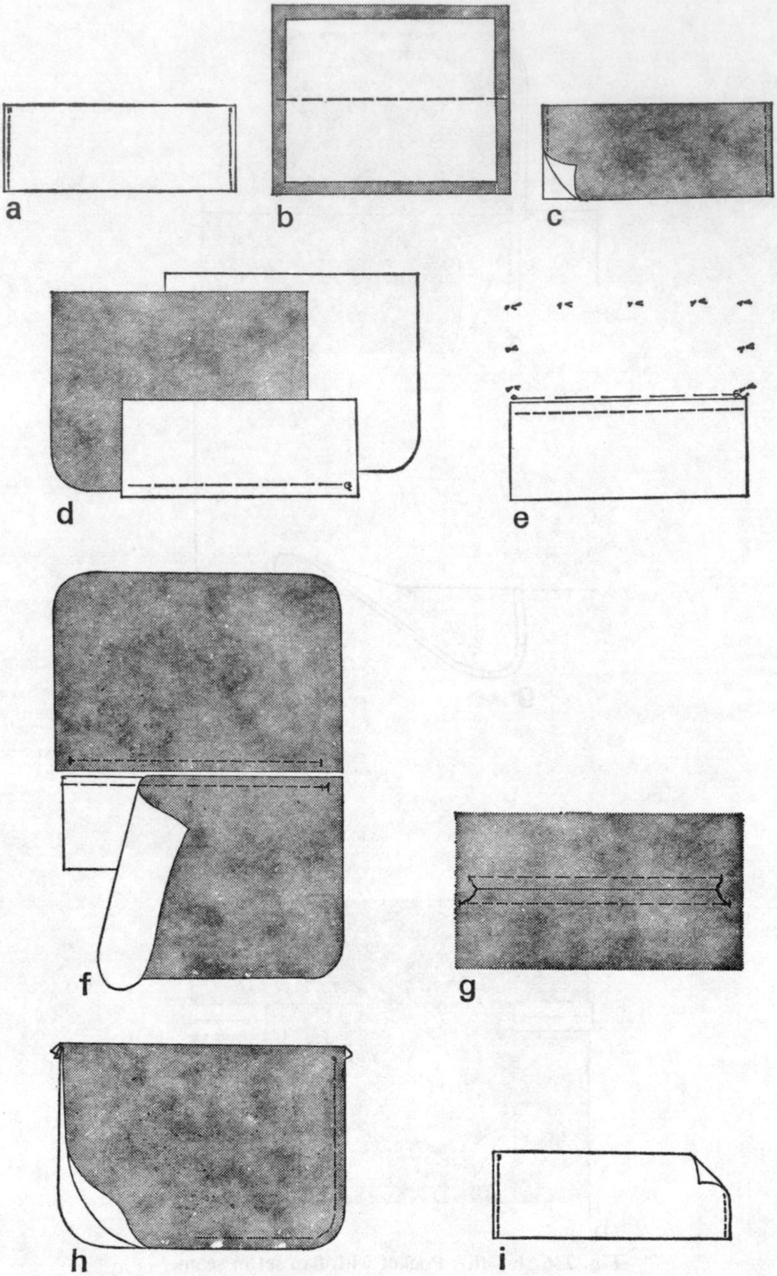

Fig. 237. (a)–(i) Welt pocket.

set into an existing seam, but has an opening cut through the garment so that mistakes are hard to rectify.

Mark the welt shape on the garment. Then mark a second line, just under 1 cm ($\frac{3}{8}$ in) above the welt line—call this the pocket line.

Cut the welt piece (twice the depth of the finished welt size, plus 1 cm ($\frac{3}{8}$ in) seam allowances all around, and equal to the length of the pocket opening. Interface on the wrong side. Fold this piece in half lengthwise, right sides together. Machine stitch each end, clip and trim seam allowances, turn through to the right side and press. Tack loose edges together.

Cut the pocket bag, with seam allowances, again slightly longer than the opening, one half deeper than the other.

Lay the welt piece, right side down, with raw edges to the pocket line (the folded edge facing lower edge of garment). Tack in position, then lay the deeper section of the bag above the welt, with opening edge to meet the welt edge. Lay the other half of the bag on top of the welt, the opening edge level with the welt edge, again to meet the pocket line.

Machine stitch along the welt seam through all layers, but stitch the top line (bag section only) slightly shorter at both ends. This prevents the ends of opening from showing when the welt is turned up and in final position.

Cut into the pocket line and diagonally into corners (as for piped buttonhole on page 138).

Pull bags through to the wrong side and machine stitch or hand neaten the ends of pocket opening. Press the seams, turn the welt up and stabstitch or machine stitch welt ends to the garment. Finally, sew the pocket sections of the bag together. (Fig. 237.)

Flap Pocket

Almost the same method used for the welt makes this pocket. The basic differences being that the flap is sewn above the pocket line as it faces downwards—instead of below the pocket line for the welt, which faces upwards.

As before, first make up the flap, then pin right side to right side of garment, with the tacked edge to the pocket line and the finished edge facing away from the pocket marking. Sew the deeper bag section on top, exactly over the flap, the seam allowance extending beyond the flap each end. Machine stitch the length of the finished flap.

Sew the lower pocket bag on, with opening edge to pocket line below the flap, all these edges to meet.

Stitch the lower section slightly shorter, again to ensure that the ends of the opening do not show when the flap is turned down. Cut between the stitching and, diagonally to the corners, pull the pocket bags through to the wrong side. Machine stitch or hand neaten the ends of the opening and stitch the pocket bag together. Then press flap down in position on the right side. (Fig. 238.)

Piped/Jetted Pocket

Very much like a piped buttonhole opening, with the addition of a pocket bag.

Mark the opening on the garment. Cut piping strips at least 3·2 cm ($1\frac{1}{4}$ in) wide, and slightly longer than the pocket opening.

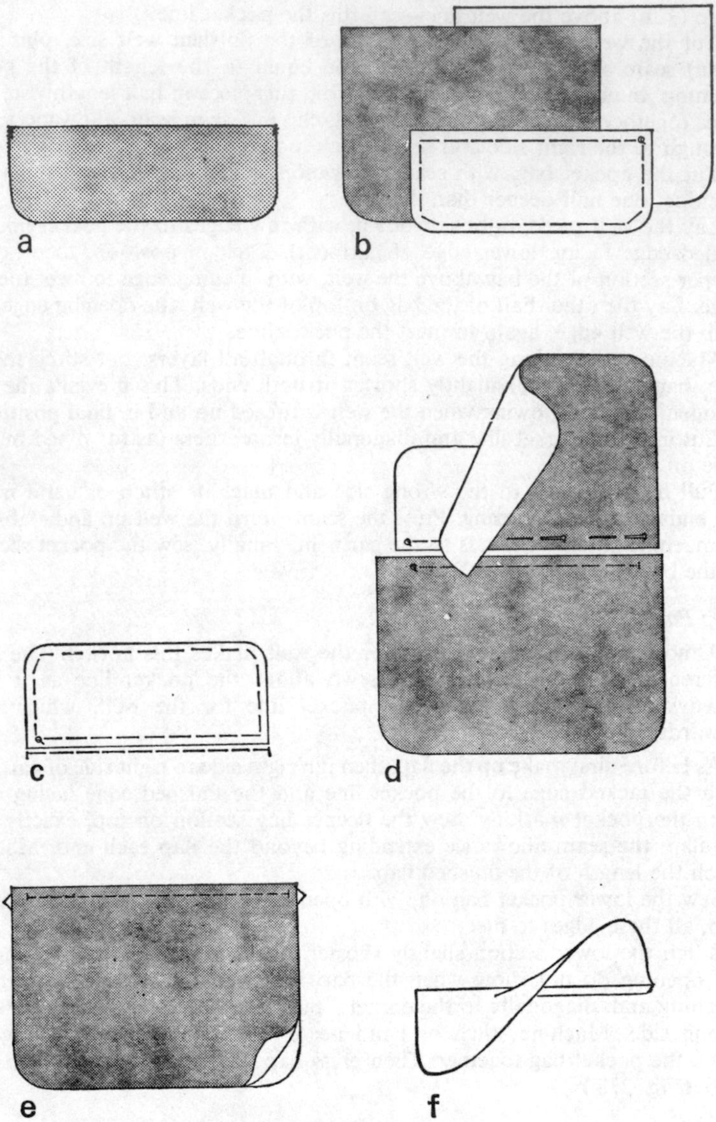

Fig. 238. (a)–(f): Flap pocket.

Cut two sections to form the pocket bag, one of them 1 cm ($\frac{3}{8}$ in) deeper than the other.

Fold piping strips in half, right sides out and tack along the centre of each strip. Lay each piping strip, with raw edges to pocket marking, on the right side.

Place and tack pocket bag with opening edge to pocket line—the deeper section to top. Machine stitch on tacked line. Cut into pocket line, and diagonally into corners. Turn through, press and stitch ends of piping. Lastly, join seam allowances of the pocket bag together and machine or hand stitch the ends of the pocket opening on the right side. (Fig. 239.)

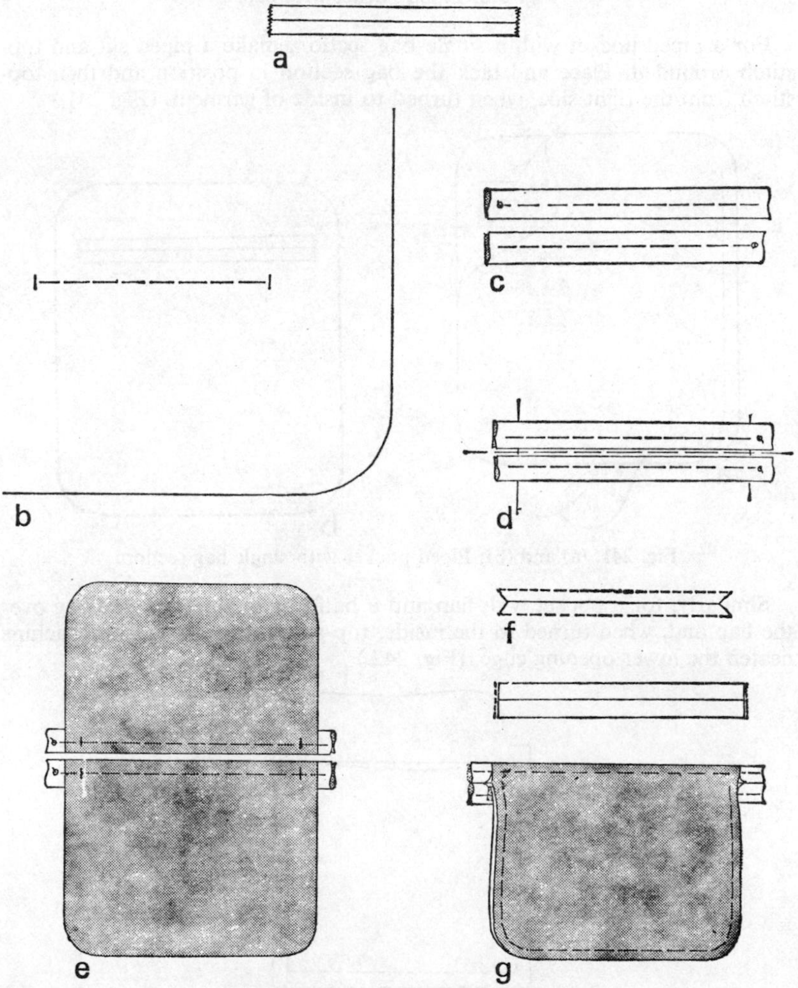

Fig. 239. (a)–(g): Piped/jetted pocket.

Pocket Variations

The pockets so far described can be easily combined to produce variations. The first example is the flap with piping.

Before stitching the flap and bag, lay the prepared piping strips with raw edges to the pocket line. Then continue as for the flap pocket. (Fig. 240.)

Fig. 240. Piped pocket with flap.

For a piped pocket with a single bag section, make a piped slit and top-stitch around it. Place and tack the bag section in position and then top-stitch from the right side, when turned to inside of garment. (Fig. 241.)

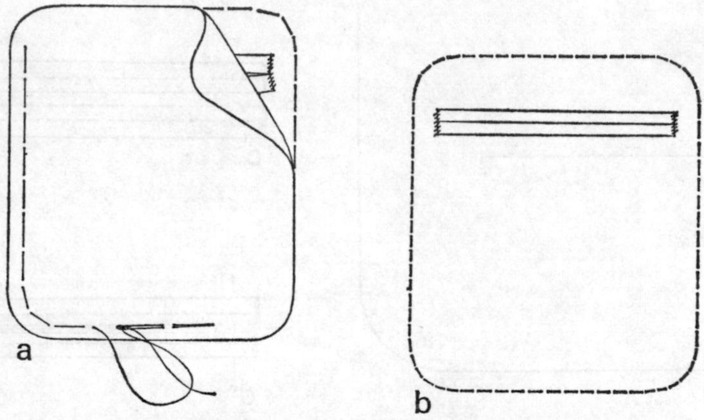

Fig. 241. (a) and (b): Piped pocket with single bag section.

Similarly, for a pocket with flap and a half bag section, sew the bag over the flap and, when turned to the inside, top-stitch to the garment. Machine neaten the lower opening edge. (Fig. 242.)

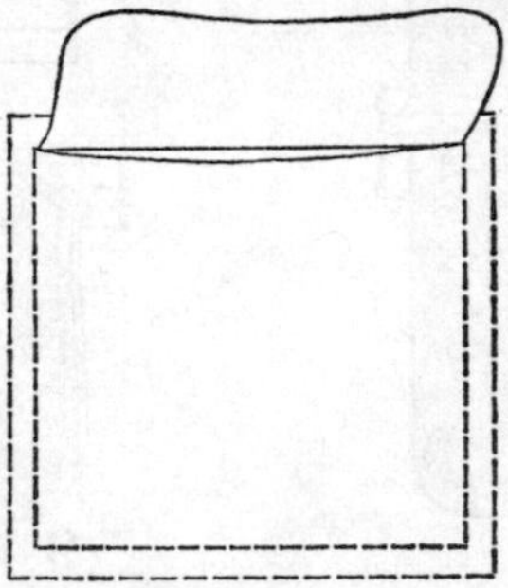

Fig. 242. Pocket with flap and single bag section.

Front Hip Pocket

This pocket is made before the side seams are joined. The pocket edge should be staystitched first, then interfaced on the wrong side to stop stretching and to keep the shape.

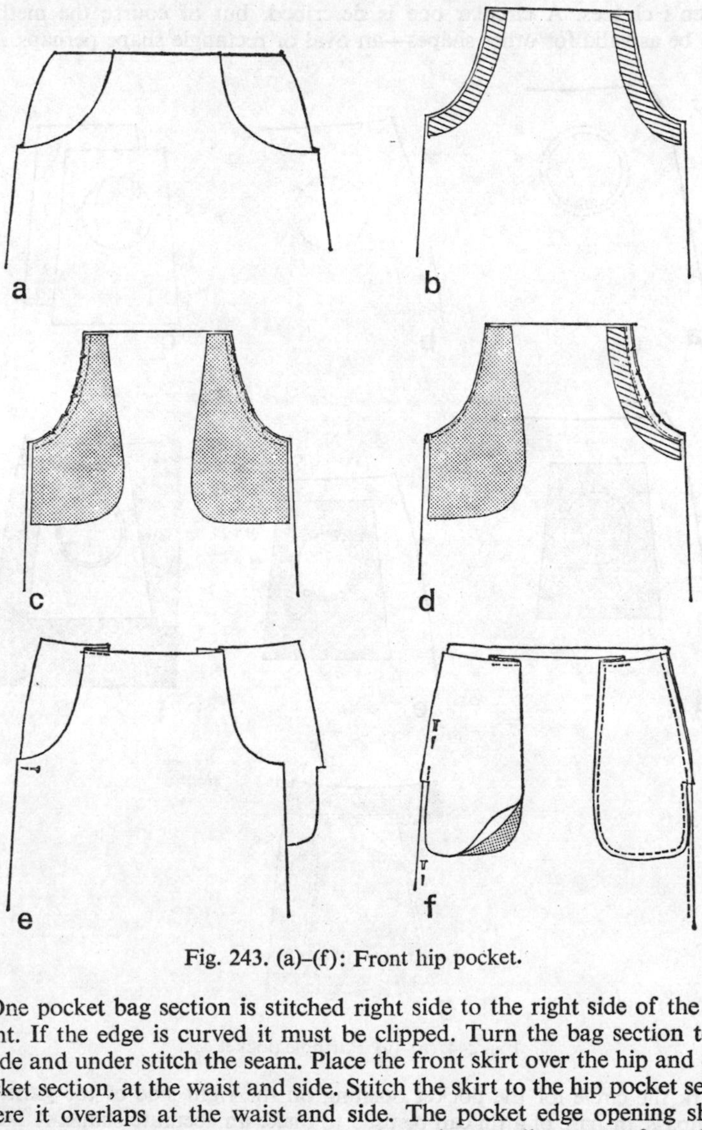

Fig. 243. (a)–(f): Front hip pocket.

One pocket bag section is stitched right side to the right side of the skirt front. If the edge is curved it must be clipped. Turn the bag section to the inside and under stitch the seam. Place the front skirt over the hip and other pocket section, at the waist and side. Stitch the skirt to the hip pocket section where it overlaps at the waist and side. The pocket edge opening should stand slightly away from the underneath section to allow room for a hand. Stitch the pocket bag sections together and join the front to the back skirt. (Fig. 243.)

Porthole Pocket

Finally, a very decorative, but simple to make pocket called a **porthole pocket.** This can have piping cord inserted round the edge and a contrast fabric or embroidered backing to the pocket, which makes it popular for children's clothes. A circular one is described, but of course the method would be as valid for other shapes—an oval or rectangle shape perhaps.

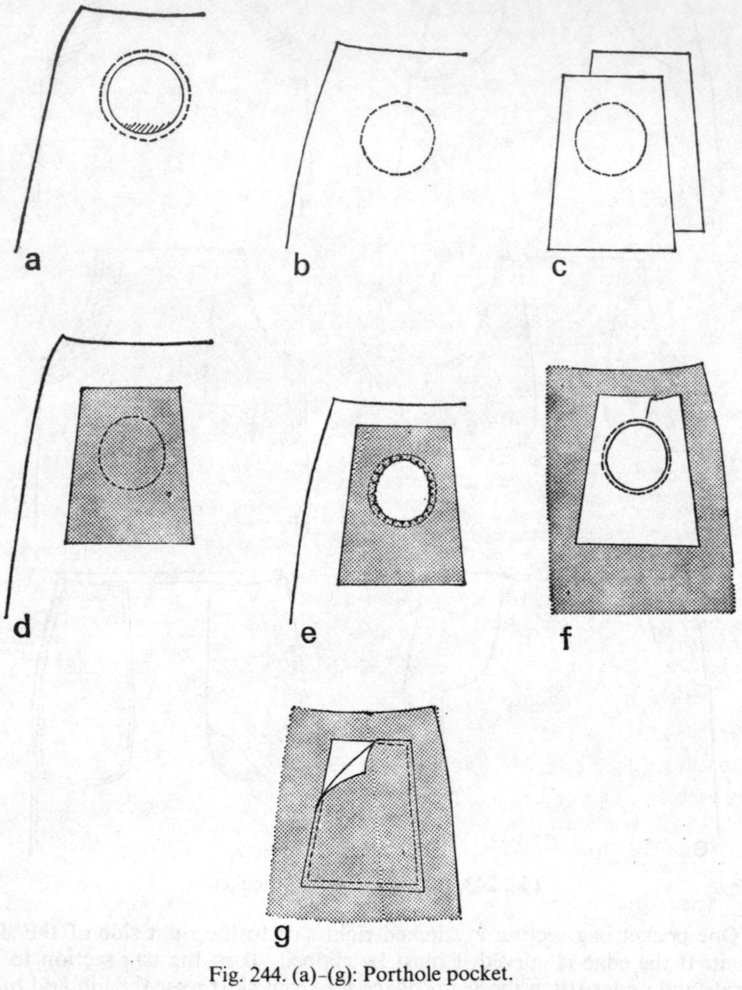

Fig. 244. (a)–(g): Porthole pocket.

Mark the circle for the pocket opening on the right side of the garment. A compass, or base of a tin can be used to make an accurate shape. A facing piece, and pocket bag, are cut large enough to contain the circle plus an allowance of at least 5 cm (2 in) on three sides, and a much deeper allowance on the lower edge to make the pocket bag. The pocket opening is marked on the facing piece, and laid right side down to the right side of the garment, matching the pocket opening. Tack in position and stitch.

Cut away the centre of the circle, leaving a seam allowance of 1 cm ($\frac{3}{8}$ in) and clip this in turn to the stitching line. On the circle shape this will have to be clipped at every centimetre, to allow the seam allowance to turn back neatly.

The facing is turned to the inside, pressed back, and the edge is top-stitched. The back pocket bag section is then sewn to the facing edge inside. (Fig. 244.)

Porthole Pocket with a Raised Edge. For a piped edge, which gives a raised effect, the cord is sewn in when the facing has just been turned through to the inside. The cord is laid between the facing and the garment fabric, right next to the stitching line on the inside. Push it well up to the seam and tack it in position, keeping the facing well to the inside. This will give a good raised edge. Stitch on the tacking line with the zip foot, which can lay close to the cord keeping it firm.

Then the pocket is finished exactly the same way as the previous one. (Fig. 245.)

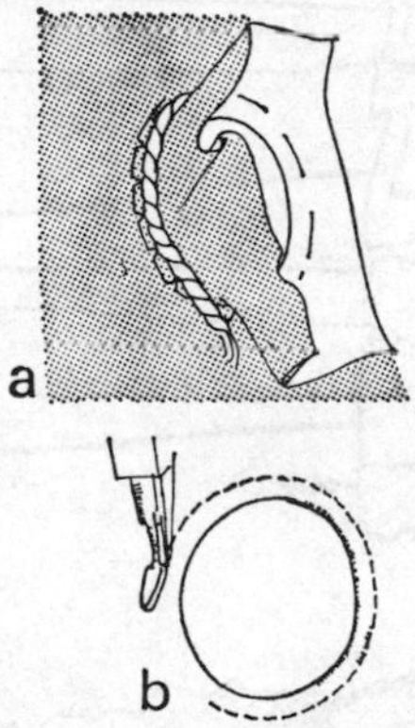

Fig. 245, (a) and (b): Porthole pocket with raised edge.

Buttons and Buttonholes

These, like many other processes of dressmaking, fulfil a functional purpose, while at the same time being decorative. The choice of size and type is most important, as badly placed or sized buttons can spoil an otherwise good garment.

There are two main types of hand-made buttonholes, bound (or piped) and worked. Machine-made buttonholes are made on basically the same principle. Bound ones have the edges finished with fabric, worked ones are made with thread. Bound, like the piped version on the coat design on page 136, are made on the garment with an interfacing only and faced afterwards. Worked buttonholes are cut and sewn through the garment, interfacing, and facing, when the garment is finished.

The buttonholes described are: bound; as loops (rouleau); tailor-worked; as thread loops; and set-in seam buttonholes.

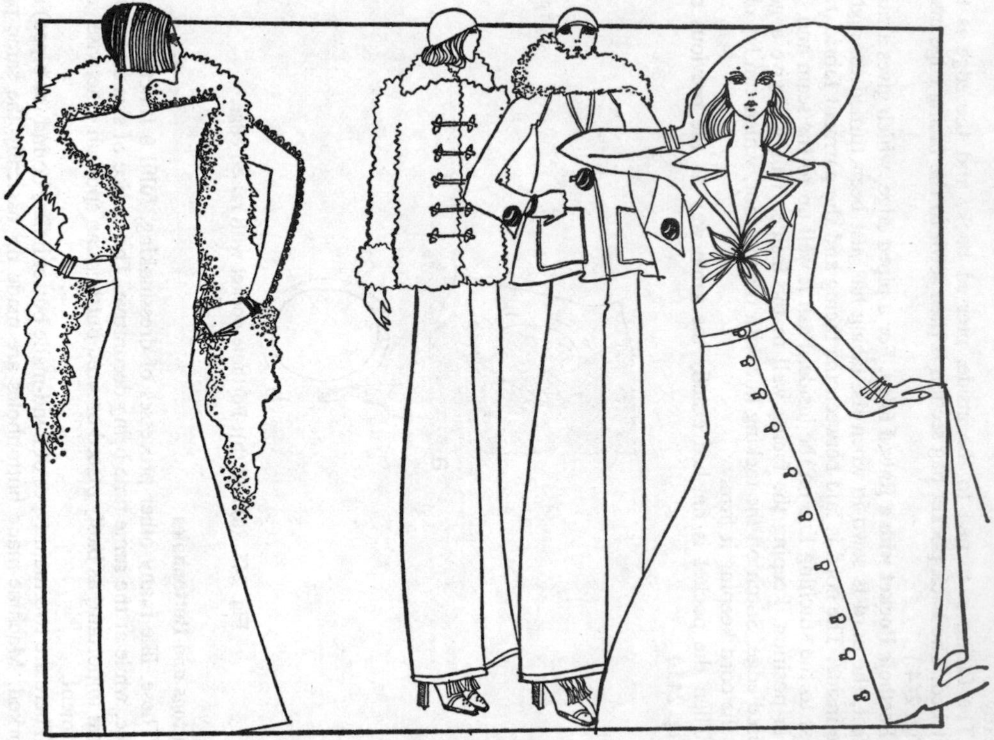

Fig. 246

Button Ligne

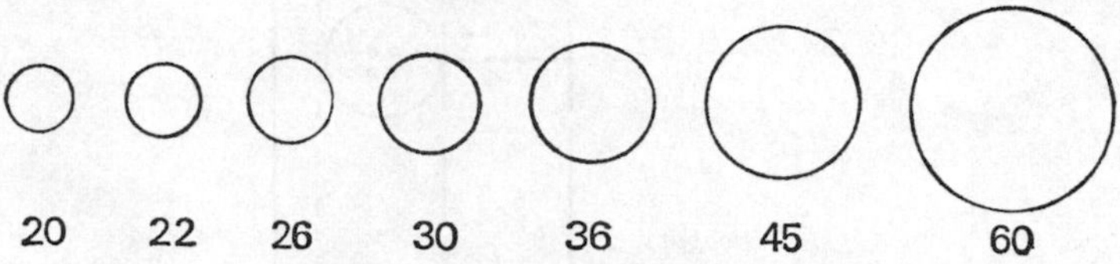

Fig. 247. Button 'lignes' (half actual size).

Button sizes are known by 'ligne' sizes—a small measurement first used probably in the eighteenth century—which refers to button lines as, for example, line 36 or 45, this term being the standard measurement for all buttons. The average sizes shown in Fig. 247, and all others, correspond to the metric and imperial measures of the button diameter.

Further button varieties, amongst other forms of fastenings are described on page 274.

Button Placing

Before making buttonholes, it is essential to have the button and wrap allowances properly placed, to keep the balance of the design. The making of a piped buttonhole and a simple worked one, has been demonstrated on the coat and shirt in previous chapters, but there are basic rules about placing them which apply to all. It is worthwhile to mention them again, so that they become well known, particularly if button markings are left off patterns, or when adapting.

There must be a sufficient allowance between buttons and holes for fastening to avoid gaping at openings. They must be placed evenly. They must be large enough, without being clumsy—bearing in mind that the buttonhole must be 3 mm ($\frac{1}{8}$ in) longer than the button, to allow it to slip through without strain and allow room for the button shank.

The button wrap allowance measured from the centre front to the opening edge, or inwards from any opening edge on side fastenings, should always be at least half the size of the button, plus 1 cm ($\frac{3}{8}$ in), which often corresponds to the actual size of the button. This allowance is essential to ensure that the button does not fasten off centre, or overlap the edge of the opening. Buttonholes can be placed vertically or horizontally across centre lines. Placed horizontally they are more practical, as garments so fastened do not tend to gape when used with average size buttons. The vertical position is used mainly on tab and shirt fastenings. An added help is to make a cardboard template of the button size, as a check for accurate placing.

From the centre front/back line, the wrap allowance is measured to the edge, with a seam allowance or grown-on facing added to this (see Fig. 248).

Parallel to the centre front/back line, and on the opposite side to it, an edge line is marked, according to the width of the button. The distance from the top neck edge to the first buttonhole is also equal to the button width (if applicable according to the design). Horizontal buttonhole lines are marked between the centre front line and the parallel line to it, but should extend 3 mm ($\frac{1}{8}$ in) beyond the centre line into the wrap, to allow for the shank.

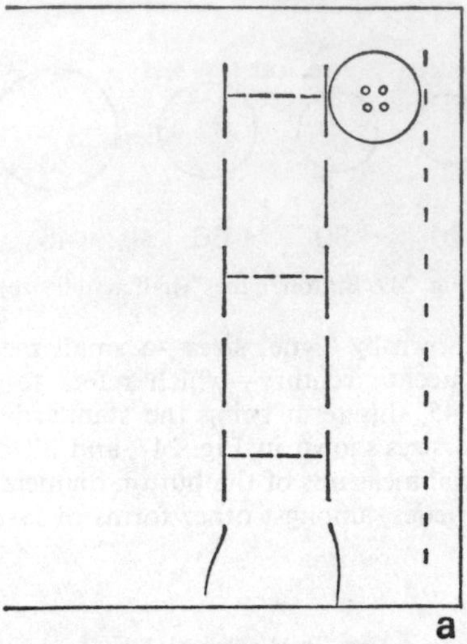

Fig. 248. Button placing.

For a double-breasted fastening, decide on the width of the wrap and follow the general principles of a single fastening. Mark the centre front line and measure and mark the wrap, to the edge of the opening, allowing a button width to the beginning of the first row of buttonholes. On the opposite side of the centre front line, mark the beginning of holes exactly the same distance away from it. (Fig. 249.)

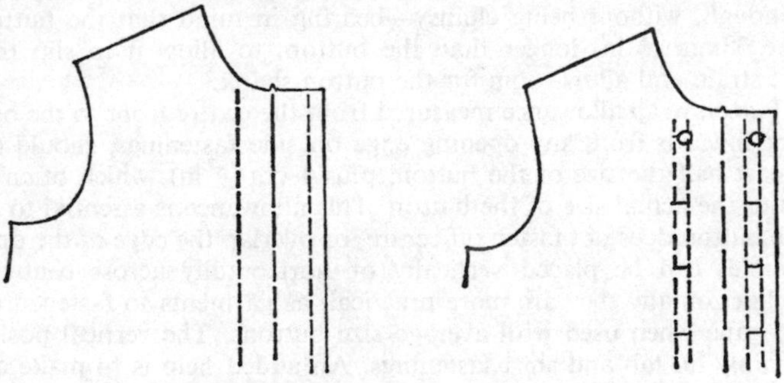

Fig. 249. (a) and (b): Double breasted button placing.

Tabs, with vertical buttonholes, should have the top button position equidistant to side and top edges.

Bound Buttonhole

This is similar to the piped buttonhole described on page 138, the difference being that a much narrower binding edge is possible, as it is made with only one piece of fabric. It is suitable for use on thinner fabrics, or almost any which are not very loosely woven and fray easily.

Cut a rectangular piece of fabric, on the bias or on the straight grain, 5 cm (2 in) wide, by a length equal to the diameter of the button plus 2 cm ($\frac{3}{4}$ in). Mark a line at the centre, on the wrong side. Place this piece right side down to the right side of the garment, matching the centre line to the buttonhole line and overlapping 1 cm ($\frac{3}{8}$ in) at each end. Tack marking lines 3 mm ($\frac{1}{8}$ in) each side of the centre line (this distance can vary depending on fabric and size of button, so first try it out on a sample). Machine stitch along the tacked lines and across each end to make a rectangle. Cut very carefully through the centre, stopping 3 mm ($\frac{1}{8}$ in) before each end, then cutting diagonally into the corners. Accuracy in stitching and cutting will produce neat binding edges, now turned through to the wrong side.

Press the seams towards the opening, press the binding piece and pull each end so that tiny pleats are formed. Then sew these down firmly to the binding. A small backstitch can be made for extra strength on the right side, through the binding seam. Finish the back of the buttonhole when covered by the facing, in the same way as the piped version, by cutting a slit, then turning in the raw edges and hemming the turned-in edges to the binding. (Fig. 250.)

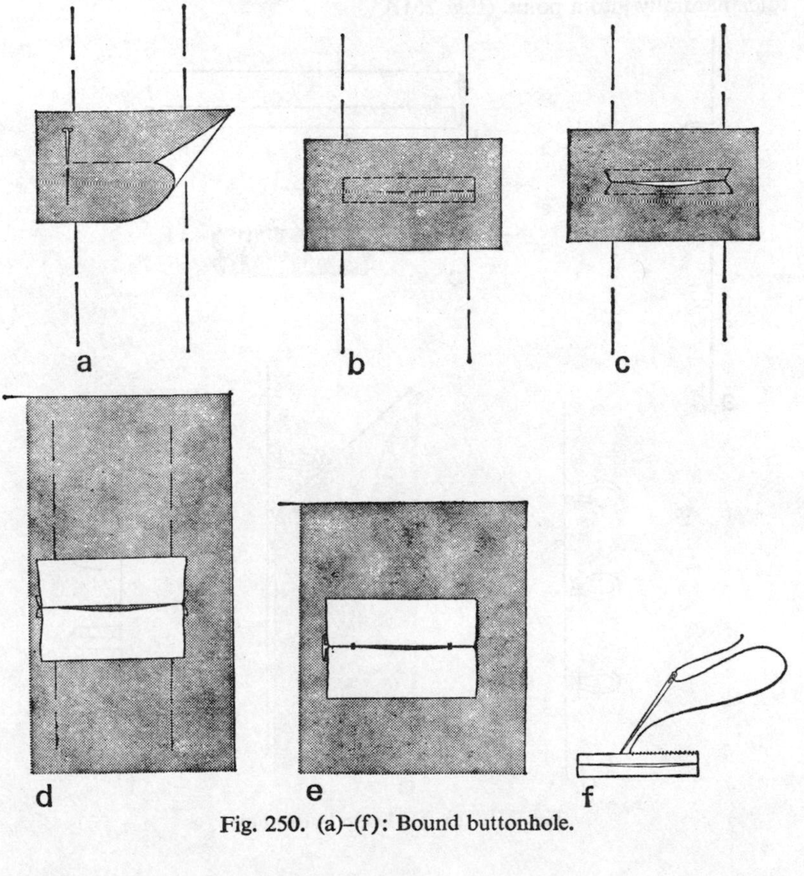

Fig. 250. (a)–(f): Bound buttonhole.

Loop Buttonhole/Rouleau

A very easy method, suitable for different fabrics, especially the silk, lighter weight fabrics often used for evening wear. They can be made from ribbon, but are generally cut on the bias in self fabric, as pulling through the ribbon on the straight grain is a little more difficult. A longish strip of fabric cut on the bias, about 2 cm (¾ in) wide, and long enough to make the loop is required.

This is folded along the centre of the length, right sides together, and stitched 6 mm (¼ in) from the fold. Leave threads at one end, thread them through a bodkin and pull the material through to the right side, working it with your fingers. If you do not possess a bodkin, a small safety pin can sometimes be used.

The loops can be cut (Fig. 251d), or left in one continuous piece. Either way the loop must face away from the edge. Sew them in position, on the right side, and sew the facing right side down on top. When this is turned to the inside of the garment the loops will be placed in the right direction. Naturally without a separate facing the loops can be sewn to the inside of the garment, facing the right way. If the tubing is pressed when it is turned through, a flat tab-like loop can be made, by pressing the end as well where it folds naturally into a point. (Fig. 251.)

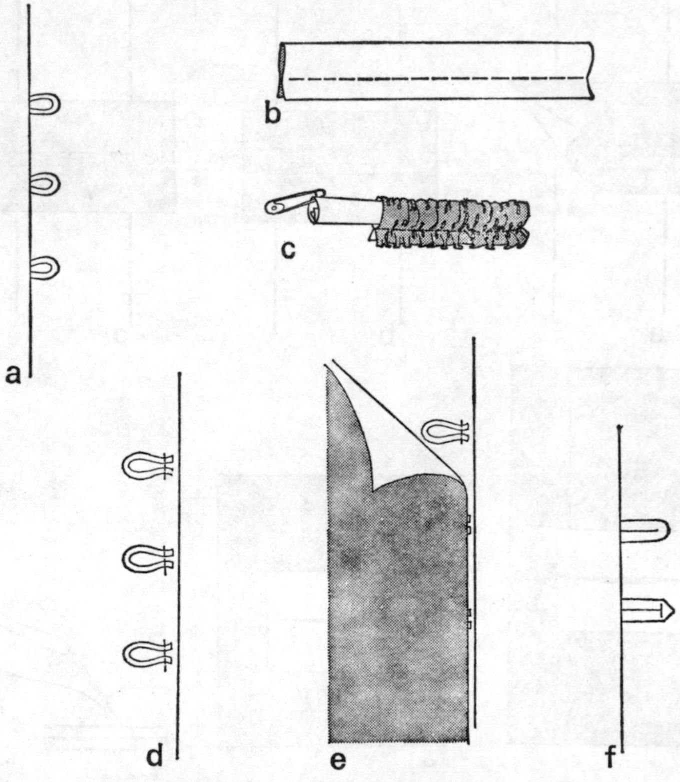

Fig. 251. (a)–(f): Loop buttonhole.

Tailor-worked Buttonhole

This has an eyelet hole at one end, since it is intended to accommodate a **tailored button,** sewn on with a longish shank, as is usual on coats and suits. Make the eyelet hole at the beginning of the buttonhole with a stiletto, cut the line, then oversew the slit opening and hole over a narrow, strong cord, called **gimp.** This, when held in place next to the cut edge, is worked with a buttonhole stitch, using heavier twist or silk over the gimp. Working from left to right, insert the needle into the slot, bringing it out below the oversewing. Bring the thread from the needle eye around, and under, the needle point, from right to left. Draw the thread up to form a **purl** on the edge. Do not pull too tightly, and continue in the same manner around the buttonhole, keeping the stitches close together, so that the purls cover the edges completely. Work a bar tack at the end and buttonhole stitch over it. (Fig. 252.)

With more practice, this gimp can be left free, and the buttonhole stitch worked over it. Before the final end bar is worked, the ends of the gimp are pulled up to tighten the opening then sewn in with the bar.

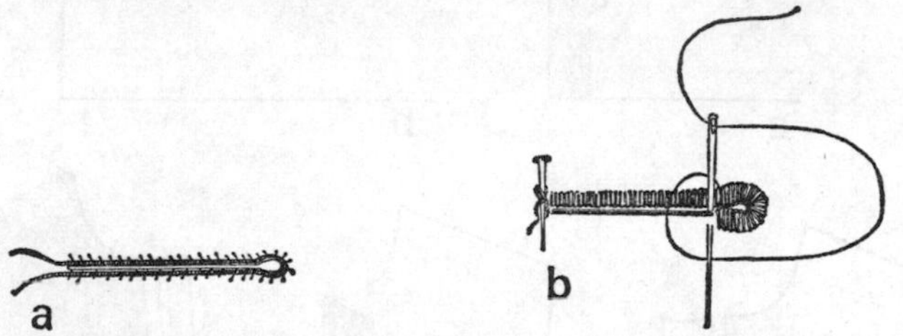

Fig. 252. (a) and (b): Tailor-worked buttonhole.

Thread Loop Buttonhole

A simple buttonhole for use at neck edges on lingerie, babies clothes and under a collar where the buttonhole should not be seen.

On the opening edge sew a few threads, rather like a loose bar tack, and just big enough for the button to slip through. Next work a blanket stitch over the threads, as shown in Fig. 253.

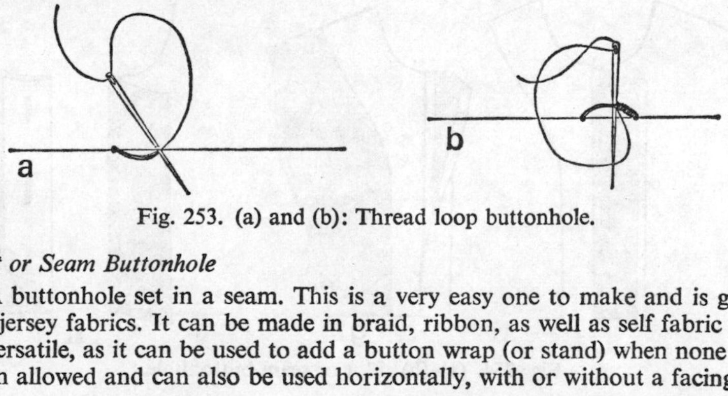

Fig. 253. (a) and (b): Thread loop buttonhole.

Slot or Seam Buttonhole

A buttonhole set in a seam. This is a very easy one to make and is good for jersey fabrics. It can be made in braid, ribbon, as well as self fabric and is versatile, as it can be used to add a button wrap (or stand) when none has been allowed and can also be used horizontally, with or without a facing.

Basically, a band is cut twice the width of the button, plus seam allowances, or with enough turn-back to form a facing. Similarly, the garment section can have a facing cut in with it, or just have a seam allowance. Buttonholes are marked on the wrong side of band, which is then laid right side down to right side of garment, seam allowances matching. This seam is stitched, between buttonholes and the ends stitched securely. The seam is pressed open, band turned to inside, seam allowance turned in—the hem to seamline, but not over it. (Fig. 254 c–e.)

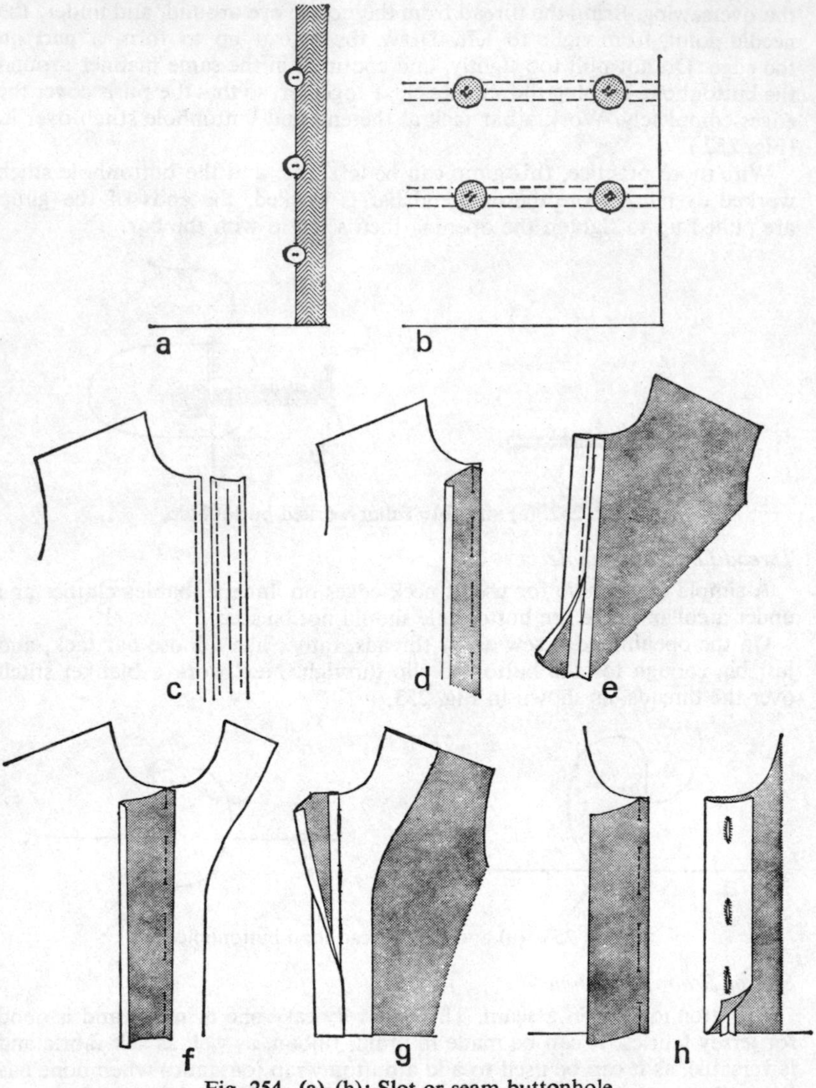

Fig. 254. (a)–(h): Slot or seam buttonhole.

Figure 254(f)–(g) shows a facing cut in one with garment (grown-on). The band is stitched to the centre line, then the seam is pressed open and the facing pressed back at the same time. The turned-in edge of the band is sewn back to the seam line. In Fig. 254(h) the facing has been cut in one with the band, so after the seam has been stitched and pressed, the facing side is turned in to the wrong side and blindstitched to the garment. The buttonholes are cut in the facing and hemmed, as in bound and piped buttonhole methods.

The horizontal slot/seam buttonholes are marked in the seam, stitched and pressed as on the band, the back finished through facing as above.

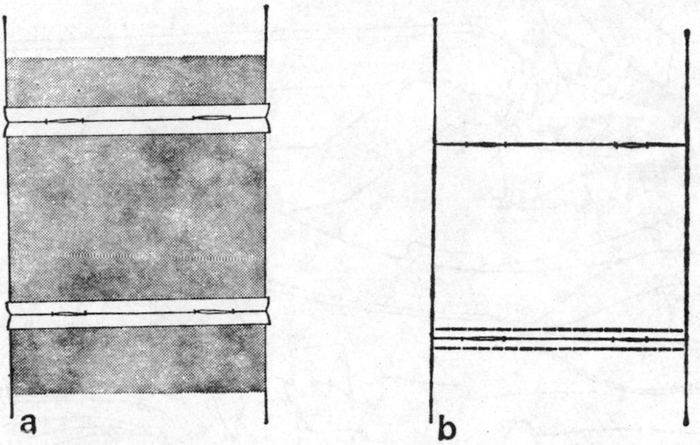

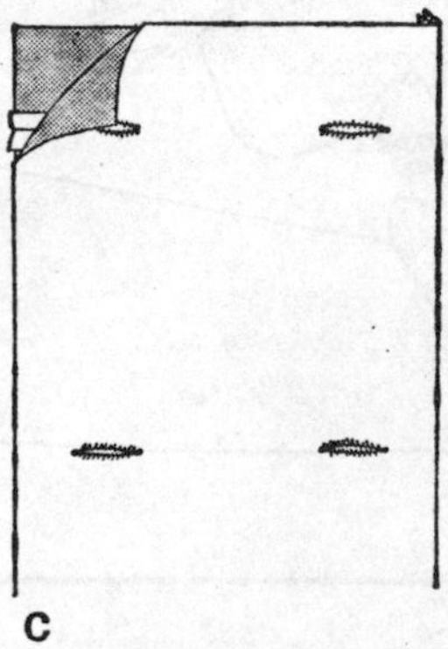

Fig. 255. (a), (b) and (c). Horizontal slot or seam buttonhole.

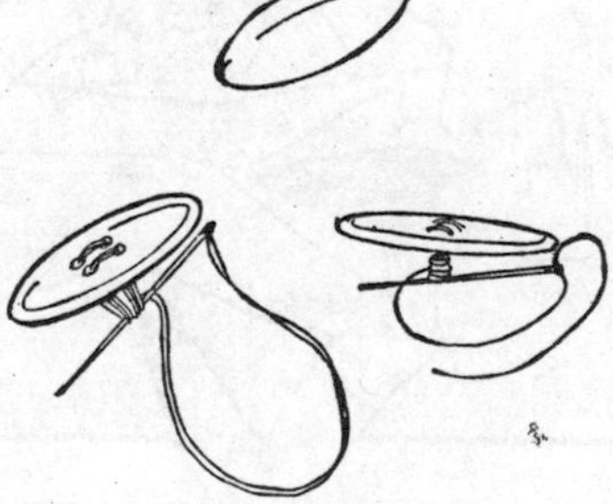

Fig. 256

Sewing on Buttons

As already mentioned on page 141, mark the button placing with a pin through the buttonhole. For buttons with two or four holes, start with a few stitches on the button-mark position, sew through the holes and back

Fig. 257

through the fabric, fairly loosely. On four-hole buttons these stitches can cross several times, or be sewn to make two parallel sets of threads. In both cases, the thread is wound several times around those holding the button to the garment, to form a shank. Buttons which have their own shanks attached, do not require loose stitches.

Collars

There are three main categories of collars: (1) the flat, (2) the stand and (3) the roll collar.

Peter Pan, Eton and sailor collars fall into the first group; and in the second are shirt, turtle neck and mandarin collars. The roll type includes the shawl and rever collars with their variations.

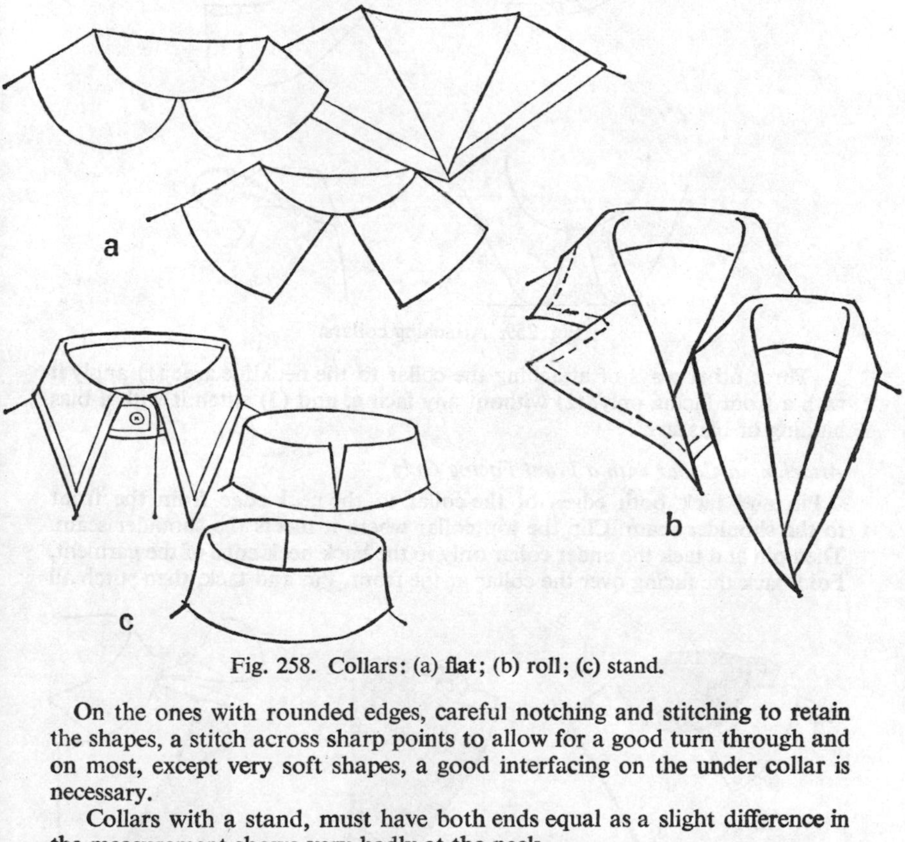

Fig. 258. Collars: (a) flat; (b) roll; (c) stand.

On the ones with rounded edges, careful notching and stitching to retain the shapes, a stitch across sharp points to allow for a good turn through and on most, except very soft shapes, a good interfacing on the under collar is necessary.

Collars with a stand, must have both ends equal as a slight difference in the measurement shows very badly at the neck.

Two ways of attaching two different collars have already been described on pages 139 and 148, attaching a collar with a front and back facing, and the shirt collar set on with a stand. With all the varying shapes and ways of attaching collars, there are essential points in making them up which are common to all of them.

These are:

(1) Staystitch the neckline of the garment.

(2) Clip the neckline to the staystitching before attaching the collar, and matching it to the neckline seam without puckering.

(3) Where possible understitch the collar for a good turned edge.

(4) Check to see that both ends of the collar are the same length and shape.

(5) Match the collar markings exactly to the corresponding marks on the garment neck.

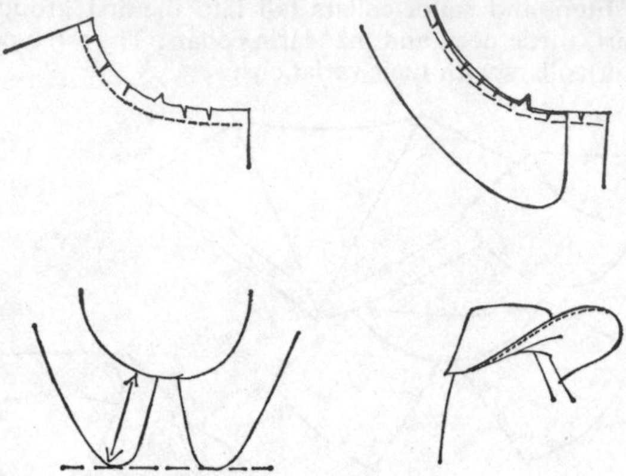

Fig. 259. Attaching collars.

Three other ways of attaching the collar to the neckline are: (1) apply it with a front facing only, (2) without any facing, and (3) stitch it with a bias binding or bias strip.

Attaching a Collar with a Front Facing Only

Pin and tack both edges of the collar to the neck edge from the front to the shoulder seam. Clip the top collar where it meets the shoulder seam. Then pin and tack the under collar only to the back neck edge of the garment. Fold back the facing over the collar at the front. Pin and tack, then stitch all

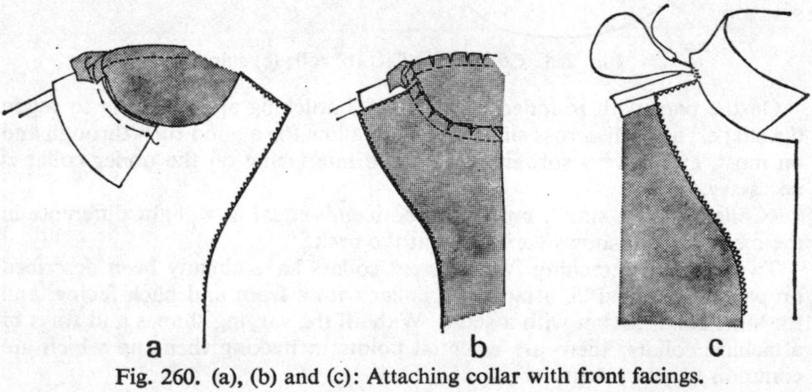

Fig. 260. (a), (b) and (c): Attaching collar with front facings.

the way round. Clip the neck edge, turn the facing to the inside and press and then under-press the back-neck seam towards the collar.

Turn under the seam allowance of the top collar at the back, and with a felling stitch sew it to the back-seam line. Slipstitch the shoulder edge of facing to the shoulder seam of the garment. (Fig. 260.)

Attaching a Collar without Facings

This is a similar method, except that the under collar edge is stitched all the way round the neck, and then the top collar seam turned in and hemmed to the inside back-neck seam. One major point to note here is that the top collar must have fractionally more allowed than the normal top collar allowance, to ensure that it rolls over well and lies correctly.

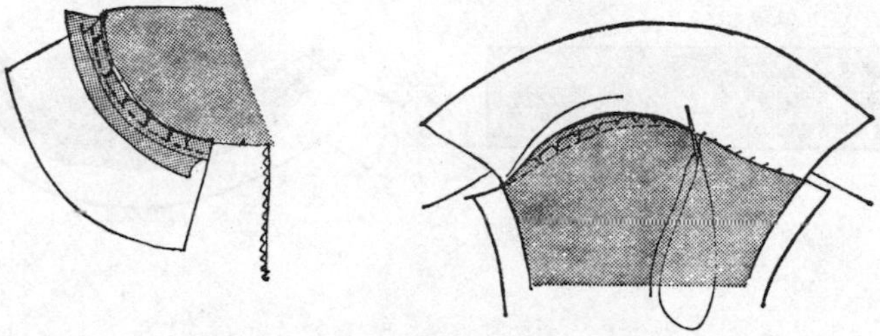

Fig. 261. Attaching collar without facings.

Attaching a Collar with a Bias Binding or Bias Strip

Pin and tack both edges of collar neck to the garment neckline. Tack the bias binding or strip, right side to the right side of the collar, stitch, clip, turn to the inside. Press the seam allowances and bias towards the garment. Slipstitch the hem to the inside neck.

If there is a narrow turn back on an open neck, the bias should overlap it slightly before it is stitched, so that it looks neat when turned to the inside.

All these methods apply equally to necklines which have openings or not,

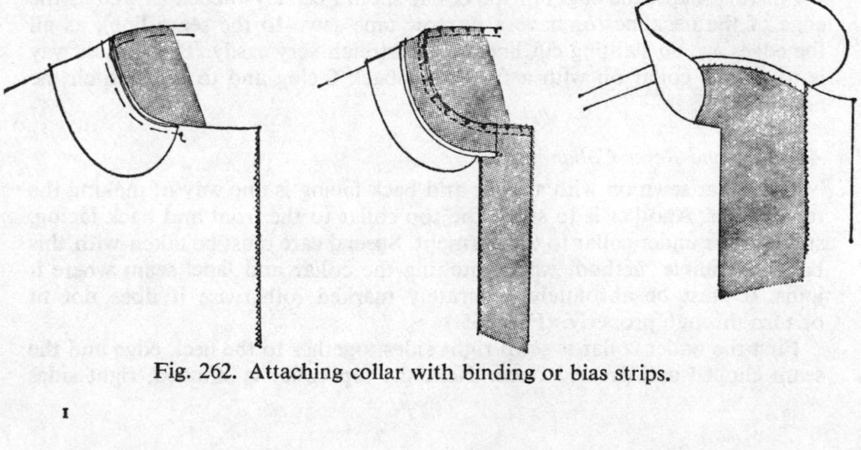

Fig. 262. Attaching collar with binding or bias strips.

of course. The figures will help show the variety of shapes and necklines where they apply.

Turtle-neck Collar

This soft roll type collar is very easy to make. Cut on the bias, the fabric is folded in half lengthwise, right sides together. The ends are stitched, corners trimmed and then it is turned to the right side. One edge has the turning pressed in. The other edge is laid to the neckline right sides together, and stitched. The seam allowance is clipped and pressed upwards. Then the pressed in edge is slipstitched to the inside neck seam. This collar can also be cut deep enough to make a turned over polo-neck collar and sewn in the same way. Hooks and eyes are sewn to the edges which meet edge-to-edge, or buttons and loop buttonholes work very well too.

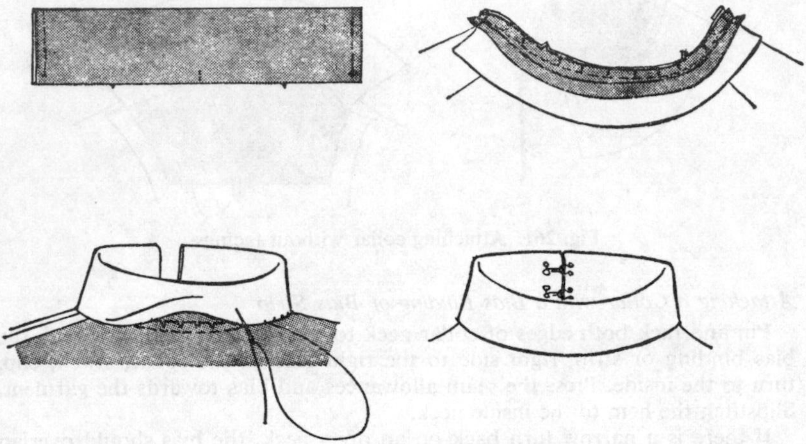

Fig. 263. Turtleneck collar.

Shawl Collar

For this shape, the edges of the collar should be staystitched as well as the edge of the neckline (or have a narrow tape sewn to the seam line), as all the edges are on slanting cut lines which stretch very easily. The neatest way is to set the collar on with a front and back facing and to understitch the neckline.

A Facing and Rever Collar

The collar sewn on with a front and back facing is one way of making the rever collar. Another is to stitch the top collar to the front and back facing, stiching the under collar to the garment. Special care must be taken with this basically simple method, when stitching the collar and lapel seam where it joins. It must be absolutely accurately marked, otherwise it does not fit or turn through properly. (Fig. 265.)

First the under collar is sewn right sides together to the neck edge and the seam clipped and pressed open. Next the top collar is stitched, right sides

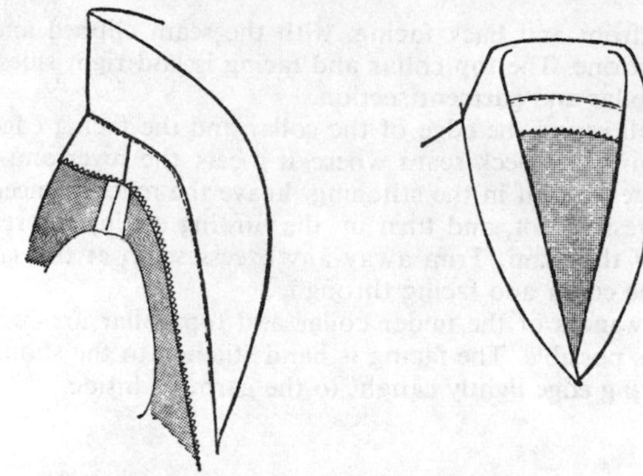

Fig. 264. Shawl collar.

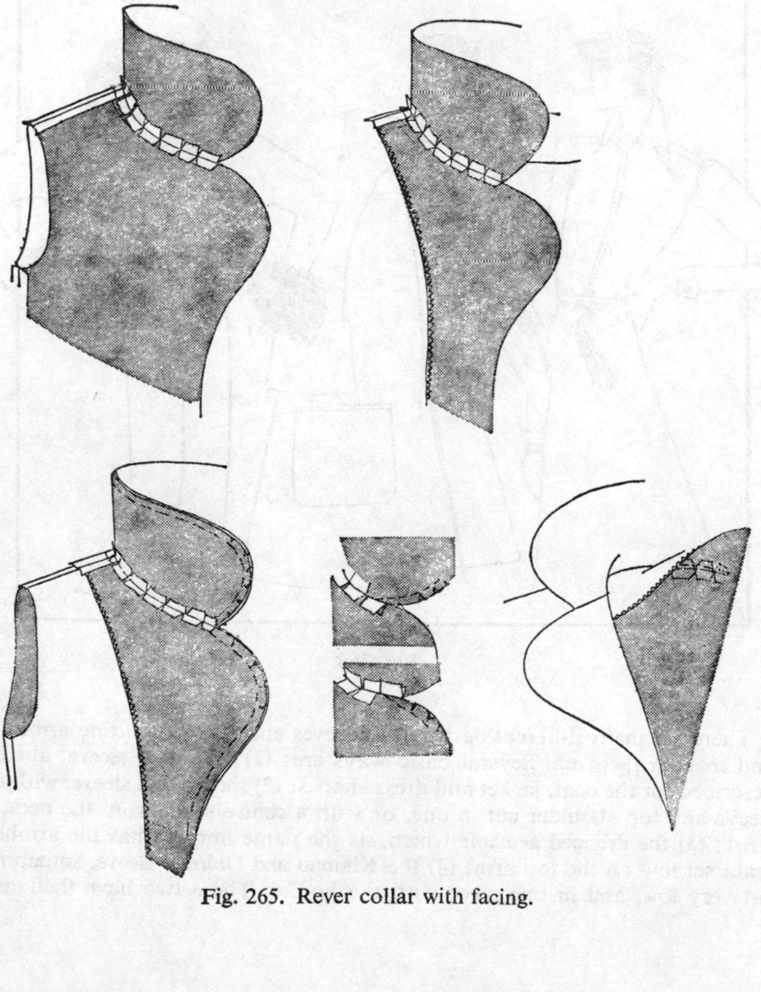

Fig. 265. Rever collar with facing.

together, to the front and back facing, with the seam clipped and pressed open like the first one. The top collar and facing is laid right sides together with the under collar and garment section.

Pin and tack all round the edge of the collar and the facing edges. When stitching, turn down the neck seam where it meets the rever and facing so that it does not get caught in the stitching. Leave the machine needle in the fabric, lift the presser foot, and turn up the turning again, before stitching round the rest of the seam. Trim away any excess seam at the same point before turning the collar and facing through.

The seam allowances of the under collar and top collar are backstitched together as far as possible. The facing is hand stitched to the shoulder seam and the front-facing edge lightly caught to the garment inside.

Sleeves

Fig. 266

There are many different designs for sleeves and ways of cutting armholes and making them up. Several basic ways are: (1) the **set-in sleeve,** already described for the coat, jacket and dress shapes; (2) the **Raglan sleeve,** with the sleeve and top shoulder cut in one, or with a centre seam from the neck to wrist; (3) the **dropped armhole** which, as the name implies, has the armhole seam set low on the top arm; (4) the **Kimono and Dolman sleeve,** sometimes cut very low, and in one piece with the bodice. These two have their own variations (such as the **batwing**), but the basic shape has a sleeve with the armhole starting at or just above the waist; (5) a narrower fitted version of the Dolman is a sleeve cut in one with the bodice with a gusset under the arm, sometimes called the **Dior sleeve**; and (6) a classic **shirt sleeve** and armhole.

Set-in Sleeve

This should be smooth and fitted to the armhole, with no puckering or twist from off grain cutting or fitting. All design detail, such as cuffs, buttonholes and openings should be made before the sleeve is set in. Puffed, pleated and gathered tops to sleeves, should be gathered or pleated to fit the armhole, then tacked and stitched to hold the fullness in the right position before it goes in the garment. The stitching-in and pressing is the same as for a plain sleeve.

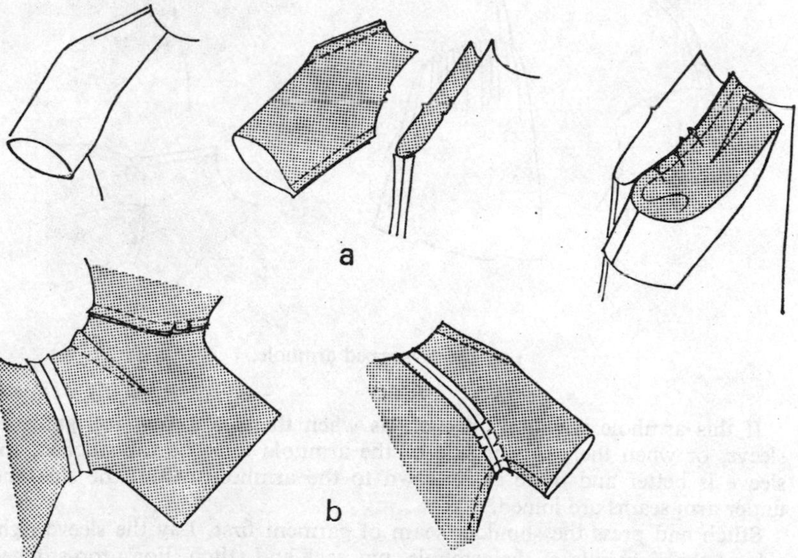

Fig. 267. (a) and (b): Raglan sleeve.

Raglan Sleeve

Made with a top shoulder dart or seam. The shoulder dart or seam is stitched first, and pressed open. For a close-fitting raglan sleeve the under-arm seam is stitched on the sleeve and on the garment, then the raglan seams are matched and stitched The seam is clipped and can be pressed open, both seam allowances pressed together, up or down, and may also be top-stitched. If the raglan is looser fitting under the arm the sleeve sections can be sewn to the front and back bodice parts first, then the under-arm and sleeve seam stitched together. The dart or top sleeve seam is sewn last.

Dropped Armhole

Sleeves can be set in two ways with this type of armhole. (1) the sleeve under-arm seam and garment side seams stitched first, then the sleeve pinned in the same way as a set-in sleeve. (2) the difference is that there is usually no crown to the top of the sleeve and it needs to be carefully matched to the notches or balance marks.

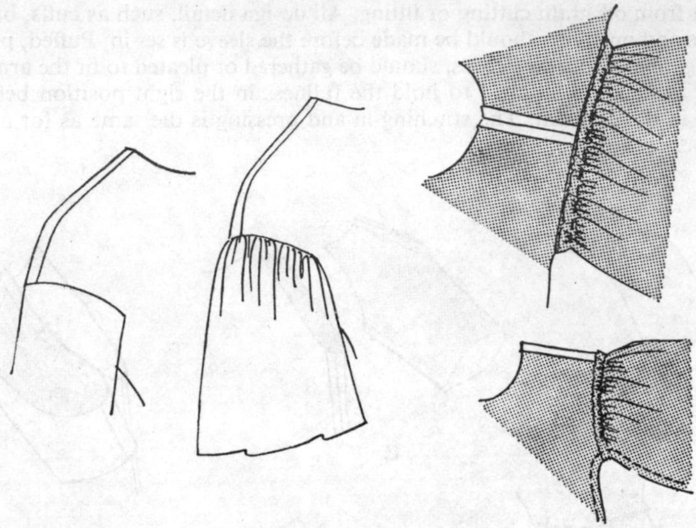

Fig. 268. Dropped armhole.

If this armhole is slightly deeper, as when there is a very full gathered sleeve, or when the garment side of the armhole is to be top-stitched, the sleeve is better and more easily sewn to the armhole before the side and under-arm seams are joined.

Stitch and press the shoulder seam of garment first. Lay the sleeve right side to the right side of the armhole, pin, tack and stitch. For a top-stitched edge, press both seams towards the garment and stitch on the right side. On a flat open seam, the under-arm seam may need clipping if there is a curve. A gathered sleeve can have the seams pressed towards the gathering or both seams pressed up.

Lastly the side seams of the garment and under-arm seams of the sleeves are sewn as one seam.

Dolman and Kimono Sleeve

This is an easy one as there is no armhole seam, sleeves are cut in one with the bodice (the kimono seam is set very low). The shoulder seams are sewn first, then the under-arm and garment seam. No difficulties here but, if the shaping makes the sleeve less deep, a strengthening tape or staystitch should be made at the under-arm itself, and the seam clipped to the staystitching.

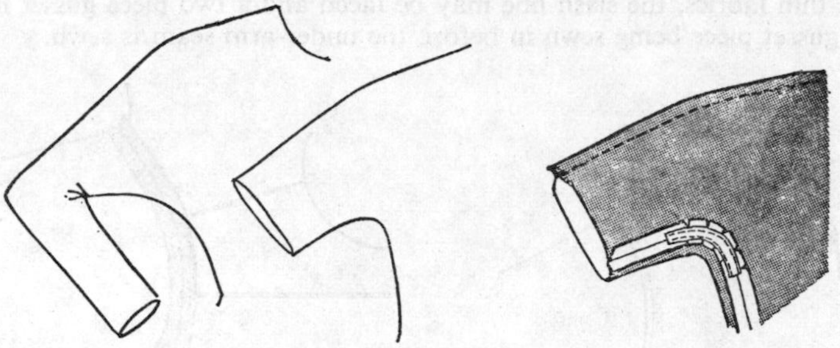

Fig. 269. Dolman/kimono sleeve.

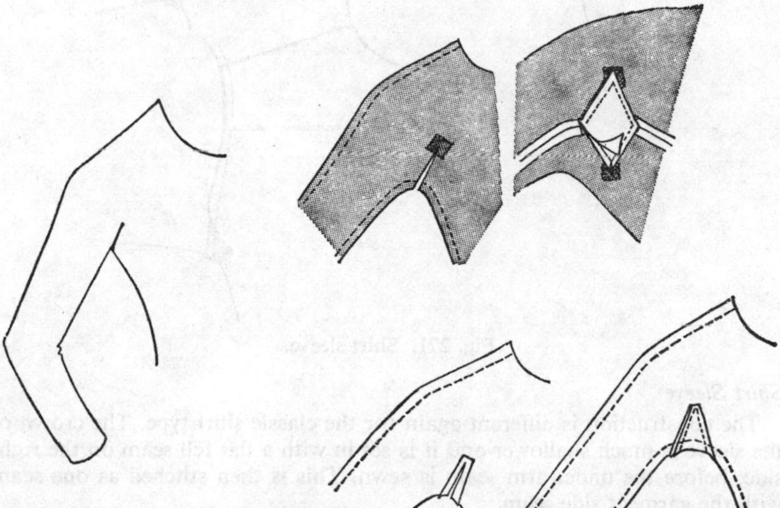

Fig. 270. 'Dior' sleeve.

Dior Sleeve

A fitted version of the dolman sleeve, which must have a gusset under the arm to allow for movement. A diagonal slash line is made at the under-arm, about 9 cm (3½ in) into the bodice part where a sleeve seam would normally be. The end of this cut is staystitched with a small piece of fabric sewn on the wrong side at this point to strengthen it.

A gusset piece to fit the slash line, is cut on the bias, about 10 cm (4 in) square. The shoulder under-arm and side seams are stitched on the garment. The gusset is tacked in the opening left by the slash lines. This is neatest method if it is stitched from the inside, but it is quite hard to turn back the corners and stitch on the machine, so a hand stitch at these points may be necessary. The gusset can be edge stitched from the right side, which is easier but the stitching will show.

On thin fabrics, the slash line may be faced and a two piece gusset made, each gusset piece being sewn in before the under-arm seam is sewn.

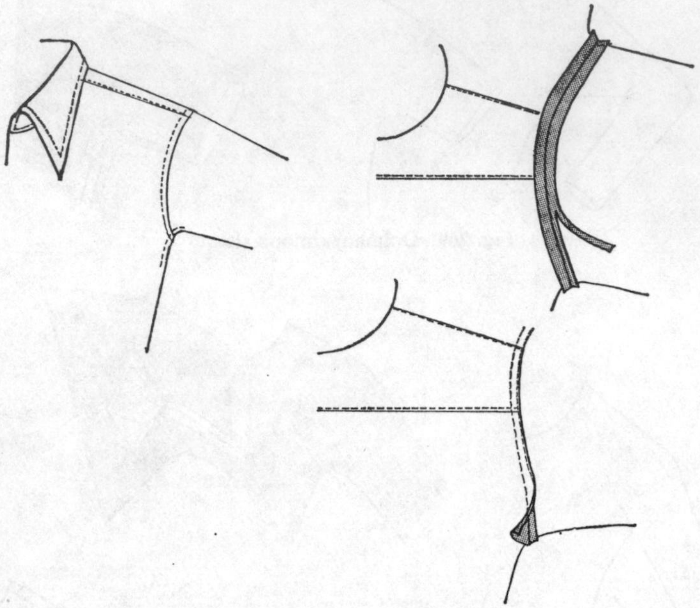

Fig. 271. Shirt sleeve.

Shirt Sleeve

The construction is different again for the classic shirt type. The crown of the sleeve is much shallower and it is set in with a flat fell seam on the right side, before the under-arm seam is sewn. This is then stitched as one seam with the garment side seam.

These are the basic ways of setting in the main sleeve types. The sleeve shapes themselves vary, but this is mostly a question of cutting. As already pointed out any decoration is made before the sleeve is set in. The main functional and decorative process associated with sleeves are **cuffs and openings.**

Openings

These have already been described (see pages 211–14). The faced slit, continuous opening and tab opening are all made at the edge of the sleeve in line with the little finger of the hand. An approximate measure is halfway on the back between the under-arm seam and the centre of the sleeve edge. A fitted sleeve can also have an opening in the under-arm seam, with a zip closing, or hooks and eyes.

Basic Cuffs

One general point, all bound or piped buttonholes, top-stitching or decoration should be made before the cuff is sewn to the sleeve.

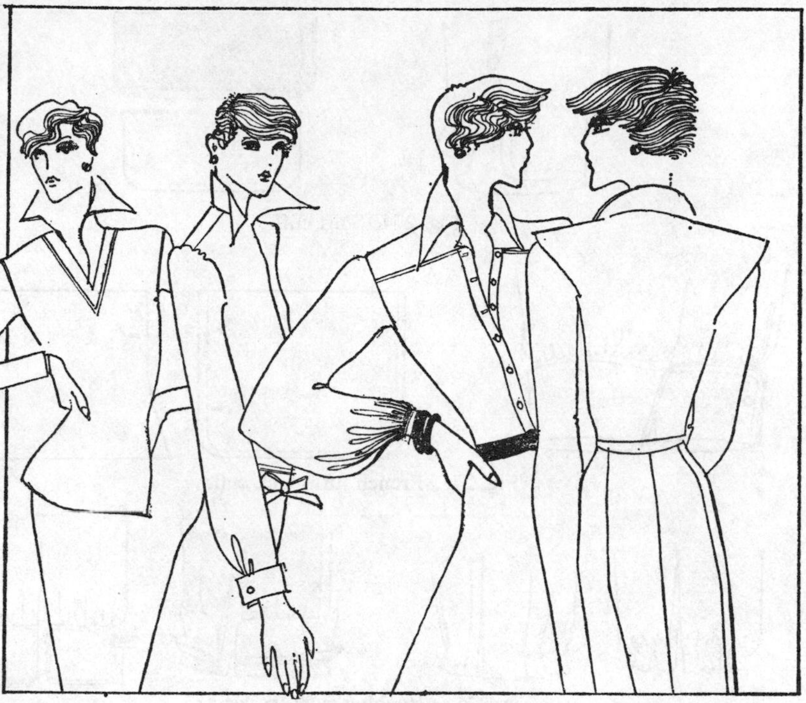

Fig. 272

Again there are various shapes of cuff, but they are sewn to the sleeve the same way.

Band Cuff. The fabric is cut and interfaced on the wrong side. For a crisp look the interfacing can be cut to the seam allowances, or cut to the finished size of the cuff. The fabric folded lengthwise, right sides together, and stitched across the ends. Then it is turned to the right side and pressed, with the seam allowance pressed in on the outside cuff.

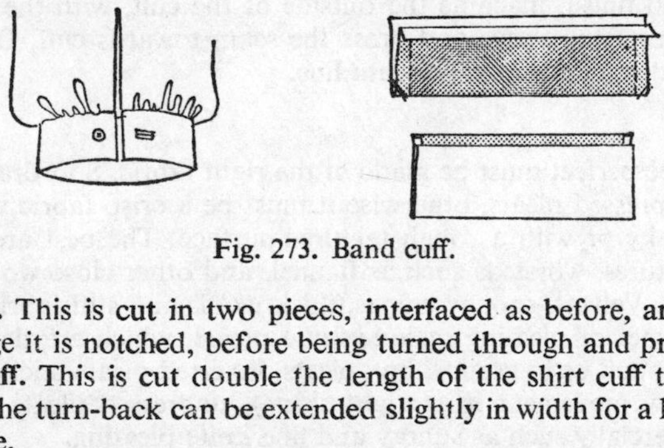

Fig. 273. Band cuff.

Shirt Cuff. This is cut in two pieces, interfaced as before, and if there is a curved edge it is notched, before being turned through and pressed.

French Cuff. This is cut double the length of the shirt cuff to allow it to turn back. The turn-back can be extended slightly in width for a link fastening or slight flare.

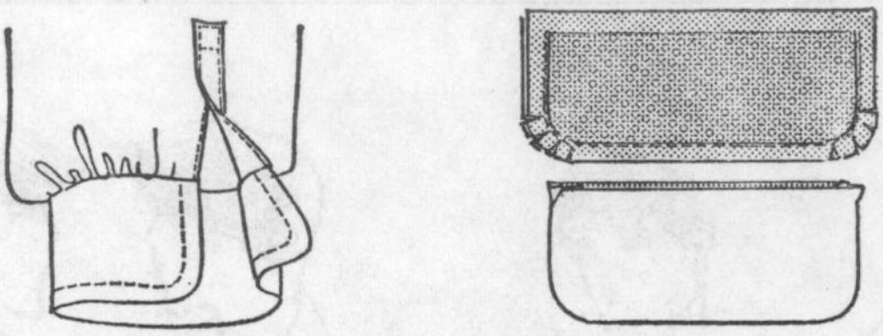

Fig. 274. Shirt cuff.

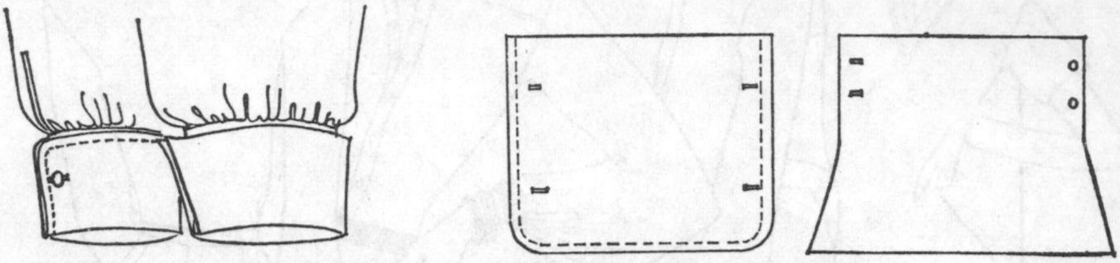

Fig. 275. French turn-back cuff.

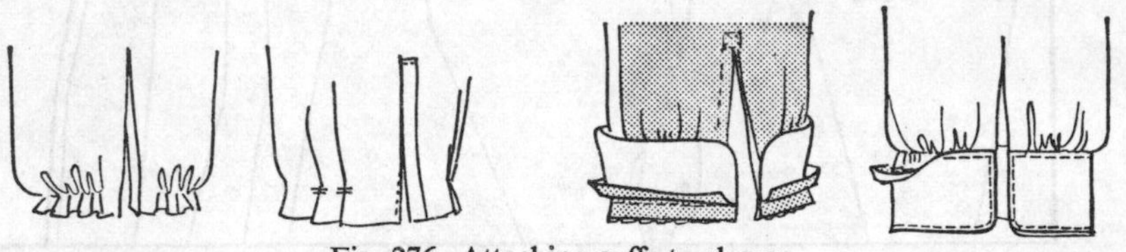

Fig. 276. Attaching cuffs to sleeves.

Attaching Cuffs to Sleeves. The sleeve has the opening already finished before attaching the cuff. The edge of the sleeve is gathered or pleated to fit the cuff, and the cuff edges should match markings exactly.

For a machine stitched finish, press under the seam allowance of the outer side of the cuff. Lay the underside of the cuff seam to the inside of the sleeve (the right side of the fabric to the inside) pin, tack and stitch the seam and press it towards the cuff. On the outside, tack the pressed-in edge of the cuff to the seam line on the outside and stitch it.

For a hand finish, machine the outside of the cuff, with the right side to the right side of the sleeve and press the seam towards cuff. On the inside, hem the inside cuff edge to the seam line.

Pleats

Pleats to be perfect must be made of the right fabric. Soft drapable fabrics can have unpressed pleats, otherwise it must be a crisp fabric which presses well, not bulky or with a rough textured surface. The best are gabardines, terylene mixtures, worsteds such as flannel, and other close woven, firm but light, fabrics. Velvets, spongy crêpes, thick wools and stiff fabrics are out.

Various types of pleating include knife pleats, which are flat, even pleats all the way round or in groups, box pleats, inverted pleats, kick pleats (small ones to allow movement in straight skirts), unpressed pleats and pleating made commercially such as sunray and fine knife pleating.

Fig. 277

Whenever possible the hem should be made first and on all but the last four types, the pleating section should be laid on a flat surface. The pleats pinned in position checking that they are on the grain line and that they are lying smoothly. Tack each pleat, a tack line across hip level and at waist, then the whole section in pressed. (Fig. 278.)

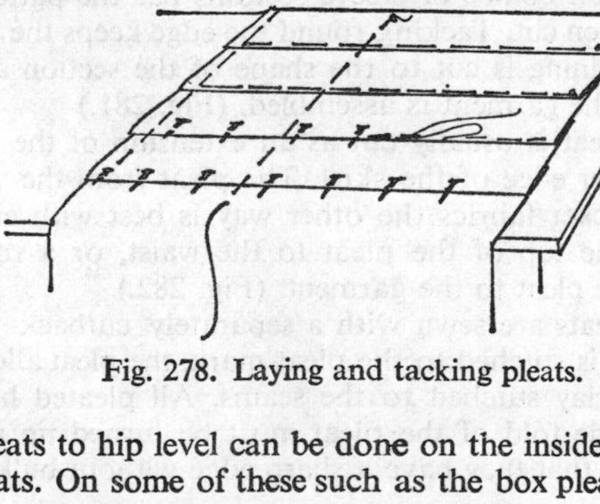

Fig. 278. Laying and tacking pleats.

Stitching pleats to hip level can be done on the inside or edge stitched on top of the pleats. On some of these such as the box pleats, the excess layers can be cut away inside, taking care to leave enough support for the pleat. (Fig. 279.)

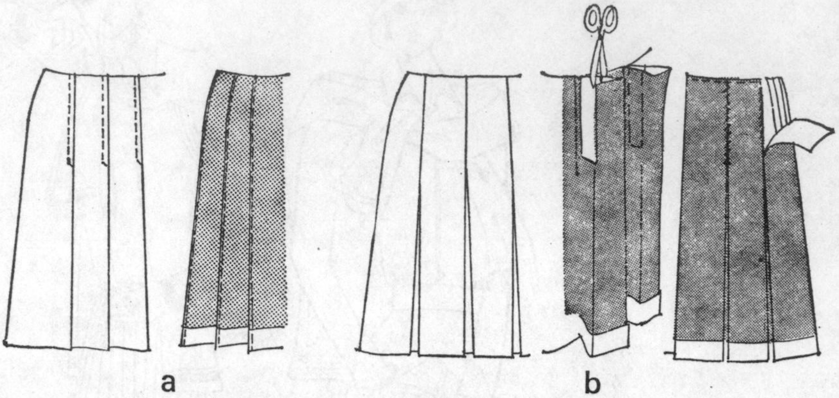

Fig. 279. (a) Edge stitching pleats; (b) cutting away bulk.

Sunray or fine knife pleating made commercially also has the hem made before pleating. A tape cut to the waist size and the pleating eased in and tacked to it, before the waistband is attached, will ensure a good fit. (Fig. 280.)

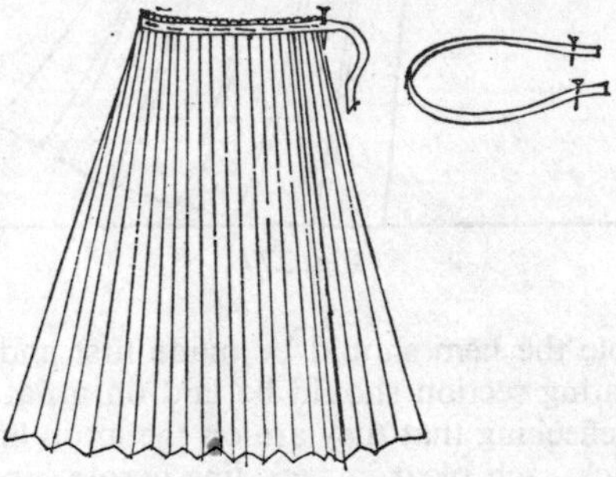

Fig. 280. Taping waist.

All-over pleating on bodice or sleeve sections has the pattern laid on the pleated fabric and then cut. Tacking round the edge keeps the pleats in place, and sometimes the lining is cut to the shape of the section and stitched to the pleating before the garment is assembled. (Fig. 281.)

The small kick pleat is usually cut as an extension of the seam from the waist, or at the lower edge of the skirt. The pleat from the waist has more support, but on thicker fabrics the other way is best with either a tape or lining sewn from the top of the pleat to the waist, or a row of stitching across the top of the pleat to the garment. (Fig. 282.)

Some inverted pleats are sewn with a separately cutback piece called an underlay. The seam is stitched to the pleat mark, the pleat allowance pressed back and the underlay stitched to the seams. All pleated hems where the seam is on the inside fold of the pleat must be turned up as described in chapter fourteen, so that they have a sharp edge without bulk. (Fig. 283.)

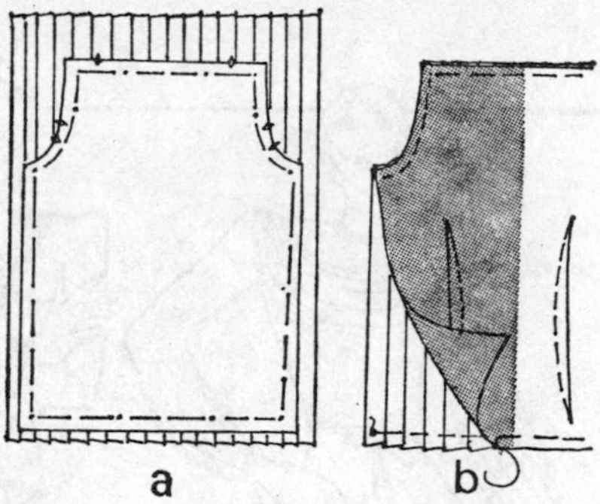

Fig. 281. (a) Laying pattern on pleating; (b) attaching lining to pleating.

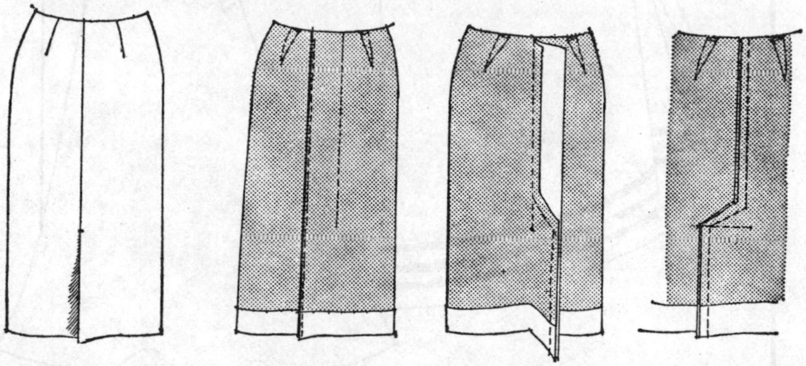

Fig. 282. Kick pleat.

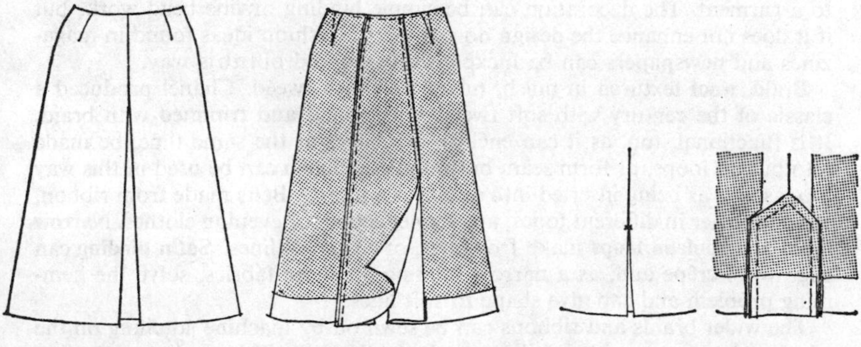

Fig. 283. Inverted pleat.

Figures 278–83 will show some of these basic points.

Decoration

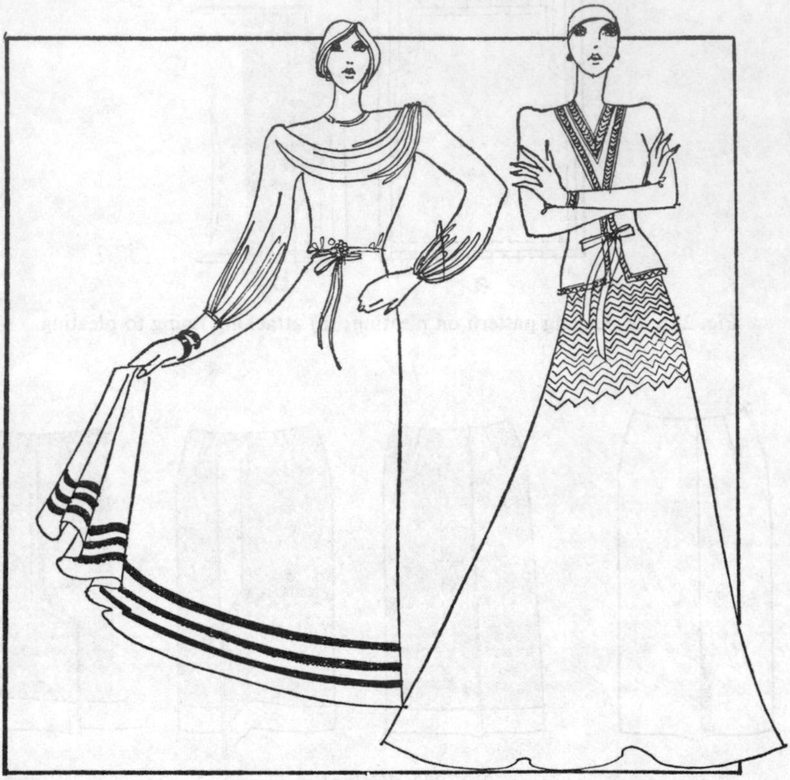

Fig. 284

Well-applied decoration integrated with the design can add individuality to a garment. The decoration can be simple binding or fine bead work, but if it does not enhance the design do not use it. Fashion ideas found in magazines and newspapers can be inexpensively worked out this way.

Braid, wool textured in finish, mixes well with tweed. Chanel produced a classic of the century with soft tweed suits bound and trimmed with braid. It is functional, too, as it can enclose raw edges at the same time, be made into button loops, or form seam buttonholes. **Ribbon** can be used in this way too, as well as being inserted into seams as a piping. Belts made from ribbon, sewn together in different tones, are very effective for evening clothes. **Narrow braid and rouleau loops** make froggings, or edge necklines. **Satin binding** can edge wool crêpe and, as a narrow binding on sheer fabrics, solve the hemming problem and can give shape to soft lines.

The wider braids and ribbons can be sewn on by machine stitching on the edge, or handsewn with a felling stitch or slipstitch. This applies to the flat, narrower ones too, but if they are of the cord, or round rouleau shape, they will have to be handsewn. (Fig. 285.)

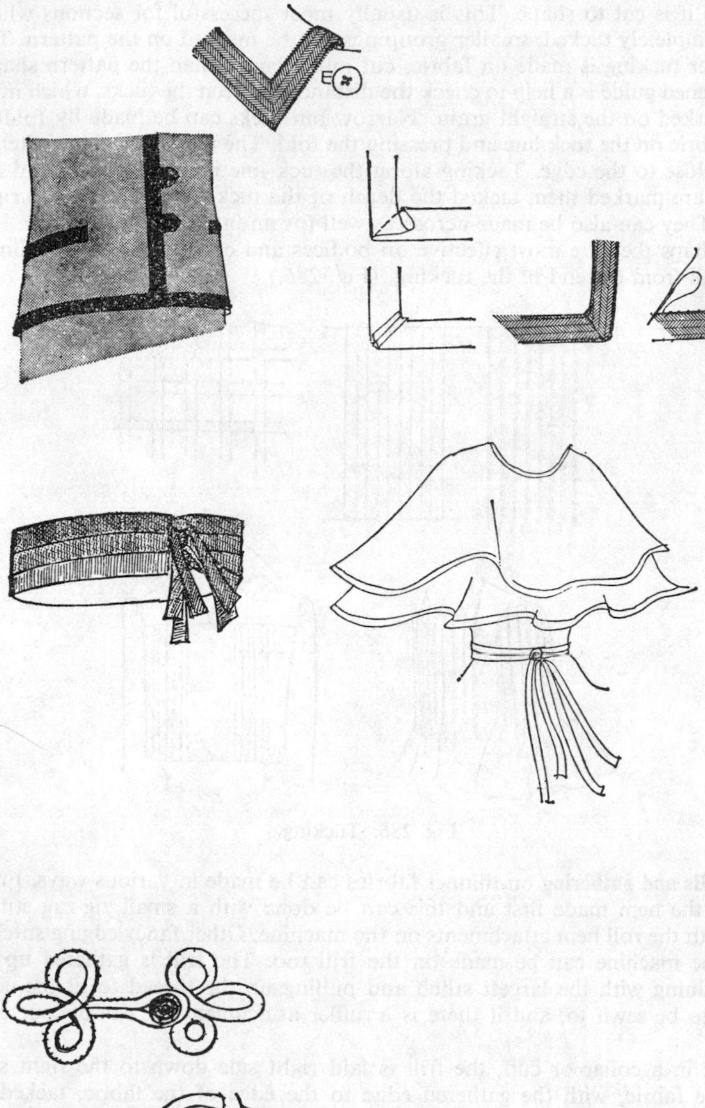

Fig. 285. Braid, ribbon, frogging.

Tucking from narrow pin tucks to wider flat tucks is made on the fabric before it is cut to shape. This is usually most successful for sections which are completely tucked, smaller groupings can be marked on the pattern. The all-over tucking is made on fabric, cut much larger than the pattern shape. A notched guide is a help to check the distance between the tucks, which must be marked on the straight grain. Narrow pin tucks can be made by folding the fabric on the tuck line and pressing the fold. The tuck is machine stitched very close to the edge. Tacking along the tuck line is another way, and flat tucks are marked then, tacked the depth of the tuck—all made on the right side. They can also be made across as well for an interesting detail.

Perhaps they are most effective on bodices and on sleeves, where fullness can fall from the end of the tucking. (Fig. 286.)

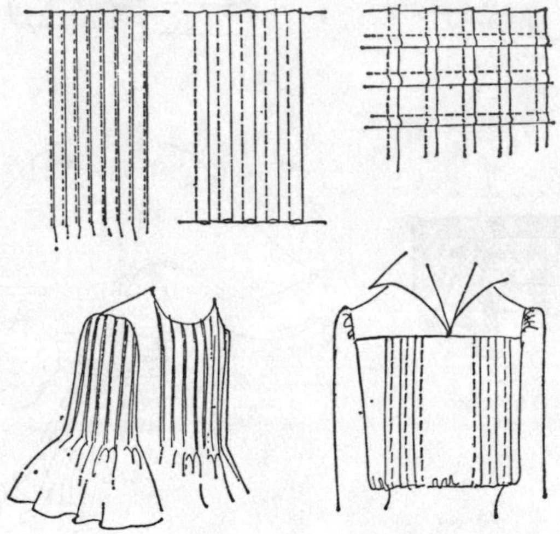

Fig. 286. Tucking.

Frills and gathering on thinner fabrics can be made in various ways. Frills have the hem made first and this can be done with a small zig-zag stitch, or with the roll hem attachments on the machine. Other fancy edging stitches on the machine can be made on the frill too. The frill is gathered up by machining with the largest stitch and pulling up the thread to fit the edge it is to be sewn to, and if there is a ruffler attachment this can of course be used.

Set in a collar or cuff, the frill is laid right side down to the right side of the fabric, with the gathered edge to the edge of the fabric, tacked in position, and the other side of the collar or cuff tacked right side down over the frill, edges meeting. After stitching on the tacked line the collar or cuff is turned to the right side.

A frill in a seam is stitched the same way, with the gathered edge to the seam edge, and right sides together, the other section right side down over it. Press the seam allowances away from the frill. A circular frill cut the length of the edge it is to be sewn to, will mean seaming sections together for wider hems. A small inside circle will make a fuller frill. This inside edge is staystitched first, and the outer edge hemmed by hand or on the machine. The seam above the staystitching nust be clipped then sewn the same way as a gathered frill. (Fig. 287.)

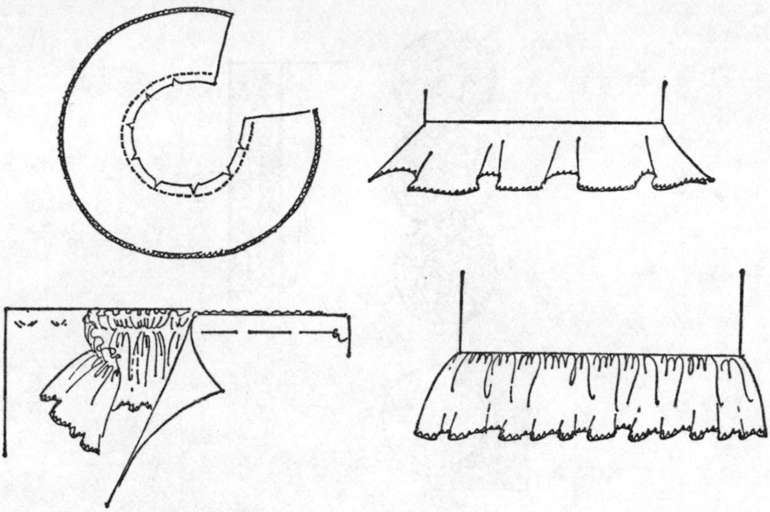

Fig. 287. Frills.

Godets are flared insets, often bias cut, and are sewn into slash lines in a skirt. This slash line should be staystitched at the point, and the adventurous can set a narrow satin piping in the seam! Pleating and lace can be set the same way as godets. (Fig. 288.)

Fig. 288. Godets.

A tape or ribbon sewn to the inside of a full garment can have a cord or elastic drawn through for a **ruched waistline.** (Fig. 289.)

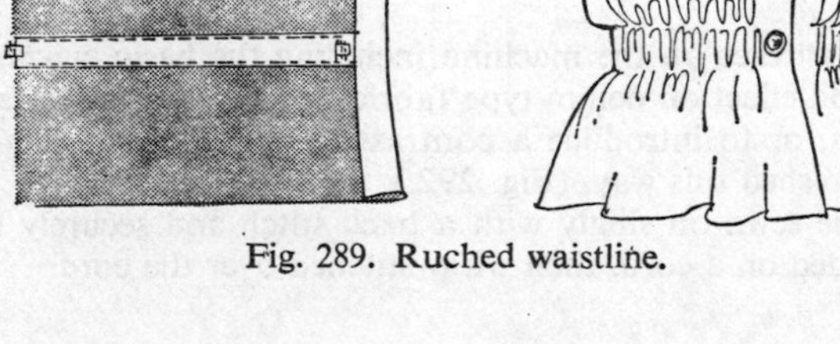

Fig. 289. Ruched waistline.

Lace can be handsewn to an edge with a whip stitch, or inserted between bands of fabric. This can also be sewn with a zig-zag stitch if it is sewn to the right side, otherwise stitched with the right side of lace to each right side of sections to be joined, with narrow plain seams. (Fig. 290.)

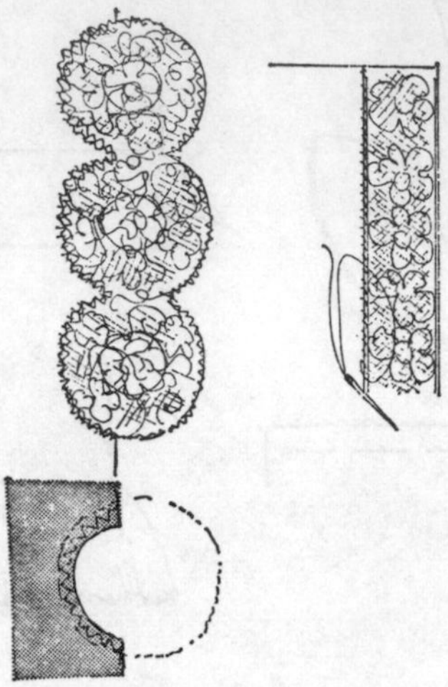

Fig. 290. Sewing on lace.

Smocking can be simulated on the machine by drawing up even rows of gathering, and using some of the embroidery stitches on the machine. Hand smocking has a variety of stitches, the most popular being a honeycomb stitch. This can be made for yoke pieces or cuffs on dresses of soft fabric. (Fig. 291.)

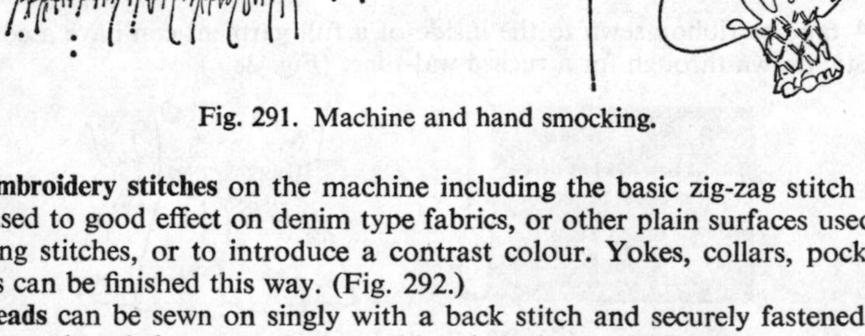

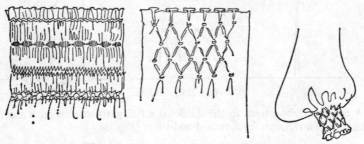

Fig. 291. Machine and hand smocking.

Embroidery stitches on the machine including the basic zig-zag stitch can be used to good effect on denim type fabrics, or other plain surfaces used as edging stitches, or to introduce a contrast colour. Yokes, collars, pockets, belts can be finished this way. (Fig. 292.)

Beads can be sewn on singly with a back stitch and securely fastened off or sewn threaded on a cord, then whip stitched over the cord.

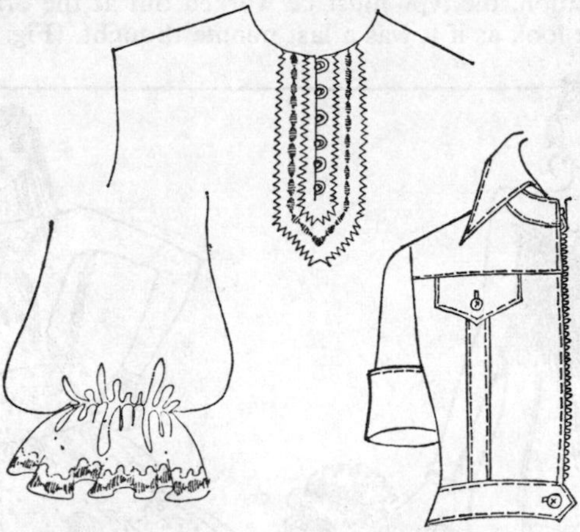

Fig. 292. Decorative stitching.

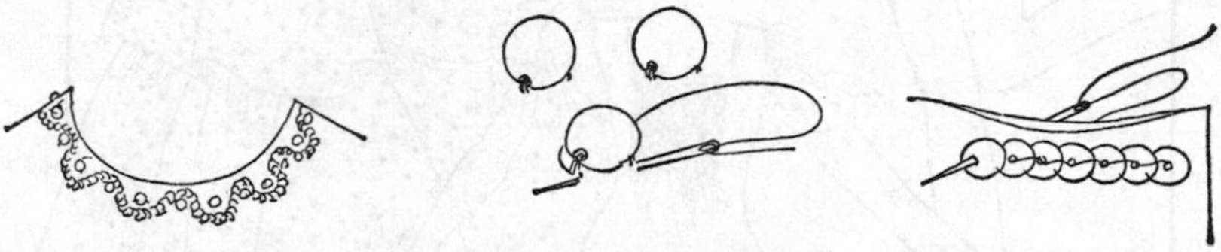

Fig. 293. Beads and sequins.

Sequins, sewn with a back stitch through each centre hole of each one. (Fig. 293.)

Belts in self or contrasting fabric, can be made from either a long or two narrower lengths of fabric, interfaced with fusible interlining on the wrong side, and top-stitched on the right side. For tie belts, the fabric can be cut in two sections for one with shaped ends, or folded in half lengthwise, both with right sides together. They are stitched all round in the first type, just leaving a gap to pull the belt through, and the other has just one long seam, stitched across one end as well, then the belt is pulled through like a large rouleau tube. The gap and end are whip stitched. Belt backing can be bought, to make stiffer belts, and buckles made or bought. (Fig. 294.)

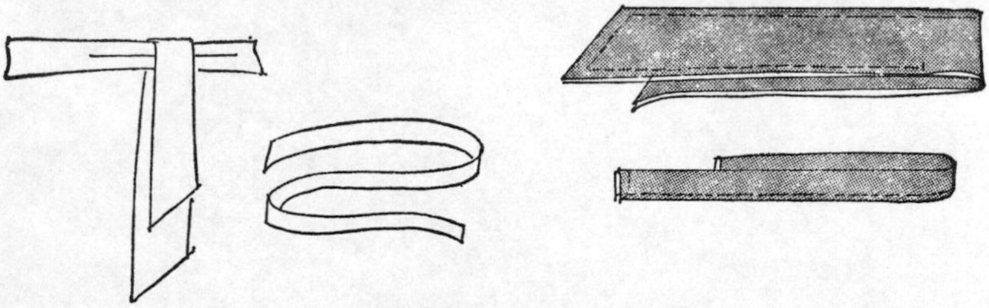

Fig. 294. Belts.

For all decoration, the type must be worked out at the original planning stage, and never look as if it was a last minute thought. (Fig. 295.)

Fig. 295

CHAPTER FIFTEEN

MORE ABOUT FABRICS

Metric and Yardage Calculations

When buying fabrics, the distinction made between length expressed in yards, and width in inches, changes to metres and decimal parts of a metre for length (e.g. 2·25 m) whilst width remains distinct in centimetres (even when greater than 1 metre, e.g. 140 cm).

Using the metric system, fabrics can be bought in multiples of 10 cm (0·10). As this is rather less than $\frac{1}{8}$ yd, it provides greater accuracy in fabric calculations for any chosen design.

The following charts on page 262 list the nearest conversions.

Making-up Special Fabrics

Some popular fabrics need special handling, as although they appeal to the beginner their difficult textures, weaves, or stripes and plaids, need special attention in cutting and making them up.

In this section we will deal as simply as possible with these fabrics which are: checks, plaids and stripes, velvet, chiffon and other sheers, lace and crêpe, knitted fabrics, mohair and include, although technically not fabric, leather and its imitations.

Checks, Plaids and Stripes

The main problem here is in the laying out and cutting of them. As it is the matching of these checks at the seams that is important, it follows that patterns should be chosen that have as few seams as possible, with good, unbroken lines. Some checks and plaids are smaller and even, which makes matching a little easier. Even so, more fabric must be allowed; for these allow an extra 0·25 m–0·50 m ($\frac{1}{4}$–$\frac{1}{2}$ yd) and on the larger and more uneven plaids as much as 0·5 m–0·90 m ($\frac{1}{2}$–1 yd). Matching stripes need slightly less than checks and plaids.

Planning the position of the plaid is important, as a larger or more dominant colour bar, will affect the design, and should be placed accordingly. Pockets, sleeves and pleats, too, will be affected. When laying the pattern on the fabric, mark on the pattern the position of these checks and, particularly, mark where the stripes or checks meet the seam line. Mark these in accurately with a pencil, in one or two places (near balance marks, and notches are a guide). With an uneven plaid or stripe, the pattern will also have to be laid the same way, and not up and down; this is why more fabric must be allowed.

With the checks, plaids and stripes marked in this way, the other sections can be laid on, matching the marked pieces to the fabric checks, etc. (Fig. 296.)

Unless cutting is on the true bias, straight, or equal slant, the plaids cannot

AVAILABLE FABRIC WIDTHS

Centimetres	*Inches*
65	25
70	27
90	35/36
100	39
115	44/45
122	48
127	50
140	54/56
150	58/60
175	68/70
180	72

FABRIC WEIGHT

gramme/m^2	oz/yd

METRES TO YARDS—ROUNDED TO THE NEAREST EQUIVALENT

m	*yd*	*m*	*yd*	*m*	*yd*
0·15	⅛	3·20	3½	6·30	6⅞
0·25	¼	3·35	3⅝	6·40	7
0·35	⅜	3·45	3¾	6·55	7⅛
0·50	½	3·55	3⅞	6·65	7¼
0·60	⅝	3·70	4	6·75	7⅜
0·70	¾	3·80	4⅛	6·90	7½
0·80	⅞	3·90	4¼	7·00	7⅝
0·95	1	4·00	4⅜	7·10	7¾
1·05	1⅛	4·15	4½	7·20	7⅞
1·15	1¼	4·25	4⅝	7·35	8
1·30	1⅜	4·35	4¾	7·45	8⅛
1·40	1½	4·50	4⅞	7·55	8¼
1·50	1⅝	4·60	5	7·70	8⅜
1·60	1¾	4·70	5⅛	7·80	8½
1·75	1⅞	4·80	5¼	7·90	8⅝
1·85	2	4·95	5⅜	8·00	8¾
1·95	2⅛	5·05	5½	8·15	8⅞
2·10	2¼	5·15	5⅝	8·25	9
2·20	2⅜	5·30	5¾	8·35	9⅛
2·30	2½	5·40	5⅞	8·50	9¼
2·40	2⅝	5·50	6	8·60	9⅜
2·55	2¾	5·60	6⅛	8·70	9½
2·65	2⅞	5·75	6¼	8·80	9⅝
2·75	3	5·85	6⅜	8·95	9¾
2·90	3⅛	5·95	6½	9·05	9⅞
3·00	3¼	6·10	6⅝	9·15	10
3·10	3⅜	6·20	6¾		

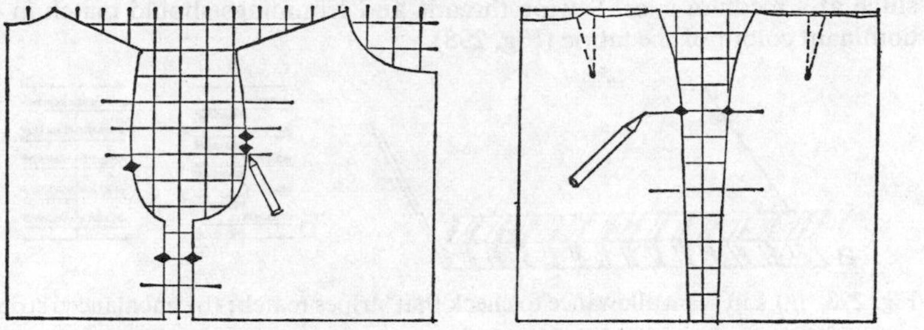

Fig. 296. Mark where stripes/checks meet on seam line.

match all along the seam. Similarly, matching at seams can be achieved horizontally, but not always with the vertical bars matching.

It is safer to cut all these uneven and large checks and plaids on a single layer of fabric, not forgetting to reverse the pattern pieces for the other section. As sleeves cannot always be matched on both front and back bodices, it is better to match the front; again the notches will help in matching the same check lines. Figures 296–7 will show some of the possibilities. It goes without saying to always look for a pattern which has been designed for plaids and checks as well as plain fabric!

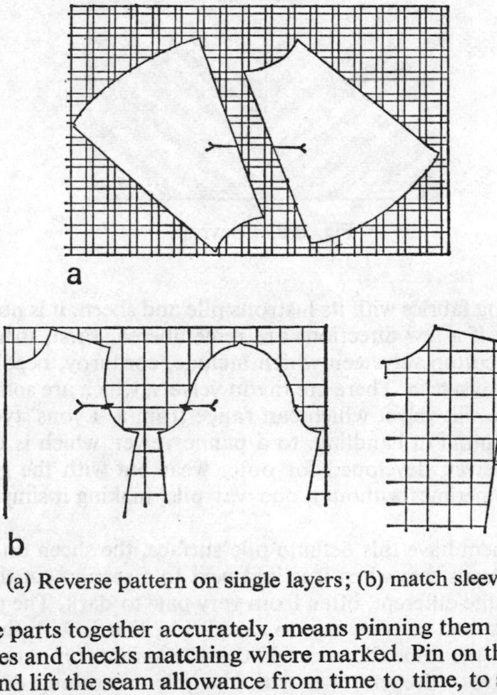

Fig. 297. (a) Reverse pattern on single layers; (b) match sleeve and bodice.

Sewing the parts together accurately, means pinning them in the first place, with all stripes and checks matching where marked. Pin on the bars of checks and stripes and lift the seam allowance from time to time, to see if at the seam itself the stripes and bars are matching. Tack the seam carefully, and machine stitch at a medium pace. Sewing threads and trimmings should match in the dominant colour of the fabric (Fig. 298).

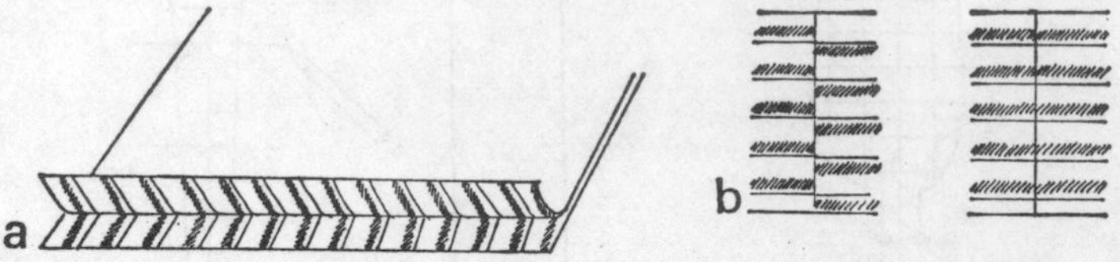

Fig. 298. (a) Lift seam allowance to check that stripes match; (b) unbalanced stripes.

A Chevron effect, is made by cutting the fabric on the bias. Try a fold on the bias first to see just how the plaids or stripes will look. The fabric with an uneven plaid, must be reversible and cut separately. Balanced plaids also have the pattern pieces cut individually, on a single layer, with the pattern turned over to have right and left sections. As with all plain bias fabrics, care must be taken not to stretch the seam when stitched. The sections should be laid flat on a table, without distorting the seams, and the pieces pinned and tacked together firmly to avoid slipping (Fig. 299.)

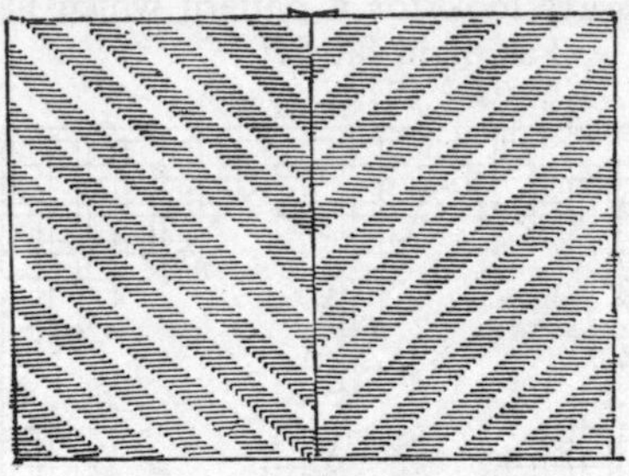

Fig. 299. Chevron.

Velvet

A queen among fabrics with its lustrous pile and sheen, it is not too difficult to sew correctly if a few directions are remembered. First, there are several types of velvet, cotton velveteen which include, corduroy, needlecord, whale cord, and plain velveteen. There are rayon velvets, which are softer and silkier in feel, and pure silk velvet which can range from a 'Lyons' type, very rich, and fairly substantial in handling, to a panne velvet, which is thin and very shiny. 'Street' velvet, developed for outer wear but with the rich look of a Lyons type is sometimes without a one way pile, making it simpler to lay out and cut.

As most of them have this definite pile surface, the sheen on the pile as it lays one way, means that when it is laid next to a section cut the other way, the shading is quite different, often from very pale to dark. The pattern pieces must be laid out, and cut one way to avoid this, that is with the top of each section laying in the same direction. If the pile smooths in an upward direction this will give a deeper tone, with the pile smoothing downwards the shading is lighter. For this reason velvets are generally cut with the upward direction of the pile. As with the plaids, more fabric must be allowed. If no metrage for velvet is shown on the pattern instructions, make sure that the design is suitable for velvets. The cutting is done with the napped (pile) surface inside, and the direction of pile marked on this wrong side with chalk. Preparing to make up velvet, the pinning should be done in the seam allowances with the pile, and not across it as it could leave marks. When possible this should be done with the very finest pins, or better still, fine needles. Tacking is best done with a fine thread and needle, as for all hand finishing, and all sewing done in the direction of pile or nap. A light tension on the machine, about 10 stitches for 2·5 cm (1 in), needle size 14, mercerized thread for the cotton velvet types and pure silk for the luxury velvets. The seams cannot have a turned-in finish, as it is too bulky and would leave marks after pressing: a machine zig-zag stitch, hand oversewing or bias seam binding are best. For facings use lightweight lining on velveteens, or organza on the finer velvets.

Pressing is the most problematical point. Velvet cannot be pressed in the ordinary way, as it would shine or flatten the pile surface. A needle board is best but expensive: the velvet is laid face down to the needle surface and pressed in the direction of the pile under a damp cloth. Otherwise stand the iron on end, place a damp cloth over it and draw the wrong side of the fabric across the covered iron to steam press it.

Most of these directions apply to other napped fabrics in woollen cloth, and in general these are cut one way, but with the nap running down—corduroy cut this way shows less wear but, on the other hand, not so deep a colour.

The same cutting and layout principles apply to one-way printed fabrics. Check that the print is the right way up—large flowers upside down on one section are very obvious! Satin fabrics can also have a shading problem, so if in doubt, cut these one way as well. (Fig. 300.)

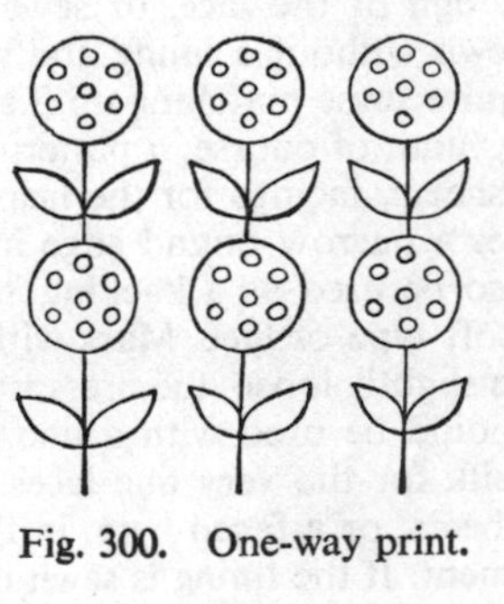

Fig. 300. One-way print.

Chiffon and Other Sheers

This group includes chiffon, which is very soft; voile and lawn, which are semi-soft, and crisp sheers such as organdie. Many will have to be lined, and the lining should be of a type to give depth to the fabric.

Again, choose a pattern with as few seams as possible and one specially designed for the fabric, for the best results.

Chiffon has a tightly-woven selvedge which should be clipped at intervals to stop the fabric lying unevenly. Mark with tailor tacking—any other method will show through to the right side and be difficult to remove. The very soft fabrics will have to be pinned and sewn through tissue paper to prevent them slipping and cut with very sharp shears or scissors.

Full skirts can also be cut across the width instead of lengthwise, as this eliminates some seams. A double hem lends weight and looks neater, with no raw edges visible through to the right side. The alternative is a very narrow, rolled hem. If a lining has been sewn together with the sheer, the facing is made in the lining fabric, but, if not, a fine bound edge in the same fabric can be neater than a facing.

To sew through tissue paper and fabric, strips of it are cut and laid underneath the tacked seam and stitched through, the paper gently torn away from the seam afterwards. Use average to loose tension, and the same pressure. The stitch length should be short about sixteen stitches to 2·5 cm (1 in) and a very fine needle, size 9 or 11, with fine pure silk thread.

Seams can be made and finished so little is seen through to the right side. The French seam is ideal, but another way is to stitch a plain seam, press both seam turnings together and stitch again close to the other seam line through the turnings. Trim away surplus turnings.

One method for hems is a very narrow machine turning, then turned again and slipstitched. Another is a hand-rolled hem. On the machine this can be a very narrow machine turning, then another just as narrow and stitched again. A double hem, is one with one turning the depth of the hem, turned again, so that the raw edge is right on the inside of hem fold, then slip stitched in place. Buttonholes can be made on the machine, otherwise loop buttonholes are more successful.

Lace

Lace comes in various weights and patterns. It can be backed onto net, which accentuates the design of the lace, or sewn to a lining, which takes away the transparency sewn without a lining and worn with a separate slip. The pattern lace may require some matching up,if so, concentrate this to the seams and front openings and, of course, a pattern without too many seams and design lines. As on sheers, facings for the heavier laces can be in lining fabric, on the lighter ones a narrow bound edge in chiffon or silk, or faced with net. Chiffon can also be used as a backing to give light support (or semi-transparency) to a soft type of lace. Mark with tailor tacks. The tension on the machine should be slightly loose; the pressure adjusted to the fabric. A medium-to-long stitch should be used with a fine needle, size 11, and mercerized thread, or pure silk for the very fine laces. Finishing on seams and hems can be as for the sheers, or a faced hem, in the same lining, or the net used throughout the garment. If the lining is sewn in with the lace, seams are pressed open and finished with zig-zag or oversewing through both seam allowances. On unlined laces, zig-zag close to the seam line and trim. On some large motif laces, for an unseamed look, the motif or pattern is cut around and matched to the other section, then it can be handsewn with a hemming stitch, on the right side, or stitched with a small zig-zag stitch on the machine.

Press lace under a cloth, as the openwork of the lace might catch on the iron tip. (Fig. 301.)

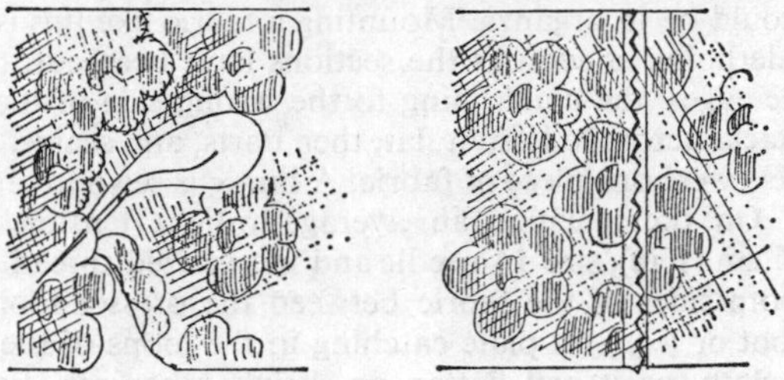

Fig. 301. Joining lace.

Crêpe

A spongy texture fabric which is rather stretchy. When cutting out it needs to be pinned to the pattern very carefully to avoid slipping. Slanted seams, and necklines, should be tacked singly while still flat on the table and stay-stitched immediately to prevent excessive stretching. Bias seams are very tricky, as the hem will drop very unevenly, so the garment needs to hang for at least a few days, before the hem can be measured and cut. As before, a pattern designed with this fabric in mind is best, the cutting is all important. On the machine use a medium to light tension, a stitch length of about 12–14 stitches to 2·5 cm (1 in), fine mercerized thread and a fine needle. Some slanting seams, those in a halter top, for instance, can have a very narrow tape sewn in with the seam to stop stretching—the same method can be used on shoulder and waist seams too. Press with care, and never damp as this shrinks the fabric alarmingly, or flattens and shines it, so press under a dry cloth on the wrong side.

Knitted Fabrics

Knitted fabrics, developed from the basic wool jerseys, now have the look of hand knits as well as crochet and rib patterns. Double knit jersey is easy to make up as it is firmer (see page 49). The finer and softer knits need more attention and circular and bias seaming should be avoided, when possible—the circular shape in particular would just go on dropping, and look very saggy. Check to see where the rib is and which is the 'grain' of the knitted fabrics. Avoid stretching the fabric when cutting out, remembering that they stretch more in the width than in the length. The tension on the machine should be medium-to-light with 12–15 stitches to 2·5 cm (1 in) or use a small zig-zag stitch. Size 11 needle is required for the fine single knits and a size 14 needle for heavier knits with a mercerized thread. Very thin nylon and silk jerseys need smaller stitches, a fine needle size 11 changed as soon as it becomes slightly dull, or a small zig-zag stitch. Sew slowly and evenly, otherwise stitches may get skipped.

With all these knits seams at the shoulder and waist should be taped. The hem zig-zagged or oversewn then blindstitched is the best way as it stretches easily with the fabric.

Mohair

Delicious to look at and difficult to sew! Usually this is best if it is completely underlined first and, on the very lightweight, loose-woven types, this underlining could be in organza. Mounting a fabric like this is done by tacking in the underlining as soon as the sections have been cut, tacking around all the outside edges, the underlining to the wrong side of the fabric. A few big diagonal tacks across to keep it flat, then darts, and seams, are sewn in as if the two layers were one piece of fabric. A lining is sewn in afterwards in the normal way. On the machine an average-to-light tension, about 12–15 stitches to 2·5 cm (1 in), size 14 needle and mercerized thread. It is a help to have paper both sides of the fabric between the presser foot and plate, to prevent the foot or teeth on plate catching in the loops of the mohair. Press under a dry cloth, as it will flatten or shrink otherwise. Bound or piped buttonholes can be made with a matching ribbon or firm fabric.

Fur Fabrics

They look very difficult but in fact are not. Some of the points to watch are the same as for velvets and other pile fabrics. The pile and backing is usually man-made, and either knitted or woven. Obviously with the bulkiness of the fabric, attention must be paid to the type of collars and sleeves if not using a pattern specifically designed for this fabric. The bigger rever type of collar is possible, though not with sharp corners which would be hard to make up. Facings are better cut in one with the garment, made in lining fabric, or the edges can be bound in braid. The fabric should be cut one way with the pile running down and the very thick pile types should be cut singly. Stitch with a loose tension, light pressure, larger stitches, about 10 stitches to 2·5 cm (1 in), a needle size 16 or heavier and heavier-weight mercerized thread.

All sections will have to be firmly tacked first, to stop them slipping or 'creeping' and stitched always in the direction of the pile. To pick out pile caught in the seam on the right side use a pin, and, on the wrong side, darts and seams can have the pile shaved to make them flatter. Not much pressing would be needed by the nature of the fabric,but if a hem or seam must be pressed, use a velvet board, or terry towelling, and lightly steam press without touching the fabric.

Leather

This has obvious differences from fabrics. In the first place they are sections of animal skins, so are individual and have to be chosen to match each other in weight and colour. The skins are not very large, so the pattern must be bought or worked out first to see how many skins are needed. They also need interfacing to hold and support the shape. Pieces must be cut singly, 1 cm ($\frac{3}{8}$ in) seams and the pattern laid to the lengthwise or crosswise right side of the leather. Suede leather has a napped surface, and the tops of all pattern sections should point to the neck of the skin.

Only pin in the seam allowance or use sellotape or similar tape to hold the pattern to leather. Mark with chalk on the wrong side all design lines, darts, etc., and make sure of fitting and accurate marking before sewing, as stitches show if they are removed, or the leather could split! Stitch with a slightly loose tension, about 8–10 stitches to 2·5 cm (1 in), a 14 or 16 needle—always new if no leather needle is available—and use a heavier weight mercercized thread. Seams can be sewn with a special adhesive leather tape, to strengthen and prevent ripping. They should be held, before stitching, with paper clips or sticky tape, instead of pins. Seams and darts are trimmed, pressed and glued down to keep them flat.

All seams and darts and the hem, which is also glued and not sewn, are hammered lightly to keep them flat and in place. Bound and piped button-holes can be made—seam buttonholes are ideal, as they eliminate extra stitching. Press with a warm, dry iron over paper or a medium-weight cloth.

Leather Imitations and Vinyl

They have some points in making up in common with leather, pinning should be done only in the seam allowance, with sellotape or paper clips to hold the layers together and work as for leather. Use very sharp scissors or shears, mark on the wrong side with chalk. The tension on the machine should be medium with a stitch length of 8–12 to 2·5 cm (1 in)' Any top stitching should be larger, use size 14–16 needles depending on the weight of the material, and heavier weight mercerized thread. When the leather or vinyl surface is down on the throat plate, or to the presser foot, use tissue paper between them to prevent them sticking. As for leather, stick down all seam allowances that are not top-stitched. Hems can be done with a blind-stitch catching the garment side with its backing material. Bound or seam buttonholes work best.

For all leather and leather imitations, welt, flat fell, and top-stitching on seams are good: as well as being decorative, they hold down the seams, and support the shape. A Teflon presser foot is recommended for smoother sewing.

Fabric and Design Suitability

With all this information it is apparent that certain fabrics are more suitable than others for the various types of garments. As a brief guide starting from the inside, so to speak, **lingerie fabrics** should be the very lightest and smooth not to interfere with the line of the dress or skirt shapes. **House-coats, dressing gowns, nightwear**, all make up well in the washable manmade fibres, especially the ones mixed with cotton to give softness.

Shirts and blouses, in fine jersey, cotton, silk, and similar weight manmade fibres. **Skirts and suits**, which have a more tailored look, make up well in all the worsted type woollens and terylene mixtures, heavy denim and cotton gabardine, lighter weight tweeds. Corduroy is good, but its slightly bulkier look like that of thicker tweeds, must be taken into account, for instance they do not pleat. The same fabrics apart from the thicker tweeds are suitable for **trousers. Dresses** too, follow the same fabric suggestions, with fluid, softer lines made up in jersey, wool crêpe, and similar weight mixtures. *Shirt dresses* make up well in most fabrics, gathered skirts and pleated dresses need thinner, flat surface fabrics; some fine wool crêpes look ideal, but in fact are rather too springy. Cottons and single jerseys, are best for gathers, and terylene mixtures for pleats—some of the new crêpes in manmade fibres also pleat very well. These softer crêpe fabrics, through to the sheers, are best for evening and special-occasion wear, looking very good on the full skirted and sleeved designs.

Jackets look well in flannel, denim, velour, tweed corduroy or velveteen—these weights are good for all the tailored and soft tailored shapes. *Coats* can be made in all the woollen fabrics—from the worsted, to the heaviest weight fabrics—with body in them, which will wear and hang well.

This general outline does not exclude experimenting with fabrics, but always work out if a fabric wili pleat; hold a collar shape; is not not too loosely woven; or if there are fine points or shapes to sew. Hold the fabric and see how it falls and if it is heavy or springy to handle. Denim, silk and corduroy all make coats as they are firmly woven, the difference is to see the purpose and the design worked out to its best advantage.

Linings, Interlinings and Interfacings

Linings. This is essential for a good professional finish to most types of garments. The lining helps to keep the shape and prevents excessive wrinkling. It also reduces the need to finish some seams, except on the most frayable types of fabric, as the lining covers the inside of the garment.

There are various types of lining fabric to suit different weights of garment fabric. The most popular and usually the cheapest, least expensive is **rayon taffeta.** The plain kind is fairly crisp to touch, but loses some of this in wear. It is not washable and damp can affect it, although it is easily pressed. It is a good all purpose lining in spite of this, especially for woollen, and fancy fabrics which would have to be dry cleaned. **Poult taffeta** is much heavier and best used for coats, **'Bemberg' rayon taffeta**, is very soft and near to a pure silk in feel, and gives a luxurious feel to the inside of dresses and, because of its quality can be used to line quite fine fabrics. Bemberg is a trade name for this rayon. **Lining crêpe,** also usually made from rayon, is hard wearing, but very soft and springy in handle. It is, therefore, good for jackets and coats, as it gives, with the same ease, as the woollen fabrics—making it better when pulling coats and jackets over other garments.

Others of this type are satin back crêpe and plain satin lining. 'Milium', a brand name, is a specially treated lining, with a satin finish, and a rather metallic sheen to the wrong side. This lining adds warmth or at least keeps the temperature even so it's a good one for winter coats. **Jap silk** is a very fine, plain, pure silk, used to line luxury fabrics like silks, fine velvets, or fine woollen cloth.

Washable linings also come in various weights, but on the whole are not quite so soft to handle. They are essential when making up clothes in man-made fibres, like Tricel, Courtelle Crimplene and others which are washable outer fabrics. Colour for the lining, is usually chosen as near as possible to the background colour of the fabric, unless on thinner or transparent fabrics when a darker or lighter shade can be used to enhance a design, and give depth to the fabric. For coats and jackets, a contrast colour or printed lining to match a dress or shirt, however, plain or printed the colour should blend, if not matching.

Interlinings They can be a confusing term as it can be taken to mean lining, which it is not, Interlining is cut exactly as the garment and sewn with the garment fabric as one layer. This gives support to a design shape, may be used to back a very loosely woven fabric, or simply add body to a rather limp fabric that needs a more structured look, or is difficult to handle.

Thin cotton lawn, organza, or lightweight rayon taffeta are the most usual types.

Interfacings. Another kind of interlining, iron-on, woven or non woven, are applied to support necklines, collars, pockets. They add crispness and body, strengthen buttonhole areas, and give prominence to shaping in design. The fusible, iron-on kinds are the easiest to use, but are not suitable for the very fine, or semi-transparent fabrics as they add a certain stiffness, this must be taken into account when support is needed but a soft look desired. On most of the heavier weight cottons they work very well, as there are thin woven or non-woven kinds which suit the weight of the fabric. For woollen fabrics there are heavier ones, and also iron-on canvas types for the heavier tweeds and coatings. Of the other non-iron kinds, canvas, hair canvas, wool canvas are all traditional interfacing fabrics, for wools and tweeds preferred by some dressmakers as they are more flexible and 'move' with the fabric. For silk and similar fabrics fine organza is used if collars or cuffs need interfacing, for a softer look lawn is good as well as being suitable to interface other fine cotton fabrics.

CHAPTER SIXTEEN

TRIMMINGS AND THREADS

Fig. 302

Bindings, belts, buttons and zips, and all functional and decorative *additions* to a garment are trimmings. The basic ones listed here are in general use; some others are listed in the glossary. One point common to all trimmings —washable ones only on washable garments.

Threads

Amongst trimmings in the most functional sense are the *threads* that hold the dressmaking together. There are specific threads for various weights and types of fabric. One which can be used on most fabrics successfully is a mercerized thread of the '*Sylko*' *type* which has a silky finish. Colour-matching should be as near perfect as possible, but always choose a reel of thread which looks slightly darker than the fabric, as when it works in with a single strand it is lighter.

The size number indicates the suitability to fabric weight. For example, a **36** is a heavy thread for the heavier tweeds and coatings, whilst a **40** is a good all purpose thread suitable for all medium-heavy to lighter fabrics. Gütermann Perivale produce amongst their threads a **60** which is good for sheer fabrics, as well as pure silk thread for the very fine chiffons, pure silk materials, velvets, and fine handsewing.

For synthetic fabrics there are corresponding threads, and although those mentioned above work well on these fabrics too, obviously the same type of synthetic will be best. 'Drima' is one brand name of a synthetic thread which works for all synthetic fabrics and weights, as well as Terylene and nylon threads, all with the same wash and wearability as the fabric.

Tacking cotton is a soft, breakable thread, used because it is less likely to mark the fabric when it has been pulled out. For velvet, as has been mentioned before, however, the fine silk thread must be used to avoid marking the material.

Buttonhole twist is a much thicker, silky finish thread for hand-made buttonholes and hand top-stitching. A similar *silk twist* is available for machine top stitching. *Gimp thread* is a fine linen cord covered in silk or cotton, and used to strengthen the edge of the buttonhole.

Fastenings

The basic *hooks, eyes and bars* are usually in black or white metal, graded from a very small size for invisible neck fastening to larger sizes for skirt waists, belts, and coats. The hook is used with the eye for edge-to-edge closings, and with the bar for overlapping closings. *Trouser hooks and bars* are much larger and designed to be set in the waistband. Special hooks and eyes are available for fur and fur fabrics.

Press fasteners are made of metal-like hooks and bars, and also range from very small to larger sizes. They are used where buttons cannot be placed and the edge needs to fasten and lie flat. Like hooks, they can be used in conjunction with buttons to relieve excess strain on the buttonhole and button itself.

Velcro, a brand name for a special fastening strip, is made of two tape-like strips with gripping pads which stick to each other when pressed together. These are ideal for sports clothes and outer wear, which need unfastening quickly and simply.

Zip fasteners are perhaps the most popular of fastenings, with different weights and lengths for different garment types and fabric weights. The lengths are from 10 cm (4 in) to 61 cm (24 in) for dress openings, the shortest usually for neck openings; 20·5–23 cm (8–9 in) for skirts; side-seam openings in dresses need about a 30·5–35·5 (12–14 in); and back neck to below waist need from about 46–61 (18–24 in), depending on the style and size. Skirt and dress weight zips for woollen and firmer fabrics need medium-weight zips, and lighter-weights exist in a large range, made with metal or nylon teeth, making them suitable for natural or synthetic fabrics.

The question of the right weight of zip is most important, as too heavy a type will drag on lighter fabric, and light-weight zips will not take the strain of heavier garments and fabrics.

Open end zips for jacket, coat, and dressing-gown openings are available in a standard range of sizes and basic range of colours. Colour choice is again very important as the idea of a zip fastener is to be a concealed opening. A very large choice is available, and the zip should match as near as possible the background or dominant colour of the fabric.

Buttons

Buttons are one of the trimmings that can ruin the best-made garment if not chosen properly. They should be matched carefully to the colour and design of the garment, and the choice depends on the importance of the closing.

Some buttons have either two or four centre holes, and are sewn through these with a hand made 'shank' between the back of the button and the fabric. The others are of the dome or covered type, with a shank moulded on the back. The first group include most of the tailor type buttons in bone or plastic substitute. These plain bone buttons have always been much favoured by the French Couture, as they can be dyed professionally to an exact match of the fabric and do not detract from the design of the garment.

A button covering service is available in most good haberdashery departments in stores and specialized shops, and 'do-it-yourself' sets are sold on cards. With these covered buttons, washability should be taken into account, and rustless moulds used.

Fancy buttons are sold in different colour ranges and a large selection of designs: military style buttons in metal, diamante buttons for evening—a fascinating choice to be made wisely.

Belts

As with buttons, a covering and making service is widely available. For those making their own, belt backing and buckle covering sets are available in haberdashery departments. Bought belts should, whenever possible be chosen at the same time as the buttons with a fabric sample, and design or pattern illustration.

Bindings and Braids

These are used decoratively on the outside, or to neaten insides of garments. Bias, paris, and satin bindings, wool, silk, and cotton braids can be used imaginatively and functionally.

Bias binding is sold by the yard from rolls, or ready-cut on cards. The bindings can be in plain cotton, or nainsook, a softer silkier finish, as well as nylon bias bindings, A soft satin one is sometimes obtainable, in black, navy, white and pastel shades for special edgings. They all have ready pressed in edges, which makes them easy to apply.

Paris binding is about 1 cm ($\frac{3}{8}$ in) wide with a silky but firm texture, and does not stretch. It is therefore used as a stay tape in seams, and to neaten raw edges, make loops, etc.

Wool braids come in many patterns, usually about 1 cm ($\frac{3}{8}$ in) to 3–4 cm ($1\frac{1}{4}$–$\frac{1}{2}$ in) wide. They can be used to great effect on tweed and wools with a surface, finishing raw edges on unlined jackets and coats as well as lined ones, and of course reversible garments. These and silkier ones can be made into froggings as well.

Cotton braids and similar weights in synthetic fibres include '*ric-rac*', a zig-zag narrow braid, widely used for trimming children's clothes, and some decorative furnishings. A narrow rayon *round braid*, almost like a cord, can be used to make buttonhole loops, and is sometimes sewn in with the lining seam to strengthen it, particularly on fur coats.

Petersham Ribbon and Skirt Petersham

Petersham ribbon is a corded ribbon used as a trimming, or to back openings, as on knitted garments.

Skirt petersham is a much stiffer corded band, used to finish the waist of skirts, or used inside the fabric waistband as a stiffener. A ready curved type is sold which fits a natural waist curve.

Piping Cord

Piping cord is made from white cotton and comes in various widths, from very fine up to a 1 cm ($\frac{3}{8}$ in). It is usually covered with a bias strip, to be inserted into piped seams or used decoratively as a finish to neck and hemlines.

Tape

Narrow plain cotton tape is used as a stay for waistlines, seams and any stretchable edges. Being narrow it can be successfully sewn in with the garment without creating too much bulk on the seam.

Paddings

Wadding is obtainable in synthetic or natural fibre. Apart from being warm, it can be used very effectively as a quilted edge,or to pad seams, apart from the wider all-over quilting. It can also be used to make shoulder pads.

Another warm padding—or interlining in its strictest sense—is 'Domette', which can be used in the same way, although it is a lighter and woven or knitted type, giving it more flexibility.

Shoulder pads can of course be bought ready-made. They come in different shapes and sizes for coats, dresses or jackets. An additional shaping can be given to fibre pads by pressing gently over a sleeve board or pad under a dampish cloth.

All these trimmings are used to enhance the design and to give the construction of the garment a professional look, Looking round haberdashery and trimming departments and keeping an eye on current fashion ideas will give you the opportunity to experiment with them and use your own ideas.

CHAPTER SEVENTEEN

BACKGROUND TO FASHION

Before a final commitment by readers to dressmaking, which could be called the beginning of fashion, some historical background to it might be useful, as a conclusion to this book.

Many definitions of fashion have been offered. In its wider sense, it covers a large variety of activities in society. We are constantly aware of examples of 'fashionable things', even in abstract forms. According to the Oxford dictionary it is a *prevailing custom* and Iris Ashley defines it as a *preferred manner of speech, of behaviour*, as it is of chosen attitudes and reactions to them. It is also a mode in the visual arts at any given time and includes our furniture, ourselves, and the architecture of our buildings—our surroundings. Indeed, the way of life of any community is exposed to fashion and influenced by its changes.

In its narrower sense, we think of fashion as relating to a mode of dress. However, it is normally understood as being part of our total environment and very existence and, as such, it is exciting and worthwhile. The study of fashion is a fascinating subject, and an involvement in activities relating to it can be so very satisfying and rewarding, and express a creative urge many people need to fulfil.

Fashion, however, must also be acknowledged as projecting an image of a life style, it mirrors the political, economic and social events of any given period.

Paradoxically, in some ways, fashion is indefinable. It is often an intuition, a feeling, an atmosphere, but it is certainly also communication. It is a reaction against the current after some time, but as soon as one fashion becomes too exaggerated it dies. A new style takes over and frequently reverses a trend, returning to a previously experienced period of time for inspiration, in similar, but never exactly the same manner. By its very nature it implies change, it evolves and is only rarely a revolution.

It gives enjoyment and pleasure to the amateur and to the professional it offers dedication, in beautifying the female figure. Both of them construct and build within an art form expression, and both need enthusiasm, coupled with the ability for concentration, to carry out work with care.

The Origins of Modern Fashion in France

Perhaps the origin of fashion can best be found in the Courts of France in the fourteenth century. One thinks of France, and especially Paris (though historically much later), as the traditional centre of fashion. This is no doubt true, in spite of recent changes with inspiration also obvious from designers in other capital cities. Paris fashion in the 1970s continues to hold its own, if in revised forms. A long tradition of accrediting a place of prominence to fashion enabled it to make an important contribution to the Arts in French Society.

It is as if the art of fashion and self-decoration has been absorbed in the blood of the French and not other nations. French women are said to have an intuitive trait for beautiful clothes, they have always loved them and have known how to wear them. They are the possessors of a heritage of centuries of elegance and *chic.* Society women and working girls alike having fostered the renown of *La Couture.*

The Spreading of French Fashions

It was customary until the nineteenth century to dress wooden dolls (known as **Pandoras**) in the then current fashions of the ladies of the court, sending them to foreign courts whose ladies, in turn, would copy them. Royal marriages, exchanges of ambassadors, the making of alliances between countries, contributed to the spread of French modes. Merchants of silk and other fine materials promoted fashion on their travels.

Gradually, with the development of printing processes, these dolls were replaced by fashion plates or drawings. As women's magazines emerged, and their circulation increased, so did the awareness of fashion and its changes. But of course, without the sewing machine, (invented c. 1850) these fashionable garments were extremely expensive and confined to the few who could afford them. Trimmings on hats were often removed and replaced on to dresses, rather than new ones made. During long periods of time details changed more often than the silhouette. None the less, by around 1775, some seventeen hundred dressmaking houses existed in Paris.

Designers and Their Influence on Fashion

Rose Bertin

The first figure of great importance in this field, at the end of the eighteenth and into the nineteenth century, was Rose Bertin. One might even call her the first Designer Dressmaker. From being apprenticed to a dressmaker as a child, learning to sew, embroider, arrange ornaments and flowers on customers dresses, she became the Court dressmaker to Queen Marie Antoinette, who even called her the *Minister of Fashion.*

Worth

The nineteenth century saw the growth of many famous Couture Houses. One man above all is remembered as the first on this list. Strange, that in a world of fashion dominated by the French it fell to an Englishman, Charles Frederick Worth, to become a most commanding and influential figure—a man, to whom fashion owes much to this day.

Born in 1825 in Lincolnshire, he worked in a dress material shop in London at the age of twelve. He delighted in handling the rich fabrics sold by his employer and became deeply interested in fashion. It led to his decision to go to Paris in 1841, in due course opening his own house, helped no doubt by an acumen for business. (He was made a cashier in London when only twenty years old). Worth was to become couturier to the Empress Eugenie in the 1850s, as well as supplying his creations the world over. He is said to be the creator of the famous crinoline, though he later took a strong dislike to it and was responsible for its decline.

On his death in 1894, his two sons took over his Couture House, which prospered amongst many other famous names, including Jacques Doucet,

Madame Paquin, Madame Lanvin, the Englishman, Redfern, and Paul Poiret, who was a contemporary of Toulouse Lautrec, the Moulin Rouge and the Can-Can. No wonder then, with many more famous names to follow, that Paris was the arbiter of fashion and dressmaking. History remembers Madeleine Vionnet, famous for inventing the bias cut, Gabrielle 'Coco' Chanel, a genius with classics in jersey and tweeds and many others. Designers such as Captain Edward Molyneux, an Englishman, and Mainbocher an American, established themselves in Paris. Only there it seemed, was it possible to be creative.

Christian Dior

The two World Wars in the first part of this century caused inevitable interruptions, yet fashion in Paris survived. In 1960 more than twenty-five Haute Couture Houses showed their collections. Those were the great days of Balanciaga, the inimitable master of superb tailoring; Elsa Schiaparelli; the House of 'Gres'; Jacques Fath; Pierre Balmain; Pierre Cardin; Nina Ricci; Hubert de Givenchy and so many more. But above all, one name stands out as a giant among the famous, a man responsible for one of the rare occasions when fashion became a revolution, Christian Dior.

Born in 1905 in Normandy, he did not start his fashion career until the age of thirty. Brought up in sheltered and peaceful surroundings, he moved with his family to Paris in 1919, where his interest was greatly aroused in the Arts, particularly in Interior Decoration and Architecture. However his parents would not hear of his suggestion to study the Fine Arts, and he agreed to enrol for studies in Political Sciences, claiming that this would give him time to find his real vocation. But he soon tired of it and, on leaving *L'Ecole des Sciences Politiques*, opened an art gallery showing and hoping to sell works by contemporary artists, some of whom were his friends. Alas, this venture proved unsuccessful, the gallery finally having to close for lack of funds. In 1935, after a period of looking for almost any job to earn a living, friends encouraged him to draw and paint, and he set his hand to producing fashion sketches and gradually succeeded in selling them. This finally led to his employment as a designer with the Couture House of Lucien LeLong, from whom he learnt his profession and for whom he worked happily.

As a result of casually meeting a friend in 1945, Dior was introduced to Marcel Boussac, a well known financier, who amongst other business involvements was the owner of a failing Couture House. Anxious to find a designer to reorganize and put his establishment back on its feet, Dior was asked to undertake this task, but he refused to do so as soon as he had seen and acquainted himself with the set up of this Couture House, certain in the knowledge that its rescue would be impossible. Instead he outlined a vision of his own House to Boussac, and convinced of his abilities and sincerity, the latter agreed to back him financially. Not quite expecting this offer and reluctant to leave Lucien Lelong, it took some time before Dior finally made up his mind to accept, partly encouraged by Pierre Balmain, a fellow designer with the House of Lelong, who had also decided to start his own Couture House. Hesitations and negotiations behind him, *Maison Christian Dior* opened its doors in the avenue Montaigne in 1947, with just three small work-rooms.

The Second World War established a fashion silhouette of a masculine nature. In Britain the attitude of so many women serving in the armed forces, working in factories and public services—previously confined to men—reflected on clothes. Uniforms, working and leisure garments were influenced by the clothes worn by men and modelled on masculine shapes or, in Paris, were often ridiculous in the extreme. Most French Couture Houses had closed (but had resisted pressure to transfer to Germany). Britain was cut off from what remained of French Fashion, and suffered austerity. Clothes and fashion were too frivolous in battles for survival (though many French women used their frivolity as a sign of resistance to the enemy). Utility clothes in Britain, which decreed a minimum of design and workmanship, brilliant in conception though they were, starved women of showing off their femininity. The end of the war created an opportunity for someone to return to women their lost six years of fashion. Christian Dior, hating the fashion around him, grasped it.

His 'New Look' of soft, rounded shoulders, tight-fitting waists, long, very full skirts, reversed the hard lines of square shoulders and the straight, narrow skirts worn during the war. Almost overnight he created a complete new silhouette and women loved it. Within a month of opening the House of Dior, the world was taken by storm. His designs welcomed everywhere, transformed the look of woman, no less than *Maison Dior* itself—the three small workrooms grew into an empire, spreading to many capital cities throughout the world. By his total involvement in the art of fashion and dressmaking, combined with perfection in craftsmanship, he had earned the esteem and admiration of all who shared his love of beautiful clothes, thus contributing to the enhancement of the female figure. A man of genius in his profession, who continued to excel in future collections, creating amongst others the *A Line*, *H Line*, and *Y Line*, until his untimely death at the age of fifty-two in 1957.

Post-war Designers in Britain and France

But Dior's efforts and successes also contributed to the post-war revival of interest in fashion both in France and now in Britain and, indeed, in many other countries. In Paris new names joined existing ones: amongst them Andre Courreges, after many years with Balanciaga; Louis Feraud and particularly Yves St. Laurent, a pupil of Dior, who became his immediate successor and is now famous in his own right as one of those who continue to influence fashion on a world-wide scale. These designers have become household names, as had their predecessors.

In Britain no famous dressmakers were known until the 1930s. From then on, designers such as Norman Hartnell and Hardy Amies, dressmakers to the Queen, Victor Stiebel, John Cavanagh, Digby Morton, the House of Lachasse and a few others emerged and made their contribution to the world of fashion. Eleven members formed the 'Incorporated Society of London Fashion Designers' in 1942. Alas, partly for economic reasons explained on page 280, only four of the 'Big Eleven' were left by 1969. Manufacturers of wholesale couture (clothes without fittings), who later formed associations such as the Fashion House Group of London, thrived for some years but ultimately fared little better.

Haute Couture Houses

Here a short description of the working set-up of Haute Couture Houses is relevant. On the one hand, Haute Couture in France, England and in other countries cater for private clientele. Houses are organized into separate workrooms for Dressmaking, Tailoring, Embroidery and Millinery. Elaborate attention is given to garments made for individual customers by cutters, fitters, seamstresses and 'hands' working under strict supervision. With three, four or more fittings before completion of any design, clients are certain of excellent workmanship and perfect fit, though they are not necessarily able to claim that theirs is an exclusive design, as each garment is selected from a 'collection' and may well have been chosen by others.

On the other hand French and to a lesser extent English Haute Couture Houses have also been very important as fashion originators, with their influence reaching every High Street. Twice yearly shows of collections are produced with great aplomb for the international Press and trade buyers from the stores and fashion manufacturers. Journalists report on the collection and thus promote a style, a look, or a type of fabric. Buyers select and buy designs often in the form of a *toile* (a linen copy of a design, accompanied by details of the original fabric and trimmings). This is used for copying and production in quantity and the design is often modified and simplified to make it suitable for mass production. Much of this activity in Paris is in the hands of an organization called *Chambre Syndicale de la Couture Parisienne* (founded in 1868), which co-ordinates opening dates of collections, sets release dates of designs, controls publicity and so on.

The declining number of individual customers over the years has been considerable, for many reasons. Haute Couture-made garments are very expensive, in many cases too expensive for enough women to keep all the couturiers in business. The availability of good off-the-peg clothes is attractive to most women, since fittings can be irksome and time is at a premium for the modern woman. A sufficient number of skilled hands to make the clothes is no longer available. In many ways, Haute Couture could not succeed in keeping abreast of life in the 1970s particularly as far as English Couture is concerned. As, although Britain has been famous for its Saville Row men's tailoring for a long time, inspiration for women's fashion did not come to the fore in quite such powerful forms as is credited to Paris. The history of fashion speaks for itself: Paris and fashion were synonymous but not so London and fashion. But change was on the way.

Mary Quant

The mid 1950s and the early 1960s saw the emergence of a movement distinct from others in the evolution of fashion. The innovator of a new attitude to clothes and a way of dressing from head to toe, Mary Quant, started a series of developments which over a period of years, considerably increased the prestige of fashion in England. Its effects were to be felt throughout the world. It saw the beginning of an era, when young people, avid for new ideas, delighted in the fashions which members of their own generation offered and, so, a dramatic change took place. Until our young designers began to make an impact, fashion for most people was decreed by Couturiers, and influenced by the then wealthy population, Haute Couture and 'High Fashion' being the only criteria for fashionable clothes, daughters following their mother's example and dressing like them. This situation was completely reversed, with the young and not so well off becoming the creators and mothers often trying to keep up with their daughters in matters of dress. Mary Quant, awarded the OBE in 1966 in recognition of services to British export, opened her boutique *Bazaar* in 1956 and captured the mood of the time with accuracy.

Together with other young designers, many of whom were trained and superbly guided at the Fashion School of the Royal College of Art and other good fashion schools, these enthusiastic young people spoke the language of youth and discarded the pretence of Haute Couture as they saw it. The cult of youth, perhaps not taken quite seriously at first by the majority of the population, none the less grew and changing fashions increased in speed.

The culmination of this trend led to the 'swinging sixties'; its effect was world-wide and obliged couturiers everywhere to cut back on what had hitherto been-very lucrative businesses. Obviously, the image of 'swinging' London, mini, midi, maxi skirts, unisex, hot pants, and all, began to tarnish. It could not, and was not meant, to last. The early part of the 1970s saw the inevitable return to a long-absent feeling for elegance and women desired to look feminine once again. Emphasis on quality, neglected for many years, returned. Designers in all major fashion centres found inspiration from earlier decades, as well as from a variety of cultures throughout the world. These took the form of the ethnic look, designs based on many national costumes, peasant clothing and decoration.

The 1970s also gave us the 'layered' look, and denim jeans—worn universally by almost everyone—became another classic.

At the beginning of the 1980s, the 'romantic', the 'puritan', and, in contrast, the 'sporty' looks were much in evidence. Above all, many designers opted for a relaxed, easy-dressing, classic theme and its popularity may well have reflected the reality of the economic recession and constantly rising prices.

Doubtless, the cycle of fashion will continue, though, as throughout the history of fashion, retrospective trends never return in *exactly* the same way.

To date, all this has led to the existence of large and efficient textile and fashion industries, employing mature, established designers, who are now and again joined by new, young talent—industries which exploit sophisticated equipment in manufacturing and offer a choice for all tastes in both fabrics and made-up garments. Women in all walks of life, the young and not so young, the wealthy and not so rich, are able to take advantage of and enjoy clothes from a wide range of inexpensive mass-produced, medium-priced and expensive semi-couture garments. With changes in life style, from the speed of jet travel to the comfort of central heating, fashion has become far less rigid. Where selecting clothes was once determined by seasonal changes, these are no longer strictly defined.

Combining aesthetics with modern technology is surely the answer to an easier and more enjoyable way of dressing for women of all ages, everywhere. And yet, it is not difficult to detect an air of disenchantment with mass production, or any kind of clothes available off-the-peg. Certainly there are those women who find it difficult to buy suitable clothes and for them standardization has not solved their problems. But more than that, the revival of dressmaking for its own sake has gathered momentum.

The aim of this book is to encourage the ambitious, new and old hands at dressmaking, to find satisfaction and pride in 'doing their own thing'. For if nothing else, dressmaking is fun.

APPENDIX ONE

SUGGESTED FURTHER READING

Adburgham, A., *Shops and Shopping*, Allen & Unwin, 1981.
Amies, H., *Just so Far*, Collins, 1954.
Balmain, P., *My Years and Seasons*, Cassell, 1964.
Battersby, M., *Art Deco Fashion: French Designers 1908–1925*, Academy, 1974.
Bertin, C., *Paris à la Mode*, Gollancz, 1956.
Brogden, J., *Fashion Design*, Studio Vista, 1973.
Carter, E., *Twentieth-Century Fashion*, Eyre Methuen, 1975.
Carter, E., *Changing World of Fashion: 1900 to the Present*, Weidenfeld & Nicolson, 1977.
Carter, E., *Magic Names of Fashion*, Weidenfeld & Nicolson, 1980.
Charles-Roux, E., *Chanel*, Cape, 1976.
Contini, M. (Laver, J., Ed.), *Fashion from Ancient Egypt to the Present Day*, Paul Hamlyn, 1965.
De Marly, D., *History of Haute Couture 1850–1950*. Batsford, 1980.
De Marly, D., *Worth: Father of Haute Couture*, Elm Tree Books, 1980.
Dior, C., *Dior by Dior*, Weidenfeld & Nicolson, 1957.
Dorner, J. (Compiler), *Fashion in the Twenties and Thirties*, Ian Allan, 1973.
Dorner, J., *Fashion in the Forties and Fifties*, Ian Allan, 1975.
Ewing, E., *History of Twentieth Century Fashion*, Batsford, 1974.
Fairly, R., *A Bomb in the Collection*, Clifton Books, 1969.
Garland, A., *Lion's Share*, Michael Joseph, 1970.
Garland, M., *Fashion*, Penguin, 1962.
Garland, M., *The Changing Face of Fashion*, J. M. Dent, 1970.
Garland, M., *History of Fashion*, Orbis, 1980.
Glynn, P., *In Fashion: Dress in the Twentieth Century*, Allen & Unwin, 1978.
Howell, G., *In Vogue: Six Decades of Fashion*, Allen Lane, 1975.
Ironside, J., *Fashion as a Career*, Museum Press, 1962.
Ironside, J., *Fashion Alphabet*, Michael Joseph, 1968.
Keenan, B., *The Women We Wanted to Look Like*, Macmillan, 1977.
Labour, A., *Kings of Fashion*, Weidenfeld & Nicolson, 1958.
Laver, J., *Taste and Fashion*, Harrap, 1945.
Laver, J., *Costume Through the Ages*, Thames & Hudson, 1963.
Laver, J., *Women's Dress in the Jazz Age*, Hamish Hamilton, 1964.
Laver, J., *A Concise History of Costume*, Thames & Hudson, 1969.
Lynam, R. (Ed.), *Paris Fashion*, Michael Joseph, 1972.
Quant, M., *Quant by Quant*, Cassell, 1966.
Settle, A., *Fashion as a Career*, Batsford, 1963.
Spanier, G., *It Isn't all Mink*, Hale, 1972.
Spencer, C., *Erté*, Studio Vista, 1970.
Turner Wilcox, R., *Dictionary of Costume*, Batsford, 1971.
White, P., *Poiret*, Studio Vista, 1973.

APPENDIX TWO

THE GLOSSARY

Dressmaking and Fashion Terms

Allowance. Extra fabric-added (1) to a seam line, (2) to accommodate pleats, gathers, tucks, or (3) for movement and comfort in wear of garment.

Appliqué. Pieces of fabric sewn on to another with decorative stitches.

Armhole. The opening in a garment for the arm. Armholes can be faced or sleeves set into them. (Also called a *Scye*.)

Asymmetrical. A design of two unequal sides of a garment.

Backstitch. Continuous handstitch, as in machine stitch.

Backstitching. Reversing the sewing direction at the beginning and end of seams to secure the stitches and thread ends.

Bag-out. A method of making up two sections of a garment, first machined separately, or two layers of fabric sewn together on all sides except for an opening, and turned through from wrong to right side.

Balance. (1) The correct hang of a garment from the shoulder, dividing the front from the back section or the correct hang of a sleeve set into an armhole. (2) The correct joining of two or more parts of a garment making them equal on two sides. (See *Balance Marks*.)

Balance marks. Placed as guide marks on seams of patterns and cut-out fabric to ensure correct balance.

Basting. Joining parts of a garment with temporary hand stitches in preparation for fittings and before machine stitching. (See also *Tacking*.)

Basque. See *Peplum*.

Belt loop. Made in fabric or thread to hold belt in position.

Bias. Diagonal to straight grain of lengthwise and crosswise threads of fabrics. Fabrics cut on the bias achieve greater elasticity and 'give'. Material cut at 45° to selvedge gives true bias.

Bias Binding. Strips of fabric or tape cut on the bias grain for seam binding and encasing of raw edges, and for decoration.

Bishop sleeve. A full length sleeve, wide at the bottom and gathered in to a cuff or band.

Block pattern. Master pattern without design lines.

Bodice. The upper part of a dress, above the waist.

Body Measurements. The actual measurements of the body without allowances for movement and comfort in wear of garment.

Bolero. A short jacket originating from Spain.

Boutique. French for small shop, now associated with selling fashion garments and accessories of a particular type.

Box pleat. A pleat with two sides of folded edges facing outward.

Braid. A woven trimming for decoration, finished on both edges, made in a variety of widths and weights.

Breakline. A line on which a lapel folds back against the front part of a garment.

Button Line. (or **Ligne**). A standard measurement for all buttons.

Button wrap or stand. Material added to the edge of a garment beyond the position of buttons and buttonholes on each side of an opening.

Cap sleeve. A very short sleeve, usually cut as an extension to the shoulder seams and sometimes in one with the bodice.

Channel. Two rows of parallel stitching, set apart for insertion of ribbon or elastic.

Circular skirt. A skirt cut with the waist and hem circumference based on a true circle.

Clip. To cut into corners or curved seam allowances, enabling seams to lie flat when pressed open.

Collar stand and fall. The stand of the collar is that part sewn to the base of the neck up to the crease line; the fall that which 'falls' back from the crease line.

Colour ways. Colours and colour combinations available in any given fabric and fabric design.

Cording. A cord inserted into a piece of fabric for decoration, sewn with *Cording foot.*

Cording Foot. A special attachment used on the machine allowing the corded fabric to be stitched close to the seam into which it is inserted.

Cross grain. See *Bias.*

Crutch (crotch). That part of trousers where the legs are joined together.

Dart. A stitched fold, tapering to a point at one or both ends, used to give shape to garments to fit the contours of the body. (Called an open dart if left unstitched at one end.)

Décolleté. A very low cut neckline.

Directional. Cutting, stitching and pressing *with* the grain of the fabric.

Double-breasted. A front fastening with two rows of buttons set equally apart from the centre front line.

Drape. Soft folds, forming pleats or gathers on garments.

Dress stand. A form made in varying materials, corresponding to the shape of the human torso from neck to thighs.

Dressmaker suit. A soft suit made by a dressmaker, as opposed to a tailored suit.

Ease. (1) Allowances on certain parts of patterns, over and above body measurements, ensuring tolerance for movement and comfort in wear of garments. (2) Extra length added to one side of a seam joining two parts of a garment, to create shape, in place of darts. (3) Allowing an extra amount of fabric for decorative fullness by gathering.

Edge stitching. Top-stitching close to edges.

Eyelet. A small hole made in garment or accessory and finished by hand stitches, or a metal ring (As in a belt to hold the prong of a buckle.)

Facing. Material sewn to raw edges, in self or other fabric.

Fastenings. Buttons, hooks, eyes and bars, press studs, Velcro and others used to keep garments closed.

Feeler. A trade term for a largish piece of a fabric often accompanied by patterns of colour ways.

Felling. Another term for hemming.

Fitting. Adjusting prepared garments to fit individual figures.

Fitting lines. Final seam lines.

Flare. Additional width of fabric at lower ends of a garment for extra fullness.

Fly. The buttoned or zipped front opening of trousers.

Fly fastening. A concealed opening, the type of fastening not being visible on the right side of a garment.

French chalk. Powdered chalk.

Fraying. Small, loose threads which unravel on cut edges of fabrics.

French dart. A bust dart placed diagonally at lower end of bodice side seam.

Frill. A piece of fabric with one edge gathered, the other left flat, giving a fluted effect.

Frog fastening. Looped braid or cord used for decorative fastening of garments.

Fusing. The melting of resin-treated interlinings and canvases to fabrics by application of heat and pressure.

Gathering. The shortening of a fabric length by drawing it up on a line of stitching.

Gimp. A thick thread used to strengthen and raise buttonhole stitching. It can also be used for embroidery.

Godet. A triangular-shaped piece of fabric sewn into lower parts of a garment for extra width.

Gore. A panel of fabric which is narrower at the top than at the bottom. Mostly used for skirt designs.

Grain (straight). A term denoting the lengthwise (warp) and crosswise (weft) threads of fabric crossing each other at right angles. Fabrics are *off-grain* if warp and weft threads do not cross each other at right angles, or garment pieces are *off-grain* if not placed and cut on the straight grain.

Grown on. Hems or facings cut in one with the main sections of a garment, rather than separately.

Gusset. A triangular-shaped piece of fabric inserted to allow extra movement, usually at under-arm seams on sleeves cut in one with the bodice, or at crutch seams.

Haberdashery. All trimmings used for garments.

Hanger appeal. A trade term to describe the look of a garment when seen on a clothes hanger.

Haute Couture. The French word for 'high sewing'. A term now mainly used to describe the work of well-known French designers, though Couture-made garments embrace all those made for private clients. Couture garments may have many fittings and are finished with a considerable amount of hand work.

Hem. The edge of a fabric which has been folded under.

Hemline. The line on which an edge of fabric is folded.

Hemming. The hem sewn back to the main part of the garment.

Interfacing or **interlining.** The use of material for shaping, reinforcing and stiffening parts of a garment to give strength and body or extra warmth, placed between the outer fabric, facings and linings.

Inset. A piece of fabric, braid or other trimming set into a seam, mainly for additional decoration.

Inverted pleat. Two sides of pleats with folded edges facing inwards. The reverse side of a box pleat.

Jet pocket. A pocket opening made with folded piping strips, in self or contrast fabric.

Joining. Stitching together of fabric pieces on sewing lines.

Kick-pleat. A short pleat at the lower end of skirts, mainly for extra stride room. Usually cut on as an extension to centre and side seams and forming a knife pleat.

Knife pleat. Folded edge of one side of a pleat facing either to the left or right side.

Lap. To place and then secure one piece of fabric *over* another (overlap) or *under* another (*underlap*).

Lapel. The upper part of a front edge of a jacket or coat folded back from the neck.

Lay. A term used in garment manufacturing, meaning the same as *Layout*.

Layering. Trimming of seam allowances to narrowing widths to reduce bulk.

Laying-up. Placing one layer of fabric on top of the other for cutting more than one garment.

Layout. Pattern pieces placed on the fabric for cutting according to the width and type of fabric.

Lining. Material which fully or partially covers the inside of a garment.

Link buttons. Two buttons held together by strands of threads forming a long shank, used as cuff links or front fastenings on coats and jackets.

Marker. The top layer on which patterns are marked in, for wholesale cutting of garments.

Marking. To transfer symbols on patterns—sewing lines, darts, balance marks, pocket positions and others—to the fabric.

Match. (1) To join and bring together construction markings. (2) Checks, plaids and stripes. (3) Colours of fabric and trimmings.

Mitre. (1) Forming of diagonal seam at a corner. (2) The addition in length to one side of a dart to equal the length of the other, if placed on a diagonal seam.

Modelling. (1) Designing three-dimensionally by pinning and marking calico or muslin on a dressmaker stand. (2) Displaying garments on the body.

Mounting. Interlinings stitched to the main fabric, and made up as one garment.

Needleboard. A board with a surface of fine steel wires for pressing velvet and other pile fabrics preventing the nap or pile from being flattened. (Also called *Velvet board.*)

Notches. Marks on paper patterns and cut garments indicating balance marks and seam allowances.

Notchers. A tool for notching.

Notions. The same as *Haberdashery*, sometimes used with instructions on commercial patterns but not a term used in the trade.

Off grain. See *Grain.*

Overlap. See *Lap.*

Overlock. A special machine stitch used in the trade for oversewing raw edges.

Oversewing. Handstitching of raw edges preventing fraying of the material.

Pad-out. To build up parts of a garment with soft material.

Pad stitch. Diagonal stitch used in tailoring, holding canvas to the fabric, especially on collars and lapels for lasting shape. Can be done by hand or special machine.

Peplum. A loose piece of fabric, from waist seam to hips, mostly on jackets. A peplum has a fluted effect; a *basque* has a flat shape.

Petersham. A webbing or heavy ribbon used to finish waist lines on skirts and trousers.

Picot. A special edge finish on hems, made by cutting through machine stitches.

Pinking. Cutting seam edges with serrated (or 'pinking') shears to prevent fraying.

Pin-tuck. A very narrow edge-stitched tuck.

Piping. A folded piece of fabric inserted into a seam for buttonholes, pockets and other decorations.

Pivot. (1) Turning at square corners when machining. (2) Swivelling of darts from bust point.

Placket (plaquet). A piece of fabric sewn on to openings of garments for a neat finish.

Plaids. Patterns of checks and lines woven in to, or printed on to, cloth.

Pleat. A fold on fabric, stitched down, left loose, or pressed into a crease. All pleats are based on three main types: the box, inverted, and knife pleat.

Pleating. The forming of patterns of pleats.

Pressing. The removing of creases or creating of creases on fabrics by heat and pressure, as in dry pressing, or by the use of moisture, as in damp and steam pressing.

Presser foot. An attachment to the sewing machine which puts pressure on the fabric and ensures an even flow of stitching.

Prêt à porter. French for 'ready to wear'.

Princess line. A garment shape, cut to fit close to the body and flared towards the hem, using only vertical seam lines.

Pucker. Too tightly stitched and held seams, giving a 'wavy' effect.

Purl. A twist in the thread to form a knot-like edge.

Quilt. Several thicknesses of fabric sewn together, or soft material inserted between two outer layers of fabric and stitched through all, forming a pattern with a raised effect,

Ready-to-wear. A term embracing all types of garments made without fittings for sale in shops and stores.

Reinforcing. Strengthening of corners or slashed openings with extra stitching, tape or interlinings.

Rever. The upper part of a front-edge opening folded back from the neck.

Ribbon. A strip of fabric in varying widths, finished on both edges.

Ric-rac. Type of braid with zig-zag edges and serrated effect used for decorative purposes.

Rouleau. A narrow strip of fabric stitched and turned through.

Ruching. A drawn up, pleated effect on material.

Saddle stitch. Decorative stitching often made with special threads, large on the right side, small on the wrong side of the fabric.

Scallop. Edgings forming decorative semi-circles.

Scye. See *Armhole*.

Seam (line). A sewing line holding parts of a garment together.

Seam allowance. A given amount of material on garments, between (stitching) sewing lines and cutting edges, added to sewing line to allow for seaming.

Seaming. Joining two or more parts to form one.

Seams. For types of seams see chapter sixteen.

Self fabric. This refers to using the same fabric as the garment.

Selvedge (Selvage). Finished lengthwise edges of fabrics.

Shank. Space between button and fabric, taken up by strands of thread or lower part of button.

Shape. (1) Created by use of darts, seams and fullness to accommodate structure of body and limbs. (2) The silhouette and line of a design.

Shirring. Gathering material with elastic thread.

Slash. To cut into fabrics.

Sleeve-crown or **head.** The upper part of the sleeve.

Smocking. Gathering of fabric with decorative stitches.

String. A piece of string, thread or similar mark on selvedges, used to denote faulty or damaged section of fabric. Shops and stores allow extra length in compensation.

Stitches. For most types of stitches see chapters six to eleven and chapter sixteen.

Sunray pleats. Graduated pleats, from narrow to wider.

Suppression. Removal of excess material at a given point at one end, creating fullness at the other for shape, by means of darts, seams, tucks, folds.

Swatch. A composite collection of small pieces of fabrics.

Symmetrical. A design of two equal halves.

Tacking (also **Basting**). Temporary stitches holding parts of a garment together before fitting and machining.

Tailored. Garments made in part by shaping and moulding with an iron and the use of heavy type canvas and interlinings to maintain shape.

Tailor tack. Marking sewing lines, darts, balance marks with double threads through both halves of parts of cut garment, leaving loop between each stitch, pulled apart and cut. (See also *Trace tack*.)

Tension. The relative tightness or looseness between top and bottom thread in machine stitching.

Toile. Try out of a garment, made in unbleached calico or muslin. Finished toiles are often bought by manufacturers for copying of designs.

Top-pressing. Final pressing of finished garment.

Top-stitching. Machine stitching on right side of garments for decoration and/or extra strength.

Trace tack. Marking with single thread on single pieces of cut garment. (See also *Tailor tack.*)

Tracing. Marks transferred from one part of pattern to another, from pattern to fabric or one part of fabric to another, using a tracing wheel (see chapter four).

Trimming. (1) Cutting back widths of seams or excess fabric. (2) Decorating garments with buttons, belts, braid and other materials.

Tuck. A straight and even fold stitched either outside of a garment for decoration or inside for body shape.

Turnings. Same as *Seam allowance.*

Turn-up. Material folded and turned up at bottom of trousers.

Underlap. See *Lap.*

Under-pressing. Pre-pressing of sections and opening of seams with an iron—progressively—when making garments, before final top pressing.

Under-stitching. Top stitching of facings through seams holding facings to main parts of garment. Keeps facings inside garments and prevents them from rolling back and showing. Also called machine backstitching of facings.

Velvet board. See *Needleboard.*

Vent. A lapped hem opening on lower parts of garments.

Welt. A strip of fabric sewn to a pocket opening, stitched down on three sides and left open at the top.

Wing seam. A curved design line commencing at the front or back armhole and extended to the waist.

Working drawing. An accurate drawing of a design, clearly showing all seam lines and details.

Yoke. A shoulder piece on front and/or back of garments, or a waist piece at the top of skirts and trousers.

Fabric Descriptions

This comprehensive list will help in identifying fabrics, and in the most suitable selection for any chosen design or purpose. The glossary of textile, dressmaking and fashion terms (see page 283) will assist in clarifying the finer points of cloth constructions and finishes and in the making-up of fabrics.

Afgalaine. A light-weight wool fabric.

Alpaca. The fibre from the fleece of the alpaca or llama of South America. A soft, very fine quality fabric, with a smooth, lustrous surface. Mixtures with wool and cotton are used for light-weight garments.

Angora wool. Long, soft wool spun from the hair of the Angora goat or rabbit. Very good for knitting yarns. Angora wool is used to make mohair fabric.

Art silk. An old name for rayon (artificial silk).

Astrakhan. Wool or lamb's fur of a curly nature coming from Astrakhan, in the USSR. Also a pile fabric made to imitate Astrakhan or Persian lamb cloth. The foundation cloth is either knitted or woven and contains mohair, sometimes cotton or rayon.

Banlon. Registered trade name of a bulked nylon yarn-knitted fabric.

Barathea. A fabric made from woollen and worsted or silk and manmade fibres, with a twilled rib weave. Usually in black.

Batiste. A smooth, soft, light-weight plain-weave cotton fabric, also sometimes made in linen or rayon. Suitable for shirts and soft dresses. Available in white, colours and prints.

Bedford cord. A strong, smooth, generally woollen fabric, with lengthwise cords. Best for suit and coat weights.

Bengaline. A plain-weave, ribbed fabric resembling poplin. Wool, cotton, silk or rayon, in dress and coat weights.

Bird's eye. A weave pattern (see Textile Glossary, page 299).

Blazer cloth. A cloth similar to flannel and melton.

Botany. A fine wool from the Merino Sheep. Also cloth woven from Botany wool.

Bouclé. A woven or knitted, usually woollen fabric with a roughly curled loop effect on the surface, produced by means of fancy yarns.

Broadcloth. A fine, close, plain-weave woollen cloth. Smooth and lustrous, and highly napped one way, this produces different light reflections, so that all pattern pieces must be cut in one direction only.

Brocade. A heavy, rich fabric with elaborate, slightly raised, jacquard-weave patterns. Often made in silk or rayon, satin backed, sometimes incorporating gold and silver threads.

Broderie Anglaise. Open embroidery work is the characteristic of this cotton fabric.

Calico. A plain-weave cloth without finished surface available in light, medium and heavy weights. Coarse in handle, creases easily. Mainly used for making toiles. (See Glossary, page 288.)

Cambric. A fine, muslin type fabric of firm, plain weave and glazed surface finish.

Camel hair. Very fine wool fabric woven with camel's hair, and wool fibres. Slightly napped, soft, and combines qualities of warmth with light weight.

Canvas. An unbleached, strong, firm plain-woven cloth. It is made in cotton and flax, also in wool, hair and rayon in a variety of weights and for many uses, particularly for interfacings in tailored garments.

Cashmere. Fabric woven from a soft, very fine wool of goats in the Himalayan region. Expensive, but used for many types of outer-wear garments.

Cavalry twill. A strong, double twill-weave fabric with pronounced diagonal cords, in wool, rayon and cotton.

Chambray. A plain fabric, woven with coloured warp and white weft threads. Usually in cotton, but can be made with fibre blends. Washes and handles well.

Cheese-cloth. A coarse muslin fabric.

Cheviot. A rough, heavy-weight, twill-weave woollen fabric, not unlike tweed.

Chiffon. A plain-woven sheer fabric, soft, light-weight and delicate, with a 'floating quality'. Not easy to handle.

Chintz. Glazed surface sheen fabric normally used as a furnishing fabric, but occasionally also for clothes. Closely woven, good quality cotton, brightly patterned. Finished for stiffness, though this is not permanent.

Cire. This fabric has a bright, shiny, wet-look surface appearance, produced on satin by application of wax, heat and pressure.

Cloqué. Raised pattern effect on the surface of fabric resembling embossing.

Corduroy. '*Cor du Roi*' gave the name to this fabric. Worn by the servants of French kings. A ribbed cotton velvet, very strong and durable with a short, one-way pile. Ribs vary from thin, pin needle cord, to thick whale-cord and elephant cord.

Crêpe. The name denotes the structure of this type of fabric. It is woven with highly twisted yarns to form a crinkled surface effect. Wool, cotton and man-made fibres are used for crêpe fabrics, including: *Alpaca crêpe*—a soft dull rayon type with the appearance of a woollen fabric; *Bark crêpe*—with the appearance of tree bark, woollen or rayon; *Canton crêpe*—rough looking, with much crosswise stretch; *Chiffon crêpe*—soft, smooth, plain weave; *Crêpe de Chine*—a sheer washable silk crêpe; *Crêpe Georgette*—light-weight, semi-sheer, made in wool, silk or man-made fibres. (See also *Marocain.*)

Crepon. Woven or knitted with puckered, blistered surface effect, achieved by chemical or heat setting processes. Light to medium in weight.

Delaine. Light-weight, plain-weave wool fabric, often printed.

Denim. This is a very strong and hard wearing twill fabric, woven with coloured warp and white weft yarns with a slightly stiff, but firm handle. Obtainable in medium to heavy weights. Makes up and washes well. Suitable for many types of garments.

Dimity. A crisp, sheer, corded cotton fabric.

Doe-skin. A one-way napped fabric, reflecting light in different directions. Close twill or satin weave, made in wool, cotton and rayon, with a very fine, suede-like surface.

Donegal (tweed). Originally hand-spun in County Donegal, now used as the term for this type of tweed of herringbone or twill weave construction, incorporating coloured spots or slubs.

Dotted Swiss. Sheer cotton fabric with woven dots.

Drill. A double-weave strong cotton fabric of medium weight.

Duchesse satin. See *Satin.*

Duck. Closely woven, heavy canvas-like cotton fabric with a slight rib effect. Also made in linen.

Dupion (douppion). A slub fabric made from silk, or simulated in manmade fibres. The use of two threads woven as one produces the irregular slub effect.

Duvetyn (duveteen). Soft, velvet-like napped fabric, similar to suede, from silk or wool fibres, with good draping qualities. (See *Pile fabrics.*)

Etamine. Woollen fabric which is soft, light-weight, in plain, open weave.

Face-cloth. A woollen or worsted fabric, finished with a soft, smooth, regular nap.

Faconne. Silk or rayon fabric with a small, jacquard design.

Faille. Flat, ribbed fabric, with flatter ribs than found in *grosgrain.* Made in silk or rayon.

Felt. A non-woven fabric, mainly made from wool fibres, by pressure, moisture and heat.

Flannel. An all-wool or part-wool fabric of plain or twill weave, with a soft handle. It has a slightly raised surface, but not one way. A firm cloth, which makes up well.

Flannelette. Made from cotton, with raised surface as flannel. It is soft, warm and cosy and launders well. Also made in manmade fibres.

Fleece. Long-napped fabric from the fleece of sheep. Often used as the inside of sheepskin coats. Rather bulky and not easy to handle.

Foulard. Soft, light-weight silk fabric with a twill weave. It is also made from wool, cotton or rayon fibres. Often used for ties and scarves.

Fur fabrics. Pile fabrics, woven or knitted from manmade fibres to imitate natural fur.

Gabardine. Describes the structure of the twill weave, with a diagonal rib. The fabric is firm, made mainly in wool, worsted and cotton. The rib effect is less pronounced in cotton gabardine. Extensively used for suits, coats, trousers, casual and sportswear.

Gauze. A sheer, light-weight fabric, with an open lace-like effect produced by the Leno/gauze weave. Made in cotton, linen and rayon.

Georgette. See *Crêpe.*

Gingham. Cotton, with woven coloured check or plaid designs. Sometimes blended with silk or rayon. Crisp, but soft in handle. Washes extremely well.

Gossamer. A gauze weave, very light-weight silk or cotton fabric.

Grosgrain. Firm, stiff, closely woven fabric with a pronounced horizontal rib, which is heavier than in poplin or faille. Silk or man-made.

Guipure. See *Lace.*

Harris tweed. This fabric is spun, dyed and finished in the Outer Hebrides. Made from pure Scottish wool.

Homespun. A coarse, plain-weave wool or cotton fabric with a hand-woven look. The thick yarns used produce a heavy-weight fabric suitable for coats and suits.

Hopsack. A coarse, plain-weave cloth of wool or cotton, not very closely woven. Some hopsack may be of a basket weave. Primarily suitable for coats and suits.

Houndstooth. Woven tweed-type fabric with a tooth-like design.

Interlock. A light-weight, circular-knitted cotton cloth.

Irish tweed. A fancy tweed fabric, woven with homespun yarns.

Jersey. A knitted fabric of wool, cotton, rayon, silk or synthetic blends, so weights range from sheer for lingerie to heavy for coats. Stretchability of lighter weights (single-knit) make it most suitable for draping, but it is firm enough for tailored garments in heavier weights (double-knit).

Knits. Any knitted fabric made by the interlocking of loops of one or more yarns (See Glossary, page 298)

Lace. Open-work fabric, made with bobbins, needles and hooks, either by hand or machine. Made from nearly every fibre, the threads are formed into designs, such as: *Alencon Chantilly*—light, delicate, usually with floral pattern, backed to a fine net; *Cluny Venice*—coarser, stronger, with geometric designs, mainly in cotton without backing; *Guipure*—rich, stiff, heavy textured lace.

Lamé. A brocade woven with natural and manmade fibres and containing metallic yarns for decorative purposes, hence suitable for evening wear.

Lawn. Light-weight, sheer, thin and fine cotton or linen of plain weave. Crisper than voile, less crisp than organdie. Ideal for many light-weight garments, or as backing for extra body. In white, colours or prints.

Linen. Woven from the strong flax fibre, in three main weights: handkerchief, which is sheer; medium dress weights; and heavier suiting weights.

Lurex. A registered trade name for fabrics with non-tarnishing metallic yarns.

Madras. Cotton with plain weave, in multi-coloured checks and stripes; not colour fast and bleeds in washing and sunlight. Used for shirts, blouses and dresses.

Marocain. Heavy dress weight in silk or manmade fibres: *moss crêpe*—moss-like looking finish; *satin crêpe* or *satin bark crêpe*—heavy-weight type; *wool crêpe*—soft, from wool fibres only. (See also *Crêpe*.)

Marquisette. An open-weave mesh fabric, very light-weight. It is made in cotton, silk or nylon, often suitable for evening wear.

Matelassé. This, made in cotton, wool, silk or rayon, is woven on dobby or jacquard looms to produce patterns with a quilted effect.

Melton. Heavily felted, non-lustrous woollen fabric with slight one-way nap. The finishing processes ensure that this is a solid cloth, so garments wear well.

Merino. Very fine wool from the merino sheep used for worsted cloth.

Milanese. A warp-knitted fabric, the product of the 'Milanese' machine.

Mohair. Luxurious fabric from the fine, soft, silky hair of the Angora goat. Made in plain and twill weaves, its characteristics are strength, lightness and lustre.

Moirê. Any fabric, often silk taffeta, finished with a watered/wavy surface effect.

Moss crêpe. See *Crêpe*.

Moleskin. A strong twill fabric, resembling the skin of the mole in touch and appearance.

Mousseline de soie. Silk or rayon muslin with firm and crisp finish. Most suitable for evening wear.

Mull. Soft, thin cotton muslin, semi-sheer. Coarse and loose weave, finished without stiffening agents.

Muslin. Usually cotton with twill or gauze weave, muslin is a coarser version of mull. Sometimes dressed with starch, which is not permanent.

Needle cord. See *Corduroy.*

Net. An open-weave, mesh-like fabric. Can be made in cotton, rayon, silk or nylon in weights from light to heavy.

Non-woven fabrics. Any fabric in which fibres have been bonded or fused together rather than spun, woven or knitted.

Nun's veiling. A soft, light-weight plain-weave cloth, not unlike flannelette in feel.

Organdie. Thin, stiff, transparent fabric in plain-weave cotton.

Organza. As *organdie*, in silk or rayon. Both suitable for evening wear.

Ottoman. Heavy, cross-wise corded fabric with larger and rounded ribs than *grosgrain.* Can be made of wool, cotton or rayon, with silky appearance.

Paisley. Any wool, cotton or rayon fabric which is printed with the traditional scroll design originating from Paisley in Scotland.

Panne velvet. See *Velvet.*

Peau de soie. The 'skin of silk'. A good-quality heavy, dull satin dress material made from silk, but also from manmade fibres or blends.

Pile fabrics. Any material woven with looped yarns, raised on the surface and cut or uncut, to stand up to form a rich texture. Fur fabrics, velvet, velour, corduroy, etc., are all pile fabrics.

Piqué. Crisp, mainly cotton fabric with raised lengthwise or diagonal ribs, as in *Wale pique*, *Waffle pique*, or honeycomb (diamond shape) weave or birds-eye effects.

Plissé. Plain or printed cotton, with a blistered surface effect achieved by a special finish. Made in a variety of weights.

Poplin. Smooth, firm, ribbed, plain-weave cloth originally made in silk, but can also be in wool or rayon, though it is mostly a medium to heavy-weight cotton fabric.

Poult. A stiff, ribbed silk or rayon material heavier than taffeta.

Prints. Can be any fabric with printed patterns applied by various methods after the cloth is made.

Rattinet (ratieen or **ratiné).** A pile wool fabric, with a surface effect of small round knobs. Mostly suit and coat weights.

Repp (rep). A ribbed fabric produced by weaving with a thick weft into a thin warp.

Raw silk. *See silk*

Sailcloth. Strong and slightly stiff, mostly heavy-weight fabric, made of cotton, linen or nylon. Used largely for play clothes and casual wear.

Sateen. A cotton cloth woven with the normal satin weave used for silk and rayon satin. Glazed for high lustre.

Satin. Satin weaves make a large range of lustrous fabrics in silk or manmade fibres, extensively used for dresses, linings and lingerie, and include: *crêpe satin*—soft, drapy; *duchess satin*—stiff and solid; *lining satin*—light in weight; *panne satin*—very high lustre; *slipper satin*—fairly stiff; and *washable satin.*

Seersucker. Light-weight, plain weave cotton fabric with crinkled surface effect. Can be laundered without ironing. It has no right or wrong side.

Serge. Twill, or plain-weave cloth of wool, worsted but also other fibres, with a roughish texture. Suit weights, hard wearing.

Shantung. See *Silk.*

Sharkskin. Wool, worsted, silk, rayon, and synthetic fibres are used for this cloth, which is medium to heavy in weight and most suitable for tailored garments and sportswear.

Silk. A selection of silk fabrics includes: *Jap silk*—very light-weight, soft plain silk, mostly used for linings; *Pongee*—A rough, strong, natural silk fabric; *raw silk*—

the continuous filament from the silk worm before processing to remove the gum. The uneven weave produces a rough surface effect.

Shantung. Plain-weave, rough silk caused by use of uneven yarns, giving this fabric a slubbed effect. Made in cotton rayon and blends to simulate this slub.

Shot silk. Silk characterized by changing colour effects.

Spun silk. Made from silk waste.

Stretch fabrics. All fabrics constructed to achieve elasticity and stretch when pulled, returning to the original shape when released. Stretch qualities include comfort, shape retention and crease resistance. Stretchability varies from: *warp*, or parallel to selvedge, good for trousers; *weft*, or across the width of fabric, good for skirts and tops; *two-way* stretch, in both directions, used mostly for swimwear and foundation garments.

Suedette. Velveteen, napped one way and finished to simulate suede (leather).

Surah. Soft twill-weave, light-weight silk, but also made in rayon or synthetic fibres.

Taffeta. A plain, closely woven, smooth and crisp fabric. Originally in silk, now mainly made with rayon or synthetic fibres: *faille taffeta* has a cross-wise rib; *moiré taffeta* has a wafered, wavy surface effect; and *paper taffeta* is light-weight and stiff.

Tarlatan. Cotton cheese-sloth, with plain weave and starched finish.

Tartan. Colourful checks denoting Scottish clans.

Terry cloth towelling. Cotton fabric with uncut or looped pile (not one way) mostly on both sides. Very absorbent and therefore popular for beachwear.

Thai silk. Woven in Thailand, with traditional patterns.

Tricot. A plain warp-knitted fabric made with a single thread. Mostly made in cotton, rayon or nylon. It is light in weight and very suitable for underwear and T-shirts.

Tulle. A stiff, fine net-like sheer fabric in silk, nylon or rayon. Popular for bridal wear.

Tussore (Tussah). Wild silk, rough and coarse, quite loosely woven.

Tweed. Genuine tweed is made with pure virgin wool. It has a rough surface, is usually woven with two or more colours, often forming patterns of checks and plaids. There are now not only woollen tweeds but cotton, silk, and synthetic tweeds are available. The term tweed sometimes now covers almost any fabric which has a roughened look.

Twill. A basic weave fabric with a diagonal rib in natural, manmade fibres and blended yarns.

***Velour.** Has a velvety texture, and is a soft, thick fabric closely napped one way. Wool velour is similar to Broadcloth, most suitable for suits and coats. Nylon is also used to make this cloth.

***Velvet.** A one-way pile fabric in silk, rayon, cotton or nylon, sometimes in natural fibres backed to synthetic ones. Velvet is double-woven face to face, and cut apart on the loom by a knife placed in position resembling a shuttle. Types of velvet include: *chiffon velvet*—light-weight with silk orrayon backing; *Lyons velvet*—a stiff velvet; *mirror velvet*—a calendered, highly polished velvet; *panne velvet*—has a flattened pile, is very lustrous in appearance.

***Velveteen.** A cotton one-way weft pile velvet, the fibres are cut after weaving and form the dull surface.

Vicuna. A soft woollen cloth from the hair of the South American goat, of high quality, made in dress and heavy weights.

Virgin wool. Wool that has never previously been processed.

Viyella. Registered trade name: part wool, part cotton fabric with slight nap. The cotton content makes it more washable.

*** See** *Pile fabrics.*

Voile. A soft, light semi-transparent fabric, usually a plain weave, or variations of a plain weave. Similar to organdie and lawn, though less stiff, with good draping quality.

Vynel 'fabric'. A type of plastic and not strictly a fabric. Vynel films are used either on their own, or with a bonded woven or knitted backing. It can be embossed to simulate natural leather.

Waffle cloth. See *Piqué*.

Whipcord. A closely woven worsted, with a diagonal rib, similar to gabardine, but the ribs are more pronounced. A strong fabric with a lot of body.

Wool crêpe. See *Crêpe*.

Worsted. Made from best quality wool fibres, the highly twisted yarns make a strong, firm and smooth cloth.

Winceyette. A light-weight, strong fabric of wool or wool and cotton, with plain or twill weave, and surface—raised on both sides.

Zibelene. A lustrous woollen fabric with a hairy nap raised in one direction.

Textile Terms

The great majority of fabrics in common use are woven, which means that yarns are interlaced at right angles to each other. The many different ways in which this interlacing takes place, and the quality, structure and colour of the yarns used, determine the feel and performance as well as appearance of fabrics. Many more are knitted, a construction of the interlocking of loops of one or more yarns, and are either 'circular' or 'warp knit'. The use of one yarn makes a 'Single Knit', two or more make a 'Double Knit'. Novelty knits can have tweed effects, looped and boucle surfaces, lacy, crocheted, and open, fishnet appearances. Other fabrics still, are bonded by chemical processes as previously described. The great variety available is further extended by numerous finishing processes.

In dressmaking, you will want to know something about the fabric you choose so that you can link its characteristic performance and with the selected design, to obtain the best from both. Even though the finer technical details of fabric constructions are not important to you, and can be quite confusing, a basic understanding of the main differences of materials can only be an advantage and help to achieve garments which are a great pleasure to wear.

Weaves

Dobby. Geometric designs woven by special looms, for example *Birds eye*, a twill weave forming a diamond pattern with small dots in the centre resembling the bird's eye.

Gauze/Leno. An open effect weave, produced by the Leno loom for light weight fabrics like *Gauze*, *Net*.

Jacquard. A loom with perforated patterns, which enables every individual thread to weave differently from all others in a given design, so being capable of producing most intricate shapes of patterns, as found in *Damask*, in which patterns stand out from the ground with a contrasting lustre.

Pile. A combination plain and twill weave, with an additional warp thread forming a loop on the surface. This is cut as in *velvet*, flattened as in *Panne Velvet* or left uncut as in *Terry*.

Plain. This and the following two weaves are the basic methods used. The difference between them are the way the warp (lengthwise) threads cross the weft (crosswise) threads. In the plain weave, the weft yarn is passed *over* the warp yarn and *under* the next alternately. *Closely woven*, this is the strongest of all weaves. All others are variations of these three. The *Basket weave* is one of them, using double yarns instead of single ones. This makes a loosely woven fabric which stretches easily. Plain weave fabrics include, *Batiste*, *Broadcloth*, *Cambric*, *Lawn*.

Satin. Similar to the Twill weave, but with longer gaps in the interlacing between warp and weft threads. The weft thread is passed *under* four or more warp threads and then *over* one. This helps to produce lustrous fabrics such as *Satin Sateen*.

Twill. The weft thread passes *over* and then *under* two or more warp threads and in so doing they produce diagonal ribs from left to right in fabrics such as *Barathea*, *Denim Foulard*, *Gabardine*, or variations as in *Herringbone* and *Dogtooth* patterns.

Textile Finishes and End Treatments

These are basically divided into three groups:

(1) **Permanent.** Should last throughout the life of the fabric.
(2) **Durable.** Should last through several times of washing or dry-cleaning.
(3) **Non-durable** Lasts only until first time of washing or cleaning.

Anti-stat. A finish to reduce the effects of static electricity, slight shocks and the tendency of the fabric clinging to the body, caused by friction of a fabric rubbing against itself or other objects.

Bleaching. The cleaning and whitening of 'grey' fabrics. Natural fibres are off-white because of the impurities they contain. Cotton fabrics can easily be bleached, woollen ones less so.

Bonding. The pressing of fibres or layers of fabric together with chemical substances.

Brushed. Fabrics in which loose fibres are raised to the surface.

Bulking. To fluff up the surface of manmade, mainly acrylic fibres.

Calendering/Glazing. Produces high gloss and firm finish of fabrics.

Calpetra. A registered trade name for finishing processes including non-shrink, permanent glaze, crease resist.

Colourfast. Colours which do not change during the life of the fabric. They should not rub off, fade through washing, dry-cleaning, exposure to sunlight, perspiration, temperature, pressing and ironing.

Crease resisting. Treatment of fabrics, by the application of resin finish, reducing the tendency to crease, and which recover from creasing when left to hang.

Dressing/Sizing. To produce a stiff effect by use of starch, though this is not always permanent.

Drip-dry. Describes garments which after washing are left to dry, shedding wrinkles at the same time and thus requiring little or no ironing.

Durable-Press. See Permanent Press.

Dyeing. The colouring of yarns or fabrics.

Embossing. The transfer of designs from heavy engraved rollers on to cloth.

Embroidered. Many different types of decorative needlework.

Everglaze. A registered trade name of fabrics treated for crease, shrink and stretch resistance.

Flame proofing. This treatment enables fabrics to resist fast burning if they catch fire.

Flocking. To apply patterns and designs to fabrics by adhesives.

Glazing. See *Calendering*.

Laminating. A fabric joined to a synthetic foam backing.

Mercerizing. Adds strength, produces lustrous sheen finish on some fabrics, e.g. cotton, sateen, chintz.

Mildew resistant. A finishing treatment that discourages the growth of bacteria. Mildew grows on and damages fabrics (not thermoplastic fibres), especially in periods of high humidity. Cotton, linen and rayon fabrics without this finish should be kept particularly dry and clean.

Permanent Press/Pleating. The ability of garments to retain their shape through wear and washing, including pleats and creases deliberately put in during manufacture for fashion interest. Simultaneously, these garments have the ability to shed creases and wrinkles appearing in the course of wear. Fabrics before making up are *Pre-cured*, a term to describe a chemical process at the finishing stage, which is similar to crease-resisting. Materials so treated are called *Durable Press.*

Post-Cured describes the pressing in of pleats or creases after the garment has been made and then called permanent Press/Pleating.

Polyester is the most suitable fibre used for these processes.

Pre-Shrunk. Fabrics do not shrink more than 3 per cent after shrink resistant treatment.

Sanforizing. A registered trade name of a controlled pre-shrinking process for cotton and colour blends.

Shower proofing. See Water repellent/resisting.

Shrinking. To obtain a permanent contraction of fabrics by heat treatment.

Sizing. See Dressing.

Stain/Spot resistant. Some stains on treated fabrics can be wiped off.

Trubenizing. A registered trade name of a process to stiffen collars and cuffs.

Washable. All fabrics which can be washed without shrinkage or loss of shape. Many materials are now washable. Look out for directions supplied by the manufacturers.

Wash and Wear. A term to describe a number of treatments developed from crease-resisting. Wash and wear fabrics need little or no ironing or pressing after laundering, depending on the fibres used to make the fabric, their construction and finish applied.

Water proofing. Fabrics so treated resist water completely. This is usually a process of applying a coating of rubber or plastic, such as Vinyl, to close all open spaces between yarns.

Water repellent/resisting. Not fully water proofed, but reduces penetration of water.

General Textile Terms

Abrasion. The ability of a fibre to withstand rubbing or abrasion in everyday use. Nylon is most resistant to abrasion but wool, cotton, rayon and acetate are less so.

Blending. Natural or manmade fibres or yarns mixed to combine their desirable qualities.

Carding. The process of cleaning fibres in their raw state and separating them from each other.

Combing. A continuation of the carding process which produces smoother and finer yarn.

Converting. Any finishing process carried out after the basic fabric is made.

Cords/Ribs. A distinct raised rib with pronounced sunken lines in between on the surface of fabrics which is formed by heavier thread running lengthwise, crosswise or diagonally.

As in Bedford Cord = lengthwise.
Broadcloth, Poplin, Ottoman = crosswise.

Colour Bleeding. The running of colour in water.

Crimping. To 'curl' manmade fibres for elasticity.

Crimped. Fabrics constructed with a wrinkled or puckered effect, by wearing or use of chemicals and heat setting, or the shrinking of sections of the fabric.

Denier/Gauge. The fineness of a manmade yarn affected by weight. The lower the denier, the finer the yarn.

Elasticity. The amount of 'give' in a fabric when stretched, recovering to its original shape when released.

Fibre. Basic substances of natural or manmade origin used to make yarns. Staple ones are short, continuous filament and as the name implies, can be very long, as in silk or manmade fibres.

Grey Goods. Fabrics before any processing takes place.

Handle. The feel and touch of fabric.

Milling. A shrinking process to produce a firmer fabric and to obscure the weave.

Nap. Hairy fibres brought to the surface and either brushed or pressed flat to give a sheen. Napped fabrics reflect a different light in each direction, so all garment pieces must be cut with the nap in one direction only.

Piece Dye. Fabrics dyed after weaving or knitting.

Pile. Fabrics woven with sets of looped yarns raised on to the surface.

Pilling. The fluffing of wool and wool, like fabrics in wear.

Reversibles. Two face sides of fabrics which can be used on either side, consisting of (1) the bonding of two identical fabrics, for extra weight and stability, or on one side as alternative to a lining. (2) contrasting woven or knitted sides in colour weave or texture for added fashion interest.

Sheer Fabrics. The transparent quality, ranging from chiffon; soft and light-weight, to voile, lawn, batiste; semi soft, with more body, to organza, organdie, dimity, crisp, by starched finish.

Slubbed. Use of uneven yarns (thin or thick areas) in weaving, produce a rough effect on surfaces often found in fabrics such as Dupion, Shantung or Linen.

Teazling. To raise the nap of a cloth by scrubbing it with the heads of the teazel plant, or with wire hooks.

Tensile Strength. The ability of yarn or fabric to withstand breakage by tension.

Thermoplastic. Fibres which can be softened by heat, and permanently shaped by heat-setting.

Texture. The surface effect of cloth.

Warp. Yarns running lengthwise in fabrics.

Weft. Yarns running crosswise in fabrics.

Yarn. Strands of spun fibres for weaving and knitting.

Yarn Dye. Yarns dyed before weaving or knitting.

INDEX

The page numbers in **bold type** refer to entries in the Glossary.